M000248329

English Verb Classes and Alternations

English Verb Classes and Alternations

A Preliminary Investigation

Beth Levin

The University of Chicago Press
Chicago and London

The University of Chicago Press, Chicago 60637
The University of Chicago Press, Ltd., London
© 1993 by The University of Chicago
All rights reserved. Published 1993
Printed in the United States of America
16 15 14 13 12 11 10 09 08 07   5 6 7 8 9

ISBN-13: 978-0-226-47532-5 (cloth)
ISBN-13: 978-0-226-47533-2 (paper)
ISBN-10: 0-226-47532-8 (cloth)
ISBN-10: 0-226-47533-6 (paper)

An earlier, less extensive form of Part I of this book first appeared as "English Verbal Diathesis," Lexicon Project Working Papers 32, Center for Cognitive Science, MIT, Cambridge, MA. © 1989 by The University of Chicago. All rights reserved.

Library of Congress Cataloging-in-Publication Data

Levin, Beth, 1955–
    English verb classes and alternations : a preliminary
  investigation / Beth Levin.
        p.   cm.
    Includes bibliographical references and index.
    1. English language—Verb.   I. Title.
  PE1271.L48   1993
  425—dc20   92-42504
                                                CIP

⊗ The paper used in this publication meets the minimum requirements of the American National Standard for Information Sciences—Permanence of Paper for Printed Library Materials, ANSI Z39.48-1992.

To my parents

Contents

Preface

The set of resource materials on the English verb lexicon which make up this book grew out of work begun as part of the cross-linguistic study of lexical organization and lexical representation undertaken by the Lexicon Project of the MIT Center for Cognitive Science, which I was affiliated with during the years 1983–1987. I thank Ken Hale and Jay Keyser, the co-directors of the project, for giving me the opportunity to participate in the stimulating research atmosphere of the project. This book would never have happened without the Lexicon Project: it started life as a handout on lexical organization prepared for the project's seminar series. The book contains expanded and revised versions of earlier lists of verb classes and diathesis alternations (dated 1984, 1985, 1986, and 1989), which have been previously circulated.

More people than I can hope to acknowledge have contributed to this work. The late Bill Martin first encouraged me to think deeply about these issues. Boris Katz, Judy Kegl, Betsy Ritter, Jane Simpson, and especially Sue Atkins deserve my special thanks for their continuing encouragement to get the material in this book into a form that could be published. I would like to thank Sue Atkins, Ken Hale, Mary Laughren, Malka Rappaport Hovav, and Betsy Ritter for many valuable discussions. Roz Fergusson and Jim McCawley offered extensive and detailed comments on an earlier draft. Michael Brent, Annette Herskovitz, Geoff Huck, Talke Macfarland, and Tova Rapoport also commented on portions of the draft. I am grateful to Olivia Chang, Li Ya Fei, Tina Nielsen, Tova Rapoport, and Betsy Ritter for help in compiling this book and its precursors; to Olivia Chang, Jazmine Loiselle, Alice Rusnock, and Kirsten Winge for help with the bibliography; to David Weir for help with LATEX; to Ken Church for generating the verb index; and to Christine Bartels for her excellent job copyediting the manuscript. I am also indebted to the many linguists and lexicographers whose work I have drawn on in preparing this book.

The compilation of this book was aided by a series of discussions among

members of the Lexicon Project during 1985–6 and by two meetings of the
Lexicon Seminar in the fall of 1985 that were devoted to discussions of verb
properties. The contents have also benefited from meetings of the Working
Group on the Polytheoretical Lexicon in 1987, as well as from the Workshops
on the Lexicon held at both the 1986 Linguistic Institute at CUNY and the 1987
Linguistic Institute at Stanford University.

The *Oxford Advanced Learner's Dictionary* in electronic form has been an
invaluable tool for filling out specific sets of verbs. A variety of dictionaries
in printed form have also aided this work. They include: *The Collins-Robert
English-French Dictionary*, *The Collins COBUILD English Language Dictionary*, *The Longman Dictionary of Contemporary English*, and *The Longman
Lexicon of Contemporary English*.

During the years 1983–1987, this work was supported by a grant from the
System Development Foundation to the Lexicon Project of the MIT Center for
Cognitive Science. Since 1989, this work has been supported in part by NSF
Grant BNS-8919884.

I hope that this book serves to stimulate further research into the lexical
organization and lexical representation of English verbs.

Introduction:
The Theoretical Perspective

The resource materials on the English verb lexicon presented in this book represent some initial results of an ongoing investigation of the syntactic and semantic properties of English verbs. This introduction gives an overview of the conception of lexical knowledge that forms the foundation for this investigation and shows how a research program devoted to compiling the kinds of materials included here can assist in increasing such knowledge.

This work is guided by the assumption that the behavior of a verb, particularly with respect to the expression and interpretation of its arguments, is to a large extent determined by its meaning. Thus verb behavior can be used effectively to probe for linguistically relevant pertinent aspects of verb meaning. This book offers an attempt at delimiting and systematizing the facets of verb behavior. Its contents should help pave the way toward the development of a theory of lexical knowledge. Ideally, such a theory must provide linguistically motivated lexical entries for verbs which incorporate a representation of verb meaning and which allow the meanings of verbs to be properly associated with the syntactic expressions of their arguments.

The Nature of Lexical Knowledge

One of the most widely known views of the lexicon is that articulated by Bloomfield (1933), who wrote, "The lexicon is really an appendix of the grammar, a list of basic irregularities" (p. 274). Bloomfield's view conforms to a frequently articulated desideratum for an ideal lexicon—a lexicon that contains the minimum information necessary and that, therefore, as Bloomfield proposes, has to provide a record of precisely the idiosyncratic information associated with each lexical item. However, this view of the lexicon offers an incomplete picture of lexical knowledge as a whole. The knowledge that a speaker demonstrates with respect to lexical items suggests that there is more to lexical knowledge than knowledge of idiosyncratic word-specific properties.

This characteristic of lexical knowledge is easily illustrated with respect to verbs. Verbs, as argument-taking elements, show especially complex sets of properties. As shown in B. Levin (1985b, in prep.) and other works, native speakers can make extremely subtle judgments concerning the occurrence of verbs with a range of possible combinations of arguments and adjuncts in various syntactic expressions. For instance, speakers of English know which *diathesis alternations*—alternations in the expressions of arguments, some-times accompanied by changes of meaning—verbs may participate in. They know that verbs such as *spray* and *load* may express their arguments in two different ways, displaying the so-called *locative alternation*.

(1)   a.   Sharon sprayed water on the plants.
        b.   Sharon sprayed the plants with water.

(2)   a.   The farmer loaded apples into the cart.
        b.   The farmer loaded the cart with apples.

But the same speakers know that some verbs which are apparently closely related to *spray* and *load* do not allow both options: *fill* and *cover* show one possibility, while *dump* and *pour* show the other.

(3)   a.   * Monica covered a blanket over the baby.
        b.   Monica covered the baby with a blanket.

(4)   a.   * Gina filled lemonade into the pitcher.
        b.   Gina filled the pitcher with lemonade.

(5)   a.   Carla poured lemonade into the pitcher.
        b.   * Carla poured the pitcher with lemonade.

(6)   a.   The farmer dumped apples into the cart.
        b.   * The farmer dumped the cart with apples.

Furthermore, speakers agree in their judgments concerning subtle differ-ences in meaning associated with alternate expressions of a verb's arguments. For instance, they know that sentence (2b) suggests that the cart is full, but that sentence (2a) need not suggest this. Thus (2a), but not (2b), could be used to describe a cart that is half-full of apples. (This is the much-discussed "holistic/partitive" effect; see references cited in Part I under Locative Alternation.)

A speaker of English also knows whether a verb may participate in one of various *transitivity alternations* found in English—diathesis alternations that involve a change in a verb's transitivity. So for example, although the verb *break* shows transitive and intransitive uses, where the transitive use of the verb means roughly "cause to *break*-intransitive," this possibility—known as the *causative/inchoative alternation*—is not available for the verb *appear.* That is, the verb *appear* cannot be used transitively to mean "cause to *appear*-intransitive."

(7)   a. The window broke. (inchoative variant)
        b. The little boy broke the window. (causative variant)

(8)   a. A rabbit appeared out of the magician's hat.
        b. * The magician appeared a rabbit out of his hat.

The ability to make such judgments extends to novel combinations of arguments and adjuncts. For instance, speakers of English know that benefactive phrases, though typically expressed as *for* prepositional phrases, can sometimes be expressed as the first object in the double object construction.

(9)   a. Martha carved a toy out of wood for the baby.
        b. Martha carved the baby a toy out of wood.

Yet a speaker also knows when this option is not available. Though (10a) is a near-paraphrase of (9a), speakers of English know that there is no sentence (10b) comparable to (9b) where the benefactive is expressed as an object.

(10)   a. Martha carved some wood into a toy for the baby.
        b. * Martha carved the baby some wood into a toy.

English has productive morphological processes for deriving new verbs that are zero-related to nouns,[1] and speakers of English have no difficulty in using or understanding these verbs. The advent of electronic communication has been accompanied not only by the widespread use of the noun *modem*, but also by its use as a verb meaning 'communicate via modem'.

(11)   "I'll modem him tomorrow," said one of them, urged by Mr. Krens to get in touch with an out-of-town colleague. (Arts and Leisure Section, *New York Times*, May 29, 1988, p. 1)

Modem, then, is taking its place among a set of verbs that take their names from instruments of communication (*cable, wire, radio,* etc.). Once again, speakers are aware of the limitations on the process of creating denominal verbs. Even though new verbs of this type are being coined daily, certain imaginable uses of nouns as verbs are not possible. As Hale and Keyser (1992)

---

1 Here and throughout this work, I use the term *zero-related* rather than *zero-derived* when referring to the relation between the uses of a particular word in two lexical categories, such as the use of *tile* as a noun and as a verb. This choice reflects a desire to remain neutral about the direction of the relation, since although in some instances the direction is clear, in others it is not. Also, in using the term "zero-related" I do not intend to take any position with respect to the debate as to whether the derivational process involves the addition of a category-changing zero-morpheme or not.

point out, a speaker of English would never use the noun *church* as a verb meaning "give to a church," as in **They churched the money.*

Speakers of English also know that certain English verbs manifest what B. Levin and Rapoport (1988) have called *extended meanings* (or senses) and what Apresjan (1973) calls *regular polysemy*. This phenomenon is best introduced with an example. Verbs like *whistle* and *roar*, which basically describe the emission of a sound, can regularly take on certain additional senses (see Atkins and B. Levin (1991), B. Levin (1991)). For instance, they can be used as verbs of directed motion, describing an object moving and simultaneously emitting a sound, as in *The bullet whistled through the window* or *The car roared up the driveway*. Yet speakers know that they cannot use the apparently comparable **The dog barked down the street behind the jogger* to say that a dog ran down the street barking behind a jogger.

The examples described in this section are representative of a wide range of phenomena that suggest that a speaker's knowledge of the properties of a verb goes well beyond an awareness of the simple expression of its arguments—the type of lexical knowledge traditionally represented in subcategorization frames. Furthermore, the speaker's ability to make subtle judgments about possible and actual verbs and their properties makes it unlikely that all that a speaker knows about a verb is indicated in its lexical entry.

Verb Meaning: A Key to Verb Behavior

What underlies the ability to make such judgments? Hale and Keyser (1987) present a telling example that suggests the following answer: what enables a speaker to determine the behavior of a verb is its meaning.

Hale and Keyser consider the archaic English verb *gally*, a whaling term, used as in *The sailors gallied the whales*. A speaker of English who is unfamiliar with this verb might assume that *gally* means "see" (*The sailors saw the whales*), while a second speaker might take *gally* to mean "frighten" (*The sailors frightened the whales*). What is striking is that, on the basis of these assumptions about the meaning of *gally*, the two speakers are able to make judgments about its syntactic behavior. To illustrate this point, Hale and Keyser look at the *middle* transitivity alternation. The subject of the intransitive middle use of a verb corresponds to the object of the transitive use; compare the transitive use of *slice* in *The baker sliced the bread* with the middle use of the same verb, *Stale bread slices easily*.[2] The speaker who believes that *gally*

---

2 The middle alternation should not be confused with the causative/inchoative alternation illustrated in (7) with the verb *break*. Although both are transitivity alternations where the subject of the intransitive use of the verb bears the same semantic relation to the verb as the object of the transitive use, there are differences between the two constructions. First, the middle construction differs from the inchoative construction, the intransitive variant of the causative/inchoative alter-

means "see" would not allow the middle construction *Whales gally easily* (cf. *Whales see easily*), although the speaker who interprets *gally* as "frighten" will find this construction perfectly acceptable (cf. *Whales frighten easily*).

Thus the two speakers' different treatment of *gally* may be explained by their different assumptions concerning its meaning. Hale and Keyser propose that the middle construction is available only to a certain semantically defined class of verbs: verbs whose meaning involves a notion of causing a change of state. They point out that change of state verbs such as *frighten, cut, split, open*, and *crush* have middles, but that other types of verbs such as *see, consider,* and *believe* do not. Only the speaker who attributes the change of state meaning "frighten" to *gally* will allow the verb to be used in the middle construction. The speaker who—contrary to fact as it turns out—believes that *gally* means "see" correctly does not allow this option.

The *gally* example shows vividly that for speakers of English, knowing the meaning of a verb can be a key to knowing its behavior. Presumably, predictions about verb behavior are feasible because particular syntactic properties are associated with verbs of a certain semantic type. The *gally* example and others like it suggest that general principles of grammar are at work, allowing the syntactic behavior of a verb to be predicted from its meaning. Their existence should explain a speaker's ability to make the judgments discussed in the previous section.[3]

A More Complex Example

Further examination of the nature of lexical knowledge confirms that various aspects of the syntactic behavior of verbs are tied to their meaning. Moreover, verbs that fall into classes according to shared behavior would be expected to show shared meaning components. This point about the nature of lexical knowledge can be demonstrated with a more extensive example: an investigation of the verbs *break, cut, hit,* and *touch*, which draws on several studies of these verbs, including Fillmore (1967), Guerssel, Hale, Laughren, B. Levin, and White Eagle (1985), Hale and Keyser (1986, 1987), and Laughren (1988).

---

nation, in not denoting an event; that is, it need not have a specific time reference. Second, the middle construction always implies an agent (*Crystal vases shatter easily*), while the inchoative construction need not (*The crystal vase shattered*). See the discussion of these two alternations in Part I and the references cited there.

3 Providing an explanation for each of these judgments goes beyond the scope of this introduction. See Rappaport and B. Levin (1988) and Pinker (1989) for a discussion of the *spray/load* facts. See Hale and Keyser (1991) for a discussion of the *church* example and E.V. Clark and H.H. Clark (1979) for more general discussion of productive strategies for coining verbs from nouns. The extended meaning example is discussed in B. Levin (1991) and B. Levin and Rappaport Hovav (1991). The causative/inchoative alternation is discussed at greater length in the following section.

The verbs *break, cut, hit,* and *touch* are transitive, taking two arguments expressed as subject and object, but we will see that they have little else in common.

(12)   a.   Margaret cut the bread.
        b.   Janet broke the vase.
        c.   Terry touched the cat.
        d.   Carla hit the door.

In particular, these verbs differ with respect to their participation in diathesis alternations. First, the middle alternation differentiates among these four verbs. Only *cut* and *break,* but not *hit* and *touch,* are found in the middle construction.[4]

(13)   a.   The bread cuts easily.
        b.   Crystal vases break easily.
        c. * Cats touch easily.
        d. * Door frames hit easily.

On the other hand, *cut* and *hit* appear in the *conative construction,* as shown in (14), but *break* and *touch* do not.

(14)   a.   Margaret cut at the bread.
        b. * Janet broke at the vase.
        c. * Terry touched at the cat.
        d.   Carla hit at the door.

The conative alternation is also a transitivity alternation, but unlike the middle and causative/inchoative alternations, the subject of the transitive variant (12) and intransitive variant (14) bears the same semantic relation to the verb. The variants differ in the expression of the other argument: in the conative construction, the argument corresponding to the object of the transitive variant is expressed in a prepositional phrase headed by *at*. The conative construction is set apart by its meaning: there is no entailment that the action denoted by the verb was completed. Thus (14a) means something like "Margaret tried to cut the bread."

Yet another diathesis alternation—the *body-part possessor ascension alternation*—distinguishes *cut, hit,* and *touch* from *break*. Only *break* does not display this alternation.

---

4 The uses of *hit* in this section involve the simple "contact through the motion of an instrument" sense of this verb. The verb *hit* is not found in the middle construction on this sense, which does not necessarily involve any subsequent motion of the entity that is hit. However, the verb *hit* has a second sense that might be described as "contact using an instrument and set in motion," as in *The batter hit the ball over the fence.* This second sense of *hit* allows the middle for some speakers. To ensure that the examples in this section unambiguously involve the simple sense of *hit,* the examples have an immovable entity as the object of the verb.

(15)   a.   Margaret cut Bill's arm.
         b.   Margaret cut Bill on the arm.

(16)   a.   Janet broke Bill's finger.
         b.   * Janet broke Bill on the finger.

(17)   a.   Terry touched Bill's shoulder.
         b.   Terry touched Bill on the shoulder.

(18)   a.   Carla hit Bill's back.
         b.   Carla hit Bill on the back.

This alternation is characterized by a change in the expression of a possessed body part: either the possessed body part may be expressed as the direct object of the verb, as in the (a) sentences, or the possessor may be expressed as the object of the verb, with the possessed body part expressed in a prepositional phrase, as in the (b) sentences.

Each verb shows a distinct pattern of behavior with respect to these three alternations, as summarized in the table.

	touch	hit	cut	break
Conative:	No	Yes	Yes	No
Body-Part Possessor Ascension:	Yes	Yes	Yes	No
Middle:	No	No	Yes	Yes

The four patterns of behavior observed here cannot simply be dismissed because they are linked to four different verbs. Corresponding to each one of these four verbs are other verbs that show the same pattern of behavior.

(19)   a.   *Break* Verbs: break, crack, rip, shatter, snap, ...
         b.   *Cut* Verbs: cut, hack, saw, scratch, slash, ...
         c.   *Touch* Verbs: pat, stroke, tickle, touch, ...
         d.   *Hit* Verbs: bash, hit, kick, pound, tap, whack, ...

Not only can four verb classes be recognized that are defined by the shared behavior of their members with respect to the above diathesis alternations, but several studies (Fillmore (1967), Guerssel et al. (1985), Hale and Keyser (1986, 1987)) have examined each set of verbs in (19) closely and found that their members share certain aspects of meaning. Thus their members have common syntactic as well as semantic properties. These studies propose that the differences in verb behavior can be explained if the diathesis alternations are sensitive to particular components of verb meaning.

As a first step in identifying the relevant meaning components, let us look more closely at the body-part possessor ascension alternation. What distinguishes *cut*, *hit*, and *touch*, which enter into this alternation, from *break*, which does not, is that the actions the first three verbs denote necessarily involve contact. Although the real-world event denoted by the verb *break* often involves contact, it need not. Evidence drawn from an examination of a variety of diathesis alternations indicates that, linguistically speaking, *break* is a pure change of state verb and a notion of contact is not inherent to its meaning (see below). It appears that a verb shows the body-part possessor ascension alternation only if its meaning involves the notion of contact.

But even if the meaning component 'contact' is common to *cut*, *hit*, and *touch*, there must be further meaning components that distinguish between them. After all, *touch*, unlike the other two, does not show the conative alternation. Guerssel et al. (1985) suggest that verbs which enter into the conative alternation have meanings that involve both motion and contact components. Only the meanings of *hit* and *cut* involve both. The motion component is missing from the meaning of *touch*, which is a pure verb of contact, while the meaning of *break* lacks both these components. If both contact and motion are necessary for the conative alternation, then pure verbs of motion would also be predicted not to show this alternation, and in fact, they do not.[5]

(20)   a.   Jean moved the table.
          b. * Jean moved at the table.

As we have also seen, *cut* and *break* both show the middle alternation, while *hit* and *touch* do not. As discussed above, this alternation is manifested by verbs of causing a change of state. The behavior of the verbs *hit* and *touch* suggests that they are not change of state verbs. And indeed, hitting and touching need not entail a change of state, unlike cutting and breaking. Although they behave differently in some respects from one another, *cut* and *break* nevertheless show similarities that go beyond the middle construction. For instance, both have associated zero-related nominals with a similar interpretation: they refer to the result of the action. In contrast, the nominals zero-related to *hit* and *touch* do not allow this interpretation, but refer instead to the action itself.

---

5 The interpretation that would be expected to be associated with the conative use of *move* in (20b), if this construction were possible, would be roughly "Jean attempted to move the table." However, this particular conjunction of meaning and syntactic frame is not observed. The verb *move* can be found with an *at* phrase, as in *The two opponents moved at each other*, but the interpretation associated with this use of *move* is not that expected in the conative construction. Rather, the use of *at* here parallels that found in *run at* or *charge at*. Furthermore, this use of *at* is not paired with a transitive use of the verb that is derived by "dropping" the preposition *at*; *The opponents moved each other* is not at all related to *The opponents moved at each other*. The existence of this use of *at*, as well as many other uses of *at* with verbs that do not show the conative alternation, raises another question: Are there some meaning components that are common to all these uses of the preposition? If there are, they may not be precisely the ones that determine participation in the conative alternation. The investigation of a unified characterization of *at* falls outside the scope of this book.

(21)   a.   a break
         b.   a cut
         c.   a hit
         d.   a touch

   This additional difference supports the proposal that *cut* and *break* are both verbs of causing a change of state; presumably, the actions they denote have a result that can be referred to by a nominal.

   Finally, a few words concerning the difference between *cut* and *break*. Although the meaning of both verbs involves a change of state, *cut*'s meaning also involves notions of contact and motion. The verb *cut* describes bringing about a change of state by means of contact through motion; cutting involves bringing a sharp object into contact with a surface and causing a "separation in its material integrity" in the words of Hale and Keyser (1986). The verb *break* is a pure change of state verb: in both its transitive and intransitive uses it simply expresses a change of state (plus a notion of cause when transitive), without specifying how this change of state comes about. For example, throwing a rock at a window, bending a twig sharply, and dropping a cup are only a few of the many imaginable ways of breaking things. Not only does *break* differ from *cut* in not showing the conative or body-part possessor ascension alternations, but *break*, unlike *cut*, participates in the causative/inchoative alternation, as illustrated above in (7), which is repeated here as (22).

(22)   a.   The window broke.
         b.   The little boy broke the window.

(23)   a.   Margaret cut the string.
         b.   * The string cut. (on the interpretation "became cut")

   This fact has been attributed to this alternation's sensitivity to pure change of state verbs. And as expected, since they are not change of state verbs, the verbs *hit* or *touch* are not found in the causative/inchoative alternation.[6]

(24)   a.   Terry touched the cat.
         b.   * The cat touched.

(25)   a.   Carla hit the door.
         b.   * The door hit.

   Studies such as Guerssel et al. (1985) offer an explanation for the contrasting behavior of *break* and *cut*. A pure change of state verb like *break* is basically a single-argument verb, denoting an entity undergoing a change of state, as in the inchoative variant. The two-argument form of the verb found in the causative

---

   6 The absence of a causative form for *appear* illustrated in (8) would be attributed to its not being a verb of change of state; it belongs to the class of verbs of appearance.

variant is derived by the addition of a notion of cause. Because the meaning of a verb like *cut* inherently involves an instrument, this verb requires the existence of an agent that uses this instrument to bring about a change of state in the patient; hence, *cut* is basically a two-argument verb and would never be found in the inchoative construction. Both *cut* and *break* are found in the middle construction because this construction is open to verbs of causing a change of state, whether or not their meaning also specifies how this change of state comes about.

The four verbs examined in this section then differ as follows: *touch* is a pure verb of contact, *hit* is a verb of contact by motion, *cut* is a verb of causing a change of state by moving something into contact with the entity that changes state, and *break* is a pure verb of change of state. These characterizations are not intended to exhaust the meaning of these verbs; rather, they simply capture those aspects of meaning that serve minimally to distinguish the verbs participating in the alternations discussed here. The notions of motion, contact, change of state, and causation that figure in these characterizations must be taken into account in selecting a lexical representation of verb meaning. These same notions are correlated with participation in diathesis alternations, including those discussed here. The body-part possessor ascension alternation is sensitive to the notion of contact, while the conative alternation is sensitive to both contact and motion. The causative/inchoative alternation is found only with verbs of pure change of state, while the middle alternation is found with verbs whose meaning involves causing a change of state.

The existence of ties between verb behavior and verb meaning is not particular to English. Alternations—including analogues of many of those found in English—are manifested across languages by verbs of the same semantic types. To take one example, the Australian language Warlpiri also shows the conative alternation. As in English, this alternation is not found with *break*-type verbs and *touch*-type verbs, though it is found with *hit*-type and *cut*-type verbs.[7] Such examples reinforce the evidence from English that certain components of verb meaning determine verb behavior. This is not to say that all languages have the same inventory of verbs or diathesis alternations.[8] But to the extent that languages are similar—and the similarities between them are often great—the same meaning components, and hence the same classes of verbs, figure in the statement of regularities concerning the expression of arguments. Even when alternations are specific to only some languages, they are often

---

7 For more discussion of Warlpiri, see Guerssel et al. (1985) and Laughren (1988).

8 Talmy (1985, 1991) and others, including Choi and Bowerman (1991), Pouradier Duteil and François (1981), Green (1973), Iordanskaja and Mel'chuk (1981), and B. Levin and Rapoport (1988), have described interesting differences between languages involving both the possible words of a language and the possible senses that can be associated with a given word.

sensitive to aspects of verb meaning that have been shown to be significant to the characterization of verb behavior in other languages as well.

The discussion of *break*, *cut*, *hit*, and *touch* underscores the conclusions drawn in the earlier sections. Studies of diathesis alternations show that verbs in English and other languages fall into classes on the basis of shared components of meaning. The class members have in common a range of properties, including the possible expression and interpretation of their arguments, as well as the existence of certain morphologically related forms. Furthermore, the existence of regular relationships between verb meaning and verb behavior suggests that not all aspects of a verb's behavior need to be listed in its lexical entry, a conclusion also suggested by a speaker's ability to make judgments about possible and actual verbs and their properties. The picture that emerges is that a verb's behavior arises from the interaction of its meaning and general principles of grammar. Thus the lexical knowledge of a speaker of a language must include knowledge of the meaning of individual verbs, the meaning components that determine the syntactic behavior of verbs, and the general principles that determine behavior from verb meaning.

The Larger Context

These observations about the nature of lexical knowledge fit well with proposals that the ideal lexical entry for a word should minimize the information provided for that word. This goal can be achieved by factoring predictable information out of lexical entries, leaving only idiosyncratic information. If the syntactic properties of a verb indeed follow in large part from its meaning, then it should be possible to identify general principles that derive the behavior of a verb from its meaning. Given such principles, the meaning of a verb will clearly have a place in its lexical entry, but it is possible that the entry will need to contain little more. And since a word's meaning is necessarily idiosyncratic, the inclusion of a word's meaning in its lexical entry conforms to Bloomfield's characterization of the lexicon as a locus of idiosyncrasy. In fact, Bloomfield (1933) follows his famous statement to this effect by writing that this view of the lexicon "... is all the more evident if meanings are taken into consideration, since the meaning of each morpheme belongs to it by an arbitrary tradition" (p. 274). Certainly this statement is just as true of words—at least monomorphemic words and multi-morpheme words whose meanings are not compositional. (It is not clear that this statement should apply to multi-morpheme words whose meanings are compositionally determined. The properties of such words are determined from their component parts, as discussed in recent work on argument structure and morphology; see, for example, Lieber (1983), Rappaport Hovav and B. Levin (1992), Sproat (1985), Williams (1981).)

Taking this approach seriously requires a re-evaluation of previous assumptions concerning the contents of lexical entries, since it suggests that they may contain less information than has sometimes been proposed. Specifically, if there are indeed correlations between verb meaning and verb behavior, some properties that might have been included in lexical entries because they were thought to be idiosyncratic could turn out on further examination to be predictable from verb meaning and could be eliminated from a verb's lexical entry.

Subcategorization frames are a case in point. Recently, there has been much investigation of the proposal that the subcategorization requirements of a lexical item might be predictable from its meaning, a position that is consistent with the view of lexical knowledge proposed here, though the motivation has come from efforts to constrain the power of syntactic rules. Those facets of syntactic constructions that cannot be made to follow from general principles of grammar are considered to be projections of the lexical properties of the words in these constructions. Concomitantly, the lexicon has assumed an increasingly central place in several syntactic frameworks (e.g., Government-Binding, Lexical Functional Grammar, Head-driven Phrase Structure Grammar), and much effort has been devoted to investigating the nature of lexical representation. This move has led to an increased interest in *argument structure*—the representation and characterization of argument-taking properties of verbs and other predicators. As discussed here, studies of these properties suggest that argument structures might in turn be derivable to a large extent from the meaning of words. Chomsky (1986), for example, speculates that only the meaning of a verb needs to be learned, and "semantic bootstrapping" models of child language acquisition (Pinker (1989)) are built on the assumption that a word's syntactic properties are predictable from its meaning. Within this context then, the ability to build representations of linguistically relevant aspects of word meaning and to formulate the principles that determine syntactic properties from word meaning becomes essential.

Challenges

Although no one is likely to deny that words with similar meaning show at least some tendency toward displaying the same syntactic behavior, the hypothesis that the syntactic behavior of a word is fully semantically determined is not uncontroversial. Many researchers have argued that this hypothesis must be rejected, citing numerous purported counterexamples to it. Nevertheless, the meaning of a verb does have considerable predictive ability, as the examples above and examples cited in other work illustrate, suggesting that the ties between a verb's meaning and its syntactic behavior cannot simply be ignored. And there are studies that show that this hypothesis receives substantial support, particularly in restricted domains (Laughren (1988), B. Levin and Rappaport Hovav (1991), Zwicky (1971a), among others). This work pursues the hypothesis of semantic determination seriously to see just how far it can be taken, even if it does ultimately turn out to meet with limited success (see Jackendoff (1990b) for some discussion).

The key to maintaining this hypothesis is the identification of the appropriate representation of verb meaning. Determining the appropriate meaning components is not easy, since a priori it is possible to classify verbs in many ways according to their meaning. So it would not be surprising if some proposed semantic/syntactic correlations did not make reference to the proper choice of meaning components. Such correlations will be found to have limited applicability, suggesting that the relation between verb meaning and verb behavior is more idiosyncratic than it actually is and that the search for generalizations is doomed to fail. However, these conclusions may not be warranted. Apparent deviations from semantic/syntactic correlations might reflect the use of the wrong meaning components in the statement of the correlations, rather than the absence of such correlations. It is possible that many examples intended to demonstrate the limitations of the hypothesis that syntactic properties are semantically determined might, if reanalyzed, turn out to support it. An illustration, discussed in B. Levin and Rappaport Hovav (1991, 1992) and repeated here, underscores the importance of carefully evaluating purported counterexamples to the hypothesis.

This illustration involves the Unaccusative Hypothesis, a hypothesis concerning the syntactic configurations associated with intransitive verbs first proposed by Perlmutter (1978) and further elaborated by Burzio (1986). The proposal is that the single argument of some intransitive verbs, the unaccusative verbs, is an underlying object, while the single argument of the others, the unergative verbs, is an underlying subject. The Unaccusative Hypothesis has provided a rich context for debating whether syntactic behavior is semantically determined. Some researchers, including Perlmutter himself, have argued that the membership of an intransitive verb in the unaccusative or unergative class can be determined from its meaning. However, other researchers, including Rosen (1984), have concluded that meaning alone is not predictive of class membership. To support this view, Rosen points out that bodily process verbs in Italian do not show uniform behavior: *russare* 'snore' patterns like an unergative verb, while *arrossire* 'blush' patterns like an unaccusative verb.

But in fact, this particular example only emphasizes the importance of identifying the appropriate meaning components and does not necessarily argue against the semantic determination of syntactic properties. The verbs *russare* 'snore' and *arrossire* 'blush' would be expected to show similar behavior only if the semantic notion "bodily process" plays a part in determining a verb's status with respect to the Unaccusative Hypothesis. If it does not, then these verbs need not necessarily pattern in the same way. The fact that they do not suggests that the semantic notion "bodily process" is probably not relevant to verb classification. There are other possible characterizations of bodily process verbs. The concept denoted by English *snore* can be classified as an activity in the sense of Vendler (1957), while that denoted by English *blush* is open either to an activity or to a change of state interpretation. Interestingly, Italian *arrossire* 'blush' literally means "become red," suggesting that *arrossire* is a change of state verb. There is evidence, in fact, that the semantic notions of activity and change of state are facets of meaning that figure in the determination of a verb's status with respect to the Unaccusative Hypothesis (B. Levin and Rappaport Hovav (1992), McClure (1990), Tenny (1987), Van Valin (1990), Zaenen (in press)).

If the hypothesis that syntactic properties are semantically determined is taken seriously, then the task is to determine, first, to what extent the meaning of a verb determines its syntactic behavior, and second, to the extent that syntactic behavior is predictable, what components of verb meaning figure in the relevant generalizations. The identification of the relevant components of meaning is essential if this approach is to be successful. And once these questions are answered, others remain. What kind of lexical representation of verb meaning is necessary? How are the mapping rules formulated that determine the syntactic properties? And more important, why are certain phenomena sensitive to certain meaning components? The attested patterns of behavior exhibited by verbs in English and other languages must be accounted for in a principled and systematic way. The present study is intended to lay the groundwork that will facilitate the future investigation of these questions, even though it does not offer explicit answers.

The Underlying Research Methodology

The assumption that the syntactic behavior of verbs is semantically determined gives rise to a powerful technique for investigating verb meaning that can be exploited in the development of a theory of lexical knowledge. If the distinctive behavior of verb classes with respect to diathesis alternations arises from their meaning, any class of verbs whose members pattern together with respect to diathesis alternations should be a semantically coherent class: its members should share at least some aspect of meaning. Once such a class is identified, its members can be examined to isolate the meaning components they have in common. Thus diathesis alternations can be used to provide a probe into the elements entering into the lexical representation of word meaning.[9]

---

9 A similar approach is proposed and illustrated by Deane and Wheeler (1984), who call it "correlation analysis." See also Green (1974, 66–69) and Wierzbicka (1987, 24–26).

The availability of this technique for investigating word meaning is important since it can be quite difficult to pin down the meanings of words using introspection alone. For instance, dictionaries provide rather different definitions of the sense of the verb *whistle* found in the context *The bullet whistled through the air*. They seem unsure whether to treat this sense as involving a verb of sound or a verb of motion. Thus *Webster's Ninth* (Mish (1986)) sees this sense as involving sound emission, giving the definition "to make a shrill clear sound, esp. by rapid movement;" in contrast, the *Collins English Dictionary* (Hanks (1986)) gives the definition "to move with a whistling sound caused by rapid passage through the air." By itself, intuition provides little guidance as to which one of these definitions is correct.

Distinctions induced by diathesis alternations help to provide insights into verb meaning, and more generally into the organization of the English verb lexicon, that might not otherwise be apparent, bringing out unexpected similarities and differences between verbs. A striking example is provided by verbs of motion. Verbs of motion are frequently cited as a large and important class within the English verb inventory. Yet a study of the syntactic behavior of these verbs (B. Levin and Rappaport Hovav (1992)) shows that this class is not homogeneous. It includes at least a subclass of verbs of inherently directed motion (e.g., *arrive, come, go*) and a subclass of verbs of manner of motion (e.g., *jump, run, trot, skip*). In the absence of a directional prepositional phrase, verbs of directed motion describe the direction of motion but not the manner of motion, while verbs of manner of motion describe the manner of motion but not the direction. In fact, some verbs of manner of motion do not necessarily entail any displacement, as in *run in place*. However, the verbs *run* and *whistle*—one a verb of motion and the other a verb of sound emission—are in some respects more similar to each other than the verbs *run* and *come*—although both are verbs of motion. The verbs *run* and *whistle* manifest a similar extended meaning: both can be used as verbs of directed motion in the presence of a directional prepositional phrase (*The bullet whistled through the window*, *The man ran into the room*), though neither is basically a verb of this type. Returning to the question of the best definition for one of the senses of *whistle*, it is likely that the *Collins English Dictionary* is on the right track in treating the relevant sense as a motion sense, since the verb shows the complement-taking properties of verbs of motion in this sense, which is only available in the presence of a directional phrase.

As these examples show, by providing independent criteria for isolating narrow classes of verbs known to share certain aspects of meaning, the study of diathesis alternations can lead to the identification of the linguistically relevant meaning components which determine a verb's behavior. In order to identify the full set of meaning components that figure in the lexical representation of verb meaning, the investigation of semantically relevant syntactic properties and the ensuing clustering of verbs into classes need to be carried out over a larger and larger number of verbs occurring in a wide range of constructions. A growing number of studies of the syntactic behavior of English verbs are being conducted with the goal of identifying such meaning components; see, for example, Guerssel (1986), Guerssel et al. (1985), Hale and Keyser (1986, 1987), B. Levin and Rappaport Hovav (1991, 1992), Rappaport and B. Levin (1988). Furthermore, as discussed above, work on other languages can provide additional support both for this technique of studying lexical representation and for the results that it achieves. Interestingly, as noted in B. Levin and Pinker (1991), certain meaning components identified via the study of semantic/syntactic correlations show considerable overlap with the set of elements posited as being central to the meanings of English verbs in studies that approach the problem of verb meaning from the perspectives of language acquisition and cognition (Jackendoff (1983, 1990b), G.A. Miller and Johnson-Laird (1976), Pinker (1989)).

The nature of these meaning components, in turn, would be expected to influence the selection of a lexical representation of verb meaning that allows for the observed behavior. In fact, some of the studies listed above move beyond an examination of verb behavior to a consideration of its implications for the choice of a lexical representation of verb meaning and for the principles mapping from such a representation to the syntax. One of the conclusions that emerges from such studies is that the complex pattern of behavior manifested by verbs with respect to diathesis alternations cannot be explained with a lexical semantic representation that takes the form of a list of semantic roles (see Grimshaw (1990), Rappaport and B. Levin (1988), among others). These studies, as well as other recent work, propose lexical semantic representations that take the form of predicate decompositions, though there are significant differences in detail.

Although the hypothesis that meaning determines syntax has been used before in lexical semantic studies, its success within limited, well-defined domains shown in current work such as the studies cited above depends in part on the investigation of intricate and extensive patterns of syntactic behavior. Research of this kind looks not only at the subcategorization frame of a verb, but also examines a wider constellation of properties, particularly a verb's participation in diathesis alternations, and also to a more limited extent its morphological properties and extended meanings. Such wide-ranging studies are necessary because it is unlikely that a single property can be isolated that will prove sufficient to characterize a particular class of verbs (see also Mufwene (1978)). Each class of verbs displays a set of properties which together reflect the meaning components of its members. Since many of these meaning components are common to more than one class of verbs, properties that are attributable to a single meaning component will be manifested by verbs from various classes. Although any single property of a class of verbs will in itself not be very informative, the conjunction of properties shown by a class of verbs may well be more revealing, since it will reflect the entire set of meaning components shared by the class members. For this reason, continued progress in the development of a theory of lexical knowledge of verbs will depend on an extensive exploration of verb behavior.

The Scope of this Book

This book offers the results of a preliminary large-scale investigation of the behavior of English verbs. It is divided into two major parts that reflect the nature of lexical knowledge as it has been described in this introduction. Part I of the book sets out a range of diathesis alternations that are relevant to a speaker's lexical knowledge of English. Part II presents a large number of semantically coherent classes of verbs whose members pattern in the same way with respect to diathesis alternations and other properties. The classes that are identified in Part II of the book have emerged from the study of the diathesis alternations set out in Part I.

This book tries to strike a balance between breadth and depth of coverage. Many of the diathesis alternations and verb classes included are familiar and well studied. Others have received relatively little attention, and I hope that their inclusion may stimulate further study. This introduction is intended to justify the general approach toward the exploration of the English verb inventory, though it cannot hope to argue for the inclusion of any given diathesis alternation or verb class. The classificatory distinctions in this book have been drawn using criteria of the type discussed throughout this introduction. They involve the expression of arguments of verbs, including alternate expressions of arguments and special interpretations associated with particular expressions of arguments of the type that are characteristic of diathesis alternations. Certain morphological properties of verbs, such as the existence of various types of related nominals and adjectives, have been used as well, since they are also tied to the argument-taking properties of verbs.

The verb classes that are identified in this book should be "handled with care," since there is a sense in which the notion of "verb class" is an artificial construct. Verb classes arise because a set of verbs with one or more shared meaning components show similar behavior. Some meaning components cut across the classes identified here, as attested by the existence of properties common to several verb classes. For instance, the meaning components contact and motion are common to the *hit* verbs and the *cut* verbs, as manifested by their participation in the conative alternation. However, the meaning component contact alone would also have picked out the *touch* verbs, as well as the *hit* and *cut* verbs. Thus, since most verbs are characterized by several meaning components, there is potential for cross-classification, which in turn means that other, equally valid classification schemes might have been identified instead of the scheme presented in Part II of the book.

The important theoretical construct is the notion of meaning component, not the notion of verb class. This point is also argued for by Mufwene (1978) in a follow-up to Zwicky's (1971a) exploration of the properties of manner of speaking verbs. Mufwene argues that the identification of this class of verbs is of limited value since each of the twenty properties which Zwicky ascribes to manner of speaking verbs is shared by other types of verbs as well. A more explanatory account would result, Mufwene argues, if rather than tying the properties to a list of verb classes, they were associated with particular meaning components that are common to all verbs showing the property, whether or not they are manner of speaking verbs. Thus Mufwene favors "identifying a specific feature . . . as a component of a lexical entry . . . which triggers a given behavior or is held responsible for a given property" (p. 278).

Mufwene is right, but the identification of the meaning components poses a real challenge. Their identification is an eventual aim of the line of research described here. As discussed in the previous section, an examination of classes of verbs defined by shared behavior can play an important part in zeroing in on these meaning components. In this book, I have chosen a level of classification characterized by interesting clustering of verbs that should further the isolation of meaning components. The classification system does not take into account every property of every verb, since such a system would be liable to consist of classes having only one member, a state of affairs that would not provide much insight into the overall structure of the English verb lexicon.

Having set out what the book attempts to do, I would now like to turn briefly to what it does not attempt to do. This book presents a snapshot of ongoing research. It is by no means a definitive and exhaustive classification of the verb inventory of English. Some of its limitations reflect explicit design decisions. The verb classes were chosen because their members participated in diathesis alternations or showed behavior that was closely related to that of other verbs found in particular alternations. This strategy has led to the omission of certain verbs and verb classes. This book also restricts itself to verbs taking noun phrase and prepositional phrase complements. Verbs taking sentential complements are for the most part ignored, except when they show interesting behavior with noun phrase or prepositional phrase complements.[10] Nor does this book look systematically at verbs derived by productive morphological processes, such as

---

10 For some catalogs of verbs that take sentential complements, see Alexander and Kunz (1964), Bridgeman et al. (1965), Ingria (1987), Rudanko (1989), Sager (1981), among others.

so-called zero-derived denominal verbs[11] and verbs derived through prefixation (*un–*, *de–*, *dis–*, *re–*, etc.) or suffixation (*–ify*, *–ize*, *–en*, etc.). This study also does not treat the inherent lexical aspect of verbs (aktionsart).[12] The connection between the verb classes and diathesis alternations discussed here and lexical aspect needs to be carefully investigated, since lexical aspect also plays an important part in determining verb behavior.

The material that is within the scope of this book is likely to contain inconsistencies, omissions, and inaccuracies, which reflect the practical difficulties that face attempts to accurately and exhaustively carry out hypothesis checking over a large number of English verbs. The set of verbs listed as belonging to any given class does not necessarily exhaust the membership of that class, though an effort has been made to make the lists as comprehensive as possible. It would not be surprising to find disagreement over the inclusion of a certain verb in a particular class, as well as differences of opinion concerning whether all the members of a certain class do indeed manifest a particular property. What is important is the existence of core sets of verbs with specific sets of properties that can provide the basis for the later identification of meaning components.

The goals of this work have also figured in the decision not to illustrate a consistent set of properties across all the verb classes identified in Part II of this book. Where information about a property is relevant it is included. For instance, given that the verb *fill* expresses its arguments in a frame resembling one of the variants of the locative alternation, and that as a first approximation it seems rather similar in meaning to locative alternation verbs like *spray* and *load*, it makes sense to include among the properties of *fill*'s verb class that its members do not undergo the locative alternation. However, the inclusion of this information in the discussion of another class of verbs might merely obscure the central properties of the members of this class. Similarly, in Part I of the book only some classes of verbs that do not display a particular diathesis alternation are noted.

Finally, this book does not assess the implications of the material it includes for the identification of meaning components, nor does it move beyond their identification to the formulation of a lexical semantic representation. Rather, it is intended to set the stage for these necessary next steps. In the meantime, I hope that it will be a valuable resource for linguists and researchers in related fields.

---

11 For extensive studies of these verbs, see Bladin (1911), E.V. Clark and H.H. Clark (1979), Karius (1985), Leitner (1974), Marchand (1969), among others.

12 There is a vast literature devoted to lexical aspect that includes Bach (1981, 1986), Brinton (1988), Declerck (1979), Dowty (1979), Freed (1979), Hinrichs (1985), Kenny (1963), Lys (1988), Mourelatos (1978), Tenny (1987, 1988b, 1989), Vendler (1957), Verkuyl (1972, 1989), among many others.

The Layout of the Book

This book consists of two major parts: a list of diathesis alternations and a list of verb classes. It also contains a bibliography of relevant works and a verb index. There is a certain area of overlap between the two major parts, because they present the same material from different perspectives.

The presentation of material relies primarily on illustrative examples, with written descriptions kept brief; however, comments signaling noteworthy properties of verb classes and alternations have been included. Bibliographic references have also been included where possible; these references should provide a starting point for further investigations. Throughout this work, if the illustrative examples given seem problematic, the reader should try substituting another verb of the same type, in case the judgment simply reflects disagreement about the classification of a particular verb. However, the reader needs to keep in mind that verbs belonging to the same class are syntactic "synonyms." That is, they should be substitutable in the same set of syntactic frames, though not necessarily in exactly the same contexts.

Although different behavior with respect to a diathesis alternation is more often than not a good reason to split a set of verbs into two subclasses, in some instances where members of a set of verbs share all but one or two properties, the class has not been subdivided further to avoid too much fragmentation and the resulting loss of insight. In these circumstances, in Part I of the book, when the relevant diathesis alternation is illustrated with respect to this class of verbs, it is accompanied by an annotation indicating that it applies to only some members of the class and that only the relevant verbs are listed. In Part II of the book, when the relevant verb class is treated, the properties that do not apply to the whole class are flagged.

Part I: Alternations

This part of the book includes a wide variety of diathesis alternations characteristic of English verbs, as well as special diatheses exhibited by certain English
verbs. Each diathesis alternation is exemplified upon introduction; often, too,
examples are given of verbs which might be expected to undergo the alternation but do not. In an attempt to suggest semantic restrictions which may bear
on the alternations, the semantic classes of verbs which do and do not show
the alternation are identified, insofar as these are understood. If only some
members of one of the semantic classes undergo the alternation, only those
members are listed; a full list of members of such classes will be found in Part
II. Lists of verbs that do not undergo a particular alternation are preceded by
an asterisk; lists of verbs that undergo an alternation are not set off in a special
way. References to relevant discussions in the literature are included, as are
comments on noteworthy features of the alternations.

   Most verbs mentioned in Part I of the book figure in one or more classes in
Part II. But a small number of verbs cited in Part I have not been associated
with a class in Part II because of limited or ill-understood behavior.

   The alternations are subdivided into groups on the basis of the syntactic
frames involved. The first group includes transitivity alternations, while the
second group covers alternate expressions of arguments (mostly within the verb
phrase) that do not affect transitivity. A third group includes alternations that
arise when verbs permit "oblique" subjects. These major groups of alternations
are followed by a variety of other types.

Part II: Verb Classes

This part of the book contains various syntactically relevant, semantically
coherent verb classes of English. These classes are described individually. A
list of as many members of each class as possible is given; however, additional
class members are likely to exist in many instances. Lists considered to be
exhaustive are signaled by the word "only" following the last verb in the list. A
representative verb is then used to exemplify the characteristic properties of the
class, including argument-taking properties, behavior with respect to diathesis
alternations, and occasionally morphological properties (related nominals or
adjectives). These properties have been chosen to illustrate what is distinctive
to the members of that class. References to other discussions of the verb class
in the literature are provided where possible. Special properties of each class
are also signaled.

   Some verbs have several meanings and therefore will be included in several
classes. Often when a verb has more than one meaning, one of its meanings is
basic and the others are systematically related to it; that is, they are instances
of extended meanings (see Introduction). Usually the ability to show particular

extended meanings is a property of a class of verbs, so where applicable, the existence of related meanings is mentioned in the comments associated with the description of a verb class. This phenomenon is not well understood, so no attempt has been made to include extended meanings systematically.

This part of the book is organized into sections that reflect a limited attempt to group verb classes related by meaning together. However, there is little hierarchical organization compared to the number of classes identified. This lack of structure reflects not only the preliminary nature of the investigation, but also the fact that it is an open research question whether a complete hierarchical organization of English verb classes is possible or even desirable (see Fellbaum (1990) and G.A. Miller and Fellbaum (1991) for some discussion).

Part One

Alternations

1 Transitivity Alternations

This section includes alternations involving a change in a verb's transitivity. These alternations take the form 'NP V NP' alternating with 'NP V' or else 'NP V NP' alternating with 'NP V PP'. The question of whether the intransitive use of the verb qualifies as unaccusative (ergative) or unergative (pure intransitive) has been largely ignored. See Burzio (1986), Grimshaw (1987), B. Levin and Rappaport (1989), Perlmutter (1978) for an overview of the unaccusative/unergative distinction.

1.1 Object of Transitive = Subject of Intransitive Alternations

This subsection includes transitivity alternations taking the form of 'NP V NP' alternating with 'NP V (PP)', where the semantic role of the subject of the intransitive use of the verb is the same as the semantic role of the object of the transitive use of the verb. This pattern has led some researchers to suggest that these verbs are unaccusative in their intransitive use; that is, the surface subject in the intransitive use has been claimed to be an underlying object. These alternations have been split into three subtypes: the middle alternation, a set of alternations labeled "causative alternations," and an alternation termed the "substance/source" alternation.

1.1.1 Middle Alternation

References: Condoravdi (1989), Croft (1991), Curme (1931), Davidse (1991), Dezsö (1980), Dixon (1991), Doron and Rappaport Hovav (1991), Emonds (1976), Erades (1950), Fagan (1988, 1992), Fellbaum (1985, 1992), Fellbaum and Zribi-Hertz (1989), Gawron (1983), Geniušienė (1987), Grady (1965), Hale and Keyser (1986, 1987, 1988), Halliday (1967, 1968), Hatcher (1943), Jaeggli (1986), Jespersen (1927), Keyser and Roeper (1984, 1992),

Poutsma (1904), Roberts (1987), Stroik (1992), Sundén (1916a, 1916b), Van Oosten (1977), Wilkins (1987), Williams (1981), Zubizarreta (1987). See Ruwet (1972) for a discussion of French.

(1)   a.   The butcher cuts the meat.
        b.   The meat cuts easily.

(2)   a.   Janet broke the crystal.
        b.   Crystal breaks at the slightest touch.

(3)   a.   Kelly adores French fabrics.
        b.   * French fabrics adore easily.

(4)   a.   Joan knew the answer.
        b.   * The answer knows easily.

(5)   a.   Bill pounded the metal.
        b.   * This metal won't pound.

(6)   a.   Bill pounded the metal flat.
        b.   This metal won't pound flat.

Comments: The intransitive variant of this alternation, the middle construction, is characterized by a lack of specific time reference and by an understood but unexpressed agent. More often than not, the middle construction includes an adverbial or modal element. These properties distinguish the middle alternation from the causative/inchoative alternation. In particular, the intransitive variant of the causative/inchoative alternation, the inchoative construction, need not have an understood agent, may have specific time reference, and does not have to include adverbial or modal elements. However, there has been some debate in the literature about whether there really is a middle alternation that is distinct from the causative/inchoative alternation or whether there is only a single alternation. Verbs that display the causative/inchoative alternation are found in the middle construction, but there are a number of verbs found in the middle construction that do not display the causative/inchoative alternation. The middle alternation is described as being restricted to verbs with affected objects. This constraint is used to explain the data above involving *pound:* the object of this verb is not affected by the action of the verb, so that the verb is found in the middle construction only in the presence of a resultative phrase, which contributes a state that results from the action of pounding.

1.1.2 Causative Alternations

The next three subsections present "causative alternations," so called since they involve verbs with transitive and intransitive uses, where the transitive use of a verb V can be paraphrased as roughly "cause to V-intransitive." Two major subtypes of causative alternations are usually distinguished in English: the causative/inchoative alternation (sec. 1.1.2.1) and the induced action alternation (sec. 1.1.2.2). However, a wider range of verbs show both transitive and intransitive uses related through the notion of "cause" than fit into these two categories; consequently, a third subsection is included entitled "Other Instances of Causative Alternations" (sec. 1.1.2.3). Some alternating verbs that might have been listed among the verbs showing the causative/inchoative alternation in other work, but that do not clearly fit the semantic characterization of these verbs, have been put into this subsection. This subsection also includes a variety of verbs that are not commonly discussed from the perspective of transitivity alternations.

In Part II of this book, when a verb shows one of the recognized subtypes of the causative alternations (i.e., the causative/inchoative alternation or the induced action alternation), the particular alternation is identified. If a verb is identified as showing the causative alternation, then it shows an instance of the alternation that does not qualify as an instance of one of the two recognized subtypes (cf. sec. 1.1.2.3). However, when a verb does not show any form of the causative alternation, the indication given is "*Causative Alternations."

1.1.2.1 Causative/Inchoative Alternation

References: Abusch (1985, 1986), Anderson (1977), Binnick (1974), Boguraev (1991), Borer (1991), Bowerman (1976, 1982), Brousseau and Ritter (1991), Burzio (1986), Chafe (1970), Chitoran (1986), Croft (1986, 1990, 1991), Cruse (1972, 1973), Curme (1931), Davidse (1992), Dezsö (1980), Dixon (1982b, 1991), Dowty (1979), Farsi (1974), Fellbaum (1990), Fillmore (1966, 1967, 1968a, 1968b, 1977a, 1977b), Fodor (1970), Fodor et al. (1980), Fontenelle and Vanandroye (1989), Gawron (1983), Geis (1973), Gergely and Bever (1986), Guerssel et al. (1985), Hale and Keyser (1986, 1987, 1988, 1992), Halliday (1967, 1968), T. Hoekstra (1992), Ikegami (1988), Jackendoff (1990b), Jespersen (1927, 1942), Jolly (1987), Kastovsky (1973), Keyser and Roeper (1984), Kilby (1984), Kirchner (1955, 1959), G. Lakoff (1968, 1970a), G. Lakoff and J.R. Ross (1972), Langacker (1991), Lee (1971), B. Levin and Rappaport Hovav (1992b), Lipka (1976), Lord (1979), Manzini (1992), Marantz (1984, 1988), Marchand (1969, 1974), J. McCawley (1968a), G. Miller and Fellbaum (1991), Morgan (1969), Mukhin (1985), Parsons (1990), Pinker (1989), Pustejovsky (1988, 1991b), Ravin (1990), Richardson (1983), C.S. Smith (1970, 1972), Sundén (1916a, 1916b), Vendler (1972), Wall (1968), Wasow (1977), Zubizarreta (1987). See Rothemberg (1974) and Ruwet (1972) for an in-depth discussion of a similar phenomenon in French.

(7)   ROLL VERBS: bounce, drift, drop, float, glide, move, roll, slide, swing
        including MOTION AROUND AN AXIS: coil, revolve, rotate, spin, turn,
        twirl, twist, whirl, wind

(8)   BREAK VERBS: break, chip, crack, crash, crush, fracture, rip, shatter,
        smash, snap, splinter, split, tear

(9)   BEND VERBS: bend, crease, crinkle, crumple, fold, rumple, wrinkle

(10)   OTHER ALTERNATING VERBS OF CHANGE OF STATE:
        a. abate, advance, age, air, alter, atrophy, awake, balance, blast, blur,
            burn, burst, capsize, change, char, chill, clog, close, collapse, col-
            lect, compress, condense, contract, corrode, crumble, decompose,
            decrease, deflate, defrost, degrade, diminish, dissolve, distend,
            divide, double, drain, ease, enlarge, expand, explode, fade, fill,
            flood, fray, freeze, frost, fuse, grow, halt, heal, heat, hush, ig-
            nite, improve, increase, inflate, kindle, light, loop, mature, melt,
            multiply, overturn, pop, quadruple, rekindle, reopen, reproduce,
            rupture, scorch, sear, short, short-circuit, shrink, shrivel, singe,
            sink, soak, splay, sprout, steep, stretch, submerge, subside, taper,
            thaw, tilt, tire, topple, triple, unfold, vary, warp
        b. ZERO-RELATED TO ADJECTIVE: blunt, clear, clean, cool, crisp, dim,
            dirty, double, dry, dull, empty, even, firm, level, loose, mellow,
            muddy, narrow, open, pale, quiet, round, shut, slack, slim, slow,
            smooth, sober, sour, steady, tame, tense, thin, triple, warm
        c. CHANGE OF COLOR: blacken, brown, crimson, gray, green, purple,
            redden, silver, tan, whiten, yellow
        d. –en VERBS: awaken, brighten, broaden, cheapen, coarsen, dampen,
            darken, deepen, fatten, flatten, freshen, gladden, harden, has-
            ten, heighten, lengthen, lessen, lighten, loosen, moisten, neaten,
            quicken, quieten, ripen, roughen, sharpen, shorten, sicken,
            slacken, smarten, soften, steepen, stiffen, straighten, strengthen,
            sweeten, tauten, thicken, tighten, toughen, waken, weaken, widen,
            worsen
        e. –ify VERBS: acetify, acidify, alkalify, calcify, carbonify, dehumid-
            ify, emulsify, fructify, gasify, humidify, intensify, lignify, liquefy,
            magnify, nitrify, ossify, petrify, purify, putrefy, silicify, solidify,
            stratify, vitrify
        f. –ize VERBS: americanize, caramelize, carbonize, crystallize, de-
            centralize, demagnetize, democratize, depressurize, destabilize,
            energize, equalize, fossilize, gelatinize, glutenize, harmonize,
            hybridize, iodize, ionize, magnetize, neutralize, oxidize, polar-
            ize, pulverize, regularize, stabilize, unionize, vaporize, volatilize,
            westernize

g. *–ate* VERBS: accelerate, agglomerate, ameliorate, attenuate, coagulate, decelerate, de-escalate, degenerate, desiccate, deteriorate,
detonate, disintegrate, dissipate, evaporate, federate, granulate,
incubate, levitate, macerate, operate, proliferate, propagate,
ulcerate, vibrate

(11)   AMUSE-TYPE PSYCH-VERBS (some): cheer, delight, enthuse, gladden,
grieve, madden, obsess, puzzle, sadden, sicken, thrill, tire, weary,
worry

(12)   a. Janet broke the cup.
        b. The cup broke.

(13)   * VERBS OF CHANGE OF POSSESSION (only selected subtypes listed):
        a. * GIVE VERBS: feed, give, lease, lend, loan, pass, pay, peddle,
            refund, render, rent, repay, sell, serve, trade
        b. * CONTRIBUTE VERBS: administer, contribute, disburse, distribute,
            donate, extend, forfeit, proffer, refer, reimburse, relinquish, remit,
            restore, return, sacrifice, submit, surrender, transfer
        c. * VERBS OF FUTURE HAVING: advance, allocate, allot, assign, award,
            bequeath, cede, concede, extend, grant, guarantee, issue, leave,
            offer, owe, promise, vote, will, yield

(14)   a. They gave the bicycle to me.
        b. * The bicycle gave to me.

(15)   * VERBS OF CUTTING:
        a. * CUT VERBS: chip, clip, cut, hack, hew, saw, scrape, scratch, slash,
            snip
        b. * CARVE VERBS: bore, bruise, carve, chip (potatoes), chop, crop,
            crush, cube, dent, dice, drill, file, fillet, gash, gouge, grate, grind,
            mangle, mash, mince, mow, nick, notch, perforate, pulverize,
            punch (paper), prune, shred, slice, slit, spear, squash, squish

(16)   a. Margaret cut the bread.
        b. * The bread cut.

(17)   * VERBS OF CONTACT BY IMPACT:
        a. * HIT VERBS: bang, bash, batter, beat, bump, butt, dash, drum, ham-
            mer, hit, kick, knock, lash, pound, rap, slap, smack, smash (where
            no effect implicated), strike, tamp, tap, thump, thwack, whack
        b. * SWAT VERBS: bite, claw, paw, peck, punch (person), scratch, shoot
            (gun), slug, stab, swat, swipe
        c. * SPANK VERBS: belt, birch, bludgeon, bonk, brain, cane, clobber,
            club, conk, cosh, cudgel, cuff, flog, knife, paddle, paddywhack,

pummel, sock, spank, strap, thrash, truncheon, wallop, whip, whisk

(18)   * TOUCH VERBS: caress, graze, kiss, lick, nudge, pat, peck (=kiss), pinch, prod, sting, stroke, tickle, touch

(19)   * DESTROY VERBS: annihilate, blitz, decimate, demolish, destroy, devastate, exterminate, extirpate, obliterate, ravage, raze, ruin, waste, wreck

(20)   * VERBS OF KILLING:
       a. * MURDER VERBS: assassinate, butcher, dispatch, eliminate, execute, immolate, kill, liquidate, massacre, murder, slaughter, slay
       b. * POISON VERBS (most): crucify, electrocute, garrotte, hang, knife, poison, shoot, smother, stab, strangle

(21)   * VERBS OF APPEARANCE, DISAPPEARANCE, AND OCCURRENCE:
       a. * APPEAR VERBS (many): appear, arise, awake, come, dawn, emanate, emerge, erupt, evolve, flow, gush, issue, materialize, plop, result, rise, steal, stem, stream, supervene, surge, wax
       b. * VERBS OF DISAPPEARANCE: die, disappear, expire, lapse, perish, vanish
       c. * VERBS OF OCCURRENCE: ensue, eventuate, happen, occur, recur, transpire

(22)   a. A dove appeared from the magician's sleeve.
       b. * The magician appeared a dove from his sleeve.

Comments: This alternation is known by a variety of other names, including "anti-causative" and "ergative." C.S. Smith (1970) provides a good discussion of the factors licensing this alternation and causative alternations in general. The verbs undergoing the causative/inchoative alternation can roughly be characterized as verbs of change of state or change of position. Selected verbs that do not undergo the alternation have also been listed, including some verbs that are only used transitively, such as verbs of change of possession, and some that are only used intransitively, such as verbs of appearance, disappearance, and occurrence. Few psych-verbs—verbs of psychological state—participate in the causative/inchoative alternation in English, but all verbs of this type appear to participate in the French, Italian, and Russian counterparts of this alternation; see Ruwet (1972) for a discussion of French psych-verbs. See also comments under Middle Alternation above for a comparison of the causative/inchoative and middle alternations.

1.1.2.2   Induced Action Alternation

References: Abusch (1985, 1986), Brousseau and Ritter (1991), Cruse (1972, 1973), Davidse (1992), Dixon (1991), Gawron (1983), Hale and Keyser (1986), Halliday (1967), Huddleston (1970), Ikegami (1970), Lee (1971), Pinker (1989)

(23)   RUN VERBS (some): canter, drive, fly, gallop, jump, leap, march, race, run, swim, trot, walk

(24)   a.   Sylvia jumped the horse over the fence.
      b.   The horse jumped over the fence.

(25)   a.   The scientist ran the rats through the maze.
      b.   The rats ran through the maze.

Comments: This alternation is found primarily with a subset of the *run* verbs. It differs from the causative/inchoative alternation in that the causee is typically an animate volitional entity that is induced to act by the causer. Often in the transitive variant the causer is understood not only to cause the causee to move but also to be accompanying the causee. However, the accompaniment interpretation is not necessary, as shown by the example involving rats in a maze. Nevertheless, due to this potential interpretation, this alternation has sometimes been referred to as the "accompanied causation" alternation.

In the transitive causative use, the verb must be accompanied by a directional phrase. Even if such a phrase is not overtly expressed, it is understood. For instance, *Sylvia jumped the horse* means that Sylvia jumped the horse over something; it cannot mean that Sylvia made the horse jump in place. This property sets the induced action alternation apart from other instances of causative alternations.

1.1.2.3   Other Instances of Causative Alternations

References: C.S. Smith (1970). See also references under Causative/Inchoative Alternation.

(26)   VERBS OF EMISSION (some):
      a.   VERBS OF SOUND EMISSION (some): bang, beep, blare, buzz, clack, clang, clash, clatter, click, hoot, jangle, jingle, ring, rustle, squeak, squeal, tinkle, twang
      b.   VERBS OF LIGHT EMISSION (some): beam, blink, flash, shine
      c.   VERBS OF SUBSTANCE EMISSION (few): bleed, squirt

(27)   a.   The visitor rang the bell.
      b.   The bell rang.

(28)   VERBS OF SPATIAL CONFIGURATION (some): dangle, fly, hang, lean, perch, rest, sit, stand, swing

(29)   a.   They stood the statue on the pedestal.
        b.   The statue stood on the pedestal.

(30)   LODGE VERBS (some): bivouac, board, lodge, settle, shelter

(31)   a.   The soldiers lodged in the schoolhouse.
        b.   The army lodged the soldiers in the schoolhouse.

(32)   SUFFOCATE VERBS: asphyxiate, choke, drown, ?stifle, suffocate

(33)   OTHER VERBS: bleed, burp

(34)   a.   I burped the baby.
        b.   The baby burped.

Comments: This section could be viewed as a "catchall" category that includes all those verbs whose transitive use means roughly "cause to V-intransitive" which do not fit into the other two types of causative alternations identified here. Despite this negative characterization, many of the verbs listed here do have something in common. With the exception of the *suffocate* verbs, which may deserve separate treatment, these verbs are felt to be basically "intransitive" verbs describing internally controlled actions which in certain circumstances can be externally controlled (caused), giving rise to the transitive use of the verb. This characteristic is reflected in the fact that many of them show a more limited range of objects in their transitive use than they show subjects in their intransitive use, even though both types of arguments bear the same semantic relation to the verb. For instance, as C.S. Smith (1970) points out, one can burp a baby, but not a doctor, although both babies and doctors can burp.

1.1.3   Substance/Source Alternation

References: Pinker (1989), Salkoff (1983)

(35)   VERBS OF SUBSTANCE EMISSION: belch, bleed, bubble, dribble, drip, drool, emanate, exude, gush, leak, ooze, pour, puff, radiate, seep, shed, spew, spout, sprout, spurt, squirt, steam, stream, sweat

(36)   a.   Heat radiates from the sun.
        b.   The sun radiates heat.

Comments: This transitivity alternation is only found with verbs of substance emission. These verbs take two arguments: a source (emitter) and the substance emitted from this source. Like the middle alternation and the causative alternations, this transitivity alternation is characterized by the subject of the intransitive form of the verb bearing the same semantic relation to the verb as the object of the transitive form: in this instance, the substance emitted. Unlike the middle alternation and the causative alternations, both arguments of the verbs of substance emission are expressed in both the transitive and intransitive uses of these verbs. Not only is the substance expressed in both, but the source is expressed as the subject in the transitive use of the verb and as the object of the preposition *from* in the intransitive use.

1.2 Unexpressed Object Alternations

This section includes transitivity alternations where the subject of the transitive use of the verb bears the same semantic relation to the verb as the subject of the intransitive use does. The intransitive variant in each of these alternations involves an unexpressed but understood object. The different alternations in this section have been recognized because each one is associated with a distinct interpretation of the unexpressed object. However, further study may suggest that some of these alternations should be collapsed. See also Fillmore (1986) for some discussion of a range of constructions involving unexpressed objects with definite interpretations, which might suggest the inclusion of an additional category.

1.2.1 Unspecified Object Alternation

References: Allerton (1975), Brame (not dated), Bresnan (1980), Browne (1971), Carrier and Randall (1992, in press), Curme (1931), Dixon (1991), Dowty (1978b, 1981), Fellbaum and Kegl (1989), Fillmore (1986), Fodor and Fodor (1980), Jespersen (1927), Keyser and Roeper (1992), Kilby (1984), G. Lakoff (1970a), Lehrer (1970), Manzini (1992), Mittwoch (1982), Postal (1977b), Rice (1988), Williams (1981), Zubizarreta (1987)

(37)   bake, carve, chop, clean, cook, crochet, draw, drink, dust, eat, embroi-
         der, hum, hunt, fish, iron, knead, knit, mend, milk, mow, nurse, pack,
         paint, play, plow, polish, read, recite, sew, sculpt, sing, sketch, sow,
         study, sweep, teach, type, sketch, vacuum, wash, weave, whittle, write

(38)   a. Mike ate the cake.
         b. Mike ate. (→ Mike ate a meal or something one typically eats.)

Comments: This alternation is manifested with a wide range of activity verbs. Despite the lack of overt direct object in the intransitive variant, the verb in this variant is understood to have as object something that qualifies as a typical object of the verb; however, there is some discussion concerning how best to characterize this interpretation. There is also some debate about whether the understood object is or is not explicitly represented at some level of syntactic or lexical representation. This alternation also often goes by names such as "indefinite object" or "indefinite NP deletion" alternation.

1.2.2   Understood Body-Part Object Alternation

References: Rice (1988)

(39)   VERBS OF GESTURES/SIGNS INVOLVING BODY PARTS:
   a.   WINK VERBS: blink (eye), clap (hands), nod (head), point (finger), shrug (shoulders), squint (eyes), wag (tail), wave (hand), wink (eye)
   b.   * CRANE VERBS: arch (back, neck), bare (teeth), bat (eyelashes), beat (feet), blow (nose), clench (fists), click (heels, tongue), close (eyes), cock (head), crane (neck), crook (finger), cross (arms, eyes, legs), drum (finger), flap (wings), flash (teeth), flex (muscles), flick (finger), flutter (eyelashes), fold (arms), gnash (teeth), grind (teeth), hang (head), hunch (shoulders), kick, knit (eyebrows), open (eyes), pucker (lips), purse (lips), raise (eyebrows, hand), roll (eyes), rub (hands), shake (head, fist, hands), show (teeth), shuffle (feet), smack (lips), snap (fingers), stamp (foot), stretch (legs), toss (mane), turn (head), twiddle (thumbs), twitch (ears, nose), wag (finger, tail), waggle (ears), wiggle (ears, hips, nose), wring (hands), wrinkle (forehead, nose)

(40)   a.   The departing passenger waved his hand at the crowd.
   b.   The departing passenger waved at the crowd.

(41)   a.   Jennifer craned her neck.
   b.   * Jennifer craned.

(42)   VERBS OF CARING FOR A SPECIFIC BODY PART:
   a.   FLOSS VERBS: brush (teeth), floss (teeth), shave (beard, legs), wash (hands, face)
   b.   * BRAID VERBS: bob (hair), braid (hair), brush (hair), clip (nails), coldcream (face), comb (hair), condition (hair), crimp (hair), crop (hair), curl (hair), cut (hair), dye (hair), file (nails), henna (hair), lather (hair, body), manicure (nails), part (hair), perm (hair), plait (hair), pluck (eyebrows), powder (face, nose), rinse (hair, mouth), rouge (cheeks, face), set (hair), shampoo (hair), soap (hands, body), talc (body), tease (hair), towel (face, hands), trim (hair, beard), wave (hair)

(43)   a.   I flossed my teeth.
   b.   I flossed.

(44)   a.   Celia braided her hair.
   b.   * Celia braided.

(45)   * HURT VERBS: bark (shin), bite (lip), bump, burn, break, bruise, chip (tooth), cut, fracture, hurt, injure, nick (chin, leg), prick (finger), pull

(muscle), rupture, scald, scratch (chin), skin (knee), split (lip), sprain (ankle, back, knee, wrist), strain, stub (toe), turn (ankle), twist (ankle)

(46)   a. Tessa sprained her ankle.
         b. * Tessa sprained.

Comments: This alternation is found with verbs describing conventionalized gestures and signs made with a particular part of the body. These verbs take this body part as their direct object in their transitive use. In their intransitive use, the body part is understood but not expressed. Some of these verbs allow a range of objects, including several body parts; however, usually only one of these body parts is associated with the intransitive use. Interestingly, in Russian many of these verbs mark the body part in the instrumental case rather than the accusative case (see J.S. Levine (1980)).

1.2.3   Understood Reflexive Object Alternation

References: Curme (1931), Dixon (1991), Faltz (1985), Geniušienė (1987), Halliday (1968), Jespersen (1927), Langacker (1991), Quirk et al. (1985), Sigler (1985)

(47)   VERBS OF CARING FOR THE WHOLE BODY:
         a. DRESS VERBS: bathe, change, disrobe, dress, exercise, preen, primp, shave, shower, strip, undress, wash
         b. * GROOM VERBS: curry, groom

(48)   a. Jill dressed herself hurriedly.
         b. Jill dressed hurriedly.

(49)   * VERBS OF CARING FOR A SPECIFIC BODY PART:
         a. * FLOSS VERBS: brush (teeth), floss (teeth), shave (beard, legs), wash (hands, face)
         b. * BRAID VERBS: bob (hair), braid (hair), brush (hair), clip (nails), coldcream (face), comb (hair), condition (hair), crimp (hair), crop (hair), curl (hair), cut (hair), dye (hair), file (nails), henna (hair), lather (hair, body), manicure (nails), part (hair), perm (hair), plait (hair), pluck (eyebrows), powder (face, nose), rinse (hair, mouth), rouge (cheeks, face), set (hair), shampoo (hair), soap (hands, body), talc (body), tease (hair), towel (face, hands), trim (hair, beard), wave (hair)

(50)   a. I flossed.
         b. * I flossed myself.

(51)   a. * Celia brushed herself.
         b. * Celia brushed.

(52)   *HURT VERBS: bark (shin), bite (lip), bump, burn, break, bruise, chip
        (tooth), cut, fracture, hurt, injure, nick (chin, leg), prick (finger), pull
        (muscle), rupture, scald, scratch (chin), skin (knee), split (lip), sprain
        (ankle, back, knee, wrist), strain, stub (toe), turn (ankle), twist (ankle)

(53)   a. Tessa cut herself. (few verbs)
        b. *Tessa cut.

(54)   LOAD VERBS (some): jam, cram, load, pack

(55)   a. We loaded ourselves onto the bus.
        b. We loaded onto the bus.

(56)   PUSH/PULL VERBS (some): jerk, pull, yank

(57)   a. We pulled ourselves free.
        b. We pulled free.

Comments: The action described by the verb in the intransitive variant of
this alternation is understood to be directed toward the subject of the verb; that
is, the intransitive variant can be roughly paraphrased by the combination of
the transitive use of the verb plus a reflexive object. This alternation is often
discussed with respect to Romance and Slavic languages, where the verb in
the intransitive variant is associated with an overt reflexive morpheme or clitic
(see Babby (1975), Burzio (1981, 1986), Kayne (1975), among others). It is
possible that the alternation shown by the *load* verbs and *push/pull* verbs,
though superficially similar to that shown by the verbs of caring for the whole
body, may reflect a different phenomenon.

1.2.4   Understood Reciprocal Object Alternation

References: Baldi (1974), Carrier and Randall (in press), Condoravdi (1990),
Croft (1991), Curme (1931), Dong (1970), Dougherty (1970, 1971, 1974),
Fiengo and Lasnik (1973), Geniušienė (1987), Gleitman (1965), Jespersen
(1949), G. Lakoff and Peters (1969), Langendoen (1978), Lichtenberk (1985),
J. McCawley (1968b, 1972a), G. Miller and Johnson-Laird (1976), Schachter
(1977), Schwartz (1990). See also references under Understood Reflexive
Object Alternation above.

(58)   VERBS OF SOCIAL INTERACTION:
        a. MARRY VERBS: court, cuddle, date, divorce, embrace, hug, kiss,
            marry, nuzzle, pass, pet
        b. MEET VERBS: battle, box, consult, debate, fight, meet, play, visit
        c. *CORRESPOND VERBS: agree, argue, banter, bargain, bicker,
            ?brawl, clash, coexist, collaborate, collide, ?combat, commis-
            erate, communicate, compete, concur, confabulate, conflict,

consort, cooperate, correspond, dicker, differ, disagree, dispute, dissent, duel, elope, feud, flirt, haggle, hobnob, jest, joke, joust, mate, mingle, mix, neck, negotiate, pair, plot, quarrel, quibble, rendezvous, scuffle, skirmish, spar, spat, spoon, squabble, struggle, tilt, tussle, vie, war, wrangle, wrestle

(59) a. Anne met Cathy.
      b. Anne and Cathy met.

(60) a. * Brenda bantered Molly.
      b. Brenda and Molly bantered.

(61) a. The drunk hugged the lamppost.
      b. * The drunk and the lamppost hugged.

(62) VERBS OF CONTIGUOUS LOCATION (some): cross, hit, intersect, meet, miss, touch

(63) a. Italy touches France.
      b. Italy and France touch.

(64) * TALK VERBS: speak, talk

(65) * CHITCHAT VERBS: argue, chat, chatter, chitchat, confer, converse, gab, gossip, rap, schmooze, yak

(66) a. * Ellen chitchatted Helen.
      b. Ellen and Helen chitchatted.

Comments: The action described by the verb in the intransitive variant of this alternation can be roughly paraphrased by the transitive verb when it takes the reciprocal *each other* as object. When used intransitively, these verbs must take a collective NP as subject. There are additional restrictions on the subject when the verb is used intransitively: all participants in the action must be of comparable status. For instance, with some verbs, such as *hug* in example (61) above, each member of the group must be animate and able to participate in initiating and carrying out the action. This alternation is often discussed with respect to Romance and Slavic languages, where the verb in the intransitive variant is associated with an overt reflexive morpheme or clitic (see Babby (1975), Burzio (1981, 1986), Kayne (1975), among others).

1.2.5 PRO-arb Object Alternation

References: Rizzi (1986)

(67) ADVISE VERBS (except *alert*): admonish, advise, caution, counsel, instruct, warn

(68)   a. The sign warned us against skating on the pond.
       b. The sign warned against skating on the pond.

(69)   AMUSE-TYPE PSYCH-VERBS: abash, affect, afflict, affront, aggravate,
       agitate, agonize, alarm, alienate, amaze, amuse, anger, annoy, antago-
       nize, appall, appease, arouse, assuage, astonish, astound, awe, baffle,
       beguile, bewilder, bewitch, boggle, bore, bother, bug, calm, captivate,
       chagrin, charm, cheer, chill, comfort, concern, confound, confuse,
       console, content, convince, cow, crush, cut, daunt, daze, dazzle, deject,
       delight, demolish, demoralize, depress, devastate, disappoint, dis-
       arm, discombobulate, discomfit, disconcert, discompose, discourage,
       disgrace, disgruntle, disgust, dishearten, disillusion, dismay, dispirit,
       displease, disquiet, dissatisfy, distract, distress, disturb, dumbfound,
       elate, electrify, embarrass, embolden, enchant, encourage, engage,
       engross, enlighten, enliven, enrage, enrapture, entertain, enthrall,
       enthuse, entice, entrance, exasperate, excite, exhaust, exhilarate, fas-
       cinate, faze, flabbergast, flatter, floor, fluster, frighten, frustrate, gall,
       galvanize, gladden, gratify, grieve, harass, haunt, hearten, horrify,
       humble, humiliate, hurt, hypnotize, impress, incense, infuriate, in-
       spire, insult, interest, intimidate, intoxicate, intrigue, invigorate, irk,
       irritate, jar, jollify, jolt, lull, madden, mesmerize, miff, mollify, mor-
       tify, move, muddle, mystify, nauseate, nettle, numb, obsess, offend,
       outrage, overawe, overwhelm, pacify, pain, peeve, perplex, perturb,
       pique, placate, plague, please, preoccupy, provoke, puzzle, rankle,
       reassure, refresh, relax, relieve, repel, repulse, revitalize, revolt, rile,
       ruffle, sadden, satisfy, scandalize, scare, shake, shame, shock, sicken,
       sober, solace, soothe, spellbind, spook, stagger, startle, stimulate,
       sting, stir, strike, stump, stun, stupefy, surprise, tantalize, tease, tempt,
       terrify, terrorize, threaten, thrill, throw, tickle, tire, titillate, torment,
       touch, transport, trouble, try, unnerve, unsettle, uplift, upset, vex,
       weary, worry, wound, wow

(70)   a. That movie always shocks people.
       b. That movie always shocks.

Comments: In this alternation, the unexpressed object in the intransitive
variant receives what has been called an "arbitrary" or "PRO-arb" interpretation.
That is, this variant could be paraphrased with the transitive form of the verb
taking "one" or "us" or "people" as object. This alternation is restricted to verbs
with affected objects. It is found with a more limited set of verbs in English
than in Italian: primarily the verbs listed here. It is possible that not all the
psych-verbs listed above may participate in this alternation.

1.2.6   Characteristic Property Alternations

These two alternations are used to indicate that an agent or instrument has a propensity for or is suited to the action named by the verb.

1.2.6.1   Characteristic Property of Agent Alternation

References: Fellbaum and Kegl (1989), Geniušienė (1987). See Babby (1975) for discussion of the same phenomenon in Russian.

(71)   ALTERNATING VERBS: bite, butt, itch, kick, pinch, prick, scratch, sting

(72)   a.   That dog bites people.
          b.   That dog bites.

Comments: Both variants of this alternation are used to indicate that the subject typically shows a propensity for the action named by the verb. That is, the action named by the verb is in some sense characteristic of the subject. The understood object in the intransitive variant is interpreted as something like "people." The subject need not be animate. Interestingly, in Russian this use of the verb involves the affixation of the reflexive morpheme -*sja* to the verb (see Babby (1975)). It is difficult to characterize precisely the set of verbs that show this alternation, although it appears to be a fairly restricted set.

1.2.6.2   Characteristic Property of Instrument Alternation

References: Dixon (1991), C.S. Smith (1970)

(73)   clip, cook, cut, hammer, record, slice, pinch, prick, scratch, sting, write

(74)   a.   I cut the bread with this knife.
          b.   This knife cut the bread.
          c.   This knife doesn't cut.

(75)   a.   This pen doesn't write.
          b.   These shears clip well.
          c.   This machine records well.
          d.   This oven cooks well.
          e.   This lotion softens, soothes, moisturizes, and protects.
          f.   This polish cleans, protects, and shines.

(76)   a. * This key won't open.
          b.   This key won't open the lock.

(77)   a. * This hammer won't break.
               (on the interpretation where the hammer breaks something)
          b.   This hammer won't break the window.

Comments: The intransitive variant of this alternation is used to indicate an instrument's suitability for carrying out the action named by the verb. This alternation has not been collapsed with the characteristic property of agent alternation because in this alternation the instrument is used by the agent to carry out the action named by the verb, and it is not always capable of carrying out the action alone. It is difficult to characterize the verbs that show this alternation; they are drawn from a wide range of classes of verbs that may take instruments, including the *cut* and *carve* verbs.

1.2.7 *Way* Object Alternation

References: Jackendoff (1990b), B. Levin and Rapoport (1988), Marantz (1992)

(78)   PUSH/PULL VERBS (some): press, push, shove

(79)   a.   They pushed their way through the crowd.
         b.   They pushed through the crowd.

Comments: A large number of verbs can be followed by X's *way* plus a directional phrase; however, the members of the set of verbs given here appear to have an intransitive use (see (79b)) that almost paraphrases the use of the verb followed by X's *way* (see (79a)).

1.2.8 Instructional Imperative

References: Atkins, Kegl, and B. Levin (1988), Haegeman (1987), Massam and Roberge (1989), Sadock (1974)

(80)   ALTERNATING VERBS: attach, bake, beat, boil, cook, cover, mix, pour, put, remove, set, stir

(81)   a.   Bake the cake for 30 minutes.
         b.   Bake for 30 minutes.

(82)   a.   * Like the ice cream.
         b.   * Like after tasting.

Comments: This construction always requires the verb to be in the imperative. Consequently it will not be found with verbs that do not allow the imperative. The instructional imperative construction is found with a wide range of verbs that take an affected object. This property means that it is not displayed by many other types of verbs, including verbs of perception or *admire*-type psych-verbs. However, it is found with a much wider range of verbs than many of the other alternations such as the unexpressed reflexive and reciprocal object alternations. The understood object in the intransitive variant receives its interpretation from context; generally, it receives a definite interpretation.

1.3 Conative Alternation

References: Dixon (1991), Gawron (1983), Guerssel et al. (1985), Ikegami (1985), L. Levin (1987). See also Hale (1982) and Laughren (1988) for a discussion of this alternation in Warlpiri.

(83)   VERBS OF CONTACT BY IMPACT:
       a.   HIT VERBS: bang, bash, batter, beat, bump, butt, dash, drum, hammer, hit, kick, knock, lash, pound, rap, slap, smack, smash (where no effect implicated), strike, tamp, tap, thump, thwack, whack
       b.   SWAT VERBS: bite, claw, paw, peck, punch (person), scratch, shoot (gun), slug, stab, swat, swipe
       c. * SPANK VERBS: belt, birch, bludgeon, bonk, brain, cane, clobber, club, conk, cosh, cudgel, cuff, flog, knife, paddle, paddywhack, pummel, sock, spank, strap, thrash, truncheon, wallop, whip, whisk

(84)   a.   Paula hit the fence.
       b.   Paula hit at the fence.

(85)   POKE VERBS (some): dig, jab, poke, stick

(86)   VERBS OF CUTTING:
       a.   CUT VERBS: chip, clip, cut, hack, hew, saw, scrape, scratch, slash, snip
       b. * CARVE VERBS: bore, bruise, carve, chip (potatoes), chop, crop, crush, cube, dent, dice, drill, file, fillet, gash, gouge, grate, grind, mangle, mash, mince, mow, nick, notch, perforate, pulverize, punch (paper), prune, shred, slice, slit, spear, squash, squish

(87)   a.   Margaret cut the bread.
       b.   Margaret cut at the bread.

(88)   SPRAY/LOAD VERBS (some): dab, rub, splash, spray, squirt, swab

(89)   a.   Faustina sprayed the lilies.
       b.   Faustina sprayed at the lilies.

(90)   * ALTERNATING VERBS OF CHANGE OF STATE including:
       a. * BREAK VERBS: break, chip, crack, crash, crush, fracture, rip, shatter, smash, snap, splinter, split, tear
       b. * BEND VERBS: bend, crease, crinkle, crumple, fold, rumple, wrinkle

(91)   a.   Janet broke the bread.
       b. * Janet broke at the bread.

(92)   * TOUCH VERBS: caress, graze, kiss, lick, nudge, pat, peck (=kiss), pinch, prod, sting, stroke, tickle, touch

(93)   a. Terry touched the cat.
       b. * Terry touched at the cat.

(94)   PUSH/PULL VERBS: ?draw, heave, jerk, press, pull, push, shove, ?thrust, tug, yank

(95)   a. I pushed the table.
       b. I pushed at/on/against the table.

(96)   * DESTROY VERBS: annihilate, blitz, decimate, demolish, destroy, devastate, exterminate, extirpate, obliterate, ravage, raze, ruin, waste, wreck

(97)   VERBS OF INGESTING:
       a. EAT VERBS: drink, eat
       b. CHEW VERBS: chew, chomp, crunch, gnaw, lick, munch, nibble, pick, peck, sip, slurp, suck
       c. * GOBBLE VERBS: bolt, gobble, gulp, guzzle, quaff, swallow, swig, wolf
       d. * DEVOUR VERBS: consume, devour, imbibe, ingest, swill

(98)   a. The mouse nibbled the cheese.
       b. The mouse nibbled at/on the cheese.

(99)   * VERBS OF SENDING AND CARRYING including:
       a. * SEND VERBS: airmail, convey, deliver, dispatch, express, FedEx, forward, hand, mail, pass, port, post, return, send, shift, ship, shunt, slip, smuggle, sneak, transfer, transport, UPS
       b. * SLIDE VERBS: bounce, float, move, roll, slide

(100) a. Monica moved the cat.
       b. * Monica moved at the cat.

Comments: The conative alternation is a transitivity alternation in which the object of the verb in the transitive variant turns up in the intransitive conative variant as the object of the preposition in a prepositional phrase headed by the preposition *at* (sometimes *on* with certain verbs of ingesting and the *push/pull* verbs). The use of the verb in the intransitive variant describes an "attempted" action without specifying whether the action was actually carried out. The conative alternation seems to be found with verbs whose meaning includes notions of both contact and motion.

1.4 Preposition Drop Alternations

These transitivity alternations involve a verb found either in an intransitive frame with a prepositional phrase complement or else in a transitive frame. The transitive frame appears to be derived from the intransitive frame by "dropping" the preposition.

1.4.1 Locative Preposition Drop Alternation

References: Davidse (1992), Dixon (1991), Emonds (1991), Gawron (1983), Gruber (1965), Halliday (1967), Jackendoff (1985b, 1992c), Keyser and Roeper (1992), Kirchner (1955, 1959), Langacker (1991), Moravcsik (1978), Mukhin (1985), Poutsma (1904), Rappaport and B. Levin (1985), Stratton (1971), Zubizarreta (1987)

(101)   RUN VERBS (some): canter, climb, cross, fly, gallop, hike, jog, jump, leap, prowl, ramble, ride, roam, rove, row, run, shoot (rapids), stroll, swim, traipse, tramp, travel, trudge, vault, wade, walk, wander

(102)   a.   Martha climbed up the mountain.
         b.   Martha climbed the mountain.

(103)   VERBS THAT ARE VEHICLE NAMES (some): bicycle, bike, canoe, jeep, raft, row, sail, skate, ski

(104)   a.   They skated along the canals.
         b.   They skated the canals.

(105)   * ROLL VERBS: bounce, drift, drop, float, glide, move, roll, slide, swing including MOTION AROUND AN AXIS: coil, revolve, rotate, spin, turn, twirl, twist, whirl, wind

(106)   a.   The spaceship revolves around the earth.
         b. * The spaceship revolves the earth.
             (on the interpretation "The spaceship circles the earth.")

(107)   VERBS OF INHERENTLY DIRECTED MOTION (some): ascend, depart, descend, escape, flee, leave
         BUT NOT: arrive, come, go, return

(108)   a.   Martha slowly descended down the stairs.
         b.   Martha slowly descended the stairs.

(109)   a.   Sharon came into the room.
         b. * Sharon came the room.

Comments: This alternation is found with certain verbs of motion that take directional phrase complements. These verbs are found intransitively with a directional phrase or transitively with a path or goal (or in a few instances a source) as direct object. It has been claimed that this alternation is associated with the "holistic/partitive" effect associated with locative alternation verbs; see Locative Alternation (sec. 2.3) for discussion. Specifically, the path or goal argument receives a "holistic" interpretation when it is expressed as direct object. To state this differently, when these verbs are found in the transitive variant, the path is understood as being completely traversed or the goal as attained.

1.4.2 *With* Preposition Drop Alternation

References: Fillmore (1972), Kirchner (1959)

(110)   VERBS OF SOCIAL INTERACTION:
     a.   MEET VERBS: battle, box, consult, debate, fight, meet, play, visit
     b.   * MARRY VERBS: court, cuddle, date, divorce, embrace, hug, kiss, marry, nuzzle, pass, pet
     c.   * CORRESPOND VERBS: agree, argue, banter, bargain, bicker, brawl, clash, coexist, collaborate, collide, combat, commiserate, communicate, compete, concur, confabulate, conflict, consort, cooperate, correspond, dicker, differ, disagree, dispute, dissent, duel, elope, feud, flirt, haggle, hobnob, jest, joke, joust, mate, mingle, mix, neck, negotiate, pair, plot, quarrel, quibble, rendezvous, scuffle, skirmish, spar, spat, spoon, squabble, struggle, tilt, tussle, vie, war, wrangle, wrestle

(111)   * TALK VERBS: speak, talk

(112)   * CHITCHAT VERBS: argue, chat, chatter, chitchat, confer, converse, gab, gossip, rap, schmooze, yak

(113)   a.   Jill met with Sarah.
     b.   Jill met Sarah.

(114)   a.   * Jill embraced with Sarah.
     b.   Jill embraced Sarah.

Comments: A small set of verbs that involve potentially reciprocal actions alternate between an intransitive form involving a prepositional phrase headed by *with* and a transitive form that is an apparent paraphrase of the intransitive form and seems to differ merely in the absence of the preposition *with*. Unlike the locative preposition drop alternation, this alternation does not involve verbs of manner of motion, but rather involves certain verbs of social interaction. Very few intransitive verbs that take a *with* complement allow this preposition to "drop."

2   Alternations Involving Arguments Within the VP

This section includes a variety of alternations that do not involve a change in the transitivity of the verb. All of these alternations are displayed by transitive verbs taking more than one internal argument and arise because these verbs allow more than one way of expressing these arguments. A few of these alternations also show a second form involving intransitive verbs that can be seen as parallel to the alternation with transitive verbs if the subject of the intransitive verb plays the role of the object of the transitive verb in the alternation. If these intransitive verbs are said to be unaccusative verbs, so that their surface subject is an underlying object, then both the transitive and intransitive forms of the alternations included in this section can be said to involve alternate expressions of VP-internal arguments.

2.1   Dative Alternation

References: Abney (1987), Abraham (1983), Allerton (1978), Anderson (1988), Aoun and Li (1989), C.L. Baker (1992), M. Baker (1988a, 1988b), Barss and Lasnik (1986), Blansitt (1984), Boguraev and Briscoe (1989), Bolinger (1971), Bouldin (1990), Bowers (1981, 1989), Branchadell (1991), Bresnan (1980), Brittain (1971), Cattell (1985), Channon (1982), Croft (1991), Czepluch (1982), DeLancey (1985), Dik (1978), Dixon (1973, 1982a, 1989, 1991), Dowty (1978a, 1978b, 1979, 1982), Dryer (1987), Emonds (1972, 1991), Erteschik-Shir (1979), Faltz (1978), Fillmore (1965), Gawron (1983), Givòn (1984), Goldberg (1989, in press), Goldsmith (1980), Green (1974, 1986), Grimshaw (1989), Grimshaw and Prince (1986), Gropen et al. (1989), Haider (1992), Haïk (1990), Hawkins (1981), E. Hoekstra (1989, 1991a, 1991b), Hoffman (1991), Hudson (1991, 1992), Jackendoff (1990a, 1992c), Jackendoff and Culicover (1971), Jespersen (1927), Johnson (1991), Jolly (1987), Kayne (1981), Kegl and Fellbaum (1988, 1989), Keyser and Roeper (1992), Kipka (1990), Kuroda (1968), Langacker (1991), Larson (1988a, 1988b, 1990), J. Lumsden (1991), Machonis (1985), Marantz (1984), J.E. Miller (1989), Napoli (1988a), Oehrle (1976, 1977, 1983), Pesetsky (1992), Pinker (1989), Poser (1982), Randall (1990), Ritchie (1985), Shopen (1986), D.L. Smith (1981), Speas (1990), Stowell (1981), Tremblay (1990, 1991), Wechsler (1991), Wierzbicka (1986, 1988b), Williams (1981), Woolford (1984), Ziv and Sheintuch (1979), Zubizarreta (1987), Zwicky (1986), Zwicky and Pullum (1986)

(115)   Alternating Verbs (characterizations in quotes are from Gropen et al. (1989)):

    a.   GIVE VERBS ("verbs that inherently signify acts of giving"): feed, give, lease, lend, loan, pass, pay, peddle, refund, render, rent, repay, sell, serve, trade

b. VERBS OF FUTURE HAVING ("commitments that a person will have something at some later point"): advance, allocate, allot, assign, award, bequeath, cede, concede, extend, grant, guarantee, issue, leave, offer, owe, promise, vote, will, yield

c. BRING AND TAKE ("verbs of continuous causation of accompanied motion in a deictically specified direction"): bring, take (only)

d. SEND VERBS ("verbs of sending"): forward, hand, mail, post, send, ship, slip, smuggle, sneak

e. SLIDE VERBS: bounce, float, roll, slide

f. CARRY VERBS ("verbs of continuous causation of accompanied motion in some manner"): carry, drag, haul, heave, heft, hoist, kick, lug, pull, push, schlep, shove, tote, tow, tug

g. ? DRIVE VERBS: barge, bus, cart, drive, ferry, fly, row, shuttle, truck, wheel, wire (money)

h. VERBS OF THROWING ("instantaneously causing ballistic motion"; most): bash, bat, bunt, catapult, chuck, flick, fling, flip, hit, hurl, kick, lob, pass, pitch, punt, shoot, shove, slam, slap, sling, throw, tip, toss

i. VERBS OF TRANSFER OF A MESSAGE ("verbs of type of communicated message [differentiated by something like 'illocutionary force']"): ask, cite, ?pose, preach, quote, read, relay, show, teach, tell, write

j. VERBS OF INSTRUMENT OF COMMUNICATION: cable, e-mail, fax, modem, netmail, phone, radio, relay, satellite, semaphore, sign, signal, telephone, telecast, telegraph, telex, wire, wireless

(116) a. Bill sold a car to Tom.
       b. Bill sold Tom a car.

(117) "Animacy" restriction on double object construction:
       a. Bill sent a package to Tom/London.
       b. Bill sent Tom/*London a package.

(118) Non-Alternating *to* Only:
       a. * Primarily Latinate verbs belonging to some of the semantically plausible classes listed above: address, administer, broadcast, convey, contribute, delegate, deliver, denounce, demonstrate, describe, dictate, dispatch, display, distribute, donate, elucidate, exhibit, express, explain, explicate, forfeit, illustrate, introduce, narrate, portray, proffer, recite, recommend, refer, reimburse, remit, restore, return, sacrifice, submit, surrender, transfer, transport
       b. * SAY VERBS ("verbs of communication of propositions and propositional attitudes"): admit, allege, announce, articulate, as-

sert, communicate, confess, convey, declare, mention, propose, recount, repeat, report, reveal, say, state

c. * VERBS OF MANNER OF SPEAKING: babble, bark, bawl, bellow, bleat, boom, bray, burble, cackle, call, carol, chant, chatter, chirp, cluck, coo, croak, croon, crow, cry, drawl, drone, gabble, gibber, groan, growl, grumble, grunt, hiss, holler, hoot, howl, jabber, lilt, lisp, moan, mumble, murmur, mutter, purr, rage, rasp, roar, rumble, scream, screech, shout, shriek, sing, snap, snarl, snuffle, splutter, squall, squawk, squeak, squeal, stammer, stutter, thunder, tisk, trill, trumpet, twitter, wail, warble, wheeze, whimper, whine, whisper, whistle, whoop, yammer, yap, yell, yelp, yodel

d. * VERBS OF PUTTING WITH A SPECIFIED DIRECTION: drop, hoist, lift, lower, raise

e. * VERBS OF FULFILLING ("X gives something to Y that Y deserves, needs, or is worthy of"): credit, entrust, furnish, issue, leave, present, provide, serve, supply, trust

(119)   Non-Alternating Double Object Only:

a. * accord, ask, bear, begrudge, bode, cost, deny, envy, flash (a glance), forbid, forgive, guarantee, issue (ticket, passport), refuse, save, spare, strike (a blow), vouchsafe, wish, write (check)

b. * BILL VERBS: bet, bill, charge, fine, mulct, overcharge, save, spare, tax, tip, undercharge, wager

c. * APPOINT VERBS: acknowledge, adopt, appoint, consider, crown, deem, designate, elect, esteem, imagine, mark, nominate, ordain, proclaim, rate, reckon, report, want

d. * DUB VERBS: anoint, baptize, brand, call, christen, consecrate, crown, decree, dub, label, make, name, nickname, pronounce, rule, stamp, style, term, vote

e. * DECLARE VERBS: adjudge, adjudicate, assume, avow, believe, confess, declare, fancy, find, judge, presume, profess, prove, suppose, think, warrant

Comments: The dative alternation is characterized by an alternation between the prepositional frame 'NP1 V NP2 *to* NP3' and the double object frame 'NP1 V NP3 NP2'. The NP that is the object of the preposition *to* in the prepositional frame turns up as the first object in the double object construction. The dative alternation does not have an intransitive counterpart. There are differences of opinion as to exactly which verbs show the alternation. For instance, Gropen et al. (1989) include the *carry* verbs among the verbs that do not show this alternation, while Green (1974) cites many of these verbs in her list of alternating verbs.

The dative alternation has been extensively studied. A major research issue is the syntactic structure associated with the double object construction. In addition, much of the discussion of the dative alternation has focused on constraints on the alternation. Probably the most-discussed question concerns the characterization of the set of verbs showing this alternation. Many, but not all, of these are verbs of change of possession, where possession is rather broadly construed. Related to this issue is the existence of a constraint sometimes known as the Latinate restriction. This constraint involves the morphological or phonological shape of the verbs undergoing the alternation: it appears that verbs of Latinate origin that are found in the 'NP V NP *to* NP' frame are not found in the double object construction. However, exceptions have been noted to this particular generalization, and some researchers have tried to restate it in terms of other phonological and morphological properties of the verbs involved. A variety of hypotheses are evaluated in Boguraev and Briscoe (1989). A second restriction on the dative alternation involves the nature of the goal phrase. As illustrated above, there appears to be an animacy restriction on this phrase, where the notion animate extends to include organizations and corporate bodies. Thus, in example (117), the (b) sentence is acceptable if *London* is used to represent via metonymy the London office of a company or the British government (J. McCawley, personal communication).

2.2 Benefactive Alternation

References: See references listed under Dative Alternation above.

(120)   Alternating Verbs:
   a.   BUILD VERBS: arrange, assemble, bake, blow (bubbles, glass), build, carve, cast, chisel, churn, compile, cook, crochet, cut, develop, embroider, fashion, fold, forge (metal), grind, grow, hack, hammer, hatch, knit, make, mold, pound, roll, sculpt, sew, shape, spin (wool), stitch, weave, whittle
   b.   CREATE VERBS (few): design, dig, mint
   c.   PREPARE VERBS: bake (cake), blend (drink), boil (egg, tea), brew (coffee), clean, clear (path), cook (meal), fix (meal), fry (egg), grill, hardboil (egg), iron, light (fire), mix (drink), poach (egg), pour (drink), prepare (meal), roast (chicken), roll, run (bath), scramble (egg), set (table), softboil (egg), toast, toss (salad), wash
   d.   VERBS OF PERFORMANCE (some): dance, draw (picture), hum (tune), paint (picture), play (music, game), recite (poem), sing (song), spin (story), whistle (tune), write (book)
   e.   GET VERBS: book, buy, call, cash, catch, charter, ?choose, earn, fetch, find, gain, gather, get, hire, keep, lease, leave, order, phone (doctor), pick (fruit, flower), pluck (flower), procure, pull (a

beer), reach, rent, reserve, save, secure, shoot (game), slaughter (animal), steal, vote, win

(121)   a.   Martha carved a toy for the baby.
        b.   Martha carved the baby a toy.

(122)   Non-Alternating *for* Only:
        a.   * OBTAIN VERBS: accept, accumulate, acquire, appropriate, borrow, ?cadge, collect, exact, grab, inherit, obtain, purchase, receive, recover, regain, retrieve, seize, select, snatch
        b.   * VERBS OF SELECTION: ?choose, designate, favor, indicate, prefer, pick (=select), select
        c.   * CREATE VERBS (most): coin, compose, compute, construct, create, derive, fabricate, form, invent, manufacture, mint, organize, produce, recreate, style
        d.   * STEAL VERBS: abduct, cadge, capture, confiscate, cop, emancipate, embezzle, exorcise, extort, extract, filch, flog, grab, impound, kidnap, liberate, lift, nab, pilfer, pinch, pirate, plagiarize, purloin, recover, redeem, reclaim, regain, repossess, rescue, retrieve, rustle, seize, smuggle, snatch, sneak, sponge, steal, swipe, take, thieve, wangle, weasel, winkle, withdraw, wrest

(123)   a.   The architect selected a house for the couple.
        b.   * The architect selected the couple a house.

Comments: This alternation resembles the dative alternation, and it is even sometimes subsumed under it. It differs from the dative alternation in involving the benefactive preposition *for* rather than the goal preposition *to* in the prepositional variant. The benefactive alternation is found with verbs that can broadly be characterized as either verbs of obtaining or verbs of creation, including some verbs that are verbs of creation in an extended use. The studies of this alternation show that the first object in a double object construction with a benefactive alternation verb is less "object"-like in some respects than the first object in a double object construction with a dative alternation verb. Like the dative alternation, this alternation does not have an intransitive counterpart.

2.3   Locative Alternation

References: Anderson (1971, 1977), Bach (1980), Boons (1974, 1985, 1986), Bowerman (1982), Carter (1988), Croft (1986, 1991), Culicover and Wilkins (1984, 1986), Dik (1978, 1980), Dixon (1989), Dowty (1991), Emonds (1991), Fillmore (1966, 1968a, 1968b), Foley and Van Valin (1984), Fraser (1971), Gawron (1983, 1986), de Groot (1984), Gropen (1989), Gropen et al. (1991a, 1991b), Haïk (1990), Hall (1965), Hoffman (1991), Jackendoff (1990a, 1990b), Jeffries and Willis (1984), Jolly (1987), Kipka (1990),

Langacker (1991), Larson (1990), B. Levin and Rappaport Hovav (1991), Ljung (1970), J. Lumsden (1991), J.E. Miller (1989), Moravcsik (1978), Pesetsky (1992), Pinker (1989), Pusch (1972), Rappaport and B. Levin (1985, 1988), Rappaport, B. Levin, and Laughren (1988), Ravin (1990), Salkoff (1983), Schwartz-Norman (1976), Tenny (1992), Tremblay (1990, 1991), Vestergaard (1973). For work on the alternation in languages other than English: Berber—Guerssel (1986); Dutch—Dik (1978); French—Boons (1974, 1985, 1986), Postal (1982); German—Becker (1971); Igbo—Nwachukwu (1987); Japanese—Fukui, Miyagawa, and Tenny (1985), Kageyama (1980); Kannada—Bhat (1977); Russian—Veyrenc (1976).

The locative alternation, like the dative alternation, has received considerable attention. It is found with certain verbs that relate to putting substances on surfaces or things in containers, or to removing substances from surfaces or things from containers. The alternation involves the possible expressions of what E.V. Clark and H.H. Clark (1979) have called the locatum argument—the substance or entity whose location is changed—and the location argument. Specifically, in each variant one of these arguments is expressed as the object of an appropriate preposition, while the second is not. The expression of the second argument depends on whether the alternation is based on a transitive verb or an intransitive verb: it is expressed as the object of the former and the subject of the latter. The forms of the alternation manifested by transitive and intransitive verbs can be viewed as a single alternation if the intransitive verbs are given an unaccusative analysis, so that their subject is an underlying object.

One of the most-studied properties of the locative alternation is the so-called "holistic/partitive effect." When the location argument is not expressed as the object of a preposition, it is associated with what has been called a "holistic" or "affected" interpretation; that is, the location is understood to be in some sense "completely" affected by the action. The location does not necessarily have to receive such an interpretation when it is expressed as the object of a preposition. However, a number of studies have shown that providing a precise characterization of this effect is not easy; specifically, they have shown that a statement involving the notion "holistic" is not entirely accurate.

2.3.1 *Spray/Load* Alternation

(124)   Alternating Verbs:
        SPRAY/LOAD VERBS: brush, cram, crowd, cultivate, dab, daub, drape, drizzle, dust, hang, heap, inject, jam, load, mound, pack, pile, plant, plaster, ?prick, pump, rub, scatter, seed, settle, sew, shower, slather, smear, smudge, sow, spatter, splash, splatter, spray, spread, sprinkle, spritz, squirt, stack, stick, stock, strew, string, stuff, swab, ?vest, ?wash, wrap

(125)   a.   Jack sprayed paint on the wall. (locative variant)
        b.   Jack sprayed the wall with paint. (*with* variant)

(126)   Non-Alternating *with* Only:
        * FILL VERBS: adorn, anoint, bandage, bathe, bestrew, bind, blanket,
        block, blot, bombard, carpet, choke, cloak, clog, clutter, coat, con-
        taminate, cover, dam, dapple, deck, decorate, deluge, dirty, douse,
        dot, drench, edge, embellish, emblazon, encircle, encrust, endow, en-
        rich, entangle, face, festoon, fill, fleck, flood, frame, garland, garnish,
        imbue, impregnate, infect, inlay, interlace, interlard, interleave, in-
        tersperse, interweave, inundate, lard, lash, line, litter, mask, mottle,
        ornament, pad, pave, plate, plug, pollute, replenish, repopulate, riddle,
        ring, ripple, robe, saturate, season, shroud, smother, soak, soil, speckle,
        splotch, spot, staff, stain, stipple, stop up, stud, suffuse, surround,
        swaddle, swathe, taint, tile, trim, veil, vein, wreathe

(127)   a.   * June covered the blanket over the baby.
        b.   June covered the baby with a blanket.

(128)   Non-Alternating Locative Preposition Only:
        a.   * PUT VERBS: arrange, immerse, install, lodge, mount, place,
             position, put, set, situate, sling, stash, stow
        b.   * VERBS OF PUTTING IN A SPATIAL CONFIGURATION (except *hang*):
             dangle, lay, lean, perch, rest, sit, stand, suspend
        c.   * FUNNEL VERBS: bang, channel, dip, dump, funnel, hammer, ladle,
             pound, push, rake, ram, scoop, scrape, shake, shovel, siphon,
             spoon, squeeze, squish, squash, sweep, tuck, wad, wedge, wipe,
             wring
        d.   * VERBS OF PUTTING WITH A SPECIFIED DIRECTION: drop, hoist, lift,
             lower, raise
        e.   * POUR VERBS: dribble, drip, pour, slop, slosh, spew, spill, spurt
        f.   * COIL VERBS: coil, curl, loop, roll, spin, twirl, twist, whirl, wind

(129)   a.   Tamara poured water into the bowl.
        b.   * Tamara poured the bowl with water.

Comments: This form of the locative alternation is found with transitive verbs
relating to putting and covering. Like all forms of the locative alternation, it
manifests the "holistic/partitive" effect. The verb *vest* may be inappropriately
included; it appears to participate in the locative alternation, but unlike the other
verbs in this set, its locatum argument is typically an abstract noun phrase.

2.3.2   *Clear* Alternation (transitive)

References: Hook (1983), B. Levin and Rappaport Hovav (1991). See also
the references under Locative Alternation (sec. 2.3).

(130)   Alternating Verbs:
         CLEAR VERBS: clear, clean, drain, empty

(131)   a. Henry cleared dishes from the table. (locative variant)
         b. Henry cleared the table of dishes. (*of* variant)

(132)   Non-Alternating *from* Only:
         a. * REMOVE VERBS: abstract, cull, delete, discharge, disgorge, dis-
            lodge, dismiss, disengage, draw, eject, eliminate, eradicate, evict,
            excise, excommunicate, expel, extirpate, extract, extrude, lop,
            omit, ostracize, oust, partition, pry, reap, remove, separate, sever,
            shoo, subtract, uproot, winkle, withdraw, wrench
         b. * BANISH VERBS: banish, deport, evacuate, expel, extradite, recall,
            remove
         c. * STEAL VERBS: abduct, cadge, capture, confiscate, cop, eman-
            cipate, embezzle, exorcise, extort, extract, filch, flog, grab,
            impound, kidnap, liberate, lift, nab, pilfer, pinch, pirate, plagia-
            rize, purloin, recover, redeem, reclaim, regain, repossess, rescue,
            retrieve, rustle, seize, smuggle, snatch, sneak, sponge, steal,
            swipe, take, thieve, wangle, weasel, winkle, withdraw, wrest

(133)   a. The thief stole the painting from the museum.
         b. * The thief stole the museum of the painting.

(134)   Non-Alternating *of* Only:
         * CHEAT VERBS: absolve, acquit, balk, bereave, bilk, bleed, break (of a
         habit), burgle, cheat, cleanse, con, cull, cure, defraud, denude, deplete,
         depopulate, deprive, despoil, disabuse, disarm, disencumber, dispos-
         sess, divest, drain, ease, exonerate, fleece, free, gull, milk, mulct,
         pardon, plunder, purge, purify, ransack, relieve, render, rid, rifle, rob,
         sap, strip, swindle, unburden, void, wean

(135)   a. * The doctor cured pneumonia from Pat.
         b. The doctor cured Pat of pneumonia.

Comments: This form of the locative alternation is found with verbs that as
a first approximation are semantic inverses of the *spray/load* verbs. This form
of the alternation also displays the "holistic/partitive" effect. The object of the
verb receives the "holistic" interpretation in the *of* variant. The use of the *of*
variant is preferred when the locatum is abstract: *clear someone of guilt/?clear
guilt from someone*. The use of the passive also improves the acceptability of
the *of* variant. There are differences of opinion as to how large a class of verbs
shows this form of the locative alternation as opposed to the form shown by the
wipe verbs. For two different points of view compare the list in Hook (1983)
or Fraser (1971) to that in B. Levin and Rappaport Hovav (1991). The list of

alternating verbs given here reflects the more conservative approach taken in B. Levin and Rappaport Hovav; however, certain *wipe* verbs can sometimes show this alternation.

2.3.3   *Wipe* Alternation

(136)   Alternating Verbs: WIPE VERBS
   a. MEANS SUBCLASS: bail, buff, dab, distill, dust, erase, expunge, flush, leach, lick, pluck, polish, prune, purge, rinse, rub, scour, scrape, scratch, scrub, shave, skim, smooth, soak, squeeze, strain, strip, suck, suction, swab, sweep, trim, wash, wear, weed, whisk, winnow, wipe, wring
   b. INSTRUMENT SUBCLASS: brush, comb, file, filter, hoover, hose, iron, mop, plow, rake, sandpaper, shear, shovel, siphon, sponge, towel, vacuum

(137)   a. Helen wiped the fingerprints off the wall. (locative PP variant)
   b. Helen wiped the wall (*of fingerprints). (locative object variant)

Comments: This form of the locative alternation is found with a set of verbs that, like the *clear* verbs, could at a first approximation be considered semantic inverses of the *spray/load* verbs. However, the *wipe* verbs, unlike the *clear* verbs, do not allow the locatum argument to be expressed when the location argument is expressed as the direct object. That is, they do not allow an *of* phrase. This form of the locative alternation also displays the "holistic/partitive" effect. The location argument receives the "holistic" interpretation when it is expressed as the object of the verb. See the previous section on the transitive *clear* alternation for a list of non-alternating verbs. This form of the alternation has no intransitive counterpart.

2.3.4   *Swarm* Alternation

References: Salkoff (1983). See also the references under Locative Alternation (sec. 2.3).

(138)   Alternating Verbs:
   a. VERBS OF LIGHT EMISSION: beam, blink, burn, blaze, flame, flare, flash, flicker, glare, gleam, glimmer, glint, glisten, glitter, glow, incandesce, scintillate, shimmer, shine, sparkle, twinkle
   b. VERBS OF SOUND EMISSION: babble, bang, beat, beep, bellow, blare, blast, blat, boom, bubble, burble, burr, buzz, chatter, chime, chink, chir, chitter, chug, clack, clang, clank, clap, clash, clatter, click, cling, clink, clomp, clump, clunk, crack, crackle, crash, creak, crepitate, crunch, cry, ding, dong, explode, fizz, fizzle,

groan, growl, gurgle, hiss, hoot, howl, hum, jangle, jingle, knell, knock, lilt, moan, murmur, patter, peal, ping, pink, pipe, plink, plonk, plop, plunk, pop, purr, putter, rap, rasp, rattle, ring, roar, roll, rumble, rustle, scream, screech, shriek, shrill, sing, sizzle, snap, splash, splutter, sputter, squawk, squeak, squeal, squelch, strike, swish, swoosh, thrum, thud, thump, thunder, thunk, tick, ting, tinkle, toll, toot, tootle, trill, trumpet, twang, ululate, vroom, wail, wheeze, whine, whir, whish, whistle, whoosh, whump, zing

   c. VERBS OF SUBSTANCE EMISSION: drip, foam, gush, ooze, radiate, spout, sprout, squirt, stream, sweat

   d. VERBS OF SOUND EXISTENCE: ?din, echo, resonate, resound, reverberate, sound

   e. VERBS OF ENTITY-SPECIFIC MODES OF BEING: bloom, blossom, bristle, foam, sprout

   f. VERBS OF MODES OF BEING INVOLVING MOTION: dance, flutter, pulsate, quiver, shake, stir, sway, tremble, writhe

   g. SWARM VERBS: abound, bustle, crawl, creep, hop, run, swarm, swim, teem, throng

(139)   a. Bees are swarming in the garden. (locative variant)
       b. The garden is swarming with bees. (*with* variant)

(140)   Non-Alternating *with* Only:
     * BULGE VERBS: bristle, bulge, seethe

(141)   a. * People are seething in the square.
       b. The square is seething with people.

(142)   Non-Alternating Locative Preposition Only:
     * HERD VERBS: accumulate, aggregate, amass, assemble, cluster, collect, congregate, convene, flock, gather, group, herd, huddle, mass

(143)   a. The cattle are herding in the pasture.
       b. * The pasture is herding with cattle.

Comments: This form of the locative alternation is displayed by intransitive verbs, but it can be viewed as parallel to the form of the alternation displayed by the *spray/load* verbs if the intransitive subject is seen as playing the role that the object plays in the *spray/load* form of the alternation. This form of the locative alternation differs from the form displayed by the *spray/load* verbs in lacking an agent. The *swarm* form of the alternation again is associated with the "holistic/partitive" effect, but this time the "holistic" interpretation is associated with the subject of the *with* variant. See Salkoff (1983) for extensive lists of verbs showing this alternation. The non-alternating locative preposition-only verbs take collective NPs as subjects, and some of them are even zero-related to collective nouns.

2.3.5 *Clear* Alternation (intransitive)

(144)   Alternating Verbs:
         CLEAR VERBS (except *clean*): clear, drain, empty

(145)   a.   Clouds cleared from the sky. (locative variant)
         b.   The sky cleared (?of clouds). (*of* variant)

Comments: Just as the form of the locative alternation shown by the *swarm* verbs is the intransitive counterpart of the form of the locative alternation shown by the *spray/load* verbs, this form of the locative alternation is the intransitive counterpart of the form of the locative alternation shown by the *clear* verbs in their transitive use. The parallel is apparent if the intransitive subject in the intransitive *clear* alternation is seen as playing the role that the object plays in the transitive *clear* form of the alternation. In addition, the intransitive form of the *clear* alternation lacks an agent. The *clear* verbs, then, participate in both transitive and intransitive forms of the locative alternation.

This form of the alternation is again associated with the "holistic/partitive" effect, but this time the "holistic" interpretation is associated with the subject of the *of* variant. Unlike the transitive form of this alternation, its intransitive form may be best in the absence of the *of* phrase, particularly with the verbs *drain* and *empty*.

2.4   Creation and Transformation Alternations

References: Atkins, Kegl, and B. Levin (1988), Bertram (1992), Dixon (1991), Dowty (1991), Fillmore (1972), Gawron (1983), Jackendoff (1990b), Jolly (1987), Nash-Webber (1971), Napoli (1989a)

This set of alternations is found primarily with verbs of creation and transformation. There are two types of alternations, each with a transitive and an intransitive form. As with the locative alternation, the subject of the intransitive form of each type of alternation plays the same role as the object in the transitive form of the alternation. In addition, the transitive form includes an agent argument that is lacking in the intransitive form of the alternation. The forms of the alternation manifested by transitive and intransitive verbs can be viewed as a single alternation if the intransitive verbs are given an unaccusative analysis, so that their subject is an underlying object.

2.4.1 Material/Product Alternation (transitive)

(146)   Alternating Verbs:
        BUILD VERBS: arrange, assemble, bake, blow (bubbles, glass), build,
        carve, cast, chisel, churn, compile, cook, crochet, cut, develop, em-
        broider, fashion, fold, forge (metal), grind, grow, hack, hammer, hatch,
        knit, make, mold, pound, roll, sculpt, sew, shape, spin (wool), stitch,
        weave, whittle

(147)   a. Martha carved a toy out of the piece of wood.
        b. Martha carved the piece of wood into a toy.

(148)   Non-Alternating *from/out of* Only:
        * CREATE VERBS: coin, compose, compute, concoct, construct, create,
        derive, design, dig, fabricate, form, invent, manufacture, mint, model,
        organize, produce, recreate, style, synthesize

(149)   a. David constructed a house out of/from bricks.
        b. * David constructed the bricks into a house.

(150)   Non-Alternating *into* Only:
        a. * KNEAD VERBS: beat, bend, coil, collect, compress, fold, freeze,
            knead, melt, shake, squash, squish, squeeze, twirl, twist, wad,
            whip, wind, work
        b. * TURN VERBS: alter, change, convert, metamorphose, transform,
            transmute, turn

(151)   a. I kneaded the dough into a loaf.
        b. * I kneaded a loaf from the dough.

(152)   a. The witch turned him into a frog.
        b. * The witch turned him from a prince.

(153)   Non-Alternating (neither variant possible):
        * DESTROY VERBS: annihilate, blitz, decimate, demolish, destroy, dev-
        astate, exterminate, extirpate, obliterate, ravage, raze, ruin, waste,
        wreck

Comments: This alternation is found with transitive verbs taking an agent argument expressed as subject and raw material and product arguments expressed
within the verb phrase. Both the raw material and product arguments may be
expressed as either the direct object or the object of a preposition, typically *into*
for the product and *out of* or *from* for the raw material. Dixon (1991) suggests
that the preposition *with* can be used instead of *from* or *out of* to introduce the
raw material in this alternation. A few of the verbs showing this alternation are
found in causative/inchoative pairs, and in their inchoative use they show the
intransitive form of the material/product alternation.

2.4.2   Material/Product Alternation (intransitive)

(154)   Alternating Verbs:
        GROW VERBS: develop, evolve, grow, hatch, mature

(155)   a.   That acorn will grow into an oak tree.
        b.   An oak tree will grow from that acorn.

(156)   Non-Alternating *into* Only:
        * TURN VERBS: alter, change, convert, metamorphose, transform,
        transmute, turn

(157)   a.   * He turned from a prince.
        b.   He turned into a frog.

Comments: This alternation is the form of the material/product alternation
that is manifested by intransitive verbs. The subject plays the part that the direct
object plays in the transitive form of this alternation. Unlike the transitive form,
there is no agent argument. Thus the raw material and product arguments may
be expressed either as the subject or as the object of a preposition, typically
into for the product and *out of* or *from* for the raw material. Most of the verbs
showing this alternation are found in causative/inchoative pairs, and in their
causative use they show the transitive form of the material/product alternation.

2.4.3   Total Transformation Alternation (transitive)

(158)   Alternating Verbs:
        TURN VERBS: alter, change, convert, metamorphose, transform,
        transmute, turn

(159)   a.   The witch turned him into a frog.
        b.   The witch turned him from a prince into a frog.

(160)   Non-Alternating *into* Only:
        a. * BUILD VERBS: arrange, assemble, bake, blow (bubbles, glass),
             build, carve, cast, chisel, churn, compile, cook, crochet, cut, de-
             velop, embroider, fashion, fold, forge (metal), grind, grow, hack,
             hammer, hatch, knit, make, mold, pound, roll, sculpt, sew, shape,
             spin (wool), stitch, weave, whittle
        b. * KNEAD VERBS: beat, bend, coil, collect, compress, fold, freeze,
             knead, melt, shake, squash, squish, squeeze, twirl, twist, wad,
             whip, wind, work

(161)   a.   Martha carved the piece of wood into a toy.
        b. * Martha carved the piece of wood from a branch into a toy.

(162)   a.   I kneaded the dough into a loaf.
        b. * I kneaded the dough from a lump into a loaf.

(163)   Non-Alternating (neither variant possible):
          *DESTROY VERBS: annihilate, blitz, decimate, demolish, destroy, dev-
          astate, exterminate, extirpate, obliterate, ravage, raze, ruin, waste,
          wreck

Comments: This alternation is found with transitive verbs. It differs from
the material/product alternation in involving three VP-internal arguments: the
entity undergoing a complete alternation and the initial state ("source") and final
state ("goal") of this entity. The entity undergoing the transformation is always
expressed as the direct object of the verb; the other arguments are expressed
in prepositional phrases. The final state always must be expressed, while the
initial state only optionally needs to be expressed. Most of the verbs showing
this alternation are found in causative/inchoative pairs, and in their inchoative
use, they show the intransitive form of the total transformation alternation.

2.4.4   Total Transformation Alternation (intransitive)

(164)   Alternating Verbs:
          TURN VERBS (some): alter, change, metamorphose, ?transform,
          ?transmute, turn

(165)   a.   He turned into a frog.
          b.   He turned from a prince into a frog.

(166)   Non-Alternating *into* Only:
          * GROW VERBS: develop, evolve, grow, hatch, mature

(167)   a.   That acorn will grow into an oak tree.
          b. * That acorn will grow from a seed into an oak tree.

Comments: This alternation is the form of the total transformation alternation
that is manifested by intransitive verbs. The subject plays the part that the direct
object plays in the transitive form of the alternation. There is no agent argument.
All of the verbs showing this alternation are found in causative/inchoative
pairs, and in their causative use, they show the transitive form of the total
transformation alternation.

2.5   Reciprocal Alternations

References: Atkins, Kegl, and B. Levin (1986), Carrier-Duncan (1985),
Condoravdi (1990), Croft (1991), Dixon (1991), Dong (1970), Dowty (1991),
Emonds (1976), Fillmore (1972), Gawron (1983), Ginzburg (1990), Gleitman
(1965), G. Lakoff and Peters (1969), Lichtenberk (1985), Vestergaard (1973),
Zwicky and Sadock (1975). See Borillo (1971) for a discussion of a similar
phenomenon in French.

Unlike the transitivity alternations involving reciprocal interpretations (secs. 1.2.4, 1.4.2), reciprocal alternations in this section do not involve a change in verb transitivity. The verbs found in the various alternations involving reciprocal interpretations here can appear either with or without a PP complement headed by one of a range of prepositions. In the absence of the PP complement, the subject, if the verb is intransitive, and the object, if the verb is transitive, must be a collective NP—an NP that can have a group interpretation. The forms of the alternation manifested by transitive and intransitive verbs can be viewed as a single alternation if the intransitive verbs are given an unaccusative analysis, so that their subject is an underlying object; the verbs found in the transitive form of the alternation will take an agent argument that the verbs found in the intransitive form lack. However, the unaccusative analysis may not be viable for the social interaction verbs and the *talk* and *chitchat* verbs found in the intransitive reciprocal alternations; the subjects of these verbs are typically animate and volitional, unlike the typical subject of an unaccusative verb, and these verbs do not have a transitive causative counterpart (with the exceptions of *marry* and *divorce*).

There are additional restrictions on the participants when the verb is used without a prepositional phrase complement: all participants constituting the object NP if the verb is transitive, or the subject NP if the verb is intransitive, must be of comparable status, as shown by the difference in acceptability in the examples below.

(168)   a.   The car collided with the bicycle.
               The car and the bicycle collided.
         b.   The car collided with the fence.
               * The car and the fence collided.

2.5.1   Simple Reciprocal Alternation (transitive)

(169)   Alternating Verbs:
         a.   P=*with:* affiliate, alternate, amalgamate, associate, blend, co-
               alesce, coincide, combine, commingle, compare, concatenate,
               confederate, confuse, conjoin, connect, consolidate, contrast,
               correlate, criss-cross, entangle, entwine, fuse, harmonize, incor-
               porate, integrate, interchange, interconnect, interlace, interlink,
               interlock, intermingle, interrelate, intersperse, intertwine, inter-
               weave, join, link, mate, merge, mingle, mix, muddle, ?pair, pool,
               rhyme, ?team, total, unify, unite
         b.   P=*into:* blend, cream, mix
         c.   P=*to:* add, connect, engage, introduce, join, link, marry, oppose,
               network, wed

    d. P=*from:* decouple, differentiate, disconnect, disentangle, dissociate, distinguish, divide, divorce, part, segregate, separate, sever

(170) a. I separated the yolk *from* the white.
        b. I separated the yolk and the white.

(171) a. I mixed the sugar *into* the butter.
        b. I mixed the sugar and the butter.

(172) a. I confused Maria *with* Anna.
        b. I confused Maria and Anna.

(173) Non-Alternating Verbs:
       a. * SHAKE VERBS:
          P=*with:* band, beat, bundle, cluster, collate, gather, glom, group, herd, jumble, lump, mass, package, pair, roll, scramble, shake, shuffle, stir, whip, whisk
          P=*into:* beat, collect, scramble, shake, shuffle, splice, stir, swirl, whip, whisk
          P=*to:* append, attach, baste, bind, bond, fasten, fuse, graft, moor, sew, splice, stick, weld
       b. * TAPE VERBS: anchor, band, belt, bolt, bracket, buckle, button, cement, chain, clamp, clasp, clip, epoxy, fetter, glue, gum, handcuff, harness, hinge, hitch, hook, knot, lace, lash, lasso, latch, leash, link, lock, loop, manacle, moor, muzzle, nail, padlock, paste, peg, pin, plaster, rivet, rope, screw, seal, shackle, skewer, solder, staple, stitch, strap, string, tack, tape, tether, thumbtack, tie, trammel, wire, yoke, zip
       c. * DISASSEMBLE VERBS: detach, disassemble, disconnect, partition, sift, sunder, unbolt, unbuckle, unbutton, unchain, unclamp, unclasp, unclip, unfasten, unglue, unhinge, unhitch, unhook, unlace, unlatch, unlock, unleash, unpeg, unpin, unscrew, unshackle, unstaple, unstitch, untie, unzip

(174) a. Linda taped the label *to* the cover.
        b. * Linda taped the label and the cover.

Comments: This alternation involves verbs found in two frames in a near-paraphrase relationship: 'NP1 V NP2 [$_{PP}$ P NP3]' and 'NP1 V [$_{NP}$ NP2 *and* NP3]'. The verbs have been grouped according to the preposition selected and not according to semantic type. Most of the verbs showing this alternation are drawn from the following classes: *amalgamate* verbs, *mix* verbs, and *separate* verbs. Some of these verbs also are found in the *together* or *apart* reciprocal alternations, while others are not.

2.5.2 *Together* Reciprocal Alternation (transitive)

(175)   Alternating Verbs:
      a. P=*with:* band, beat, blend, bundle, cluster, combine, commingle, concatenate, connect, consolidate, fuse, gather, glom, group, herd, join, jumble, link, lump, mass, merge, mingle, mix, package, pair, pool, roll, scramble, shake, shuffle, stir, whip, whisk
      b. P=*into:* beat, blend, collect, cream, mix, scramble, shake, shuffle, stir, swirl, whip, whisk
      c. P=*to:* add, append, attach, baste, bind, bond, connect, fasten, fuse, graft, join, link, moor, network, sew, splice, stick, weld
      d. P=*to, tape*-type: anchor, band, belt, bolt, bracket, buckle, button, cement, chain, clamp, clasp, clip, epoxy, fetter, glue, gum, handcuff, harness, hinge, hitch, hook, knot, lace, lash, lasso, latch, leash, link, lock, loop, manacle, moor, muzzle, nail, padlock, paste, peg, pin, plaster, rivet, rope, screw, seal, shackle, skewer, solder, staple, stitch, strap, string, tack, tape, tether, thumbtack, tie, trammel, wire, yoke, zip
      e. P=*into:* beat, blend, collect, cream, mix, scramble, shake, shuffle, splice, stir, swirl, whip, whisk

(176)   a. I creamed the sugar *into* the butter.
      b. I creamed the sugar and the butter *together*.

(177)   Non-Alternating Verbs:
    * AMALGAMATE VERBS:
    P=*with:* affiliate, alternate, amalgamate, associate, coalesce, coincide, compare, confederate, confuse, conjoin, consolidate, contrast, correlate, criss-cross, entwine, entangle, harmonize, incorporate, integrate, interchange, interconnect, interlace, interlink, interlock, intermingle, interrelate, intersperse, intertwine, interweave, mate, muddle, ?pair, rhyme, ?team, total, unify, unite
    P=*to:* engage, introduce, marry, oppose, wed

(178)   a. Harriet alternated folk songs with pop songs.
      b. * Harriet alternated folk songs and pop songs together.

Comments: This alternation involves verbs found in two frames in a near-paraphrase relationship: 'NP1 V NP2 [PP P NP3]' and 'NP1 V [NP NP2 *and* NP3] together'. The verbs have been grouped according to the preposition selected and not according to semantic type. Most of the verbs found here are drawn from the following classes: *mix* verbs, *shake* verbs, and *tape* verbs. Verbs that take *to* phrases have been split into two groups: the verbs in the *tape* class are all zero-related to nouns that name various items used to fasten two or more physical objects together, while the remaining verbs are not zero-related to such nouns.

Together can be seen as a representative of a range of phrases indicating the resulting configuration. It is possible that the *together* reciprocal construction may turn out to be a type of resultative construction. Judgments regarding the distribution of *together* do not seem to be totally clear, but it appears that *together* is required with verbs of combining whose meaning includes a manner component but not a result component.

2.5.3 *Apart* Reciprocal Alternation (transitive)

(179) Alternating Verbs:
SPLIT VERBS: blow, break, cut, draw, hack, hew, kick, knock, pry, pull, push, rip, roll, saw, shove, slip, split, tear, tug, yank

(180) a. I broke the twig *off (of)* the branch.
b. I broke the twig and the branch *apart*.
(on roughly the interpretation of the (a) sentence)

(181) Non-Alternating Verbs:
a. * SEPARATE VERBS: decouple, differentiate, disconnect, disentangle, dissociate, distinguish, divide, divorce, part, segregate, separate, sever
b. * DISASSEMBLE VERBS: detach, disassemble, disconnect, partition, sift, sunder, unbolt, unbuckle, unbutton, unchain, unclamp, unclasp, unclip, unfasten, unglue, unhinge, unhitch, unhook, unlace, unlatch, unlock, unleash, unpeg, unpin, unscrew, unshackle, unstaple, unstitch, untie, unzip

(182) a. I unscrewed the handle *from* the box.
b. * I unscrewed the handle and the box *apart*.

Comments: This alternation involves verbs found in two frames in a near-paraphrase relationship: 'NP1 V NP2 [PP P NP3]' and 'NP1 V [NP NP2 *and* NP3] *apart*'. Most of the verbs found here are drawn from the *split* verbs. The prepositions involved are the source prepositions *from*, *out (of)*, and *off (of)*.

Apart can be seen as a representative of a range of phrases indicating the resulting configuration. It is possible that the *apart* reciprocal construction may turn out to be a type of resultative construction.

2.5.4 Simple Reciprocal Alternation (intransitive)

(183) Alternating Verbs:
a. P=*with:* affiliate, agree, alternate, amalgamate, argue, banter, bargain, battle, bicker, blend, box, brawl, chat, chatter, chitchat,

clash, coalesce, coexist, coincide, collaborate, collide, combat, combine, commingle, commiserate, communicate, compare, compete, concatenate, concur, confabulate, confederate, confer, conflict, conjoin, connect, consolidate, consort, consult, contrast, converse, cooperate, correlate, correspond, criss-cross, debate, dicker, differ, disagree, dispute, dissent, duel, elope, entangle, entwine, feud, fight, flirt, fuse, gab, gossip, haggle, harmonize, hobnob, integrate, interchange, interconnect, interlace, interlink, interlock, intermingle, interrelate, intertwine, interweave, jest, join, joke, joust, link, mate, meet, merge, mingle, mix, neck, negotiate, pair, play, plot, quarrel, quibble, rap, rendezvous, rhyme, schmooze, scuffle, skirmish, spar, spat, speak, spoon, squabble, struggle, talk, tilt, tussle, unify, unite, vie, visit, war, wrangle, wrestle, yak

b. P=*into:* blend, cream, mix

c. P=*to:* connect, join, link

d. P=*from:* decouple, differ, differentiate, disconnect, disentangle, dissent, dissociate, diverge, divide, divorce, part, separate, sever

(184)   a. Brenda agreed *with* Molly.
        b. Brenda and Molly agreed.

(185)   a. The oil separated *from* the vinegar.
        b. The oil and vinegar separated.

(186)   Non-Alternating Verbs:
        a. * MARRY VERBS: court, cuddle, date, divorce, embrace, hug, kiss, marry, nuzzle, pass, pet
        b. * SPLIT VERBS: blow, break, cut, draw, hack, hew, kick, knock, pry, pull, push, rip, roll, saw, shove, slip, split, tear, tug, yank

(187)   a. * Bill married *with* Kathy.
        b. Bill and Kathy married.

(188)   a. The twig broke *off (of)* the branch.
        b. * The twig and the branch broke.
            (on roughly the interpretation of the (a) sentence)

Comments: The intransitive simple reciprocal alternation involves verbs found in two frames in a near-paraphrase relationship: 'NP1 V [PP P NP2]' and '[NP NP1 *and* NP2] V'. The verbs have been grouped according to the preposition selected and not according to semantic type. Most of the verbs found here are drawn from the following classes: *correspond* verbs, *meet* verbs, *talk* verbs, *chitchat* verbs, *amalgamate* verbs, *mix* verbs, *separate* verbs, and *differ* verbs. There are also a variety of adjectives that could have been listed here, as they behave in the same way as these verbs.

2.5.5 *Together* **Reciprocal Alternation (intransitive)**

(189)   Alternating Verbs:
      a. P=*with:* band, blend, cluster, combine, commingle, concatenate, connect, fuse, gather, glom, join, jumble, link, lump, mass, merge, mingle, mix, pair, pool, speak, talk
      b. P=*into:* blend, collect, cream, mix
      c. P=*to:* add, bond, connect, fasten, fuse, join, link, stick

(190)   a. The eggs mixed *with* the cream.
      b. The eggs and the cream mixed *together.*

(191)   Non-Alternating Verbs:
      * AMALGAMATE VERBS:
      P=*with:* affiliate, alternate, amalgamate, associate, coalesce, coincide, compare, confederate, confuse, conjoin, consolidate, contrast, correlate, criss-cross, entwine, entangle, harmonize, incorporate, integrate, interchange, interconnect, interlace, interlink, interlock, intermingle, interrelate, intersperse, intertwine, interweave, mate, muddle, ?pair, rhyme, ?team, total, unify, unite
      P=*to:* engage, introduce, marry, oppose, wed

(192)   a. Plays alternate *with* ballets.
      b. * Plays and ballets alternate *together.*

Comments: This alternation involves verbs found in two frames in a near-paraphrase relationship: 'NP1 V [_{PP} P NP2]' and '[_{NP} NP1 *and* NP2] V *together*'. The verbs have been grouped according to the preposition selected and not according to semantic type. Most of the verbs found here are drawn from the *mix* verbs and the *talk* verbs. The *amalgamate* verbs do not show this possibility, even if they do allow an intransitive use. Judgments about the use of *together* are not clear with the *correspond* and *chitchat* verbs, so these verbs have not been included.

Together can be seen as a representative of a range of phrases indicating the resulting configuration. It is possible that the *together* reciprocal construction may turn out to be a type of resultative construction.

2.5.6 *Apart* **Reciprocal Alternation (intransitive)**

(193)   Alternating Verbs:
      SPLIT VERBS: blow, break, draw, kick, knock, pry, pull, push, rip, roll, shove, slip, split, tear, tug, yank

(194)   a.   The twig broke *off (of)* the branch.
         b.   The twig and the branch broke *apart.*
               (on roughly the interpretation of the (a) sentence)

(195)   Non-Alternating Verbs:
         a.   * SEPARATE VERBS: decouple, differentiate, disconnect, disen-
               tangle, dissociate, distinguish, divide, divorce, part, segregate,
               separate, sever
         b.   * DIFFER VERBS: differ, diverge

(196)   a.   The yolk separated *from* the white.
         b.   * The yolk and the white separated *apart.*

Comments: This alternation involves verbs found in two frames in a near-
paraphrase relationship: 'NP1 V [pp P NP2]' and '[np NP1 *and* NP2] V *apart*'.
Most of the verbs found here are drawn from the *split* verbs. The *differ* verbs do
not show this possibility; nor do the *separate* verbs, even when they do allow
an intransitive use. The prepositions involved are the source prepositions *from*,
out (of), and *off (of)*.

Apart can be seen as a representative of a range of phrases indicating the
resulting configuration. It is possible that the *apart* reciprocal construction may
turn out to be a type of resultative construction.

2.6 Fulfilling Alternation

References: Blansitt (1984), Channon (1982), Croft (1986, 1991), Emonds
(1976), Fraser (1971), de Groot (1984), Jespersen (1927), Jackendoff (1990b,
1992c), Kayne (1984), Larson (1990), J. Lumsden (1991), J.E. Miller (1989),
Pesetsky (1992), Pinker (1989), Rappaport and B. Levin (1985)

(197)   Alternating Verbs:
         VERBS OF FULFILLING: credit, entrust, furnish, issue, leave, present,
         provide, serve, supply, trust

(198)   a.   The judge presented a prize to the winner.
         b.   The judge presented the winner with a prize.

(199)   Non-Alternating *to* Only:
         Most verbs that permit the dative alternation do not show this
         alternation, including:
         * VERBS OF FUTURE HAVING: advance, allocate, allot, assign, award,
         bequeath, cede, concede, extend, grant, guarantee, issue, leave, offer,
         owe, promise, vote, will, yield

(200)   a.   The judge offered a prize to the winner.
         b.   * The judge offered the winner with a prize.

(201)   Non-Alternating *with* Only:
         * EQUIP VERBS: arm, burden, charge (with a task), compensate, equip,
         invest, ply, regale, reward, saddle

(202)   a. * The judge saddled a prize to the winner.
         b.   The judge saddled the winner with a prize.

Comments: This alternation shows some superficial similarity to both the
dative alternation and the locative alternation. One of its variants involves
the 'NP V NP *to* NP' frame associated with the dative alternation. But the
other variant of the fulfilling alternation involves the frame 'NP V NP *with*
NP', a frame associated with the form of the locative alternation found with
the *spray/load* verbs. Some of the verbs showing the fulfilling alternation also
show the dative alternation and are listed under that alternation. This alternation
does not have an intransitive counterpart.

2.7   Image Impression Alternation

References: Fraser (1971), Rappaport and B. Levin (1985)

(203)   Alternating Verbs:
         VERBS OF IMAGE IMPRESSION: appliqué, emboss, embroider, engrave,
         etch, imprint, incise, inscribe, mark, paint, set, sign, stamp, tattoo

(204)   a.   The jeweller inscribed the name on the ring.
         b.   The jeweller inscribed the ring with the name.

(205)   Non-Alternating Locative Preposition Only:
         a. * SCRIBBLE VERBS: carve, chalk, charcoal, copy, crayon, doodle,
              draw, forge, ink, paint, pencil, plot, print, scratch, scrawl, scribble,
              sketch, spraypaint, stencil, trace, type, write
         b. * TRANSCRIBE VERBS: copy, film, forge (signature), microfilm,
              photocopy, photograph, record, tape, televise, transcribe, type

(206)   a.   The jeweller copied the name on the ring.
         b. * The jeweller copied the ring with the name.

(207)   Non-Alternating *with* Only:
         * ILLUSTRATE VERBS: address, adorn, autograph, brand, date, deco-
         rate, embellish, endorse, illuminate, illustrate, initial, label, letter,
         monogram, ornament, tag

(208)   a. * The jeweller decorated the name on the ring.
         b.   The jeweller decorated the ring with the name.

Comments: The image impression alternation superficially resembles the
spray/load form of the locative alternation and has sometimes been subsumed

under this alternation. However, the verbs showing this alternation are a semantically coherent subset of verbs whose meaning is somewhat different than that of the *spray/load* verbs. Furthermore, the image impression alternation does not appear to show the "holistic/partitive" effect associated with the locative alternation. But if the lack of "holistic/partitive" effect can receive an independent explanation, this difference may not be sufficient to consider the image impression alternation a distinct alternation. This alternation does not have an intransitive counterpart.

2.8   *With/Against* Alternation

References: Dixon (1991), Dowty (1991), Fillmore (1977a), Foley and Van Valin (1984), Gawron (1983), Jolly (1987), Pinker (1989), Richardson (1983)

(209)   Alternating Verbs:
HIT VERBS: bang, bash, batter, beat, bump, butt, dash, drum, hammer, hit, kick, knock, lash, pound, rap, slap, smack, smash (where no effect implicated), strike, tamp, tap, thump, thwack, whack

(210)   a.   Brian hit the stick against the fence.
      b.   Brian hit the fence with the stick.

(211)   Non-Alternating *with* Only:
a. * SWAT VERBS: bite, claw, paw, peck, punch (person), scratch, shoot (gun), slug, stab, swat, swipe
b. * SPANK VERBS: belt, birch, bludgeon, bonk, brain, cane, clobber, club, conk, cosh, cudgel, cuff, flog, knife, paddle, paddywhack, pummel, sock, spank, strap, thrash, truncheon, wallop, whip, whisk
c. * POKE VERBS: dig, jab, pierce, poke, prick, stick

(212)   a. * Don swatted the newspaper against the mosquito.
      b.   Don swatted the mosquito with the newspaper.

(213)   Non-Alternating *against* Only:
a. * THROW VERBS (some): bat, bunt, ?cast, chuck, ?fire, fling, flip, hurl, lob, pitch, punt, shoot, shove, slap, sling, throw, tip, toss
b. * BREAK VERBS: break, crack, crash, crush, fracture, rip, shatter, smash, snap, splinter, split, tear

(214)   a.   Brian threw the stick against the fence.
      b. * Brian threw the fence with the stick.

Comments: The verbs showing this alternation take three arguments that as a first approximation might be characterized as an agent, a location, and an instrument. The instrument is moved by the agent into contact with the location; thus the instrument also qualifies as a theme in the Gruber/Jackendoff sense. The agent is always expressed as the subject. Either the location or the instrument/theme may be the object of a verb participating in the alternation, with the other argument expressed via a prepositional phrase. A hallmark of this alternation is the use of the preposition *against* to head the prepositional phrase expressing the location. This alternation does not have an intransitive counterpart. Many of the verbs listed here come from Dowty (1991).

2.9 *Through/With* Alternation

References: Gruber (1965, 1976)

(215)   Alternating Verbs:
         POKE VERBS: dig, jab, pierce, poke, prick, stick

(216)   a.   Alison pierced the needle through the cloth.
         b.   Alison pierced the cloth with a needle.

(217)   Non-Alternating *with* Only:
         a. * HIT VERBS: bang, bash, batter, beat, bump, butt, dash, drum, ham-
               mer, hit, kick, knock, lash, pound, rap, slap, smack, smash (where
               no effect implicated), strike, tamp, tap, thump, thwack, whack
         b. * SWAT VERBS: bite, claw, paw, peck, punch (person), scratch, shoot
               (gun), slug, stab, swat, swipe
         c. * SPANK VERBS: belt, birch, bludgeon, bonk, brain, cane, clobber,
               club, conk, cosh, cudgel, cuff, flog, knife, paddle, paddywhack,
               pummel, sock, spank, strap, thrash, truncheon, wallop, whip,
               whisk
         d. * TOUCH VERBS: caress, graze, kiss, lick, nudge, pat, peck (=kiss),
               pinch, prod, sting, stroke, tickle, touch

(218)   a. * Paula hit the stick through/into the fence.
         b.   Paula hit the fence with the stick.

Comments: The verbs showing this alternation, like those showing the *with/against* alternation, take arguments that as a first approximation might be characterized as an agent, a location, and an instrument. The instrument is moved into contact with the location, thus also qualifying as a theme in the Gruber/Jackendoff sense. But this alternation involves the use of a sharp instrument that not only comes into contact with the location but also pene- trates it. The agent is always expressed as the subject. Either the location or the instrument/theme may be the object of a verb participating in the alternation, with the other argument expressed via a prepositional phrase. A hallmark of this alternation is the use of the preposition *through* to head the prepositional phrase expressing the location. This alternation does not have an intransitive counterpart.

2.10 *Blame* Alternation

References: Fillmore (1968b, 1971b), Jackendoff (1974, 1990a), Larson (1990), J. McCawley (1975)

(219)   Alternating Verbs: blame (only)

(220)   a.   Mira blamed the accident on Terry.
         b.   Mira blamed Terry for the accident.

(221)   Non-Alternating *for* Only:
         a. * POSITIVE ADMIRE-TYPE PSYCH-VERBS: admire, adore, appreci-
            ate, cherish, enjoy, esteem, exalt, fancy, favor, idolize, like, love,
            miss, prize, respect, relish, revere, savor, stand, support, tolerate,
            treasure, trust, value, venerate, worship
         b. * NEGATIVE ADMIRE-TYPE PSYCH-VERBS: abhor, deplore, despise,
            detest, disdain, dislike, distrust, dread, envy, execrate, fear, hate,
            lament, loathe, mourn, pity, regret, resent, ?rue
         c. * NEGATIVE JUDGMENT VERBS: abuse, backbite, calumniate, casti-
            gate, censure, chasten, chastise, chide, condemn, criticize, decry,
            defame, denigrate, denounce, deprecate, deride, disparage, fault,
            fine, impeach, insult, lambaste, malign, mock, penalize, perse-
            cute, prosecute, punish, rebuke, reprimand, reproach, reprove,
            revile, ridicule, scold, scorn, shame, snub, upbraid, victimize,
            vilify
         d. * POSITIVE JUDGMENT VERBS: acclaim, applaud, bless, celebrate,
            commend, compensate, compliment, congratulate, eulogize, ex-
            cuse, extol, felicitate, forgive, greet, hail, honor, laud, pardon,
            praise, recompense, remunerate, repay, reward, salute, thank,
            toast, welcome
         e. * WANT VERBS: covet, crave, desire, fancy, need, want
         f. * VERBS OF ASSESSMENT: analyze, assess, audit, evaluate, review,
            scrutinize, study

(222)   a. * Mira condemned the accident on Terry.
         b.   Mira condemned Terry for the accident.

Comments: The verb *blame* is the only verb attested in this alternation; however, it is worth identifying this alternation since there are a wide range of verbs that turn up in one of the frames associated with the alternation: 'NP V NP *for* NP'.

2.11 *Search* Alternations

References: Bach (1968), Carlson (1977), Croft (1986, 1991), Dixon (1989, 1991), Dowty (1979), J. McCawley (1968a, 1973, 1974), Partee (1974), Quine (1960), Sibley (1955)

Verbs of searching seem to have available three alternate ways of expressing their arguments: 'NP1 V NP2 *in* NP3', 'NP1 V NP3 *for* NP2', 'NP1 V *for* NP2 *in* NP3'. Different verbs of searching display different subsets of these patterns, giving rise to a variety of alternations in the expression of their arguments. Rather than labeling each of the attested subsets of the three frames as distinct alternations, the different subtypes of verbs of searching are simply listed in this section. Besides an agent argument, expressed as the subject, these verbs take as arguments the entity being sought and the location where the search is being carried out. The object sought and the location can be expressed either as the direct object of the verb or within a prepositional phrase (headed by *for* for the object sought and by a locative preposition for the location). One of the possible frames arises when both of these arguments are expressed in prepositional phrases simultaneously; the other two arise when one argument is expressed as direct object and the other via a prepositional phrase. With the exception of the *ferret* verbs, all of these verbs permit the use of a *for* phrase to express the object sought.

(223)   HUNT VERBS: dig, feel, fish, hunt, mine, poach, scrounge

(224)   a.   Ida hunted the woods for deer.
         b.   Ida hunted for deer in the woods.
         c.   Ida hunted deer in the woods.

(225)   SEARCH VERBS: advertise, check, comb, dive, drag, dredge, excavate, patrol, plumb, probe, prospect, prowl, quarry, rake, rifle, scavenge, scour, scout, search, shop, sift, trawl, troll, watch

(226)   a.   Melissa searched the papers for a clue.
         b.   Melissa searched for a clue in the papers.
         c.   * Melissa searched a clue in the papers.

(227)   STALK VERBS: smell, stalk, taste, track

(228)   a.   I stalked the woods for game.
         b.   * I stalked for game in the woods.
         c.   I stalked game in the woods.

(229)   INVESTIGATE VERBS: canvass, explore, examine, frisk, inspect, investigate, observe, quiz, raid, ransack, riffle, scan, scrutinize, survey, tap

(230)   a. We investigated the area for bombs.
        b. * We investigated for bombs in the area.
        c. * We investigated bombs in the area.

(231)   RUMMAGE VERBS: bore, burrow, delve, forage, fumble, grope, leaf,
        listen, look, page, paw, poke, rifle, root, rummage, scrabble, scratch,
        snoop, thumb, tunnel

(232)   a. * We rummaged the desk for papers.
        b. We rummaged through the desk for papers.
        c. * We rummaged papers through the desk.

(233)   FERRET VERBS: ferret, nose, seek, tease

(234)   a. * I ferreted the woods for game.
        b. * I ferreted for game in the woods.
        c. I ferreted the secret out of him.

2.12   Body-Part Possessor Ascension Alternation

References: Carter (1988), Croft (1985), Fillmore (1967, 1968b), Guerssel
et al. (1985), Massam (1985, 1989), Wierzbicka (1979). For a discussion of a
related phenomenon in French see Hatcher (1944a, 1944b) and Kayne (1975).
There is also a large literature on possessor ascension in other languages; see,
for example, M. Baker (1988a), Massam (1985), and the references cited in
Dubinsky and Rosen's (1987) Relational Grammar bibliography.

(235)   TOUCH VERBS: ?caress, graze, kiss, lick, nudge, pat, peck (=kiss),
        pinch, prod, sting, ?stroke, tickle, touch

(236)   a. Selina touched the horse on the back.
        b. Selina touched the horse's back.

(237)   VERBS OF CONTACT BY IMPACT:
        a. HIT VERBS: bang, bash, batter, beat, bump, butt, dash, drum, ham-
            mer, hit, kick, knock, lash, pound, rap, slap, smack, smash (where
            no effect implicated), strike, tamp, tap, thump, thwack, whack
        b. SWAT VERBS: bite, claw, paw, peck, punch (person), scratch, shoot
            (gun), slug, stab, swat, swipe
        c. SPANK VERBS (some): ?bonk, ?cane, clobber, ?club, ?conk, flog,
            knife, pummel, sock, spank, ?strap, thrash, wallop, whip, whisk

(238)   a. The horse kicked Penny in the shin.
        b. The horse kicked Penny's shin.

(239)   POKE VERBS: dig, jab, pierce, poke, prick, stick

(240)   a.   Alison poked Daisy in the ribs.
         b.   Alison poked Daisy's ribs.

(241)   * BREAK VERBS: break, crack, crash, crush, fracture, rip, shatter, smash,
             snap, splinter, split, tear

(242)   a. * The horse broke Penny in the shin.
         b.   The horse broke Penny's shin.

(243)   VERBS OF CUTTING:
         a.   CUT VERBS: chip, clip, cut, hack, hew, saw, scrape, scratch, slash,
              snip
         b. * CARVE VERBS: bore, bruise, carve, chip (potatoes), chop, crop,
              crush, cube, dent, dice, drill, file, fillet, gash, gouge, grate, grind,
              mangle, mash, mince, mow, nick, notch, perforate, pulverize,
              punch (paper), prune, shred, slice, slit, spear, squash, squish

(244)   a. * The glass cut Rachel in the toe.
         b.   The glass cut Rachel's toe.

Comments: With certain verbs, the availability of two possible expressions
of a possessor and a possessed body part gives rise to this alternation. They
may be expressed as a single noun phrase bearing the direct object relation
to the verb: the body part is the head of the noun phrase and the possessor is
expressed as a genitive possessor within the noun phrase. Alternatively, they
may be expressed as two distinct constituents: the possessor as direct object
and the body part in a prepositional phrase headed by a locative preposition.
(In this variant, the possessor has "ascended" out of the body part NP, as
reflected in the name of this alternation.) This alternation is very similar to
the possessor-attribute factoring alternation with possessor object (sec. 2.13.1
below). However, it involves possessors and their body parts, while the factoring
alternation involves possessors and their attributes. Concomitantly, these two
alternations involve different prepositions (a locative preposition versus *for*)
and are found with rather different types of verbs.

2.13   Possessor-Attribute Factoring Alternations

These alternations involve both transitive and intransitive verbs. They arise because a possessor and a possessed attribute may be expressed in two different
ways with certain verbs. As one option, they may be expressed in a single noun
phrase that depending on the alternation is either the direct object or the subject
of the verb. The attribute is the head of the noun phrase and the possessor is
expressed as a genitive possessor within the noun phrase. Alternatively, they
may be expressed separately (hence the label "possessor-attribute factoring"),
one as either the direct object or the subject and the other via a prepositional

phrase. There are three types of transitive possessor-attribute factoring alternations: either the possessor or the attribute may be the direct object when they are expressed separately or the possessor may be the subject when expressed separately. However, the intransitive alternation always has the possessor as subject.

2.13.1 Possessor Object

References: Deane and Wheeler (1984)

(245)   Alternating Verbs:
   a. POSITIVE ADMIRE-TYPE PSYCH-VERBS: admire, adore, appreciate, cherish, enjoy, esteem, exalt, fancy, favor, idolize, like, love, miss, prize, respect, relish, revere, savor, stand, support, tolerate, treasure, trust, value, venerate, worship
   b. NEGATIVE ADMIRE-TYPE PSYCH-VERBS: abhor, deplore, despise, detest, disdain, dislike, distrust, dread, envy, execrate, fear, hate, lament, loathe, mourn, pity, regret, resent, ?rue
   c. NEGATIVE JUDGMENT VERBS: abuse, backbite, calumniate, castigate, censure, chasten, chastise, chide, condemn, criticize, decry, defame, denigrate, denounce, deprecate, deride, disparage, fault, fine, impeach, insult, lambaste, malign, mock, penalize, persecute, prosecute, punish, rebuke, reprimand, reproach, reprove, revile, ridicule, scold, scorn, shame, snub, upbraid, victimize, vilify
   d. POSITIVE JUDGMENT VERBS: acclaim, applaud, bless, celebrate, commend, compensate, compliment, congratulate, eulogize, excuse, extol, felicitate, forgive, greet, hail, honor, laud, pardon, praise, recompense, remunerate, repay, reward, salute, thank, toast, welcome
   e. WANT VERBS: covet, crave, desire, fancy, need, want
   f. VERBS OF ASSESSMENT: analyze, assess, audit, evaluate, review, scrutinize, study

(246)   a. They praised the volunteers' dedication.
   b. They praised the volunteers for their dedication.

(247)   a. I admired his courage.
   b. I admired him for his courage.

(248)   a. The inspector analyzed the building's soundness.
   b. The inspector analyzed the building for its soundness.

(249)   Non-Alternating Possessor Object Not Allowed:
   * SEE VERBS: detect, discern, feel, hear, notice, see, sense, smell, taste

(250)   a. I sensed his eagerness.
        b. * I sensed him for his eagerness.

Comments: This particular possessor-attribute factoring alternation involves transitive verbs that allow the possessor and attribute to be expressed either as a single noun phrase functioning as the direct object of the verb or as two distinct constituents: the possessor as direct object and the attribute via a prepositional phrase headed by *for*. This alternation is very similar to the body-part possessor ascension alternation (sec. 2.12). However, it involves possessors and their attributes, while the possessor ascension alternation involves possessors and their body parts. Concomitantly, these two alternations involve different prepositions (*for* versus a locative preposition) and are found with rather different types of verbs. Deane and Wheeler (1984) describe the possessor-attribute factoring alternation as being found with verbs that "denote the direction of attention toward some entity."

2.13.2   Attribute Object

(251)   Alternating Verbs:
        a. POSITIVE ADMIRE-TYPE PSYCH-VERBS: admire, adore, appreci-
            ate, cherish, enjoy, esteem, exalt, fancy, favor, idolize, like, love,
            miss, prize, respect, relish, revere, savor, stand, support, tolerate,
            treasure, trust, value, venerate, worship
        b. NEGATIVE ADMIRE-TYPE PSYCH-VERBS: abhor, deplore, despise,
            detest, disdain, dislike, distrust, dread, envy, execrate, fear, hate,
            lament, loathe, mourn, pity, regret, resent, ?rue
        c. SEE VERBS: detect, discern, feel, hear, notice, see, sense, smell,
            taste

(252)   a. I admired his honesty.
        b. I admired the honesty in him.

(253)   Non-Alternating Attribute Object Not Allowed:
        a. * NEGATIVE JUDGMENT VERBS: abuse, backbite, calumniate, casti-
            gate, censure, chasten, chastise, chide, condemn, criticize, decry,
            defame, denigrate, denounce, deprecate, deride, disparage, fault,
            fine, impeach, insult, lambaste, malign, mock, penalize, perse-
            cute, prosecute, punish, rebuke, reprimand, reproach, reprove,
            revile, ridicule, scold, scorn, shame, snub, upbraid, victimize,
            vilify
        b. * POSITIVE JUDGMENT VERBS: acclaim, applaud, bless, celebrate,
            commend, compensate, compliment, congratulate, eulogize, ex-
            cuse, extol, felicitate, forgive, greet, hail, honor, laud, pardon,

praise, recompense, remunerate, repay, reward, salute, thank,
toast, welcome

c. * WANT VERBS: covet, crave, desire, fancy, need, want

d. * VERBS OF ASSESSMENT: analyze, assess, audit, evaluate, review,
scrutinize, study

(254)   a. They praised the volunteers' dedication.
        b. * They praised the dedication in the volunteers.

Comments: This particular possessor-attribute factoring alternation involves
transitive verbs that allow the possessor and attribute to be expressed either as a
single noun phrase functioning as the direct object of the verb or as two distinct
constituents: the attribute as direct object and the possessor via a prepositional
phrase headed by *in*.

2.13.3   Possessor and Attribute Alternation

(255)   Alternating Verbs:

        a. POSITIVE ADMIRE-TYPE PSYCH-VERBS: admire, adore, appreci-
            ate, cherish, enjoy, esteem, exalt, fancy, favor, idolize, like, love,
            miss, prize, respect, relish, revere, savor, stand, support, tolerate,
            treasure, trust, value, venerate, worship

        b. NEGATIVE ADMIRE-TYPE PSYCH-VERBS: abhor, deplore, despise,
            detest, disdain, dislike, distrust, dread, envy, execrate, fear, hate,
            lament, loathe, mourn, pity, regret, resent, ?rue

(256)   a. I admired him for his honesty.
        b. I admired the honesty in him.

(257)   Non-Alternating Possessor Object Not Allowed:
        * SEE VERBS: detect, discern, feel, hear, notice, see, sense, smell, taste

(258)   a. * I sensed him for his eagerness.
        b. I sensed the eagerness in him.

(259)   Non-Alternating Attribute Object Not Allowed:

        a. * NEGATIVE JUDGMENT VERBS: abuse, backbite, calumniate, casti-
            gate, censure, chasten, chastise, chide, condemn, criticize, decry,
            defame, denigrate, denounce, deprecate, deride, disparage, fault,
            fine, impeach, insult, lambaste, malign, mock, penalize, perse-
            cute, prosecute, punish, rebuke, reprimand, reproach, reprove,
            revile, ridicule, scold, scorn, shame, snub, upbraid, victimize,
            vilify

        b. * POSITIVE JUDGMENT VERBS: acclaim, applaud, bless, celebrate,
            commend, compensate, compliment, congratulate, eulogize, ex-
            cuse, extol, felicitate, forgive, greet, hail, honor, laud, pardon,

praise, recompense, remunerate, repay, reward, salute, thank, toast, welcome

c. * WANT VERBS: covet, crave, desire, fancy, need, want

d. * VERBS OF ASSESSMENT: analyze, assess, audit, evaluate, review, scrutinize, study

(260)   a. They praised the volunteers for their dedication.
        b. * They praise the dedication in the volunteers.

Comments: This alternation should probably not be recognized as a separate alternation, because it arises simply as a consequence of the fact that the *admire*-type psych-verbs show both possessor and attribute objects.

2.13.4 Possessor Subject (transitive)

References: Dixon (1989), Van Oosten (1980, 1986)

(261)   Alternating Verbs:
        AMUSE-TYPE PSYCH-VERBS: abash, affect, afflict, affront, aggravate, agitate, agonize, alarm, alienate, amaze, amuse, anger, annoy, antagonize, appall, appease, arouse, assuage, astonish, astound, awe, baffle, beguile, bewilder, bewitch, boggle, bore, bother, bug, calm, captivate, chagrin, charm, cheer, chill, comfort, concern, confound, confuse, console, content, convince, cow, crush, cut, daunt, daze, dazzle, deject, delight, demolish, demoralize, depress, devastate, disappoint, disarm, discombobulate, discomfit, disconcert, discompose, discourage, disgrace, disgruntle, disgust, dishearten, disillusion, dismay, dispirit, displease, disquiet, dissatisfy, distract, distress, disturb, dumbfound, elate, electrify, embarrass, embolden, enchant, encourage, engage, engross, enlighten, enliven, enrage, enrapture, entertain, enthrall, enthuse, entice, entrance, exasperate, excite, exhaust, exhilarate, fascinate, faze, flabbergast, flatter, floor, fluster, frighten, frustrate, gall, galvanize, gladden, gratify, grieve, harass, haunt, hearten, horrify, humble, humiliate, hurt, hypnotize, impress, incense, infuriate, inspire, insult, interest, intimidate, intoxicate, intrigue, invigorate, irk, irritate, jar, jollify, jolt, lull, madden, mesmerize, miff, mollify, mortify, move, muddle, mystify, nauseate, nettle, numb, obsess, offend, outrage, overawe, overwhelm, pacify, pain, peeve, perplex, perturb, pique, placate, plague, please, preoccupy, provoke, puzzle, rankle, reassure, refresh, relax, relieve, repel, repulse, revitalize, revolt, rile, ruffle, sadden, satisfy, scandalize, scare, shake, shame, shock, sicken, sober, solace, soothe, spellbind, spook, stagger, startle, stimulate, sting, stir, strike, stump, stun, stupefy, surprise, tantalize, tease, tempt, terrify, terrorize, threaten, thrill, throw, tickle, tire, titillate, torment,

touch, transport, trouble, try, unnerve, unsettle, uplift, upset, vex, weary, worry, wound, wow

(262)   a.   Mark terrified me with his singlemindedness.
        b.   Mark's singlemindedness terrified me.

(263)   a.   The clown amused the children with his antics.
        b.   The clown's antics amused the children.

Comments: This type of possessor-attribute factoring alternation is manifested by a set of transitive verbs, the *amuse*-type psych-verbs. This alternation involves the expression of a possessor and an attribute (or sometimes an activity) of the possessor. The attribute/activity of the possessor is the cause of the psychological state referred to by the verb. These verbs allow the possessor and attribute/activity to be expressed either as a single noun phrase found as the subject of the verb or as two distinct constituents, with the possessor expressed as subject and the attribute expressed in a *with* phrase. In this alternation the factoring sets up a relationship between the subject of the verb and a prepositional phrase rather than between the object of the verb and a prepositional phrase, in contrast to the other factoring alternations involving transitive verbs.

This alternation can also be viewed as an "oblique" subject alternation. It is possible to draw a parallel between the instrument subject alternation (sec. 3.3) and this alternation, with the *with* phrase playing the role of the instrument. From this perspective, the cause of the psychological state can be expressed either as an "oblique" subject or as a prepositional phrase.

2.13.5   Possessor Subject (intransitive)

References: Na (1986), Perlmutter and Postal (1983), Van Oosten (1980, 1986)

(264)   Alternating Verbs:
        VERBS OF CALIBRATABLE CHANGES OF STATE: appreciate, balloon, climb, decline, decrease, depreciate, differ, diminish, drop, fall, fluctuate, gain, grow, increase, jump, ?mushroom, plummet, plunge, rocket, rise, skyrocket, soar, surge, tumble, vary

(265)   a.   Meat fell in price.
        b.   The price of meat fell.

Comments: This alternation is the intransitive counterpart of the possessor-attribute factoring alternation with possessor object (sec. 2.13.1). Specifically, the forms of the alternation manifested by transitive and intransitive verbs can be viewed as a single alternation if the intransitive verbs are given an unaccusative analysis, so that their subject is an underlying object; the verbs found in the transitive form of the alternation will take an agent argument that the verbs found in the intransitive form lack. In this form of the alternation, the relationship is between an inanimate possessor and its attribute. The possessor and attribute may be expressed using a single noun phrase bearing the subject relation to the verb: the attribute is the head of this noun phrase, and the possessor is expressed as a genitive possessor within the noun phrase. Alternatively, the possessor may be expressed as subject, and the attribute may be expressed in a prepositional phrase headed by *in*.

2.14 *As* Alternation

References: Curme (1931), Emonds (1985b), Poutsma (1904), Quirk et al. (1985), Stowell (1991b)

(266)   Alternating Verbs:
         APPOINT VERBS: acknowledge, adopt, appoint, consider, crown, deem, designate, elect, esteem, imagine, mark, nominate, ordain, proclaim, rate, reckon, report, want

(267)   a.   The president appointed Smith press secretary.
         b.   The president appointed Smith as press secretary.

(268)   Non-Alternating *as* Only:
         * CHARACTERIZE VERBS: accept, address, appreciate, bill, cast, certify, characterize, choose, cite, class, classify, confirm, count, define, describe, diagnose, disguise, employ, engage, enlist, enroll, enter, envisage, establish, esteem, hail, herald, hire, honor, identify, imagine, incorporate, induct, intend, lampoon, offer, oppose, paint, portray, praise, qualify, rank, recollect, recommend, regard, reinstate, reject, remember, represent, repudiate, reveal, salute, see, select, stigmatize, take, train, treat, use, value, view, visualize

(269)   a. * Angela characterized Shelly a lifesaver.
         b.   Angela characterized Shelly as a lifesaver.

(270)   Non-Alternating Double Object Only:
         a. * DUB VERBS: anoint, baptize, brand, call, christen, consecrate, crown, decree, dub, label, make, name, nickname, pronounce, rule, stamp, style, term, vote
         b. * DECLARE VERBS: adjudge, adjudicate, assume, avow, believe, confess, declare, fancy, find, judge, presume, profess, prove, suppose, think, warrant
         c. * BILL VERBS: bet, bill, charge, fine, mulct, overcharge, save, spare, tax, tip, undercharge, wager

(271) a. The captain named the ship Seafarer.
      b. * The captain named the ship as Seafarer.

Comments: This alternation is manifested by transitive verbs that take complements predicated of their direct object. The alternation arises because the noun phrase that is predicated of the direct object may either be a bare noun phrase or be expressed in an *as* phrase. Thus the alternation is characterized by the two frames: 'NP V NP NP' and 'NP V NP *as* NP'. The frame 'NP V NP NP' superficially resembles the double object frame associated with the dative alternation. However, despite the superficial similarity the two frames are typically given different syntactic analyses. The 'NP NP' sequence associated with the *as* alternation is often analyzed as a small clause. The verbs found in the dative alternation do not show this alternation, but they have not been cross-listed here.

3 "Oblique" Subject Alternations

The alternations found in this section do not involve a change in transitivity, but they do involve a change in the number of noun phrases found with the verb: the verb is found with one less noun phrase in one variant than in the other. These alternations involve verbs that have "agent" subjects, but that alternatively may take as subjects noun phrases that can be expressed in some type of prepositional phrase when the verb takes its canonical "agent" subject. Such subjects have been referred to as "oblique" subjects because certain prepositional phrases, particularly those expressing nonsubcategorized arguments, are sometimes referred to as oblique phrases. When the verbs take the oblique subject, the "agent" is no longer expressed. This section only includes a subset of the verbs that show this phenomenon, listing some of the major subtypes.

3.1 Time Subject Alternation

References: Perlmutter and Postal (1984)

(272) Alternating Verbs: see, find, mark, catch

(273) a. The world saw the beginning of a new era in 1492.
      b. 1492 saw the beginning of a new era.

3.2 Natural Force Subject Alternation

References: See references listed immediately below under Instrument Subject Alternation.

(274)   a.   I dried the clothes in the sun.
         b.   The sun dried the clothes.

Comments: "Oblique" subjects of this type have been characterized as "natural forces." It is sometimes difficult to draw the line between noun phrases that qualify as agents, natural forces, and instruments; there is some discussion of this issue in the Case Grammar literature. The three notions have been kept distinct here, although the question of whether this distinction is valid is by no means settled. Typically, when expressed in a prepositional phrase, natural forces cannot, or at least need not, turn up in a prepositional phrase headed by the instrumental preposition *with*. Also, unlike instruments, natural forces cannot turn up in *use* paraphrases; compare **I used the sun to dry the clothes* with *I used the hair dryer to dry the clothes*. Natural force subjects are not illustrated in Part II of this book.

3.3   Instrument Subject Alternation

References: M. Baker (1988a, 1988b), Brousseau and Ritter (1991), Cruse (1973), Deane and Wheeler (1984), Dixon (1991), Fillmore (1967, 1968a), Langacker (1991), Lasnik (1988), B. Levin and Rappaport (1988), Marantz (1984), Nilsen (1973), Rappaport Hovav and B. Levin (1992), Ravin (1990), Schlesinger (1989), Wojcik (1976)

(275)   a.   David broke the window with a hammer.
         b.   The hammer broke the window. (intermediary instrument)

(276)   a.   Doug ate the ice cream with a spoon.
         b.   * The spoon ate the ice cream. (enabling/facilitating instrument)

(277)   a.   The crane loaded the truck. (intermediary instrument)
         b.   * The pitchfork loaded the truck. (facilitating instrument)

Comments: "Oblique" subjects of this type have been characterized as "instruments." Various studies of the notion of instrument have made a distinction between enabling (also called "facilitating") instruments, which cannot turn up as subjects, and intermediary instruments, which can. Some verbs, like *eat* or *see*, never take instrumental subjects because they only take enabling/facilitating instruments. Some choices of instruments never turn up as subjects, even though the verb in the sentence permits instrument subjects, because they do not qualify as intermediary instruments, as shown by the *crane/pitchfork* example in (277). Thus, whether an instrument may turn up as subject depends both on the verb and the choice of instrument. See also comments immediately above under Natural Force Subject Alternation.

3.4   Abstract Cause Subject Alternation

(278)   Alternating Verbs: assert, confirm, demonstrate, establish, explain, imply, indicate, justify, nullify, obscure, proclaim, predict, prove, reveal, show, suggest

(279)   a.   He established his innocence with the letter.
        b.   The letter established his innocence.

(280)   His innocence was established by the letter.

Comments: The "oblique" subjects found in this alternation have been described as "abstract causes." It is possible that this notion could be collapsed with the notion of instrument, since abstract causes are expressed in *with* phrases and play an instrument-like function, acting as an intermediary in the event named by the verb. However, as their name reflects, abstract causes are typically abstract rather than concrete NPs.

3.5   Locatum Subject Alternation

References: Deane and Wheeler (1984), B. Levin and Rappaport (1988), Rappaport Hovav and B. Levin (1992), Sundén (1916a)

(281)   Alternating Verbs:
        FILL VERBS: adorn, anoint, bandage, bathe, bestrew, bind, blanket, block, blot, bombard, carpet, choke, cloak, clog, clutter, coat, contaminate, cover, dam, dapple, deck, decorate, deluge, dirty, douse, dot, drench, edge, embellish, emblazon, encircle, encrust, endow, enrich, entangle, face, festoon, fill, fleck, flood, frame, garland, garnish, imbue, impregnate, infect, inlay, interlace, interlard, interleave, intersperse, interweave, inundate, lard, lash, line, litter, mask, mottle, ornament, pad, pave, plate, plug, pollute, replenish, repopulate, riddle, ring, ripple, robe, saturate, season, shroud, smother, soak, soil, speckle, splotch, spot, staff, stain, stipple, stop up, stud, suffuse, surround, swaddle, swathe, taint, tile, trim, veil, vein, wreathe

(282)   a.   I filled the pail with water.
        b.   Water filled the pail.

Comments: The term "locatum" is taken from E.V. Clark and H.H. Clark's (1979) study of verbs zero-related to nouns. It is used by them to refer to the locatum argument, the entity whose location is described by that verb. The argument of the verb expressed in the *with* phrase or alternatively as an oblique subject appears to satisfy this definition. Although it might be possible to argue that the locatum phrases found with these verbs are actually instruments, since they turn up in *with* phrases, and that the locatum subjects are just a special case of instrument subjects, there are several reasons for not referring to them as such; see B. Levin and Rappaport (1988).

3.6   Location Subject Alternation

References: Perlmutter and Postal (1984)

(283)   Alternating Verbs:
         FIT VERBS: carry, contain, fit, feed, hold, house, seat, serve, sleep, store, take, use

(284)   a.   We sleep five people in each room.
         b.   Each room sleeps five people.

Comments: These verbs take oblique subjects that can be characterized as locations. They are used with location subjects to describe the capacity of the location with respect to the action named by the verb.

3.7   Container Subject Alternation

References: L. Levin (1986)

(285)   Alternating Verbs: amalgamate, contain, embed, include, incorporate, integrate, omit

(286)   a.   I incorporated the new results into the paper.
         b.   The paper incorporates the new results.

Comments: Verbs showing this alternation describe a relation between a whole, expressed either in a prepositional phrase or as the subject, and its components, expressed as the direct object.

3.8   Raw Material Subject Alternation

References: Atkins, Kegl, and B. Levin (1988), Napoli (1989a), Nash-Webber (1971)

(287)   Alternating Verbs:
         BUILD VERBS (some): bake, blow (bubbles, glass), carve, cast, churn, cook, crochet, grind, grow, knit, make, sew, spin, weave, whittle

(288)   a.   She baked wonderful bread from that whole wheat flour.
         b.   That whole wheat flour bakes wonderful bread.

(289)   Non-Alternating Verbs:
         a. * CREATE VERBS: coin, compose, compute, concoct, construct, create, derive, design, dig, fabricate, form, invent, manufacture, mint, model, organize, produce, recreate, style, synthesize

b. * KNEAD VERBS: beat, bend, coil, collect, compress, fold, freeze, knead, melt, shake, squash, squish, squeeze, twirl, twist, wad, whip, wind, work

(290) a. David constructed a house from those new bricks.
       b. * Those new bricks constructed a house.

Comments: The raw material argument found with certain verbs of creation can appear as subject when the product argument is expressed as the object. Sentences with raw material subjects are understood to be characterizing the ability of the subject to be used in the action named by the verb.

3.9 Sum of Money Subject Alternation

References: Perlmutter and Postal (1984)

(291) Alternating Verbs:
       a. VERBS OF OBTAINING (some verbs): buy, charter, earn, find, get, lease, obtain, procure, purchase, rent, reserve, save, secure, win
       b. BUILD VERBS (a few verbs): build, make, sew

(292) a. I bought (you) a ticket for $5.
       b. $5 will buy (you) a ticket.

(293) a. The contractor will build (you) a house for $100,000.
       b. $100,000 will build (you) a house.

Comments: The sum of money that is involved in certain financial transactions can optionally be expressed as the subject of certain verbs describing such transactions. This phenomenon is found with those verbs of obtaining where the process of obtaining involves a transfer of money. When these verbs take a sum of money subject, this sum is understood to be sufficient to allow the transaction to take place.

3.10 Source Subject Alternation

(294) Alternating Verbs: benefit, profit

(295) a. The middle class will benefit from the new tax laws.
       b. The new tax laws will benefit the middle class.

(296) Non-Alternating Verbs: gain, prosper

(297) a. The middle class will gain from the new tax laws.
       b. * The new tax laws will gain the middle class.

Comments: Certain verbs of benefiting take as "oblique" subject the source of the benefit. This type of "oblique" subject appears to be found with very few verbs.

4   Reflexive Diathesis Alternations

This section describes regular changes in meaning that accompany the use of reflexive pronouns as objects with certain verbs. In some instances, there are others changes in the verb's argument-taking properties that accompany these specialized uses of reflexive objects.

4.1   Virtual Reflexive Alternation

References: Fellbaum (1989), Fiengo (1980), Geniušienė (1987), Hale and Keyser (1987), Jespersen (1949), G. Lakoff (1977), Lee (1971), Williams (1981)

(298)   a.   The butcher cuts the meat.
         b.   This meat cuts itself.

(299)   a.   The butler polished the silver.
         b.   This silver polishes itself.

(300)   a.   The audience watched the movie.
         b. * This movie just watches itself.

(301)   a.   The boy opened the window.
         b.   This window just opens itself.

(302)   a.   The heat melted the ice cream.
         b. * This ice cream just melts itself.

(303)   a.   This book just sells itself.
         b. * This book just buys itself.

Comments: In the virtual reflexive construction, the subject bears the same semantic relation to the verb as the object does in the typical transitive use of the verb. However, unlike other constructions with this property, the verb does not change transitivity but instead takes a reflexive pronoun as object. The argument that is the subject of the typical transitive use of the verb is not expressed. The virtual reflexive construction seems to be similar to the middle construction in meaning, but the set of verbs that appear in this construction is not co-extensive with the set of verbs appearing in the middle construction. In fact, the set of verbs found in this construction is quite restricted and not easily tied to particular semantic classes of verbs. For instance, Fellbaum (1989) points out that some alternating verbs of change of state (secs. 45.1–45.4) show this alternation (e.g., *shut, open*) while others do not (e.g., *melt*).

4.2   Reflexive of Appearance Alternation

References: Geniušienė (1987), Poutsma (1904), Sigler (1985)

(304)   REFLEXIVE VERBS OF APPEARANCE: assert, declare, define, express, form, manifest, offer, pose, present, proffer, recommend, shape, show, suggest

(305)   a. I presented a solution to the problem yesterday.
         b. A solution to the problem presented itself yesterday.

Comments: When verbs undergoing this alternation are found with reflexive objects, their subject bears the same semantic relation to the verb as the object does in the ordinary transitive use. The argument that is the subject of the typical transitive use of the verb is not expressed. This construction is used to describe coming into existence or appearance on the scene. The verbs showing this property can all be used transitively.

5   Passive

References: Abney (1987), Abraham (1983), Anderson (1977, 1988), Anward (1989), Bach (1980), M. Baker (1988a), M. Baker, Johnson, and Roberts (1989), Barkaï (1972), Beedham (1979, 1982), P.A. Bennett (1980), Bolinger (1975, 1977b, 1978), Borer (1984), Bouton (1973), Bresnan (1982b), Burzio (1981, 1986), Chomsky (1981), Couper-Kuhlen (1979), Croft (1991), Curme (1931), Davison (1980), Dixon (1991), Doron and Rappaport Hovav (1991), Dowty (1978a, 1978b, 1982), Dryer (1985), Emonds (1976), Fabb (1984, 1988), Fagan (1992), Foley and Van Valin (1984), Freidin (1975), Grimshaw (1990), Grimshaw and Vikner (1990), Grodzinsky, Pierce, and Marakovitz (1991), Halliday (1967, 1968), K. Hasegawa (1968), N. Hasegawa (1981, 1988), Hestvik (1986), Hoard (1979), T. Hoekstra (1984, 1986), Hornstein and Weinberg (1981), Hudson (1991, 1992), Jackendoff (1972), Jaeggli (1986), Jespersen (1927), Keenan (1975, 1985), Kilby (1984), G. Lakoff (1970a), R. Lakoff (1971), Langacker (1991), B. Levin and Rappaport (1986), L. Levin (1986, 1987), Lightfoot (1991), Machonis (1985), Marantz (1982, 1984), J. McCawley (1988), Nunberg (1978), Parsons (1990), Perlmutter and Postal (1984), Pesetsky (1992), Pinker (1989), Postal (1990), Postal and Pullum (1988), Poutsma (1904), Quirk et al. (1985), Rice (1987), Riddle and Sheintuch (1983), Riddle, Sheintuch, and Ziv (1977), Roberts (1987), Siegel (1973), Siewierska (1984), Sinha (1973, 1974, 1978), Stanley (1975), Stein (1979), Sundén (1916a), Svartvik (1966), Valesio (1971), Vikner (1991), Wasow (1977, 1978, 1980), Williams (1981, 1982), Ziv and Sheintuch (1981), Zubizarreta (1987)

5.1 Verbal Passive

(306)   a. The cook sliced the mushrooms.
          b. The mushrooms were sliced by the cook.

(307)   a. Columbus believed the earth to be round.
          b. The earth was believed to be round.

(308)   a. Columbus believed that the earth was round.
          b. It was believed that the earth was round.

(309)   a. The police kept tabs on the suspect.
          b. Tabs were kept on the suspect.

(310)   a. The employees took advantage of the lax supervision.
          b. The lax supervision was taken advantage of.

5.2 Prepositional Passive

(311)   a. George Washington slept in this bed. (unergative verb)
          b. This bed was slept in by George Washington.

(312)   a. George Washington slept on Tuesday. (unergative verb plus adjunct)
          b. ∗ Tuesday was slept on by George Washington.

(313)   a. A pirate ship appeared on the horizon. (unaccusative verb)
          b. ∗ The horizon was appeared on by a pirate ship.

Comments: This type of passive construction is found primarily with intransitive verbs. The discussions of these passives have focused on identifying the criteria that determine whether an intransitive verb will or will not be found in the prepositional passive construction. A verb's eligibility appears to depend on the nature of the verb itself and the nature of the prepositional phrase. Couper-Kuhlen (1979) looks at constraints on the semantic roles of the arguments of intransitive verbs and suggests that one restriction on this construction is that the verb must allow an animate subject. It has also been proposed by Perlmutter and Postal (1984) that only unergative verbs (those intransitive verbs whose surface subject is an underlying subject) and not unaccusative verbs (those intransitive verbs whose surface subject is an underlying object) are found in prepositional passives. But not all supposedly unergative verbs allow prepositional passives; these restrictions must be explained. Sentences with adjunct prepositional phrases do not have prepositional passive counterparts.

5.3 Adjectival Passive (transitive verbs)

References: Barkaï (1972), Beedham (1979), Bolinger (1967), Dryer (1985), Fabb (1984), Grimshaw (1990), Grimshaw and Vikner (1990), Grodzinsky,

Pierce, and Marakovitz (1991), T. Hoekstra (1984), B. Levin and Rappaport (1986), Pesetsky (1992), Siegel (1973), Wasow (1977), Williams (1981, 1982)

(314)   a.   The feathers remained stuffed in the pillow.
        b.   The pillow remained stuffed with feathers.

(315)   broken glass, unsent letters, cut flowers

(316)   unsold cars, *unsold customers

Comments: Certain passive participles show adjectival properties; these are termed "adjectival passives." Just as with verbal passives, all obligatory complements of the verb must be expressed in order to have a well-formed adjectival passive. There is some debate about whether a notion of "adjectival passive" that is distinct from "verbal passive" should be recognized.

5.4   Adjectival Perfect Participles (intransitive verbs)

References: Bresnan (1982b), Doron and Rappaport Hovav (1991), Dryer (1985), Fabb (1984), Grimshaw (1990), T. Hoekstra (1984, 1986), B. Levin and Rappaport (1986, 1989), Pesetsky (1992), Verhaar (1990)

(317)   UNACCUSATIVE VERBS:
        recently arrived guests, collapsed lung, curdled milk, drifted snow, elapsed time, an escaped convict, failed coup, fallen leaves, a frozen lake, a grown child, lapsed Catholic, well-rested children, recently returned traveller, risen dough, rotten apples, a slipped disc, sprouted wheat, stuck window, sunken treasure, swollen feet, tarnished silver, twisted tree trunks, vanished civilizations, wilted lettuce, withered hopes, a wrinkled dress

(318)   * UNERGATIVE VERBS:
        * walked man, *talked politician, *slept children, *flashed light, *beeped clock

Comments: The adjectival perfect participles formed from certain intransitive verbs have been included in the section on passives since they are formed with the perfect morpheme –ed, which is homophonous with, if not the same morpheme as, the passive morpheme. The question is whether there is some relation between the process forming such adjectival perfect participles and the process forming adjectival passive participles. Another open issue concerns the characterization of the intransitive verbs that have related adjectival perfect participles. It has been proposed that only unaccusative verbs may have related adjectival perfect participles (although not all do), but that unergative verbs may not. There is disagreement about whether the process of forming

–ed participles from intransitive verbs is a productive process, even within the appropriately restricted set of verbs.

6   Alternations Involving Postverbal "Subjects"

These two alternations involve constructions where the subject of the verb occurs after the verb. The two alternations differ as to what becomes the surface subject. The verbs found in these constructions are primarily intransitive and passive transitive verbs. Very few transitive verbs are attested. There is a third type of alternation involving a postverbal subject, quotation inversion, as in "*I think that Wanda forgot to come,*" *said Mathilda.* This alternation is not included here since it involves sentential complement-taking verbs. See Green (1980), Hartvigson and Jakobsen (1974), Penhallurick (1984), and Zwicky (1971a), among others.

6.1   *There*-Insertion

References: Aissen (1975), Allen (1971), Bach (1980), Belletti (1988), Bolinger (1977a), Borer (1983), Bowers (1976), Breivik (1978, 1979, 1981, 1983), Bresnan (1990), Burzio (1981, 1986), Carlson (1977), Chomsky (1989), E.V. Clark (1978), Coopmans (1989), Comorovski (1991), Emonds (1976), Erdmann (1976), Fiengo (1977), Freeze (1992), Guéron (1980), Hannay (1985), Hartvigson and Jakobsen (1974), Hestvik (1986), Hetzron (1971), T. Hoekstra and Mulder (1990), Holmback (1984), Iwakura (1978), Jenkins (1975), Jespersen (1949), Kegl and Fellbaum (1988), Keyser and Roeper (1984), Kimball (1973b), Kirsner (1973), Kuno (1971), G. Lakoff (1977, 1987), Larson (1988a), Lasnik (1990), B. Levin and Rappaport Hovav (1992b), L. Levin (1986, 1987), R.D. Levine (1989), Long (1968), M. Lumsden (1988), Lyons (1989), Martin (1991), J. McCawley (1970a, 1981, 1988), McCloskey (1991), McNally (1992), Milsark (1974, 1977, 1990), Moro (1989), Napoli (1988b), Napoli and Rando (1978), Newmeyer (1987), Penhallurick (1984), Pesetsky (1992), Platzack (1983), Poutsma (1904), Quirk et al. (1985), Reuland and ter Meulen (1987), Rochemont (1978, 1979, 1986), Rochemont and Culicover (1990), J.R. Ross (1974), Safir (1985, 1987), Sawyer (1973), Schreiber (1978), Sheintuch (1980), Stowell (1978, 1979, 1981), Szabolcsi (1986), Thorne (1973), Travis (to appear), Williams (1984), Ziv (1982a, 1982b)

(319)   With the verb *be:*
    a.   A flowering plant is on the windowsill.
    b.   There is a flowering plant on the windowsill.

(320)   a.   VERBS OF EXISTENCE (drawn from various subclasses): blaze,
                bubble, cling, coexist, correspond, decay, depend, drift, dwell,
                elapse, emanate, exist, fester, float, flow, fly, grow, hide, hover,
                live, loom, lurk, overspread, persist, predominate, prevail, project,
                protrude, remain, revolve, reside, rise, settle, shelter, smolder,
                spread, stream, survive, sweep, swing, tower, wind, writhe
         b.   VERBS OF SPATIAL CONFIGURATION: crouch, dangle, hang, kneel,
                lean, lie, perch, rest, sit, slouch, sprawl, squat, stand, straddle,
                stretch, swing
         c.   MEANDER VERBS: cascade, climb, crawl, cut, drop, go, meander,
                plunge, run, straggle, stretch, sweep, tumble, turn, twist, wander,
                weave, wind
         d.   VERBS OF APPEARANCE: accumulate, appear, arise, assemble,
                awake, awaken, begin, break, burst, dawn, derive, develop, em-
                anate, emerge, ensue, evolve, exude, flow, follow, gush, happen,
                issue, materialize, occur, open, plop, rise, spill, steal, stem,
                supervene, surge
         e.   ? VERBS OF DISAPPEARANCE: die, disappear, vanish
         f.   VERBS OF INHERENTLY DIRECTED MOTION: arrive, ascend, come,
                descend, drop, enter, fall, go, pass, rise

(321)   a.   A problem developed.
         b.   There developed a problem.

(322)   a.   A ship appeared on the horizon.
         b.   There appeared a ship on the horizon.

(323)   Definiteness Effect:
         a.   There appeared a ship on the horizon.
         b.   * There appeared the ship on the horizon.

(324)   VERBS OF MANNER OF MOTION (*Run* and *Roll* Verbs): amble, climb,
         crawl, creep, dance, dart, flee, float, fly, gallop, head, hobble, hop,
         hurtle, jump, leap, march, plod, prance, ride, roam, roll, run, rush,
         sail, shuffle, skip, speed, stagger, step, stray, stride, stroll, strut, swim,
         trot, trudge, walk

(325)   Manner and direction of motion specified:
         a.   A little boy darted into the room.
         b.   There darted into the room a little boy.
            ?? There darted a little boy into the room.
            ?? Into the room there darted a little boy.

(326)   Manner of motion specified but direction of motion not specified:
         a.   A little boy ran in the yard.

      b. * There ran a little boy in the yard.

      c. ? There ran in the yard a little boy.

      d. ? In the yard there ran a little boy.

(327)   Potentially extended uses of certain verbs as verbs of existence:

      a. RUN VERBS: see above

      b. VERBS OF BODY-INTERNAL MOTION: flap, flutter

      c. VERBS OF SOUND EMISSION: beat, boom, chime, ring, rumble, shriek, tick

      d. VERBS OF SOUND EXISTENCE: echo, resound, reverberate, sound

      e. VERBS OF LIGHT EMISSION: flare, flash, flicker, gleam, glimmer, glisten, glitter, scintillate, shimmer, shine, sparkle, twinkle

      f. VERBS OF SUBSTANCE EMISSION: belch, puff, radiate

      g. OTHER VERBS: chatter, doze, idle, labor, lounge, preside, reign, sing, sleep, toil, wait, work

(328)   TRANSITIVE VERBS USED IN THE PASSIVE:

      a. VERBS OF PERCEPTION: discern, discover, hear, see

      b. VERBS OF IMAGE CREATION: engrave, imprint, inscribe, paint, scrawl, stamp, tattoo, write

      c. VERBS OF PUTTING: hang, lay, mount, place, pile, stack, suspend, scatter

      d. TAPE VERBS: glue, hook, pin, staple, strap

      e. OTHER VERBS: add, build, display, create, enact, find, show, understand, write

(329)   a. An ancient treasure trove was found in this cave.

      b. There was found in this cave an ancient treasure trove.

(330)   TRANSITIVE VERBS (very few):

await, confront, cross, enter, follow, reach, seize, take (place/shape), want

      a. Suddenly an ugly old man entered the hall.

      b. Suddenly there entered the hall an ugly old man.

(331)   * CHANGE OF STATE VERBS:

Given the size of the class, the members are not listed here.

(332)   a. A lot of snow melted on the streets of Chicago.

      b. * There melted a lot of snow on the streets of Chicago.

Comments: The hallmark of the *there*-insertion construction, which is typically found with intransitive and passive verbs, is the presence of *there* before the verb and the postverbal appearance of a noun phrase which would otherwise appear as the surface subject. Several properties of this construction have been widely investigated. One is the so-called Definiteness Effect, roughly the requirement that an immediately postverbal NP in the *there*-insertion construction be indefinite (though there is some controversy over how this term is to be defined). A second much-studied property involves the characterization of the set of verbs found in this construction. The prototypical intransitive verbs found in the *there*-insertion construction have been described as verbs of existence and appearance. Not all of the verbs that allow this construction appear to meet this characterization readily in their basic sense, but it has been suggested that they all show an existence or appearance sense when found in this construction. However, change of state verbs appear to be incompatible with it. Milsark (1974) points out that although some of the verbs found in the *there*-insertion construction are basically change of state verbs (e.g., *break, grow, open*), they lose the change of state interpretation in this construction and are understood as verbs of existence or appearance. Some passive verbs and a few transitive verbs also permit this construction; these are generally drawn from classes that can be seen to be compatible with the overall semantic constraints on the verbs found in it. The semantic make-up of the set of verbs found in this construction together with the presence of an immediately postverbal NP with at least some verbs has led some to propose that the *there*-insertion construction is an unaccusative diagnostic (Burzio (1986), L. Levin (1986, 1987), among others).

Most of the verbs found in the *there*-insertion construction must cooccur with a prepositional phrase. Less thoroughly studied is the possible position of this prepositional phrase. There are three possible positions: sentence-initial preceding *there*, immediately after the verb but before the NP, or following a postverbal NP. However, not every position is available with every type of verb. For instance, Aissen (1975) points out that some verbs are only found in this construction if the postverbal NP follows (rather than precedes) the PP. This seems to be the case with the *run* verbs; see also Burzio (1986). Bresnan (1990) also points out that the PP cannot precede *there* with the *run* verbs.

A representative list of verbs that can be found in this construction, grouped into semantically coherent classes, is identified above. The same list of verbs has been included under both *There*-Insertion and Locative Inversion (below), with the exception of the transitive verbs found in each of these constructions. This decision was motivated by the considerable overlap between the verbs found in the two constructions. However, further research is necessary to determine whether the classes of verbs found in the two constructions really are co-extensive. The lists include almost exclusively members of the classes that have been attested in the literature in one of the constructions; Hartvigson and Jakobsen (1974) and a corpus collected at Northwestern University are the sources for many of these verbs. Some of the verb classes identified here are broken down further in Part II of this book.

6.2 Locative Inversion

References: Aissen (1975), Aissen and Hankamer (1972), Birner (1992), Bolinger (1977a), Bowers (1976), Breivik (1981), Bresnan (1976, 1990), Bresnan and Kanerva (1992), Carlson (1977), Coopmans (1989, 1992), Emonds (1976, 1991), Erteschik-Shir (1991), Freeze (1992), Green (1976, 1980, 1982, 1984, 1985), Hannay (1985), Hartvigson and Jakobsen (1974), Hetzron (1971), T. Hoekstra and Mulder (1990), Hooper and Thompson (1973), Iwakura (1978), Jackendoff (1973), Jespersen (1949), Kaisse (1985), Kuno (1971), G. Lakoff (1987), Langendoen (1973, 1979), B. Levin and Rappaport Hovav (1992b), L. Levin (1986, 1987), R.D. Levine (1989), Ljung (1980), M. Lumsden (1988), Maruta (1985), N. McCawley (1977), Penhallurick (1984), Postal (1977a), Quirk et al. (1985), Rochemont (1978, 1979, 1986), Rochemont and Culicover (1990), Safir (1985), Schachter (1992), Stowell (1981), Zwicky (1986). See Bresnan and Kanerva (1989) for a discussion of a similar phenomenon in Chicheŵa.

(333)   With the verb *be:*
    a.   A flowering plant is on the windowsill.
    b.   On the windowsill is a flowering plant.

(334)   a.   VERBS OF EXISTENCE (drawn from various subclasses): blaze, bubble, cling, coexist, correspond, decay, depend, drift, dwell, elapse, emanate, exist, fester, float, flow, fly, grow, hide, hover, live, loom, lurk, overspread, persist, predominate, prevail, project, protrude, remain, revolve, reside, rise, settle, shelter, smolder, spread, stream, survive, sweep, swing, tower, wind, writhe
    b.   VERBS OF SPATIAL CONFIGURATION: crouch, dangle, hang, kneel, lean, lie, perch, rest, sit, slouch, sprawl, squat, stand, straddle, stretch, swing
    c.   MEANDER VERBS: cascade, climb, crawl, cut, drop, go, meander, plunge, run, straggle, stretch, sweep, tumble, turn, twist, wander, weave, wind
    d.   VERBS OF APPEARANCE: accumulate, appear, arise, assemble, awake, awaken, begin, break, burst, dawn, derive, develop, emanate, emerge, ensue, evolve, exude, flow, follow, gush, happen, issue, materialize, occur, open, plop, rise, spill, steal, stem, supervene, surge
    e.   ? VERBS OF DISAPPEARANCE: die, disappear, vanish
    f.   VERBS OF INHERENTLY DIRECTED MOTION: arrive, ascend, come, descend, drop, enter, fall, go, pass, rise

(335)   a.   An old woman lives in the woods. (locative PP)
    b.   In the woods lives an old woman.

(336)   VERBS OF MANNER OF MOTION (*Run* and *Roll* Verbs): amble, climb,
         crawl, creep, dance, dart, flee, float, fly, gallop, head, hobble, hop,
         hurtle, jump, leap, march, plod, prance, ride, roam, roll, run, rush,
         sail, shuffle, skip, speed, stagger, step, stray, stride, stroll, strut, swim,
         trot, trudge, walk

(337)   Manner and direction of motion specified:
         a. A cat jumped onto the table. (directional PP)
         b. Onto the table jumped a cat.

(338)   Manner of motion specified but direction of motion not specified:
         a. A cat jumped on the table. (locative PP)
         b. * On the table jumped a cat.

(339)   Extended uses of certain verbs as verbs of existence:
         a. RUN VERBS: see above
         b. VERBS OF BODY-INTERNAL MOTION: flap, flutter
         c. VERBS OF SOUND EMISSION: beat, boom, chime, ring, rumble,
             shriek, tick
         d. VERBS OF SOUND EXISTENCE: echo, resound, reverberate, sound
         e. VERBS OF LIGHT EMISSION: flare, flash, flicker, gleam, glimmer,
             glisten, glitter, scintillate, shimmer, shine, sparkle, twinkle
         f. VERBS OF SUBSTANCE EMISSION: belch, puff, radiate
         g. OTHER VERBS: chatter, doze, idle, labor, lounge, preside, reign,
             sing, sleep, toil, wait, work

(340)   a. A choir sang in the church. (locative PP)
         b. In the church sang a choir.

(341)   TRANSITIVE VERBS USED IN THE PASSIVE:
         a. VERBS OF PERCEPTION: discern, discover, hear, see
         b. VERBS OF IMAGE CREATION: engrave, imprint, inscribe, paint,
             scrawl, stamp, tattoo, write
         c. VERBS OF PUTTING: hang, lay, mount, place, pile, scatter, stack,
             suspend
         d. TAPE VERBS: glue, hook, pin, staple, strap
         e. OTHER VERBS: add, build, display, enact, create, find, show,
             understand, write

(342)   a. An ancient treasure trove was found in this cave.
         b. In this cave was found an ancient treasure trove.

(343)   TRANSITIVE VERBS (very few): take (place/shape)
         a. A violent demonstration took place in the main square.
         b. ? In the main square took place a violent demonstration.

(344)   * CHANGE OF STATE VERBS:
        Given the size of the class, the members are not listed here.

(345)   a.   A lot of snow melted on the streets of Chicago.
         b. * On the streets of Chicago melted a lot of snow.

Comments: The superficial characteristics of this construction suggest that it
is aptly named "locative inversion." It is typically found with certain intransitive
verbs and passive verbs that take locative and directional prepositional phrase
complements, and it is characterized by a preverbal prepositional phrase and a
postverbal noun phrase which bears the same relation to the verb as the surface
subject does when the verb is not used in this construction.

There has been much discussion of the set of verbs found in this construction,
and the comments above concerning the set of verbs found in the *there*-insertion
construction carry over to locative inversion. That is, the set of verbs found in
this construction have been characterized as verbs of existence and appearance.
Some of the attested verbs do not readily fit this characterization, but it has been
suggested that they show an existence or appearance sense when found in this
construction. Milsark's observation (1974) that verbs of change of state (e.g.,
break, grow, open) receive a verb of existence or appearance interpretation
when they are found in the *there*-insertion construction extends to the locative
inversion construction. As with the *there*-insertion construction, there has been
some debate over whether or not this construction is an unaccusative diagnostic;
Bresnan (1990) and T. Hoekstra and Mulder (1990) are among those who argue
that it is, while Rochemont and Culicover (1990) take the opposing position.

A representative list of verbs that can be found in this construction, grouped
into semantically coherent classes, is identified above. The same list of verbs
has been included under both *There*-Insertion and Locative Inversion, with the
exception of the transitive verbs found in each of these constructions. This
decision was motivated by the considerable overlap between the verbs found
in the two constructions. However, further research is necessary to determine
whether the classes of verbs found in the two constructions really are co-
extensive. The lists include almost exclusively members of the classes that
have been attested in the literature in one of the constructions; Hartvigson and
Jakobsen (1974) and a corpus collected at Northwestern University are the
sources for many of these verbs. Some of the verb classes identified here are
broken down further in the verb class part of this book.

7   Other Constructions

This section includes a variety of other constructions that involve the argument-taking properties of verbs. Some involve the ability to take particular kinds of complements; others involve special interpretations associated with certain choices of arguments.

7.1   Cognate Object Construction

References: Baron (1971), Dixon (1991), Fellbaum (1992), Fellbaum and Kegl (1989), Jespersen (1927), Jones (1988), Langacker (1991), Ljung (1970), Massam (1990), Moltmann (1989), Rice (1988), Stein (1979), Poutsma (1904)

(346)   a.   VERBS OF NONVERBAL EXPRESSION (some): beam, chuckle, cough, cry, frown, giggle, grimace, grin, howl, laugh, sigh, smile, smirk, sneeze, sniff, snore, snort, sob, weep, whistle, yawn
        b.   WALTZ VERBS: boogie, bop, cancan, clog, conga, dance, fox-trot, jig, jitterbug, jive, pirouette, polka, quickstep, rumba, samba, shuffle, squaredance, tango, tapdance, waltz
        c.   OTHER VERBS: dream, fight, live, sing, sleep, think

(347)   a.   Sarah smiled.
        b.   Sarah smiled a charming smile.
             (roughly: Sarah smiled charmingly.)
        c.?? Sarah smiled a smile.

(348)   a.   Sarah sang.
        b.   Sarah sang a song.
        c.   Sarah sang a ballad/an aria/a hymn/the anthem.

(349)   ? VERBS OF MANNER OF SPEAKING: babble, bark, bawl, bellow, bleat, boom, bray, burble, cackle, call, carol, chant, chatter, chirp, cluck, coo, croak, croon, crow, cry, drawl, drone, gabble, gibber, groan, growl, grumble, grunt, hiss, holler, hoot, howl, jabber, lilt, lisp, moan, mumble, murmur, mutter, purr, rage, rasp, roar, rumble, scream, screech, shout, shriek, sing, snap, snarl, snuffle, splutter, squall, squeak, squeal, squawk, stammer, stutter, thunder, tisk, trill, trumpet, twitter, wail, warble, wheeze, whimper, whine, whisper, whistle, whoop, yammer, yap, yell, yelp, yodel

(350)   a.   Heather grunted.
        b. ? Heather grunted a disinterested grunt.

Comments: Some basically intransitive verbs take as their object a noun that is zero-related to the verb—a so-called "cognate object." Usually, the cognate object itself does not appear to make a contribution to the meaning of the sentence. However, cognate objects are best when they are modified by an adjective or other modifier, and the modifier makes a contribution to the meaning of the sentence: the modifier functions rather like an adverbial. Most verbs that take cognate objects do not take a wide range of objects. Often they only permit a cognate object, although some verbs will take as object anything that is a hyponym of the cognate object.

Cognate objects are found with many verbs of nonverbal expression, as well as with a variety of other activity verbs. Zwicky (1971a) writes that verbs of manner of speaking take cognate objects, but there seem to be differences of opinion about whether such objects are indeed permitted; it is also possible that members of this class might behave differently in this respect.

7.2   Cognate Prepositional Phrase Construction

References: Jackendoff (1990b, 1992c), Ljung (1977)

(351)   a.   BUTTER VERBS: asphalt, bait, blanket, blindfold, board, bread, brick, bridle, bronze, butter, buttonhole, cap, carpet, caulk, chrome, cloak, cork, crown, diaper, drug, feather, fence, flour, forest, frame, fuel, gag, garland, glove, graffiti, gravel, grease, groove, halter, harness, heel, ink, label, leash, leaven, lipstick, mantle, mulch, muzzle, nickel, oil, ornament, panel, paper, parquet, patch, pepper, perfume, pitch, plank, plaster, poison, polish, pomade, poster, postmark, powder, putty, robe, roof, rosin, rouge, rut, saddle, salt, salve, sand, seed, sequin, shawl, shingle, shoe, shutter, silver, slate, slipcover, sod, sole, spice, stain, starch, stopper, stress, string, stucco, sugar, sulphur, tag, tar, tarmac, tassel, thatch, ticket, tile, turf, veil, veneer, wallpaper, water, wax, whitewash, wreathe, yoke, zipcode

   b.   VERBS OF COLORING: color, distemper, dye, enamel, glaze, japan, lacquer, paint, shellac, spraypaint, stain, tint, varnish

   c.   TAPE VERBS: anchor, band, belt, bolt, bracket, buckle, button, cement, chain, clamp, clasp, clip, epoxy, fetter, glue, gum, handcuff, harness, hinge, hitch, hook, knot, lace, lash, lasso, latch, leash, link, lock, loop, manacle, moor, muzzle, nail, padlock, paste, peg, pin, plaster, rivet, rope, screw, seal, shackle, skewer, solder, staple, stitch, strap, string, tack, tape, tether, thumbtack, tie, trammel, wire, yoke, zip

(352)   a.   Kelly buttered the bread.
   b.   * Kelly buttered the bread with butter.
   c.   Kelly buttered the bread with unsalted butter.

(353)   a.   Linda taped the box with two-sided tape.
   b.   ? Linda taped the box with tape.

(354)   MINE VERBS: mine, quarry

(355)   a.   The men were able to mine more gold.
         b.   The men were able to mine more gold from the abandoned mine.

(356)   * POCKET VERBS: archive, bag, bank, beach, bed, bench, berth, billet,
         bin, bottle, box, cage, can, case, cellar, cloister, coop, corral, crate,
         dock, drydock, file, fork, garage, ground, hangar, house, jail, jar, jug,
         kennel, land, lodge, pasture, pen, pillory, pocket, pot, sheathe, shelter,
         shelve, shoulder, skewer, snare, spindle, spit, spool, stable, string, tin,
         trap, tree, warehouse

(357)   a. * Lydia pocketed the change in her pocket.
         b.?? Lydia pocketed the change in her left front jacket pocket.

(358)   a. * PIT VERBS: bark, beard, bone, burl, core, gill, gut, head, hull,
            husk, lint, louse, milk, peel, pinion, pip, pit, pith, pod, poll, pulp,
            rind, scale, scalp, seed, shell, shuck, skin, snail, stalk, stem, stone,
            string, tail, tassel, top, vein, weed, wind, worm, zest
         b. * DEBONE VERBS: deaccent, debark, debone, debowel, debug, de-
            bur, declaw, defang, defat, defeather, deflea, deflesh, defoam,
            defog, deforest, defrost, defuzz, degas, degerm, deglaze, degrease,
            degrit, degum, degut, dehair, dehead, dehorn, dehull, dehusk,
            deice, deink, delint, delouse, deluster, demast, derat, derib, de-
            rind, desalt, descale, desex, desprout, destarch, destress, detassel,
            detusk, devein, dewater, dewax, deworm

(359)   a. * The cook boned the fish of bones.
         b. * The cook boned the fish of its backbone.

Comments: A "cognate" prepositional phrase may be found with certain
verbs that are zero-related to nominals. In most instances, these phrases are
headed by the preposition *with*, and the verbs taking such phrases fall into
two major classes: verbs whose meaning can be paraphrased as "put X on/in
something" and verbs whose meaning can be paraphrased as "attach with X,"
where X is the noun that the verb takes its name from. In addition, the verbs
mine and *quarry* can take cognate source phrases.

The object of the preposition is an NP headed by the noun that the verb takes
its name from or a noun that bears the hyponym relation to the noun that the
verb derives its name from. Such cognate prepositional phrases are typically
most acceptable if they contribute additional information through the use of a
modifier of some kind.

7.3   Reaction Object Construction

References: Jespersen (1949), B. Levin and Rapoport (1988), Mufwene
(1978), Poutsma (1904)

(360)   a.   VERBS OF NONVERBAL EXPRESSION: beam, cackle, chortle, chuckle, cough, cry, frown, gape, gasp, gawk, giggle, glare, glower, goggle, grimace, grin, groan, growl, guffaw, howl, jeer, laugh, moan, pout, scowl, sigh, simper, smile, smirk, sneeze, snicker, sniff, snigger, snivel, snore, snort, sob, titter, weep, whistle, yawn

        b.   WINK VERBS: blink (eye), clap (hands), nod (head), point (finger), shrug (shoulders), squint (eyes), wag (tail), wave (hand), wink (eye)

        c.   VERBS OF MANNER OF SPEAKING: babble, bark, bawl, bellow, bleat, boom, bray, burble, cackle, call, carol, chant, chatter, chirp, cluck, coo, croak, croon, crow, cry, drawl, drone, gabble, gibber, groan, growl, grumble, grunt, hiss, holler, hoot, howl, jabber, lilt, lisp, moan, mumble, murmur, mutter, purr, rage, rasp, roar, rumble, scream, screech, shout, shriek, sing, snap, snarl, snuffle, splutter, squall, squeak, squeal, squawk, stammer, stutter, thunder, tisk, trill, trumpet, twitter, wail, warble, wheeze, whimper, whine, whisper, whistle, whoop, yammer, yap, yell, yelp, yodel

(361)   a.   Pauline smiled.
        b.   Pauline smiled her thanks.

(362)   a.   Sandra beamed.
        b.   Sandra beamed a cheerful welcome.

(363)   * A cheerful welcome was beamed by Sandra.

(364)   a.   She mumbled.
        b.   She mumbled her adoration.

Comments: Certain intransitive verbs—particularly verbs of manner of speaking and verbs of gestures and signs—take nonsubcategorized objects that express a reaction (an emotion or disposition); possible objects include: *approval, disapproval, assent, admiration, disgust, yes, no.* When these verbs take such objects they take on an extended sense which might be paraphrased "express (a reaction) by V-ing," where "V" is the basic sense of the verb. For instance, *She mumbled her adoration* can be paraphrased as "She expressed/signalled her adoration by mumbling." Most of the verbs that allow such reaction objects name activities that are associated with particular emotions, and the action they name is performed to express the associated emotion. The exceptions are the verbs of emission, which also show this phenomenon to a limited extent. Reaction object constructions do not have passive counterparts.

7.4   X's Way Construction

References: Jackendoff (1990b, 1992a, 1992c), Jespersen (1949), B. Levin and Rapoport (1988), B. Levin and Rappaport Hovav (1992b), Marantz (1992). See also references under Resultative Construction (below), as this construction is probably related to the resultative construction.

(365)   Unergative Verbs:
    a.   They shopped their way around New York.
    b.   He worked his way through the book.
    c.   She talked her way out of the class.

(366)   Transitive Verbs:
    a.   She stipulated her way out of the problem.
    b.   The boy pushed his way through the crowd.
    c.   The explorers cut their way through the jungle.

(367)   * Unaccusative Verbs:
    a.   * The children came their way to the party.
    b.   * The flower bloomed its way to a prize.
    c.   * They disappeared their way off the stage.

Comments: Certain verbs can take a noun phrase of the form "X's way" as object when it is followed by a prepositional phrase describing a resulting state or location. This construction has attracted interest because it appears to be an unaccusative diagnostic: it is found only with unergative and transitive verbs, not with unaccusative verbs. It shows certain resemblances in its distribution and its syntax to the resultative construction and might be subsumed under that construction.

7.5   Resultative Construction

References: Abney (1987), Bolinger (1971), Bowerman (1982), Bowers (1989), Bresnan and Zaenen (1990), Burzio (1981), Carrier and Randall (1992, in press), Declerck (1977), Dowty (1979), Fraser (1976), Geniušienė (1987), Gestel (1989), Goldberg (1991, 1992), Green (1973), Halliday (1967, 1968), Herbert (1975), T. Hoekstra (1988, 1992), Ike-uchi (1990), Jackendoff (1987, 1990b, 1992c), Jespersen (1927), Kayne (1981, 1987), Keyser and Roeper (1992), Larson (1988a), B. Levin and Rapoport (1988), B. Levin and Rappaport (1989), B. Levin and Rappaport Hovav (1992b), L. Levin and Simpson (1981), J. McCawley (1971), Merlo (1988, 1989), Mufwene (1979), Napoli (1989b), Pustejovsky (1988, 1991a, 1991b), Quirk et al. (1985), Randall (1982), Rapoport (1986, 1990), Rivière (1981, 1982), Roberts (1988), Rothstein (1983), Sato (1987), Simpson (1983), Talmy (1991), Van Valin (1990), Van Voorst (1986), Wilkins (1987)

(368)   Cannot be predicated of transitive subjects:
        *Polly cooked the cookies dirty.
        (on the interpretation where Polly becomes dirty.)

(369)   Cannot be predicated of obliques:
        a.   The silversmith pounded the metal flat.
        b.   *The silversmith pounded on the metal flat.

(370)   Can be predicated of object of transitive verb:
        a.   Pauline hammered the metal flat.
        b.   Jasmine pushed the door open.

(371)   Can be predicated of nonsubcategorized object of unspecified object
        verb:
        a.   The guests drank the teapot dry.
        b.   Amanda burned the stove black.

(372)   Can be predicated of nonsubcategorized object of intransitive
        unergative verb:
        a.   Belinda walked the soles off her shoes.
        b.   Philippa cried herself to sleep.

(373)   Can be predicated of subject of intransitive unaccusative verb:
        a.   The river froze solid.
        b.   The door slid shut.

(374)   Can be predicated of subject of passive verb:
        a.   The metal was hammered flat.
        b.   The door was pushed open.

(375)   Types of postverbal NPs with unergative and unspecified object verbs:
        a.   Philippa cried herself to sleep. (fake reflexive)
        b.   Philippa cried her eyes dry.
             (inalienably possessed body part; Burzio's "expletive object")
        c.   Belinda walked the soles off her shoes. (nonsubcategorized NP)

(376)   *Stative Verbs:
        a.   *The dog smelled the flower bed bare.
        b.   *The teacher hated the pupils angry.

(377)   a.   *VERBS OF INHERENTLY DIRECTED MOTION: advance, arrive, as-
             cend, ?climb, come, ?cross, depart, descend, enter, escape, exit,
             fall, flee, go, leave, plunge, recede, return, rise, tumble
        b.   *BRING AND TAKE: bring, take (only)

(378)   a.   *Willa arrived breathless.
             (on the interpretation where the arriving makes Willa breathless)

b. * Sharon brought Willa breathless.
   (on the interpretation where the bringing makes Willa breathless)

Comments: A resultative phrase is an XP which describes the state achieved by the referent of the noun phrase it is predicated of as a result of the action named by the verb. The examples above show the distribution of resultative phrases with different types of verbs. Particularly noteworthy is the fact that resultative phrases cannot be predicated of the subjects of transitive verbs. They can, however, be predicated of the subjects of passive verbs and the subjects of some intransitive verbs. They also cannot be predicated of obliques. Some researchers have explained this pattern by adopting the Unaccusative Hypothesis; the basic insight then is that a resultative phrase may be predicated of an underlying object of a verb, but may not be predicated of its subject or of an oblique complement. Van Valin (1990) proposes an alternative semantic account of the pattern.

A wide range of verbs is found in the resultative construction, so no specific classes of verbs are identified here. However, there are also some clearly semantic constraints on the verbs found in the resultative construction: stative verbs and directed motion verbs are excluded. When intransitive unergative verbs are found in resultative constructions, they may display a variety of types of postverbal NPs, as shown above.

7.6 Unintentional Interpretation of Object

When certain verbs take either a reflexive object or a body-part object possessed by the subject of the verb, the sentence containing the verb assumes a special reading that is characterized here as "unintentional," although a more precise characterization might be possible. Although such verbs typically take an agentive subject, in this construction the subject of the verb is not intentionally performing the action on himself or herself and has been characterized as an experiencer or even a patient.

7.6.1 Unintentional Interpretation with Reflexive Object

References: Wierzbicka (1979)

(379)   CUT VERBS (some): cut, scrape, scratch
         Pauline cut herself (on the sharp stone).
         (ambiguous: intentionally or unintentionally)

(380)   HIT VERBS (some): bang, bash, batter, bump, hit, kick, knock, strike, whack
         Pauline hit herself (on the doorframe).
         (ambiguous: intentionally or unintentionally)

(381)   * SWAT VERBS: bite, claw, lash, paw, peck, punch (a person), slug, stab,
        swat, swipe
        Pauline bit herself.
        (unambiguous: only intentionally)

(382)   * SPANK VERBS: belt, birch, bludgeon, bonk, brain, cane, clobber, club,
        conk, cosh, cudgel, flog, knife, paddle, paddywhack, pummel, sock,
        spank, strap, thrash, truncheon, wallop, whip, whisk
        Pauline spanked herself.
        (unambiguous: only intentionally)

(383)   * BREAK VERBS: break, chip, crack, crash, crush, fracture, rip, shatter,
        smash, snap, splinter, split, tear
        Pauline broke herself (on the tree).
        (unambiguous: only intentionally)

(384)   * TOUCH VERBS: caress, graze, kiss, lick, nudge, pat, peck (=kiss), pinch,
        prod, sting, stroke, tickle, touch
        Pauline hugged herself.
        (unambiguous: only intentionally)

(385)   HURT VERBS (some): bruise, bump, burn, cut, hurt, injure, nick, prick,
        scald, scratch
        Tessa hurt herself.
        (ambiguous: intentionally or unintentionally)

Comments: This construction is characterized by an "unintentional" interpretation that is manifested when certain verbs take a reflexive object. That is,
in this construction the subject of the verb, although usually taken as an agent, is
not understood to be intentionally performing the action on himself or herself.
For instance, the unintentional reading of *Pauline hit herself on the doorframe*
would describe a situation where Pauline runs into a room and accidentally hits
herself against the doorframe. As pointed out to me by J. McCawley (personal
communication), this phenomenon reflects the ability of English to use expressions denoting a person to refer to that person's body (see Nunberg (1978));
this possibility is not available in all languages (for example, not in Korean, as
described by Na (1986)). The unintentional interpretation of reflexive objects is
found with a more restricted range of verbs than the unintentional interpretation
of a body-part object (see below).

7.6.2   Unintentional Interpretation with Body-Part Object

References: Abney (1987), Catlin and Catlin (1972), Chomsky (1981), Huddleston (1970), Junker and Martineau (1987), G. Lakoff (1970a, 1970b), Weydt
(1973), Wierzbicka (1979)

(386)   Cut Verbs (some): cut, scratch, scrape
        Sylvia cut her finger (on the knife).
        (ambiguous: intentionally or unintentionally)

(387)   Break Verbs (some): break, chip, crack, crush, fracture, shatter,
        smash, snap, split, tear
        Carrie broke her arm.
        (ambiguous: intentionally or unintentionally)

(388)   Hit Verbs (some): bang, bash, batter, bump, hit, kick, knock, strike,
        thump, whack
        Carrie hit her elbow on the doorknob.
        (ambiguous: intentionally or unintentionally)

(389)   * Swat Verbs: bite, claw, lash, paw, peck, punch (a person), slug, stab,
        swat, swipe
        Pauline bit her arm.
        (unambiguous: only intentionally)

(390)   * Spank Verbs: belt, birch, bludgeon, bonk, brain, cane, clobber, club,
        conk, cosh, cudgel, flog, knife, paddle, paddywhack, pummel, sock,
        spank, strap, thrash, truncheon, wallop, whip, whisk
        Pauline whipped her legs.
        (unambiguous: only intentionally)

(391)   * Touch Verbs: caress, graze, kiss, lick, nudge, pat, peck (=kiss), pinch,
        prod, sting, stroke, tickle, touch
        Molly touched her nose.
        (unambiguous: only intentionally)

(392)   Hurt Verbs: bark (shin), bite (lip), bump, burn, break, bruise, chip
        (tooth), cut, fracture, hurt, injure, nick (chin, leg), prick (finger), pull
        (muscle), rupture, scald, scratch (chin), skin (knee), split (lip), sprain
        (ankle, back, knee, wrist), strain, stub (toe), turn (ankle), twist (ankle)
        Tessa sprained her ankle.
        (ambiguous: intentionally or unintentionally)

Comments: This construction is characterized by an "unintentional" interpretation that manifests itself when certain verbs take a body-part object. In this
construction, the subject is understood to be the possessor of the body part, and
the action named by the verb is not intentionally carried out by the subject on
the body part. For instance, the unintentional reading of *Carrie hit her elbow
on the doorknob* could describe a situation where Carrie runs into a room and
accidentally hits her elbow against the doorknob. (This sentence is also open
to an interpretation in which the possessor of the body part is someone other

than the subject; that interpretation is not relevant here.) Although this special interpretation is associated with particular classes of verbs, it is not available to all members of each class. This property may reflect the fact that body parts are not possible objects of all the verbs in each of the classes.

7.7   Bound Nonreflexive Anaphor as Prepositional Object

References: Bickerton (1985), Cantrall (1974), Chomsky (1965, 1981), Faltz (1985), Gawron (1983), Gruber (1965, 1976), Guéron (1985), Hestvik (1991), Kuno (1972, 1983, 1987), G. Lakoff (1977), Lees and Klima (1963), Napoli (1989a), Postal (1971), Quirk et al. (1985), Reinhart (1983), Reinhart and Reuland (1991), J.R. Ross (1966), Spangler (1970), Wilkins (1988b), Zribi-Hertz (1989)

(393)   CONTAIN VERBS: contain, have, include, omit

(394)   This list$_i$ includes my name on it$_i$/*itself$_i$.

(395)   BRING AND TAKE: bring, take (only)

(396)   Sheila$_i$ brought the book with her$_i$/*herself$_i$.

(397)   CARRY VERBS (some): carry, drag, haul, kick, lug, schlep, tote, tow

(398)   Amanda$_i$ carried the package with her$_i$/*herself$_i$.

(399)   PUSH/PULL VERBS: ?draw, heave, jerk, press, pull, push, shove, ?thrust, tug, yank

(400)   Fanny$_i$ pulled the blanket over her$_i$/herself$_i$.

(401)   a.   POUR VERBS: dribble, drip, pour, slop, slosh, spew, spill, spurt
        b.   COIL VERBS: coil, curl, loop, roll, spin, twirl, twist, whirl, wind
        c.   SPRAY/LOAD VERBS (some): brush, dab, daub, drape, drizzle, dust, hang, rub, scatter, slather, smear, spatter, splash, splatter, spray, spread, sprinkle, spritz, squirt, strew, swab, wrap

(402)   Tamara$_i$ poured the water over her$_i$/herself$_i$.

Comments: In sentences with certain transitive verbs taking both a noun phrase and a prepositional phrase complement, a pronoun in the prepositional phrase may or must be understood as coreferent with the subject. This possibility is not allowed by Binding Theory (Chomsky (1981)), which requires a reflexive in this position for the coreferential interpretation. In fact, with some of these verbs the reflexive pronoun cannot be used to express the coreferential interpretation, despite the apparent predictions of Binding Theory. Verbs like *contain* only show this behavior when they take a container as subject.

7.8   Directional Phrases with Nondirected Motion Verbs

References: Aske (1989), Declerck (1979), Dowty (1979), B. Levin (1991), B. Levin and Rapoport (1988), B. Levin and Rappaport (1989), B. Levin and Rappaport Hovav (1991), Pustejovsky (1988, 1991b), Talmy (1975, 1985, 1991), Tenny (1987), Van Valin (1990). This phenomenon is also frequently discussed in the literature on aktionsart, though from a somewhat different perspective; only selected references are given to this literature.

(403)   VERBS OF SOUND EMISSION: babble, bang, beat, beep, bellow, blare, blast, blat, boom, bubble, burble, burr, buzz, chatter, chime, chink, chir, chitter, chug, clack, clang, clank, clap, clash, clatter, click, cling, clink, clomp, clump, clunk, crack, crackle, crash, creak, crepitate, crunch, cry, ding, dong, explode, fizz, fizzle, groan, growl, gurgle, hiss, hoot, howl, hum, jangle, jingle, knell, knock, lilt, moan, murmur, patter, peal, ping, pink, pipe, plink, plonk, plop, plunk, pop, purr, putter, rap, rasp, rattle, ring, roar, roll, rumble, rustle, scream, screech, shriek, shrill, sing, sizzle, snap, splash, splutter, sputter, squawk, squeak, squeal, squelch, strike, swish, swoosh, thrum, thud, thump, thunder, thunk, tick, ting, tinkle, toll, toot, tootle, trill, trumpet, twang, ululate, vroom, wail, wheeze, whine, whir, whish, whistle, whoosh, whump, zing

(404)   a.   The truck rumbled.
        b.   The truck rumbled into the driveway.

(405)   RUN VERBS: amble, backpack, bolt, bounce, bound, bowl, canter, carom, cavort, charge, clamber, climb, clump, coast, crawl, creep, dart, dash, dodder, drift, file, flit, float, fly, frolic, gallop, gambol, glide, goosestep, hasten, hike, hobble, hop, hurry, hurtle, inch, jog, journey, jump, leap, limp, lollop, lope, lumber, lurch, march, meander, mince, mosey, nip, pad, parade, perambulate, plod, prance, promenade, prowl, race, ramble, roam, roll, romp, rove, run, rush, sashay, saunter, scamper, scoot, scram, scramble, scud, scurry, scutter, scuttle, shamble, shuffle, sidle, skedaddle, skip, skitter, skulk, sleepwalk, slide, slink, slither, slog, slouch, sneak, somersault, speed, stagger, stomp, stray, streak, stride, stroll, strut, stumble, stump, swagger, sweep, swim, tack, tear, tiptoe, toddle, totter, traipse, tramp, travel, trek, troop, trot, trudge, trundle, vault, waddle, wade, walk, wander, whiz, zigzag, zoom

(406)   a.   Audrey tiptoed.
        b.   Audrey tiptoed to the door.

(407)   WALTZ VERBS: boogie, bop, cancan, clog, conga, dance, foxtrot, jig,
         jitterbug, jive, pirouette, polka, quickstep, rumba, samba, shuffle,
         squaredance, tango, tapdance, waltz

(408)   The couple waltzed to the window.

(409)   VERBS OF BODY-INTERNAL MOTION: buck, fidget, flap, gyrate, kick,
         rock, squirm, sway, teeter, totter, twitch, waggle, wiggle, wobble,
         wriggle

(410)   The clown wobbled down the hall.

(411)   PUSH/PULL VERBS: ?draw, heave, jerk, press, pull, push, shove, ?thrust,
         tug, yank

(412)   Leona pushed the cart to the market.

Comments: Certain verbs that are not inherently verbs of displacement in a
particular direction may take on a meaning that involves directed displacement
when they are found with a directional or goal prepositional phrase. In the
presence of such a prepositional phrase, the verb takes on an extended sense
that might be paraphrased as "go by V-ing." (Note that even the *run* verbs
only indicate displacement in a particular direction when they combine with a
directional or goal phrase.) In the absence of a goal phrase, the verbs showing
this phenomenon are activity verbs in the Vendler (1957) sense; in the presence
of such a phrase, they are accomplishments. This shift in aspectual class is most
often discussed with respect to the *run* verbs and the *push/pull* verbs, but it is
attested with a wider range of verbs, as shown by the examples.

This phenomenon has been studied from several perspectives. It is frequently
discussed in the literature on aktionsart, since the addition of goal phrases
changes atelic verbs to telic verbs. It has also been examined by Talmy (1975,
1985) in his study of lexicalization patterns. Talmy shows that the phenomenon
is not attested in all languages. More recently, the observation has also attracted
attention in the literature on the Unaccusative Hypothesis, since the addition
of such phrases seems to cause the *run* verbs to shift from the unergative
to the unaccusative class. There may be other types of verbs showing this
phenomenon.

8 Verbs Requiring Special Diatheses

This section includes verbs that place special restrictions on the syntactic context they are found in. The verbs are grouped according to the type of context they require.

8.1 Obligatory Passive

References: Bach (1980), Stein (1979)

(413)   reincarnate, rumor, repute

(414)   a. It is rumored that he left town.
         b. * They rumor that he left town.

Comments: These verbs are obligatorily found in the passive.

8.2 Obligatorily Reflexive Object

References: Baldi (1971), Curme (1931), Dougherty (1970), Emonds (1976), Geniušienė (1987), Jespersen (1949), Jørgensen (1987), G. Lakoff (1970a), Lees and Klima (1963), Poutsma (1904), Quirk et al. (1985)

(415)   absent, acquit, assert, avail, bear, behave, bestir, betake, bethink, better, busy, camouflage, carry, check, collect, comport, compose, conduct, contain, content, defend, demean, disgrace, disport, efface, embroil, endear, enjoy, ensconce, excel, exert, fancy, find, help, ingratiate, insinuate, intoxicate, intrude, inure, justify, lower, martyr, nerve, outdo, overreach, perjure, plight, pride, profess, prostrate, redeem, relieve, resign, revenge, steel, sun, unbosom, vindicate, worm

(416)   a. The politician perjured himself.
         b. * The politician perjured his aide.

Comments: These verbs obligatorily take the reflexive pronoun as object. Some of them may be found with an object that is not a reflexive, but when they are, they show a different meaning. However, a few of the verbs listed here are also found with the same meaning in the passive—probably the adjectival passive. Consider, for example, the verb *embroil: He embroiled himself in the latest controversy over the budget, He was embroiled in the latest controversy over the budget.*

8.3 Inalienably Possessed Body-Part Object

References: Bresnan (1982b), Rice (1988), Ross (1970)

(417)   VERBS OF GESTURES/SIGNS INVOLVING BODY PARTS:
         a.   WINK VERBS: blink (eye), clap (hands), nod (head), point (finger),
              shrug (shoulders), squint (eyes), wag (tail), wave (hand), wink
              (eye)
         b.   CRANE VERBS: arch (back, neck), bare (teeth), bat (eyelashes),
              beat (feet), blow (nose), clench (fists), click (heels, tongue), close
              (eyes), cock (head), crane (neck), crook (finger), cross (arms,
              eyes, legs), drum (finger), flap (wings), flash (teeth), flex (mus-
              cles), flick (finger), flutter (eyelashes), fold (arms), gnash (teeth),
              grind (teeth), hang (head), hunch (shoulders), kick, knit (eye-
              brows), open (eyes), pucker (lips), purse (lips), raise (eyebrows,
              hand), roll (eyes), rub (hands), shake (head, fist, hands), show
              (teeth), shuffle (feet), smack (lips), snap (fingers), stamp (foot),
              stretch (legs), toss (mane), turn (head), twiddle (thumbs), twitch
              (ears, nose), wag (finger, tail), waggle (ears), wiggle (ears, hips,
              nose), wring (hands), wrinkle (forehead, nose)

(418)   VERBS OF CARING FOR A SPECIFIC BODY PART:
         a.   FLOSS VERBS: brush (teeth), floss (teeth), shave (beard, legs), wash
              (hands, face)
         b.   BRAID VERBS: bob (hair), braid (hair), brush (hair), clip (nails),
              coldcream (face), comb (hair), condition (hair), crimp (hair), crop
              (hair), curl (hair), cut (hair), dye (hair), file (nails), henna (hair),
              lather (hair, body), manicure (nails), part (hair), perm (hair), plait
              (hair), pluck (eyebrows), powder (face, nose), rinse (hair, mouth),
              rouge (cheeks, face), set (hair), shampoo (hair), soap (hands,
              body), talc (body), tease (hair), towel (face, hands), trim (hair,
              beard), wave (hair)

(419)   HURT VERBS: bark (shin), bite (lip), bump, burn, break, bruise, chip
         (tooth), cut, fracture, hurt, injure, nick (chin, leg), prick (finger), pull
         (muscle), rupture, scald, scratch (chin), skin (knee), split (lip), sprain
         (ankle, back, knee, wrist), strain, stub (toe), turn (ankle), twist (ankle)

(420)   a.   Jennifer craned her/*his neck.
         b.   Jennifer craned her neck/*arm.

Comments: These verbs, at least on the intended interpretation, take as
their object a body part which is inalienably possessed by the subject of the
verb. They fall into two major classes: either they describe gestures or signs
performed with a part of the body or they describe damage inflicted to a part
of the body.

8.4   Expletive *It* Object

References: Bladin (1911), Postal and Pullum (1988), Pullum (1987), Stroik (1990)

(421)   a.   Let's call it a day.
      b.   They've got it made.
      c.   You've really lived it up.

Comments: Verbs such as in the above examples take expletive *it* as an object in at least one interpretation. Many verbs may take expletive *it* as one of a range of objects, but there are some verbs, particularly certain verbs that are zero-related to nouns, that can only take *it* as an object; for example, *to lord it over someone.* See Postal and Pullum (1988) for an extensive list of examples of verbs taking expletive *it* objects, subdivided into classes according to complement type.

8.5   Obligatory Adverb

References: McConnell-Ginet (1982), Napoli (1989a)

(422)   acquit, act, augur, behave, bode, do, mean, phrase, treat, word

(423)   a.   The teacher meant well.
      b.   * The teacher meant.

Comments: These verbs always require an appropriate adverb, at least on the relevant interpretation. They can be subdivided further according to whether or not they require a direct object.

8.6   Obligatory Negative Polarity Element

(424)   budge

(425)   a.   The horse wouldn't budge.
      b.   Would the horse budge if you pushed?
      c.   * The horse budged.

Comments: These verbs must be found in the context of a negative polarity item. This requirement is not strictly a requirement on a verb's argument-taking properties; nevertheless, this set of verbs has been included here since such a requirement probably does reflect some aspect of their meaning.

Part Two

Verb Classes

9 Verbs of Putting

References: Croft (1991), Dixon (1991), Gruber (1976), Jackendoff (1985a)

9.1 *Put* Verbs

Class Members: arrange, immerse, install, lodge, mount, place, position, put, set, situate, sling, stash, stow

Properties:

(1)   I put the book on/under/near the table.

(2)   a. * I put the book to Sally.
        b. * I put the book from Edna.
        c. * I put the book from Edna to Sally.

(3)   * Locative Alternation:
        a.   I put books on the table.
        b. * I put the table with (the) books.

(4)   * Middle Alternation:
        a.   I put the books on the table.
        b. * The books put on the table easily.

(5)   * Causative Alternations:
        a.   I put the books on the table.
        b. * The books put on the table.

(6)   * I put the books.

(7)   * I put on the table.
        (on the interpretation where something is placed on the table)

(8)   Zero-related Nominal (some verbs):
           a position, a lodge

Comments: These verbs refer to putting an entity at some location. The location is expressed via a prepositional phrase headed by one of a range of locative prepositions; however, the preposition heading this phrase cannot be the goal preposition *to* or the source preposition *from*. These verbs do not have related intransitive uses. Some of them have zero-related nominals; these nominals have a variety of meanings.

9.2   Verbs of Putting in a Spatial Configuration

Class Members: dangle, hang, lay, lean, perch, rest, sit, stand, suspend

Properties:

(9)   Cheryl stood the books on the shelf/next to the magazines.

(10)   a. * Cheryl stood the books to Sarah.
           b. * Cheryl stood the books from Edna.
           c. * Cheryl stood the books from Edna to Sarah.

(11)   * Locative Alternation:
           a.   Cheryl stood the books on the shelf.
           b. * Cheryl stood the shelf with (the) books.

(12)   * Middle Alternation:
           a.   Cheryl stood the tall books on the table.
           b. * Tall books stand on tables easily.
                (on the relevant interpretation)

(13)   Causative Alternation (most verbs):
           a.   Cheryl stood the books on the table.
           b.   The books stood on the table.

(14)   ? Cheryl stood the books.

(15)   * Cheryl stood on the table.
           (on the interpretation: something is placed on the table by Cheryl)

(16)   Zero-related Nominal (some verbs):
           a perch, a stand
           * a dangle, *a hang

Comments: These verbs refer to putting an entity at some location. What sets this class of verbs apart from other verbs of putting is that they specify the particular spatial configuration that the placed entity ends up in with respect to the location. They occur with a variety of locative prepositional phrases, but not with source or goal phrases. The verbs *dangle*, *hang*, and *suspend* do occur with the preposition *from*, but this is not the *from* found in source phrases. A few of these verbs have zero-related nominals referring to objects used to place other objects in the particular spatial configuration named by the verb; that is, the noun *stand* names what one stands something on.

Most of these verbs have intransitive uses as verbs of spatial configuration; the properties associated with these uses are listed under Verbs of Spatial Configuration (sec. 47.6). The intransitive use has been included here under the label "causative alternation." This alternation is not the causative/inchoative alternation since the intransitive use does not have the change of state or change of location (with displacement) interpretation that is associated with the intransitive variant of the prototypical verbs showing the causative/inchoative alternation. When one of the verbs listed in this section cannot be used intransitively, there is typically another verb that carries the meaning associated with the intransitive use, as in the pair *lay/lie*. Some of these verbs, such as *hang* or *sit*, also are used intransitively as verbs of assuming a position and are cross-listed accordingly (sec. 50).

9.3   *Funnel* Verbs

Class Members: bang, channel, dip, dump, funnel, hammer, ladle, pound, push, rake, ram, scoop, scrape, shake, shovel, siphon, spoon, squeeze, squish, squash, sweep, tuck, wad, wedge, wipe, wring

Properties:

(17)   I funneled the mixture into the bottle.
       ?? I funneled the mixture in the bottle.

(18)   a. * I funneled the mixture from the bottle. (some exceptions)
          b. * I funneled the mixture to Rina.
          c. * I funneled the mixture from Edna to Rina.

(19)   * Locative Alternation:
          a.   I funneled the mixture into the bottle.
          b. * I funneled the bottle with the mixture.

(20)   * Middle Alternation:
          a.   I funneled the mixture into the bottle.
          b. * The mixture funnels easily.

(21)   * Causative Alternations:
          a.   I funneled the mixture into the bottle.
          b. * The mixture funnels.

(22)   * I funneled the mixture.

(23)   *I funneled into the bottle.
        (on the interpretation where something is funneled into the bottle)

(24)   Zero-related Nominal (some verbs):
        a funnel (instrument)
        a wad (result)

Comments: These verbs relate to putting an entity in some location in some manner; usually they involve putting entities in spatially confined locations. These verbs, unlike the *put* verbs, show a preference for *into* rather than *in* and for *onto* rather than *on*, though they can otherwise be found with a wide range of locative prepositions. Again, these verbs are not found with *to*. Some of these verbs can also be used as verbs of removing, taking *from*; these verbs are listed under the *wipe* verbs (sec. 10.4). Unlike the verbs of putting in a spatial configuration, *funnel* verbs are vague about the resulting spatial configuration of the entity placed. Some of these verbs have zero-related nominals. These nominals are of two types: they either specify an instrument used to perform the action referred to by the verb, or they refer to a quantity of stuff that is inserted into the location. Some of these verbs, including *bang* or *pound*, are used as verbs of putting in an extended sense; in their basic sense, they belong to a variety of other classes.

9.4   Verbs of Putting with a Specified Direction

References: Cowper (1990b). See also references under Dative Alternation (sec. 2.1).

Class Members: drop, hoist, lift, lower, raise

Properties:

(25)   I lifted the books.

(26)   I lifted the book onto the table/out of the box.
        *I lifted the book on the table.

(27)   I lifted the books from the floor to the table.

(28)   *Locative Alternation:
        a.   I lifted the books onto the table.
        b. *I lifted the table with the books.

(29)   *Dative Alternation:
        a.   I lifted the books (up) to him.
        b. *I lifted him (up) the books.

(30)   * Middle Alternation:
      a.   I lifted the paperback book onto the table.
      b. * Paperback books lift onto the table easily.

(31)   * Causative Alternations:
      a.   I lifted the book onto the table.
      b. * The books lifted onto the table.

(32)   * I lifted onto the table.
      (on the interpretation where something is lifted onto the table)

(33)   Zero-related Nominal (some verbs):
      a lift, a hoist

Comments: These verbs relate to putting an entity somewhere, typically by moving it in a specific direction. For instance, as Cowper (1990b) points out, lifting does not necessarily have to be in an upward direction, although it usually is. She proposes that what is more important is that the action involves exerting a force against the action of gravity; this description seems to apply to all of these verbs. Again, these verbs show a preference for *onto* and *into* over *on* or *in*, though they are otherwise found with a wide range of locative prepositions. They may also be found with source prepositions or with paths describing a trajectory of motion. The verbs *lift* and *hoist* have zero-related nominals naming instruments used to carry out the actions named by the verbs.

9.5 *Pour* Verbs

References: See references listed under *Spray/Load* Verbs below.

Class Members: dribble, drip, pour, slop, slosh, spew, spill, spurt

Properties:

(34)   Tamara poured water into the bowl/over the flowers.

(35)   Tamara poured water from/out of the pitcher.

(36)   * Locative Alternation:
      a.   Tamara poured water into the bowl.
      b. * Tamara poured the bowl with water.

(37)   * Conative Alternation:
      a.   Tamara poured water into the bowl.
      b. * Tamara poured at water into the bowl.

(38)   * Middle Alternation:
      a.   Tamara poured water onto the plants.
      b. * Water pours easily onto the plants.

(39)   Causative Alternation:
        a. Tamara poured water onto the plants.
        b. Water poured onto the plants.

(40)   * Tamara poured into the pitcher.

(41)   Coreferential interpretation of pronouns possible:
        Tamara$_i$ poured the water over her$_i$.

(42)   Zero-related Nominal (few verbs):
        a spill

Comments: The members of this set of verbs are often compared to
spray/load verbs like *spray* and *squirt* since they relate to putting things—
typically liquids—on surfaces or in containers. However, these verbs are only
found in a syntactic configuration that resembles the locative variant of the
locative alternation—the alternation that is a hallmark of the *spray/load* verbs.
The *pour* verbs differ from some of the other types of verbs of putting in allowing *from* phrases. Many of the members of this class participate in a causative
alternation. It is likely that this is not the causative/inchoative alternation, because these verbs appear not to turn up in the middle construction whereas most
verbs found in the causative/inchoative alternation do.

9.6 *Coil* Verbs

References: See references listed under *Spray/Load* Verbs below.

Class Members: coil, curl, loop, roll, spin, twirl, twist, whirl, wind

Properties:

(43)   Cora coiled the rope around the post.

(44)   * Locative Alternation:
        a. Cora coiled the rope around the post.
        b. * Cora coiled the post with the rope.

(45)   * Conative Alternation:
        a. Cora coiled the rope around the post.
        b. * Cora coiled at the rope around the post.

(46)   Causative/Inchoative Alternation:
        a. Cora coiled the rope around the post.
        b. The rope coiled around the post.

(47)   Middle Alternation:
        a. Cora coiled the rope around the post.
        b. That kind of rope coils easily around the post.

(48)   *Cora coiled around the post.

(49)   Coreferential interpretation of pronouns possible:
        Cora$_i$ twisted the scarf around her$_i$.

(50)   Zero-related Nominal:
        a coil, a twist

Comments: These verbs are often compared to the *spray/load* verbs, since like the *spray/load* verb *wrap* they relate to putting something around something else. However, unlike the *spray/load* verbs they are only found in a syntactic configuration that resembles the locative variant of the locative alternation. Due to their meaning, they are only found with a limited range of prepositions heading the locative prepositional phrase; they are most often found with the preposition *around*.

Coil verbs can be used as intransitive verbs of manner of motion, as well as transitive verbs of putting; therefore, they are also included under the appropriate subclass of verbs of motion: the intransitive *roll* verbs (sec. 51.3.1). This section focuses on the properties related to their transitive use; the properties related to their intransitive use are discussed under *roll* verbs. Only the *roll* verbs that have transitive uses as verbs of putting are listed here; these are primarily the subset of *roll* verbs that involve motion around an axis. In addition, some *coil* verbs can be used as verbs of creation and transformation; these verbs are also listed under the *knead* verbs (sec. 26.5).

9.7   *Spray/Load* Verbs

References: Anderson (1971, 1977), Bach (1980), Boons (1974, 1985, 1986), Bowerman (1982), Carter (1988), Croft (1986, 1991), Culicover and Wilkins (1984, 1986), Dik (1978, 1980), Dixon (1989), Dowty (1991), Emonds (1991), Fillmore (1966, 1968a, 1968b), Foley and Van Valin (1984), Fraser (1971), Gawron (1983, 1986), de Groot (1984), Gropen (1989), Gropen et al. (1991a, 1991b), Haïk (1990), Hall (1965), Hoffman (1991), Jackendoff (1990a, 1990b), Jeffries and Willis (1984), Jolly (1987), Kipka (1990), Langacker (1991), Larson (1990), B. Levin and Rappaport Hovav (1991), Ljung (1970), J. Lumsden (1991), J.E. Miller (1989), Moravcsik (1978), Pesetsky (1992), Pinker (1989), Pusch (1972), Rappaport and B. Levin (1985, 1988), Rappaport, B. Levin, and Laughren (1988), Ravin (1990), Salkoff (1983), Schwartz-Norman (1976), Tenny (1992), Tremblay (1990, 1991), Vestergaard (1973). For work on the alternation in languages other than English: Berber—Guerssel (1986); Dutch—Dik (1978); French—Boons (1974, 1985, 1986), Postal (1982); German—Becker (1971); Igbo—Nwachukwu (1987); Japanese—Fukui, Miyagawa, and Tenny (1985), Kageyama (1980); Kannada—Bhat (1977); Russian—Veyrenc (1976).

Class Members: brush, cram, crowd, cultivate, dab, daub, drape, drizzle, dust, hang, heap, inject, jam, load, mound, pack, pile, plant, plaster, ?prick, pump, rub, scatter, seed, settle, sew, shower, slather, smear, smudge, sow, spatter, splash, splatter, spray, spread, sprinkle, spritz, squirt, stack, stick, stock, strew, string, stuff, swab, ?vest, ?wash, wrap

Properties:

(51) a. Jessica loaded boxes onto/into/under the wagon.
　　　 b. Jessica sprayed paint onto/under/over the table.

(52) Locative Alternation:
　　　 a. Jessica sprayed paint on the wall. (locative variant)
　　　　　 Jessica sprayed the wall with paint. (*with* variant)
　　　 b. Jessica loaded boxes on the wagon.
　　　　　 Jessica loaded the wagon with boxes.

(53) Causative Alternation (based on locative variant; some verbs):
　　　 a. Jessica sprayed paint on the wall.
　　　 b. Paint sprayed on the wall.

(54) * Causative Alternations (based on *with* variant):
　　　 a. Jessica sprayed the wall with paint.
　　　 b. * The wall sprayed with paint.

(55) Conative Alternation (some verbs):
　　　 a. Jessica squirted/sprayed/splashed water at me.
　　　 b. * Jessica loaded/stuffed/crammed boxes at the truck.

(56) Coreferential interpretation of pronouns possible (some verbs):
　　　 Jessica$_i$ rubbed the lotion on her$_i$.

(57) Zero-related Nominal (some verbs):
　　　 a spray
　　　 a spray of paint/* a spray of the wall

Comments: These verbs relate to covering surfaces and putting things into containers. They have received considerable attention. First, the members of this set participate in an alternation in the expression of their arguments known as the locative alternation. Second, these verbs show what has been called the "holistic/partitive" effect. The direct object in the *with* variant—the location argument—is associated with what has been called a "holistic" or "affected" interpretation; that is, the location is understood to be in some sense *completely* affected by the action. However, a number of studies have shown that characterizing the interpretation associated with the *with* variant is not easy; specifically, they have shown that the notion "holistic" is not always accurate. The subset of these verbs that take a liquid or a set of small particles as the typical direct object in the locative variant show a slightly different set of properties from the remainder of these verbs. For instance, they are found in the conative alternation, and they typically allow the causative alternation in the locative variant. Some of the *spray/load* verbs have zero-related nominals; typically, these nominals receive a result interpretation. The verb *vest* may be inappropriately included; it appears to participate in the locative alternation, but unlike the other verbs in this set, its locatum argument is usually an abstract noun phrase.

9.8 *Fill* Verbs

References: B. Levin and Rappaport (1988), Rappaport Hovav and B. Levin (1992). See also references listed under *Spray/Load* Verbs above.

Class Members: adorn, anoint, bandage, bathe, bestrew, bind, blanket, block, blot, bombard, carpet, choke, cloak, clog, clutter, coat, contaminate, cover, dam, dapple, deck, decorate, deluge, dirty, douse, dot, drench, edge, embellish, emblazon, encircle, encrust, endow, enrich, entangle, face, festoon, fill, fleck, flood, frame, garland, garnish, imbue, impregnate, infect, inlay, interlace, interlard, interleave, intersperse, interweave, inundate, lard, lash, line, litter, mask, mottle, ornament, pad, pave, plate, plug, pollute, replenish, repopulate, riddle, ring, ripple, robe, saturate, season, shroud, smother, soak, soil, speckle, splotch, spot, staff, stain, stipple, stop up, stud, suffuse, surround, swaddle, swathe, taint, tile, trim, veil, vein, wreathe

Properties:

(58)   Leslie staffed the store with employees.

(59)   * Locative Alternation:
        a.   Leslie staffed the store with employees.
        b. * Leslie staffed employees in the store.

(60)   * Causative Alternations:
        a.   Leslie staffed the store with employees.
        b. * The store staffed with employees.

(61)   Locatum Subject Alternation:
        a.   Leslie staffed the store with employees.
        b.   The employees staffed the store.

(62)   *With* alternates with *in* (some verbs):
        a.   Leigh swaddled the baby with blankets.
             Leigh swaddled the baby in blankets.
        b.   Leslie staffed the store with employees.
             * Leslie staffed the store in employees.

Comments: These verbs appear similar to the *spray/load* verbs in meaning, but unlike them they are only found in what looks like the *with* variant of the locative alternation. The direct object of these verbs is also said to receive the "holistic" interpretation found in the *with* variant of the locative alternation. When the argument that is the object of *with*—the locatum—is expressed as the subject, the sentence can be understood as describing a state (Jackendoff (1990b)). These verbs typically describe the resulting state of a location as a consequence of putting something on it or in it; thus they differ from the *pour* verbs, which describe the manner in which the putting is done. Some of these verbs, particularly if they involve covering with clothes or cloths, allow *with* to alternate with *in*; these verbs include: *bathe, blanket, coat, cloak, cover, deck, festoon, garland, line, robe, shroud, swaddle, swathe, veil, wreathe.*

9.9   *Butter* Verbs

References: Bladin (1911), Buck (1993), Carter (1976, 1988), E.V. Clark and H.H. Clark (1979), Dowty (1979), Duszak (1980), Hale and Keyser (1991, 1992), Jackendoff (1990b), Jespersen (1942), Karius (1985), Leitner (1974), Marchand (1969, 1974), Pusch (1972), Rappaport and B. Levin (1985), Sehnert and Sharwood-Smith (1973), Watt (1973)

Class Members: asphalt, bait, blanket, blindfold, board, bread, brick, bridle, bronze, butter, buttonhole, cap, carpet, caulk, chrome, cloak, cork, crown, diaper, drug, feather, fence, flour, forest, frame, fuel, gag, garland, glove, graffiti, gravel, grease, groove, halter, harness, heel, ink, label, leash, leaven, lipstick, mantle, mulch, muzzle, nickel, oil, ornament, panel, paper, parquet, patch, pepper, perfume, pitch, plank, plaster, poison, polish, pomade, poster, postmark, powder, putty, robe, roof, rosin, rouge, rut, saddle, salt, salve, sand, seed, sequin, shawl, shingle, shoe, shutter, silver, slate, slipcover, sod, sole, spice, stain, starch, stopper, stress, string, stucco, sugar, sulphur, tag, tar, tarmac, tassel, thatch, ticket, tile, turf, veil, veneer, wallpaper, water, wax, whitewash, wreathe, yoke, zipcode

Properties:

(63)   Lora buttered the toast.
        (i.e., Lora put butter on the toast.)

(64)   Cognate *With* Phrase:
        Lora buttered the toast with unsalted butter.
        ? Lora buttered the toast with butter.

(65)   * Locative Alternation:
        a. * Lora buttered unsalted butter on the toast.
        b.   Lora buttered the toast with unsalted butter.

(66)   * Conative Alternation:
        a.   Lora buttered the toast (with unsalted butter).
        b. * Lora buttered at the toast (with unsalted butter).

(67)   * Causative Alternations:
        a.   Lora buttered the toast (with unsalted butter).
        b. * The toast buttered (with unsalted butter).

Comments: These verbs all have zero-related nominals; their meaning can
be paraphrased as "put X on/in (something)," where X is the noun that the verb
takes its name from. These verbs appear similar to the *spray/load* verbs and
the *fill* verbs in meaning; specifically, the object of these verbs also receives the
"holistic" interpretation found in the *with* variant of the locative alternation. A
cognate *with* phrase may be found with these verbs; the object of *with* is an NP
headed by the noun that the verb derives its name from, or a noun that bears the
hyponym relation to the noun that the verb derives its name from. Such *with*
phrases are typically most acceptable if they contribute additional information
about the thing that is being put somewhere through the use of a modifier of
some kind. The process of forming verbs of this type is highly productive, so
that this class is likely to grow in size. See also Verbs of Coloring (sec. 24) for
some other verbs that show similar behavior.

9.10   *Pocket* Verbs

References: Bladin (1911), Carter (1976, 1988), E.V. Clark and H.H. Clark
(1979), Dixon (1991), Duszak (1980), Hale and Keyser (1991, 1992), Jackendoff (1990b), Jespersen (1942), Leitner (1974), Marchand (1969, 1974),
Rappaport and B. Levin (1985), Sehnert and Sharwood-Smith (1973)

Class Members: archive, bag, bank, beach, bed, bench, berth, billet, bin,
bottle, box, cage, can, case, cellar, cloister, coop, corral, crate, dock, drydock,
file, fork, garage, ground, hangar, house, jail, jar, jug, kennel, land, lodge,
pasture, pen, pillory, pocket, pot, sheathe, shelter, shelve, shoulder, skewer,
snare, spindle, spit, spool, stable, string, tin, trap, tree, warehouse

Properties:

(68)   Lydia pocketed the change.
        (i.e., Lydia put the change in her pocket.)

(69)   * Cognate Location Phrase:
        * Lydia pocketed the change in her pocket.
        ?? Lydia pocketed the change in her left front jacket pocket.

(70)   * Locative Alternation:
        a. * Lydia pocketed the change in her pocket.
        b. * Lydia pocketed her pocket with the change.

(71)   * Causative Alternations:
      a. Lydia pocketed the change.
      b. * The change pocketed.

Comments: These verbs all have zero-related nominals; the related nouns refer to a location where things can be put. The meaning of these verbs can be paraphrased as "put (something) on/in X," where X is the noun that the verb takes its name from. Most of these verbs do not seem to easily allow cognate locative phrases. This set of verbs is much smaller than the set of *butter* verbs (cf. above). Nevertheless, the process of forming verbs of this type is productive, so that this class is likely to grow in size.

10   Verbs of Removing

10.1   *Remove* Verbs

References: Gruber (1965, 1976), B. Levin and Rappaport Hovav (1991), Ostler (1980b)

Class Members: abstract, cull, delete, discharge, disgorge, dislodge, dismiss, disengage, draw, eject, eliminate, eradicate, evict, excise, excommunicate, expel, extirpate, extract, extrude, lop, omit, ostracize, oust, partition, pry, reap, remove, separate, sever, shoo, subtract, uproot, winkle, withdraw, wrench

Properties:

(72)   Doug removed the smudges from the tabletop.

(73)   Doug removed the smudges from around the sink.
      Doug removed the smudges from under the shelf.

(74)   * Doug removed the smudges out of the drawer.
      * Doug removed the smudges off of the counter.

(75)   * Doug removed the smudges to nowhere.

(76)   * Locative Alternation:
      a. Doug removed the smudges from the tabletop.
      b. * Doug removed the tabletop of smudges.

(77)   * Conative Alternation:
      a. Doug removed the smudges from the tabletop.
      b. * Doug removed at the smudges from the tabletop.

(78)   * Causative Alternations:
        a.   Doug removed the smudges from the tabletop.
        b. * The smudges removed from the tabletop.

Comments: These verbs relate to the removal of an entity from a location. One of their arguments is expressed in a prepositional phrase headed by the preposition *from*. Most of these verbs—with the exception of some, such as *excommunicate,* which only take animate objects—can also take *from* followed by one of a variety of locative prepositions. Most of these verbs cannot take the prepositions *out of* or *off of*, even though these prepositions can head source phrases elsewhere. Each of these verbs imposes particular restrictions on the set of possible direct objects; some only take human objects. Most of these verbs do not have zero-related nominals.

10.2   *Banish* Verbs

Class Members: banish, deport, evacuate, expel, extradite, recall, remove

Properties:

(79)   The king banished the general from the army.

(80)   The king banished the general to a mountain fortress.

(81)   * The king banished the general from the palace to a mountain fortress.

(82)   * Locative Alternation:
        a.   The king banished the general from the army.
        b. * The king banished the army of the general.

(83)   * Conative Alternation:
        a.   The king banished the general from the army.
        b. * The king banished at the general from the army.

(84)   * Causative Alternations:
        a.   The king banished the general from the army.
        b. * The general banished from the army.

Comments: These verbs relate to the removal of an entity, typically a person, from a location. The location argument is expressed in a prepositional phrase headed by the preposition *from*. These verbs do not allow any of the other prepositions that can head source phrases, such as *out, off,* or a combination of *from* and another preposition. Unlike the *remove* verbs, these verbs allow *to* phrases as well as *from* phrases, though not simultaneously. Most of these verbs do not have zero-related nominals.

10.3 *Clear* Verbs

References: Croft (1991), Dowty (1991), Hook (1983), Jackendoff (1990b), B. Levin and Rappaport Hovav (1991), Parsons (1990). See also references listed under *Spray/Load* Verbs (sec. 9.7).

Class Members: clear, clean, drain, empty

Properties:

(85)   Doug cleared dishes from the table.

(86)   Doug cleared the dishes from under the rack.
          Doug cleared the dishes from around the sink.
          Doug cleared the dishes from behind the fridge.

(87)   Locative Alternation (transitive):
          a.   Doug cleared dishes from the table. (locative variant)
          b.   Doug cleared the table of dishes. (*of* variant)

(88)   Locative Alternation (intransitive):
          a.   The sky cleared (?of clouds).
          b.   Clouds cleared from the sky.

(89)   * Conative Alternation:
          a.   Doug cleared the table (of dishes).
          b.   * Doug cleared at the table (of dishes).

(90)   Causative/Inchoative Alternation (except *clean*):
          a.   The strong winds cleared the skies.
               The skies cleared.
          b.   The strong winds slowly cleared the clouds from the sky.
               The clouds slowly cleared from the sky.

(91)   * Resultative Phrase:
          * Doug cleared the table clean.

(92)   Zero-related Adjective (some verbs):
          a clear road
          the road is clear of debris

(93)   Adjectival Passive Participle:
          a cleared table

Comments: Although these verbs appear to relate to the removal of a substance from a location, in at least some of their uses they are better characterized as verbs of change of state (cf. sec. 45); like verbs of change of state, most of them show the causative/inchoative alternation. The state that each of these verbs lexicalizes is a state that can hold of a "location" as a result of removing something from that location. Like some other verbs of change of state, certain verbs in this class are zero-related to adjectives. These verbs participate in both a transitive and an intransitive form of the locative alternation, although they take the preposition *of* where the *spray/load* verbs (sec. 9.7) and *swarm* verbs (sec. 47.5.1) take *with* (the *of* phrase is more awkward in the intransitive form of the locative alternation). The verbs in this class take *from* in the locative variant when they are used to refer to possessional deprivation, but may take a variety of locative prepositions when the verb describes the removal of an entity from a location. In the *of* variant, the object of the verb—the location argument— receives the "holistic" interpretation also exhibited by the *spray/load* verbs in the *with* variant. Most of these verbs do not have zero-related nominals.

10.4   *Wipe* Verbs

References: Dixon (1991), Jackendoff (1990b), B. Levin and Rappaport Hovav (1991), J. Lumsden (1991), Sehnert and Sharwood-Smith (1973). See also references listed under *Spray/Load* Verbs (sec. 9.7).

10.4.1   Manner Subclass

Class Members: bail, buff, dab, distill, dust, erase, expunge, flush, leach, lick, pluck, polish, prune, purge, rinse, rub, scour, scrape, scratch, scrub, shave, skim, smooth, soak, squeeze, strain, strip, suck, suction, swab, sweep, trim, wash, wear, weed, whisk, winnow, wipe, wring

Properties:

(94)   a.   Brian wiped the fingerprints from the counter.
        b.   Brian wiped the fingerprints from inside/outside/under the cupboard.

(95)   Locative Alternation:
        a.   Brian wiped the fingerprints from the counter.
        b.   Brian wiped the counter (*of fingerprints).

(96)   Conative Alternation (some verbs):
        a.   Brian wiped the counter.
             Brian wiped at the counter.
        b.   Paula trimmed the bush.
            * Paula trimmed at the bush.

(97)   * Causative Alternations:
        a.   Brian wiped the fingerprints from the counter.
            * The fingerprints wiped from the counter.

     b.   Brian wiped the counter.
       * The counter wiped.

(98)   Unspecified Object Alternation (some verbs):
     a.   Brian was wiping the counter.
     b.   Brian was wiping.

(99)   Unspecified Object Alternation plus Locative PP (some verbs):
     a.   Brian was wiping the wall behind the stove.
     b.   Brian was wiping behind the stove.

(100)   Resultative Phrase:
     Brian wiped the counter clean (of fingerprints).

(101)   Zero-related Nominal:
     a wipe (*of the fingerprints/the counter)
     give a wipe (some verbs)

Comments: These verbs also relate to removing things from surfaces or containers. Like the *clear* verbs above, they participate in a form of the locative alternation and show the "holistic/partitive" effect. When the location is the direct object, it receives the "holistic" interpretation, also found when the location argument of a *clear* verb is the direct object. However, while the *clear* verbs lexicalize a state that can result from removing something from a location, these verbs lexicalize a manner or means of removal. They also differ from the *clear* verbs in typically not allowing an *of* phrase when the location is expressed as the direct object. The *of* phrase may appear as a complement of an adjective heading a resultative phrase when the location is the direct object; see the resultative construction use above. Occasionally, these verbs are found with a bare *of* phrase, but only if the manner or means meaning component is lost or at least less salient (B. Levin and Rappaport Hovav (1991)). Most members of this class have a zero-related nominal that refers to the action named by the verb.

    Most of these verbs in their basic meanings are probably not verbs of removing, though they can be used as verbs of removing. Since some of the manners or means that are part of the meanings of these verbs are specifically associated with removing things from surfaces or containers, these verbs show properties of verbs of removing. But some manners or means may be associated with putting things on surfaces or in containers as well as with removing things from surfaces or containers, and the verbs whose meaning involves these (e.g. *wipe*) can be used both as verbs of putting (e.g. *wipe the crumbs onto the floor*) and as verbs of removing; these verbs are cross-listed (sec. 9).

10.4.2 Instrument Subclass

Class Members: brush, comb, file, filter, hoover, hose, iron, mop, plow, rake, sandpaper, shear, shovel, siphon, sponge, towel, vacuum

Properties:

(102) a. Carla shoveled the snow from the walk.
       b. Carla shoveled the snow from under/near/among the bushes.

(103) Locative Alternation:
       a. Carla shoveled the snow from the walk.
       b. Carla shoveled the walk (*of snow).

(104) * Conative Alternation:
       a. Carla shoveled the walk.
       b. * Carla shoveled at the walk.

(105) * Causative Alternations:
       a. Carla shoveled the snow from the walk.
           * The snow shoveled from the walk.
       b. Carla shoveled the walk.
           * The walk shoveled.

(106) Unspecified Object Alternation (some verbs):
       a. Carla was shoveling the walk.
       b. Carla was shoveling.

(107) Unspecified Object plus Locative PP (some verbs):
       a. Carla mopped the floor under the furniture.
       b. Carla mopped under the furniture.

(108) Resultative Phrase:
       Carla shoveled the walk clean (of snow).

(109) Zero-related Nominal:
       a shovel
       * a shovel of the snow/the walk

Comments: These verbs pattern exactly like the manner subclass of the *wipe* verbs, except that they are all zero-related to a noun that is the name of an instrument. These verbs in their most basic meaning probably refer to using the instrument they take their name from in a conventional way. Since many of these instruments are used for removing things from surfaces or containers, they show properties of verbs of removing. But some of these instruments may be used either to put things on surfaces or in containers or to remove things from surfaces or containers, and the verbs taking their names from such instruments can be used either as verbs of putting (e.g., *shovel the dirt into the flowerbed, rake the fertilizer into the field*) or as verbs of removing; these verbs are cross-listed (sec. 9). None of the verbs in this subclass have zero-related result or action nominals.

These verbs, like the *clear* verbs above, participate in a form of the locative alternation and show the "holistic/partitive" effect. When the location is the direct object, it receives the "holistic" interpretation, also found when the location argument of a *clear* verb is the direct object. These verbs differ from the *clear* verbs in typically not allowing an *of* phrase when the location is expressed as the direct object. The *of* phrase may appear as a complement of an adjective heading a resultative phrase when the location is the direct object; see the resultative construction use above. These verbs are found with an *of* phrase even less often than the verbs in the manner subclass of the *wipe* verbs; again, an *of* phrase occurs only if the instrument meaning component is lost or at least less salient (B. Levin and Rappaport Hovav (1991)).

10.5   Verbs of Possessional Deprivation: *Steal* Verbs

References: Dixon (1989), Fillmore (1968b), Norvig and G. Lakoff (1987), Snell-Hornby (1983)

Class Members: abduct, cadge, capture, confiscate, cop, emancipate, embezzle, exorcise, extort, extract, filch, flog, grab, impound, kidnap, liberate, lift, nab, pilfer, pinch, pirate, plagiarize, purloin, recover, redeem, reclaim, regain, repossess, rescue, retrieve, rustle, seize, smuggle, snatch, sneak, sponge, steal, swipe, take, thieve, wangle, weasel, winkle, withdraw, wrest

Properties:

(110)   The thief stole the painting from the museum.

(111)   * Locative Alternation:
     a.   The thief stole the painting from the museum.
     b. * The thief stole the museum of the painting.

(112)   * Benefactive Alternation:
     a.   The thief stole the painting for Mr. Smith.
     b. * The thief stole Mr. Smith the painting.

(113)   * Conative Alternation:
     a.   The thief stole the painting from the museum.
     b. * The thief stole at the painting from the museum.

(114)   * Causative Alternations:
     a.   The thief stole the painting from the museum.
     b. * The painting stole from the museum.

Comments: These verbs primarily describe the removal of something from someone's possession; the previous possessor or a location associated with this possessor is expressed in a *from* prepositional phrase. These verbs can also take benefactive *for* phrases to indicate the person on whose behalf the removal was done, but they do not participate in the benefactive alternation. Although they are found in a syntactic frame that resembles the location variant of the locative alternation, they do not participate in the locative alternation either. Some of these verbs can also be used as verbs of obtaining and are cross-listed (sec. 13.5); this possibility probably arises because in many situations in which someone obtains something, someone else loses possession of that thing.

10.6   Verbs of Possessional Deprivation: *Cheat* Verbs

References: Dixon (1989), Fillmore (1968b), Hook (1983), Jackendoff (1990b), Kayne (1984), B. Levin and Rappaport Hovav (1991). See also references listed under *Clear* Verbs above.

Class Members: absolve, acquit, balk, bereave, bilk, bleed, break (of a habit), burgle, cheat, cleanse, con, cull, cure, defraud, denude, deplete, depopulate, deprive, despoil, disabuse, disarm, disencumber, dispossess, divest, drain, ease, exonerate, fleece, free, gull, milk, mulct, pardon, plunder, purge, purify, ransack, relieve, render, rid, rifle, rob, sap, strip, swindle, unburden, void, wean

Properties:

(115)   The doctor cured Pat of pneumonia.

(116)   * Locative Alternation:
          a. * The doctor cured pneumonia from Pat.
          b.   The doctor cured Pat of pneumonia.

(117)   * Causative Alternations:
          a.   The doctor cured Pat of pneumonia.
          b. * Pat cured of pneumonia.

(118)   *Of* alternates with *out (of)* with a few verbs:
          a.   The swindler cheated Pat of her fortune.
               The swindler cheated Pat out of her fortune.
          b.   The doctor cured Pat of pneumonia.
               * The doctor cured Pat out of pneumonia.

Comments: Like the *steal* verbs, these verbs can be characterized as verbs of possessional deprivation. They typically describe depriving someone/something of an inalienable possession (in a broad sense). These verbs have attracted interest because they turn up in one of the two syntactic frames shown by the form of the locative alternation associated with the *clear* verbs (cf. above). The direct object of these verbs is said to receive the "holistic" interpretation found in the *of* variant of the locative alternation as manifested by the *clear* verbs. A few of these verbs allow the preposition *of* to alternate with *out of* (e.g., *cheat (out) of a reward*).

10.7 *Pit* Verbs

References: Andrews (1986), Bladin (1911), E.V. Clark and H.H. Clark (1979), Dowty (1979), Duszak (1980), Hook (1983), Horn (1988), Jackendoff (1990b), Jespersen (1942), Karius (1985), Leitner (1974, 1977), Marchand (1969, 1973, 1974), Rose (1973), A.S.C. Ross (1976)

Class Members: bark, beard, bone, burl, core, gill, gut, head, hull, husk, lint, louse, milk, peel, pinion, pip, pit, pith, pod, poll, pulp, rind, scale, scalp, seed, shell, shuck, skin, snail, stalk, stem, stone, string, tail, tassel, top, vein, weed, wind, worm, zest

Properties:

(119)   The cook boned the fish.
          (i.e., The cook removed the bones from the fish.)

(120)   ∗ Cognate *Of* Phrase:
          ∗ The cook boned the fish of bones.
          ∗ The cook boned the fish of its backbone.

(121)   ∗ Causative Alternations:
          a.   The cook boned the fish.
          b. ∗ The fish boned.

Comments: These verbs all have zero-related nominals. The meaning of each of them could be paraphrased as "remove X from (something)," where X is the noun zero-related to the verb. The nouns that these verbs are based on might for the most part be considered to be an inalienably possessed part of an animal or plant. The direct object of these verbs receives the "holistic" interpretation associated with the *with/of* variant of the locative alternation: if a cook bones a fish, all of the bones are understood to have been removed. These verbs do not allow a cognate *of* phrase. The process of forming such verbs from nouns does not seem to be particularly productive, but this may reflect the limited number of nouns of the appropriate type that these verbs can be related to.

10.8 *Debone* Verbs

References: Andrews (1986), Bladin (1911), E.V. Clark and H.H. Clark (1979), Dowty (1979), Horn (1988), Jackendoff (1990b), Jespersen (1942), Marchand (1969, 1973, 1974), Rose (1973), A.S.C. Ross (1976)

Class Members: deaccent, debark, debone, debowel, debug, debur, declaw, defang, defat, defeather, deflea, deflesh, defoam, defog, deforest, defrost, defuzz, degas, degerm, deglaze, degrease, degrit, degum, degut, dehair, dehead, dehorn, dehull, dehusk, deice, deink, delint, delouse, deluster, demast, derat, derib, derind, desalt, descale, desex, desprout, destarch, destress, detassel, detusk, devein, dewater, dewax, deworm

Properties:

(122)   The cook deboned the fish.
         (i.e., The cook removed the bones from the fish.)

(123)   * Cognate *Of* Phrase:
         * The cook deboned the fish of all its bones.

(124)   * Causative Alternations:
         a.   The cook deboned the fish.
         b. * The fish deboned.

Comments: These verbs all have related nominals; morphologically, each verb is formed by the prefix *de–* plus this nominal. The meaning of these verbs could be paraphrased as "remove X from (something)," where X is the noun related to the verb. The nouns that these verbs are based on might for the most part be considered to be an inalienably possessed part of an animal or plant (sometimes in a broad sense of inalienable possession). Those verbs that are not formed from nouns meeting this criterion (e.g., *debug, debur, delouse, deworm*) generally do not permit the prefix *de–* to drop, contrasting with those verbs that are, which allow the prefix *de–* to drop while maintaining the same meaning. Thus there is an overlap between this set of verbs and the *pit* verbs above. The direct object of these verbs receives the "holistic" interpretation associated with the *with/of* variant of the locative alternation: if a cook debones a fish, all of the bones are understood to have been removed. These verbs do not allow a cognate *of* phrase. They seem to be slightly more productively coined than the *pit* verbs.

10.9   *Mine* Verbs

References: E.V. Clark and H.H. Clark (1979), Karius (1985), Lehrer (1990), Leitner (1974)

Class Members: mine, quarry

Properties:

(125)   The men mined the gold.
         (i.e., The men removed the gold from the mine.)

(126)   Cognate Source Phrase:
          The men were able to mine more gold from the abandoned mine.

(127)   * Causative Alternations:
          a.   The men mined the gold.
          b. * The gold mined.

Comments: These verbs all have zero-related nominals; the nouns name
locations that one typically removes something from. The meaning of each of
these verbs could be paraphrased as "remove (something) from X," where X
is the noun zero-related to the verb. A cognate source phrase may be found
with these verbs if it expresses further information about the source. There
are hardly any verbs bearing this type of relation to a noun and the process of
coining such verbs does not seem to be productive; this may reflect the paucity
of appropriate nouns for these verbs to be related to.

11   Verbs of Sending and Carrying

References: Dixon (1991), Green (1974), Gropen et al. (1989), Gruber (1965,
1976), Ikegami (1970), Oehrle (1976), Pinker (1989)

11.1   *Send* Verbs

Class Members: airmail, convey, deliver, dispatch, express, FedEx, forward,
hand, mail, pass, port, post, return, send, shift, ship, shunt, slip, smuggle, sneak,
transfer, transport, UPS

Properties:

(128)   Nora sent the book (from Paris) (to London).

(129)   Dative Alternation (some verbs):
          a.   Nora sent the book to Peter.
          b.   Nora sent Peter the book.

(130)   * Conative Alternation:
          a.   Nora sent the book to Peter.
          b. * Nora sent at the book to Peter.

(131)   * Causative Alternations:
          a.   Nora sent the book to Peter.
          b. * The book sent to Peter.

(132)   * Middle Alternation:
     a. Nora sent books to children.
     b. * Books send easily to children.

(133)   Coreferential interpretation of pronouns not possible:
     * Nora$_i$ sent the book with her$_i$.
     (cf. Nora$_i$ brought the book with her$_i$.)

Comments: These verbs relate to causing an entity to change location. The entity moves unaccompanied by the agent (compare the verbs *bring* and *carry*) and, as Pinker (1989) writes, the motion is "mediated by a separation in time and space, sometimes bridged by a particular means of transfer" (p. 110). These verbs differ from verbs of putting (sec. 9) in allowing the goal preposition *to*. Some, but not all, *send* verbs can take a *from* phrase indicating a source. For some of these verbs, the change in location can also result in transfer of possession, as attested by their ability to show the dative alternation, but they are not cross-listed under verbs of change of possession (sec. 13). The inability of some of these verbs to show the dative alternation might be attributed to the so-called Latinate restriction on the double object construction (see sec. 2.1, Dative Alternation).

11.2 *Slide* Verbs

Class Members: bounce, float, move, roll, slide

Properties:

(134)   Carla slid the books across the table.

(135)   Carla slid the books from one end of the table to the other.

(136)   Dative Alternation (except *move*):
     a. Carla slid the book to Dale.
     b. Carla slid Dale the book.

(137)   * Conative Alternation:
     a. Carla slid the book (to Dale).
     b. * Carla slid at the book (to Dale).
        (cf. Nora pushed at the rock.)

(138)   Causative/Inchoative Alternation:
     a. Carla slid the books across the table.
     b. The books slid across the table.

(139)   Middle Alternation:
     a. Carla slid those books across the table.
     b. Those books slide across the table easily.

(140)   Acceptability of coreferential interpretation varies:
         a. ? Carla$_i$ slid the book away from her$_i$.
         b. * Carla$_i$ bounced the ball with her$_i$.

Comments: These verbs can be used as intransitive verbs of manner of
motion, as well as transitive verbs of causing a change of position; therefore,
they are also included under the appropriate subclass of verbs of motion: the
intransitive *roll* verbs (sec. 51.3.1). This section focuses on the properties
related to their transitive use; the properties related to their intransitive use are
discussed under *Roll* Verbs. Not all the intransitive *roll* verbs are listed here,
because not all of them have transitive uses as verbs of sending and carrying; in
particular, most of the *roll* verbs that involve motion around an axis do not show
such transitive uses. With the exception of *move*, the verbs in this subsection
can also be used as verbs of change of possession brought about by a change
of position, as shown by their ability to show the dative alternation, but they
are not cross-listed under verbs of change of possession (sec. 13). The agent
simply brings about the change of location described by the verb, but does not
accompany the moving entity.

11.3 *Bring* and *Take*

Class Members: bring, take (only)

Properties:

(141)   Nora brought the book to the meeting.

(142)   Nora brought the book to Pamela.

(143)   Nora brought the book from home.

(144)   Dative Alternation:
         a.   Nora brought the book to Pamela.
         b.   Nora brought Pamela the book.

(145)   * Conative Alternation:
         a.   Nora brought the book to the meeting.
         b. * Nora brought at the book to the meeting.

(146)   * Causative Alternations:
         a.   Nora brought the book to the meeting.
         b. * The book brought to the meeting.

(147)   * Middle Alternation:
         a.   Nora brought the book to the meeting.
         b. * The book brings easily to the meeting.

(148)   * Resultative Phrase:
        * Nora brought Pamela breathless.
        (on the interpretation where the bringing makes Pamela breathless)

(149)   Coreferential interpretation of pronouns possible:
        Nora$_i$ brought the book with her$_i$.

Comments: These verbs have been described as "verbs of continuous causation of accompanied motion in a deictically-specified direction" (Gropen et al. (1989)). Although these verbs are not used intransitively, they have been considered the "causative" counterparts of *come* and *go*. These two verbs are set apart from other verbs of sending and carrying by the presence of the deictic component of meaning and the lack of a meaning component that specifies the manner in which the motion is brought about. These verbs can also be used as verbs of change of possession brought about by a change of position, as shown by their ability to show the dative alternation, but they are not cross-listed under verbs of change of possession (sec. 13).

11.4 *Carry* Verbs

Class Members: carry, drag, haul, heave, heft, hoist, kick, lug, pull, push, schlep, shove, tote, tow, tug

Properties:

(150)   Amanda carried the package (from Boston) (to New York).

(151)   Dative Alternation:
        a.   Amanda carried the package to Pamela.
        b.   ? Amanda carried Pamela the package.

(152)   * Conative Alternation:
        a.   Amanda carried the package (to New York).
        b.   * Amanda carried at the package (to New York).
             (cf. Nora pushed at/against the chair.)

(153)   * Causative Alternations:
        a.   Amanda carried the package (to New York).
        b.   * The package carried (to New York).

(154)   * Middle Alternation:
        a.   Amanda carried packages (to New York).
        b.   * Packages carry easily (to New York).

(155)   Acceptability of coreferential interpretation varies:
        a.   Amanda$_i$ carried the package with her$_i$.
        b.   Amanda$_i$ lugged the books to the store with her$_i$.

Comments: These verbs relate to the causation of accompanied motion. None of them lexicalize a particular direction of motion. Instead, the members of this class differ from each other in meaning with respect to the manner/means of motion. The direction of motion must be overtly specified in a prepositional phrase. In fact, many of these verbs (e.g., *pull*, *push*) are also verbs of exerting force and are cross-listed (sec. 12). Such verbs allow conative *at* when used as verbs of exerting force, but when they are used as verbs of causation of accompanied motion (as shown by their use with a goal or directional phrase), they do not take an *at* phrase: *Amanda pushed at the chair to the wall.* Although these verbs are listed as allowing the dative alternation, opinions vary as to whether the verbs in this class do manifest this alternation. It is clear that some of them are more acceptable in the double object construction than others.

11.5 *Drive* Verbs

References: Karius (1985), Leitner (1974), Marchand (1969, 1974)

Class Members: barge, bus, cart, drive, ferry, fly, row, shuttle, truck, wheel, wire (money)

Properties:

(156)   Amanda drove the package (from Boston) (to New York).

(157)   ? Dative Alternation (some verbs):
      a.   Amanda drove the package to Pamela.
      b. ? Amanda drove Pamela the package.

(158)   * Conative Alternation:
      a.   Amanda drove the package (to New York).
      b. * Amanda drove at the package (to New York).

(159)   * Causative Alternations:
      a.   Amanda drove the package (to New York).
      b. * The package drove (to New York).

(160)   * Middle Alternation:
      a.   Amanda drove packages (to New York).
      b. * Packages drive easily (to New York).

(161)   Coreferential interpretation of pronouns not possible:
      * Amanda$_i$ drove the package with her$_i$.

Comments: These verbs describe the causation of accompanied motion; they inherently specify something about the manner of motion, typically the vehicle or means used, and some of them even take their name from the vehicle used.

The direction of motion is specified by directional phrases and is not part of the meaning of these verbs. Opinions vary as to whether these verbs manifest the dative alternation. It appears that some of them are more acceptable in the double object construction than others; the dative alternation seems to be least acceptable with those verbs which are zero-related to nouns, particularly nouns that are vehicle names.

12   Verbs of Exerting Force: *Push/Pull* Verbs

References: Dixon (1991)

Class Members: ?draw, heave, jerk, press, pull, push, shove, ?thrust, tug, yank

Properties:

(162)   Nora pushed the chair.

(163)   Conative Alternation:
    a.   Nora pushed the chair.
    b.   Nora pushed at/on/against the chair.

(164)   * Causative Alternations:
    a.   Nora pushed the chair.
    b.   * The chair pushed.

(165)   *Way* Object Alternation (some verbs):
    a.   Nora pushed through the crowd.
    b.   Nora pushed her way through the crowd.

(166)   Nora pushed the chair against the wall.

(167)   Coreferential interpretation of pronouns possible:
Nora$_i$ pushed the chair away from her$_i$.

(168)   Resultative Phrase:
Nora pushed the door shut.

(169)   Zero-related Nominal:
a push (*of the chair)
give the chair a push.

Comments: These verbs relate to the exertion of a force on an entity. They differ from each other in meaning with respect to the type of force exerted.

Some of these verbs can also be used as *carry* verbs—verbs of causation of accompanied motion in some manner—and have been cross-listed (sec. 11.4), together with the properties attributable to membership in this other class.

13   Verbs of Change of Possession

References: Abraham (1983), Croft (1985, 1991), Dixon (1973, 1989, 1991), Fillmore (1977b), Ikegami (1973), Jackendoff (1992b). See also references under Dative Alternation (sec. 2.1).

13.1   *Give* Verbs

Class Members: feed, give, lease, lend, loan, pass, pay, peddle, refund, render, rent, repay, sell, serve, trade

Properties:

(170)   They lent a bicycle to me.

(171)   * They lent a bicycle near me/behind me.

(172)   Dative Alternation:
  a.   They lent a bicycle to me.
  b.   They lent me a bicycle.

(173)   * Fulfilling Alternation:
  a.   They lent a bicycle to me.
  b. * They lent me with a bicycle.

(174)   * Causative Alternations:
  a.   They lent a bicycle to me.
  b. * A bicycle lent (to me).

Comments: These verbs of change of possession display the dative alternation, though there may be some differences of opinion concerning whether some of these verbs actually are found in the double object construction. Although the prepositional phrase is optional with some of these verbs, when it does appear, it must be headed by the preposition *to*.

13.2   *Contribute* Verbs

Class Members: administer, contribute, disburse, distribute, donate, extend, forfeit, proffer, refer, reimburse, relinquish, remit, restore, return, sacrifice, submit, surrender, transfer

Properties:

(175)   We contributed our paycheck to her.

(176)   * We contributed our paycheck on the counter/under the papers.

(177)   * Dative Alternation:
      a.   We contributed our paycheck to her.
      b.   * We contributed her our paycheck.

(178)   * Fulfilling Alternation:
      a.   We contributed our paycheck to her.
      b.   * We contributed her with our paycheck.

(179)   * Causative Alternations:
      a.   We contributed our paycheck to her.
      b.   * Our paycheck contributed (to her).

Comments: These verbs of change of possession do not allow the dative alternation. Their failure to be found in the double object construction has often been attributed to their Latinate character (see sec. 2.1, Dative Alternation). Like the alternating verbs of change of possession, these verbs are characterized by taking a prepositional phrase headed by the preposition *to*.

13.3   Verbs of Future Having

Class Members: advance, allocate, allot, assign, award, bequeath, cede, concede, extend, grant, guarantee, issue, leave, offer, owe, promise, vote, will, yield

Properties:

(180)   We offered a job to her.

(181)   * We offered a job behind her.

(182)   Dative Alternation:
      a.   We offered a job to her.
      b.   We offered her a job.

(183)   * Fulfilling Alternation:
      a.   We offered a job to her.
      b.   * We offered her with a job.

(184)   * Causative Alternations:
      a.   We offered a job to her.
      b.   * A job offered (to her).

Comments: These verbs relate to a change of possession that will take place in the future. They all participate in the dative alternation. As J. McCawley (personal communication) has pointed out, some of these verbs can take sentential complements that can be related to the object of the verb in its transitive use: *offer him a job* can be paraphrased as *offer to give him a job*. Although the prepositional phrase is optional with some of these verbs, when it does appear, it must be headed by the preposition *to*. These verbs do not differ from the *give* verbs above in the properties they show, so that this class and the *give* class could be collapsed; however, they have been kept distinct here following the precedent in some work on the dative alternation.

13.4   Verbs of Providing

13.4.1   Verbs of Fulfilling

References: Blansitt (1984), Channon (1982), Croft (1986, 1991), Emonds (1976), Fillmore (1971b), Fraser (1971), Gawron (1986), de Groot (1984), Jackendoff (1990b), Jespersen (1927), Kayne (1984), Kipka (1990), Larson (1990), J. Lumsden (1991), J. McCawley (1975), J.E. Miller (1989), Pesetsky (1992), Pinker (1989), Rappaport and B. Levin (1985)

Class Members: credit, entrust, furnish, issue, leave, present, provide, serve, supply, trust

Properties:

(185)   Brown presented a plaque to Jones.

(186)   * Brown presented a plaque onto the table/next to the lectern.

(187)   Fulfilling Alternation:
     a.   Brown presented a plaque to Jones.
     b.   Brown presented Jones with a plaque.

(188)   * Brown presented a plaque near/next to/at Jones.

(189)   the presentation of a plaque (to Jones)
     the presentation to/*of Jones (*with a plaque)

Comments: These verbs are described by Gropen et al. (1989) as verbs where "X gives something to Y that Y deserves, needs, or is worthy of." Besides expressing their arguments in the 'NP1 V NP2 *to* NP3' pattern typical of verbs of change of possession, these verbs also show a second pattern involving a *with* phrase, 'NP1 V NP3 *with* NP2'. In the first pattern, the goal argument is expressed in the prepositional phrase; in the second pattern, the theme argument is expressed in the prepositional phrase. These verbs do not show alternative prepositions; *to*, for instance, cannot alternate with locative prepositions. Judgments differ as to whether some of these verbs can be found in the dative alternation. This property is not indicated here; rather any verb that clearly demonstrates this property is also included in a class of verbs in this section whose members do show the dative alternation—either the *give* verbs or the verbs of future having.

13.4.2 *Equip* Verbs

Class Members: arm, burden, charge (with a task), compensate, equip, invest, ply, regale, reward, saddle

Properties:

(190)   Brown equipped Jones with a camera.

(191)   * Brown equipped a camera near/next to/at Jones.

(192)   * Fulfilling Alternation:
      a. * Brown equipped a camera to Jones.
      b.   Brown equipped Jones with a camera.

(193)   * Dative Alternation:
      a. * Brown equipped a camera to Jones.
      b. * Brown equipped Jones a camera.

Comments: These verbs are rather close in meaning to the verbs of fulfilling, but their meaning seems to specify something about what is provided rather than about the actual type of act of providing. These verbs differ from the verbs of fulfilling in only showing one of the variants of the fulfilling alternation: the variant involving the *with* phrase. None of these verbs participates in the dative alternation; presumably this property is related at least in part to the fact that they are not found in the 'NP V NP *to* NP' frame.

13.5   Verbs of Obtaining

References: Channon (1982), Croft (1985), Fillmore (1977b), Ikegami (1973), Jackendoff (1992c), Kimball (1973a). See also references listed under Dative Alternation (sec. 2.1).

13.5.1 *Get* Verbs

Class Members: book, buy, call, cash, catch, charter, ?choose, earn, fetch, find, gain, gather, get, hire, keep, lease, leave, order, phone (doctor), pick (fruit, flower), pluck (flower), procure, pull (a beer), reach, rent, reserve, save, secure, shoot (game), slaughter (animal), steal, vote, win

Properties:

(194)   Carmen bought a dress (at Bloomingdale's).

(195)   Most verbs allow a *from* phrase:
         Carmen bought a dress from Diana.

(196)   Benefactive Alternation:
         a.   Carmen bought a dress for Mary.
         b.   Carmen bought Mary a dress.

(197) * Dative Alternation:
         a. * Carmen bought a dress to Mary.
         b.   Carmen bought Mary a dress.

(198) * Locative Alternation:
         a.   Carmen bought a dress from Diana.
         b. * Carmen bought Diana of a dress.

(199)   Sum of Money Subject Alternation (some verbs):
         a.   Carmen bought a dress at Bloomingdale's for $50.
         b. $50 won't even buy a dress at Bloomingdale's.

Comments: The members of this subset of the verbs of obtaining participate
in the benefactive alternation. They take a benefactive argument that can be
expressed either as the first object in the double object construction or in a
for prepositional phrase. Some verbs in this class are verbs of obtaining in
their basic sense; others, such as *shoot*, are members of other classes in their
basic meaning, but show an extended meaning as verbs of obtaining. Some
of these verbs can also be used as *steal* verbs and are cross-listed (sec. 10.5);
this possibility probably arises because in many situations in which someone
obtains something someone else loses possession of that thing. Some of the *get*
verbs can take a sum of money as their subject; this is only the case for those
verbs where the process of obtaining involves a transfer of money.

13.5.2   *Obtain* Verbs

Class Members: accept, accumulate, acquire, appropriate, borrow, ?cadge,
collect, exact, grab, inherit, obtain, purchase, receive, recover, regain, retrieve,
seize, select, snatch

Properties:

(200)   Carmen obtained the spare part (at the hardware store).

(201)   Most verbs allow a *from* phrase:
         Carmen obtained the spare part from Diana.

(202) * Benefactive Alternation:
         a.   Carmen obtained a spare part for Mary.
         b. * Carmen obtained Mary a spare part.

(203)   * Dative Alternation:
      a. * Carmen obtained a spare part to Mary.
      b. * Carmen obtained Mary a spare part.

(204)   * Locative Alternation:
      a. Carmen obtained a spare part from Diana.
      b. * Carmen obtained Diana of a spare part.

(205)   Sum of Money Subject Alternation (a few verbs):
      a. Carmen purchased a dress at Bloomingdale's for $50.
      b. $50 won't even purchase a dress at Bloomingdale's.

Comments: Like the *get* verbs, these verbs can take a benefactive *for* prepositional phrase, but unlike the *get* verbs, they do not show the benefactive alternation. With a few exceptions, the inability to be found in the double object construction could be attributed to the Latinate character of the *obtain* verbs (see sec. 2.1, Dative Alternation). Some of these verbs can also be used as *steal* verbs and are cross-listed (sec. 10.5); this possibility probably arises because in many situations in which someone obtains something someone else loses possession of that thing. A few of the *obtain* verbs can take a sum of money as their subject; this is the case for those verbs where the process of obtaining involves a transfer of money.

The verbs *accept, inherit,* and *receive* have been included here since they pattern like the other *obtain* verbs with respect to the listed properties (except that *inherit* does not take a benefactive prepositional phrase, since one cannot inherit something on someone else's behalf). However, the subject of these three verbs is understood to play a more "passive" part in the process of obtaining than the subject of the other *obtain* verbs.

13.6   Verbs of Exchange

References: Croft (1991)

Class Members: barter, change, exchange, substitute, swap, trade

Properties:

(206)   Gwen exchanged the dress for a shirt.

(207)   * Dative Alternation:
      a. * Gwen exchanged the dress to Mary.
      b. * Gwen exchanged Mary the dress.

(208)   * Benefactive Alternation:
      a. Gwen exchanged the dress for Mary. (some verbs)
      b. * Gwen exchanged Mary the dress.

Comments: These verbs relate to exchanging one thing for another. They are not found with *to* phrases expressing goals, nor with *from* phrases expressing sources. Some of these verbs are found with *for* phrases. These *for* phrases are used to express the object that the agent receives as part of the exchange; they are not benefactive *for* phrases. These verbs show neither the dative nor the benefactive alternation.

13.7   *Berry* Verbs

References: Bladin (1911), E.V. Clark and H.H. Clark (1979), Duszak (1980), Hale and Keyser (1991, 1992), Jespersen (1942), Karius (1985), Leitner (1974), Marchand (1969, 1974), Silva (1973)

Class Members: antique, berry, birdnest, blackberry, clam, crab, fish, fowl, grouse, hay, log, mushroom, nest, nut, oyster, pearl, prawn, rabbit, seal, shark, shrimp, snail, snipe, sponge, whale, whelk

Properties:

(209)   The children like to berry in the summer.

(210)   The children went berrying.

Comments: The verbs in this class are zero-related to nominals. Each of these verbs relates to collecting or gathering the entity named by the noun from which the verb takes its name. These verbs are used almost exclusively in the *–ing* form. It is likely that more verbs of this type might be coined.

14   *Learn* Verbs

Class Members: acquire, cram, glean, learn, memorize, read, study

Properties:

(211)   Rhoda learned French from an old book.

(212)   Rhoda learned from an old book.

Comments: These verbs describe the acquisition of information. The verb *acquire* takes a wider range of direct objects than the others: *Rhoda acquired a deep understanding of French grammar*. It is also the only verb here that can be used as a verb of transfer of possession.

15 *Hold* and *Keep* Verbs

References: Dixon (1991)

15.1 *Hold* Verbs

Class Members: clasp, clutch, grasp, grip, handle, hold, wield

Properties:

(213)   She held the rail.

(214)   * Conative Alternation:
     a.   She held the rail.
     b. * She held at the rail.

(215)   * Middle Alternation:
     a.   She held the rail.
     b. * The rail holds easily.

(216)   Body-Part Possessor Ascension Alternation (some verbs):
     a.   She held his arm.
     b.   She held him by the arm.

(217)   * She held the paper from him.

Comments: These verbs describe prolonged contact with an entity, but they do not describe a change of possession or a change of location. The fact that only some of these verbs show the body-part possessor ascension alternation may be attributable to the fact that only some of these verbs take animate direct objects.

15.2 *Keep* Verbs

Class Members: hoard, keep, leave, store

Properties:

(218)   a.   Michelle kept the papers in the desk.
     b.   Michelle kept the papers behind/over/under the desk.

(219)   * Locative Alternation:
     a.   Michelle kept the papers in the desk.
     b. * Michelle kept the desk with the papers.

(220)   Zero-related Nominal (some verbs):
     a hoard
     a store

Comments: These verbs relate to maintaining something at some location. They do not describe the actual putting of an entity at this location.

16   Verbs of Concealment

Class Members: block, cloister, conceal, curtain, hide, isolate, quarantine, screen, seclude, sequester, shelter

Properties:

(221)   Frances hid the presents from Sally.

(222)   Frances hid the presents behind the books/in the drawer.

(223)   * Locative Alternation:
      a.   Frances hid the presents from Sally.
      b. * Frances hid Sally of the presents.

Comments: This class includes verbs relating to keeping something out of view.

17   Verbs of Throwing

References: C.L. Baker (1992), Dixon (1991), Fillmore (1977b), Gropen et al. (1989), Jackendoff (1990a, 1990b), Pinker (1989), Snell-Hornby (1983)

17.1   *Throw* Verbs

Class Members: bash, bat, bunt, ?cast, catapult, chuck, fire (projectile), flick, fling, flip, hit (ball), hurl, kick (ball), knock, lob, ?loft, nudge, pass, pitch, punt, shoot (projectile), shove, slam, slap, sling, smash, tap, throw, tip, toss

Properties:

(224)   Steve tossed the ball.

(225)   Directional Phrase:
      a.   Steve tossed the ball over the fence/into the garden.
      b.   Steve tossed the ball from the tree to the gate.

(226)   Steve tossed the ball at Anna.

(227)   * Steve tossed Anna with the ball. (cf. *pelt*)

(228)   Dative Alternation (most verbs):
    a.   Steve tossed the ball to Anna.
    b.   Steve tossed Anna the ball.

(229)   * *With/Against* Alternation:
    a.   Steve tossed the ball against the wall.
    b. * Steve tossed the wall with the ball.

(230)   * Conative Alternation:
    a.   Steve tossed the ball.
    b. * Steve tossed at the ball.

(231)   * Causative Alternations:
    a.   Steve tossed the ball.
    b. * The ball tossed.

(232)   * Middle Alternation:
    a.   Steve tossed the softball.
    b. * Softballs toss easily.

(233)   Zero-related Nominal:
    a toss

Comments: These verbs have been described as verbs of "instantaneously causing ballistic motion" (Gropen et al. (1989)) by imparting a force. One argument of these verbs refers to the entity that is set in motion and that moves unaccompanied by the agent of the action. These verbs can also be used as verbs of change of possession by means of change of location, as shown by their ability to participate in the dative alternation; however, they have not been cross-listed among the verbs of change of possession (sec. 13). Some of the verbs in this class are *hit* verbs that are being used in an extended sense as verbs of throwing by means of hitting; these verbs are also listed under *hit* verbs (sec. 18.1).

17.2 *Pelt* Verbs

Class Members: buffet, bombard, pelt, shower, stone

Properties:

(234)   Steve pelted Anna with acorns.

(235)   * Steve pelted acorns at Anna.

(236)   * Directional Phrase:
        * Steve pelted acorns over the fence.

(237)   * Conative Alternation:
        a.   Steve pelted Anna (with acorns).
        b. * Steve pelted at Anna (with acorns).

(238)   * *With/Against* Alternation:
        a.   Steve pelted Anna with acorns.
        b. * Steve pelted acorns against Anna.

(239)   * Dative Alternation:
        a. * Steve pelted acorns to Anna.
        b. * Steve pelted Anna acorns.

(240)   * Middle Alternation:
        a.   Steve pelted the squirrels with acorns.
        b. * Squirrels pelt easily with acorns.

Comments: These verbs, like the *throw* verbs above, involve ballistic motion, but they describe the motion of a set of physical objects. They behave quite differently from the *throw* verbs: the moving objects are expressed in a *with* phrase, and the direct object of these verbs is the "goal" that the moving objects are set in motion toward.

18   Verbs of Contact by Impact

References: Dixon (1991), Dowty (1991), Fillmore (1967, 1968b, 1977a, 1977b), Guerssel et al. (1985), Jackendoff (1990b), Pinker (1989), Richardson (1983), Ruhl (1972, 1989), Sehnert and Sharwood-Smith (1973), Snell-Hornby (1983), Styan (1984)

18.1   *Hit* Verbs

Class Members: bang, bash, batter, beat, bump, butt, dash, drum, hammer, hit, kick, knock, lash, pound, rap, slap, smack, smash (where no effect implicated), strike, tamp, tap, thump, thwack, whack

Properties:

(241)   *With/Against* Alternation:
        a.   Paula hit the stick against/on the fence.

(Doesn't imply: Paula hit the stick.)
b.   Paula hit the fence with the stick.
(Implies: Paula hit the fence.)

(242)   * *Through/With* Alternation:
a.   * Paula hit the stick through/into the fence.
b.   Paula hit the fence with the stick.

(243)   Conative Alternation:
a.   Paula hit the fence (with the stick).
b.   Paula hit at the fence (with the stick).

(244)   Body-Part Possessor Ascension Alternation:
a.   Paula hit Deirdre on the back.
b.   Paula hit Deirdre's back.

(245)   *Together* Reciprocal Alternation (transitive):
a.   Paula hit one stick against another.
b.   Paula hit the sticks together.

(246)   * Simple Reciprocal Alternation (transitive):
a.   Paula hit one stick against another.
b.   * Paula hit the sticks.
(on the relevant reciprocal interpretation)

(247)   * Causative Alternations:
a.   Paula hit the fence (with a stick).
b.   * The fence hit (with a stick).

(248)   * Middle Alternation:
a.   Paula hit the fence.
b.   * The fence hits easily.

(249)   Instrument Subject Alternation:
a.   Paula hit the fence with the stick.
b.   The stick hit the fence.

(250)   Unintentional interpretation available (some verbs):
a.   Reflexive Object:
Paula hit herself on the doorknob.
b.   Body-Part Object:
Paula hit her elbow on the doorknob.

(251)   Resultative Phrase:
Paula hit/kicked the door open.
Paula banged the window shut.

(252)   Zero-related Nominal:
         a hit/*give a hit/*get a hit in the shoulders
         a kick/give a kick/get a kick in the shins

Comments: These verbs describe moving one entity in order to bring it
into contact with another entity, but they do not necessarily entail that this
contact has any effect on the second entity. A hallmark of these verbs is the
with/against alternation. Some of these verbs allow unintentional, as well as
intentional, action interpretations with body-part or reflexive objects in the *with*
variant.

At least some of the *hit* verbs can also be used as *throw* verbs with the
meaning "instantaneously cause ballistic motion"; those most commonly used
in this way are cross-listed (sec. 17.1). Some of these verbs are also used as
verbs of sound emission (e.g., *bang*) and are cross-listed (sec. 43.2). Such verbs
describe types of contact that are associated with the emission of a characteristic
sound. It is possible that there is a greater overlap between these two classes
of verbs than has been recorded here, since there are other sounds that can
be produced by contact through motion. Some of the *hit* verbs, mainly those
that are also verbs of sound emission, are found with the preposition *on* rather
than, or as well as, *at* in the conative construction (e.g., *bang, knock, rap, tap,
thump*).

18.2   *Swat* Verbs

Class Members: bite, claw, paw, peck, punch (person), scratch, shoot (gun),
slug, stab, swat, swipe

Properties:

(253)   * *With/Against* Alternation:
         a. * Paula swatted the dishcloth against/on the fly.
         b.   Paula swatted the fly with the dishcloth.

(254)   * *Through/With* Alternation:
         a. * Paula swatted the dishcloth through/into the fly.
         b.   Paula swatted the fly with the dishcloth.

(255)   Conative Alternation:
         a.   Paula swatted the fly.
         b.   Paula swatted at the fly.

(256)   Body-Part Possessor Ascension Alternation:
         a.   Paula swatted Deirdre on the back.
         b.   Paula swatted Deirdre's back.

(257)   * Causative Alternations:
        a.   Paula swatted the fly.
        b. * The fly swatted.

(258)   * Middle Alternation:
        a.   Paula swatted flies.
        b. * Flies swat easily.

(259)   * Instrument Subject Alternation:
        a.   Paula swatted the fly with a dishcloth.
        b. * The dishcloth swatted the fly.

(260)   Resultative Phrase (some verbs):
        Paula bit the bag open.

(261)   Zero-related Nominal:
        a swat/*give a swat/*get a swat on the shoulders
        a punch/give someone a punch/get a punch on the nose

Comments: These verbs relate to moving one entity in order to bring it into contact with another entity, but they do not necessarily entail that this contact has any effect on the second entity. Unlike the *hit* verbs above, they do not show the *with/against* alternation. These verbs are found in the 'NP V NP *with* NP' frame, but unlike the *hit* verbs, they are not found in the 'NP V NP *against* NP' frame. Like the *hit* verbs, they show the conative alternation and the body-part possessor ascension alternation. These verbs cannot also be used as *throw* verbs. They do not allow instrument subjects. They also do not appear to allow an unintentional, as well as an intentional, action interpretation with reflexive or body-part objects (the verb *bite* might be the exception here), but this property is probably not surprising since with the *hit* verbs this interpretation is associated with the *against* frame, which the *swat* verbs do not show. The reciprocal alternations are not relevant for the same reason.

18.3   *Spank* Verbs

Class Members: belt, birch, bludgeon, bonk, brain, cane, clobber, club, conk, cosh, cudgel, cuff, flog, knife, paddle, paddywhack, pummel, sock, spank, strap, thrash, truncheon, wallop, whip, whisk

Properties:

(262)   * *With/Against* Alternation:
        a. * Paula spanked her right hand against the naughty child.
        b.   Paula spanked the naughty child with her right hand.

(263)   * *Through/With* Alternation:
    a. * Paula spanked her right hand through/into the naughty child.
    b.   Paula spanked the naughty child with her right hand.

(264)   * Conative Alternation:
    a.   Paula spanked the naughty child.
    b. * Paula spanked at the naughty child.

(265)   Body-Part Possessor Ascension Alternation (some verbs):
    a.   Paula spanked the naughty child on the back.
    b.   Paula spanked the naughty child's back.

(266)   * Causative Alternations:
    a.   Paula spanked the naughty child.
    b. * The naughty child spanked.

(267)   * Middle Alternation:
    a.   Paula spanked the naughty child.
    b. * Naughty children spank easily.

(268)   * Instrument Subject Alternation:
    a.   Paula spanked the naughty child with her right hand.
    b. * Paula's right hand spanked the naughty child.

(269)   Resultative Phrase:
    They flogged/thrashed him to death.

(270)   *–ing* Nominal (most verbs):
    a spanking/give a spanking/get a spanking

Comments: These verbs refer to moving one entity in order to bring it into contact with another entity, but they do not necessarily entail that this contact has any effect on that second entity. This set of verbs is set apart because many of its members are zero-related to nouns that refer to instruments used for hitting. Like the *hit* verbs above, these verbs are found in the 'NP V NP *with* NP' pattern, but unlike the *hit* verbs, they are not found in the 'NP V NP *against* NP' pattern. Like the *hit* verbs, they also show the body-part possessor ascension alternation, but unlike them, they do not show the conative alternation. These verbs cannot also be used as *throw* verbs. They do not allow instrument subjects. They also do not appear to allow an unintentional, as well as intentional, action interpretation with reflexive or body-part objects, but this property is probably not surprising, since with the *hit* verbs this interpretation is associated with the *against* frame, which the *spank* verbs do not show. Similarly, the reciprocal alternations are not relevant since the *spank* verbs are not found in the 'NP V NP *against* NP' pattern that gives rise to the *together* reciprocal alternation with the *hit* verbs. These verbs are like the *swat* verbs in all respects except that they do not show the conative alternation and, instead of having zero-related result nominals, have related result nominals of the form V-*ing*.

18.4   Non-Agentive Verbs of Contact by Impact

Class Members: bang, brush, bump, crash, hit, knock, ram, slam, smash, thud

Properties:

(271)   The grocery cart thudded against the wall.

(272)   * The wall thudded with the grocery cart. (cf. *With/Against* Alternation)

(273)   * Simple Reciprocal Alternation (intransitive):
       a.   The old cart thudded against the new cart.
       b. * The old and new carts thudded.

(274)   *Together* Reciprocal Alternation (intransitive, some verbs):
       a.   The old cart thudded against the new cart.
       b.   The old and new carts thudded together.

Comments: These verbs describe instances of non-agentive contact by impact. They are used intransitively, taking as complement a prepositional phrase headed by the preposition *against*, a frame that could be viewed as the intransitive counterpart of the 'NP V NP *against* NP' frame associated with the *hit* verbs (cf. above). These verbs are not found in an alternate intransitive frame involving the preposition *with* that could be viewed as the intransitive counterpart of the 'NP V NP *with* NP' frame also associated with the *hit* verbs. Some of these verbs are found in the intransitive *together* reciprocal alternation.

Some of these verbs are also listed as *hit* verbs (e.g., *hit, bang*). Many of these verbs are also used as verbs of sound emission (e.g., *bang, crash;* cf. sec. 43.2): such verbs relate to types of contact that are associated with the emission of a characteristic sound. The overlap between the non-agentive verbs of contact by impact and the verbs of sound emission is different from that between the *hit* verbs and the verbs of sound emission. This difference may arise because sounds differ as to whether or not their emission can be controlled by an agent.

19   *Poke* Verbs

References: Dixon (1991), Gruber (1965, 1976)

Class Members: dig, jab, pierce, poke, prick, stick

Properties:

(275)   *Through/With* Alternation:
    a.   Alison poked the needle through/into the cloth.
    b.   Alison poked the cloth with a needle.

(276)   * *With/Against* Alternation:
    a.   * Alison poked the needle against the cloth.
    b.   Alison poked the cloth with a needle.

(277)   Conative Alternation (some verbs):
    a.   Alison poked the cloth.
    b.   Alison poked at the cloth.

(278)   Body-Part Possessor Ascension Alternation:
    a.   Alison poked Daisy in the ribs.
    b.   Alison poked Daisy's ribs.

(279)   * Causative Alternations:
    a.   Alison poked the cloth.
      * The cloth poked.
    b.   Alison poked the needle through the cloth.
      * The needle poked through the cloth.

(280)   * Middle Alternation:
    a.   Alison poked the cloth.
      * That cloth pokes easily.
    b.   Alison poked the darning needle through the denim.
      * Darning needles poke easily through denim.

(281)   Instrument Subject Alternation:
    a.   Alison poked the cloth with a needle.
    b.   The needle poked the cloth.

(282)   Zero-related Nominal (some verbs):
    a poke/give a poke
    a pierce, *a stick

Comments: These verbs describe bringing a pointed object into contact with a surface and, in some instances, puncturing the surface. The *through/with* alternation is characteristic of the verbs in this class.

20   Verbs of Contact: *Touch* Verbs

References: Dixon (1991), Fellbaum (1990), Fillmore (1968b), Guerssel et al. (1985), Jackendoff (1990b), Pinker (1989)

Class Members: caress, graze, kiss, lick, nudge, pat, peck (=kiss), pinch, prod, sting, stroke, tickle, touch

Properties:

(283)   Carrie touched the cat.

(284)   * *With/Against* Alternation:
      a.   * Carrie touched the stick against the cat.
      b.   Carrie touched the cat with the stick.

(285)   * *Through/With* Alternation:
      a.   * Carrie touched the stick through/into the cat.
      b.   Carrie touched the cat with the stick.

(286)   * Conative Alternation:
      a.   Carrie touched the cat.
      b.   * Carrie touched at the cat.

(287)   Body-Part Possessor Ascension Alternation:
      a.   Carrie touched him on the shoulder.
      b.   Carrie touched his shoulder.

(288)   * Causative Alternations:
      a.   Carrie touched the cat.
      b.   * The cat touched.

(289)   * Middle Alternation:
      a.   Carrie touched that cat.
      b.   * That cat touches easily.

(290)   * Instrument Subject Alternation:
      a.   Carrie touched the fence with a stick.
      b.   * The stick touched the fence.
         (on a nonstative interpretation)

(291)   Unintentional interpretation not available:
      a.   Reflexive Object:
         Carrie touched herself. (intentional only)
      b.   Body-Part Object:
         Carol touched her hair. (intentional only)

(292)   * Resultative Phrase:
      * Carrie touched the door open.

(293)   Zero-related Nominal:
         a touch/*give a touch
         a pat/give a pat

Comments: These verbs are pure verbs of contact; they describe surface
contact with no necessary implication that the contact came about through
impact (unlike the verbs of contact by impact; cf. sec. 18). These verbs show
a more limited range of properties than the verbs of contact by impact. For
instance, they do not show the conative alternation. But these verbs do show the
body-part possessor ascension alternation, with the possible exception of *stroke*
and *caress*, which describe a series of contacts. They only allow intentional
action interpretations with body-part or reflexive objects.

21   Verbs of Cutting

21.1   *Cut* Verbs

References: Guerssel et al. (1985), Pinker (1989), Ruhl (1979)

Class Members: chip, clip, cut, hack, hew, saw, scrape, scratch, slash, snip

Properties:

(294)   Carol cut the bread with a knife.

(295)   Conative Alternation:
         a.   Carol cut the bread.
         b.   Carol cut at the bread.

(296)   Body-Part Possessor Ascension Alternation (some verbs):
         a.   Carol cut herself on the thumb.
         b.   Carol cut her thumb.

(297)   * Causative Alternations:
         a.   Carol cut the bread.
         b.   * The bread cut.

(298)   Middle Alternation:
         a.   Carol cut the whole wheat bread.
         b.   Whole wheat bread cuts easily.

(299)   Instrument Subject Alternation:
         a.   Carol cut the bread with a knife.
         b.   The knife cut the bread.

(300)   Characteristic Property of Instrument Alternation (some verbs):
     a. This knife cut the bread.
     b. This knife cuts well.

(301)   Unintentional interpretation available (some verbs):
     a. Reflexive Object:
        Carol cut herself.
     b. Body-Part Object:
        Carol cut her finger.

(302)   Path Phrase (some verbs):
     Carol cut the paper from one end to the other.

(303)   Resultative Phrase:
     Carol cut the envelope open.
     Carol cut the bread to pieces.

(304)   Zero-related Nominal (most verbs):
     a cut, *the cut of the paper
     get a cut on the finger

Comments: The meaning of these verbs involves notions of motion, contact, and effect. Specifically, the meaning of these verbs relates to what Hale and Keyser (1987) call a "separation in material integrity," but it also includes some specification concerning the instrument or means used to bring this result about. The verbs in this class differ from each other in meaning with respect to the instrument or means. Some of these verbs can be used like *build* verbs and, like them, can be found in a benefactive double object construction on this interpretation; those verbs are cross-listed (sec. 26.1). It is possible that more *cut* verbs could potentially show this option. Some of these verbs are also used as *split* verbs and have been cross-listed (sec. 23.2). The *cut* verbs have been compared and contrasted with the *break* verbs; see *Break* Verbs (sec. 45.1) for discussion.

Only some of the *cut* verbs show the body-part possessor ascension alternation; this limitation may arise because only some of them can take body parts as objects. Some of the *cut* verbs allow unintentional, as well as intentional, action interpretations with body part or reflexive objects; certain verbs allowing this option are also listed as *hurt* verbs (sec. 40.8.3) since they involve damage to the body.

21.2   *Carve* Verbs

Class Members: bore, bruise, carve, chip (potatoes), chop, crop, crush, cube, dent, dice, drill, file, fillet, gash, gouge, grate, grind, mangle, mash, mince, mow, nick, notch, perforate, pulverize, punch (paper), prune, shred, slice, slit, spear, squash, squish

Properties:

(305)   Carol carved the stone with a chisel.

(306)   * Conative Alternation:
         a.   Carol carved the stone.
         b. * Carol carved at the stone.

(307)   * Body-Part Possessor Ascension Alternation:
         a. * Carol carved the tree on the branch.
         b.   Carol carved the tree's branch.

(308)   * Causative Alternations:
         a.   Carol carved the stone.
         b. * The stone carved.

(309)   Middle Alternation:
         a.   Carol carved the marble.
         b.   Marble carves easily.

(310)   Instrument Subject Alternation:
         a.   Carol carved the marble with a chisel.
         b.   The chisel carved the marble.

(311)   Characteristic Property of Instrument Alternation (some verbs):
         a.   That chisel carved the statue.
         b.   That chisel carves well.

(312)   Zero-related Nominal:
         a dent, *the dent of the car
         put a dent in the car/get a dent in the car

Comments: The meaning of these verbs involves notions of contact and effect. Their meaning includes a specification of an instrument or a means (*bore*) or a specification of the nature of the result (*dice*); it is possible that these two types should be assigned separate subclasses. The *carve* verbs differ from the *cut* verbs in not showing the conative alternation. They also do not show the body-part possessor ascension alternation. Some of these verbs have zero-related result nominals. Most, but not all, of them allow instrument subjects. Most of them do not seem to be able to take resultative phrases. Some *carve* verbs can be used like *build* verbs and, like them, can be found in the double object construction on this interpretation; those verbs are cross-listed (sec. 26.1). It is possible that more of these verbs could potentially show this option.

22   Verbs of Combining and Attaching

References: Condoravdi and Sanfilippo (1990), Gentner (1978)

These verbs are all related to combining or attaching. Their hallmark is participation in the simple reciprocal alternations, the *together* reciprocal alternations, or both. Members of this class are never found in the *apart* reciprocal alternations. The various subclasses differ according to whether the meanings of their members involve a result or means component.

22.1   *Mix* Verbs

Class Members:
with: blend, combine, commingle, concatenate, connect, fuse, join, link, merge, mingle, mix, pool
into: blend, cream, mix
to: add, connect, join, link, network

Properties:

(313)   Simple Reciprocal Alternation (transitive):
     a. Herman mixed the eggs with the cream. (prepositional variant)
     b. Herman mixed the eggs and the cream. (reciprocal variant)

(314)   Simple Reciprocal Alternation (intransitive; most verbs):
     a. The eggs mixed with the cream.
     b. The eggs and the cream mixed.

(315)   *Together* Reciprocal Alternation (transitive):
     a. Herman mixed the eggs with the cream.
     b. Herman mixed the eggs and the cream together.

(316)   *Together* Reciprocal Alternation (intransitive; most verbs):
     a. The eggs mixed with the cream.
     b. The eggs and the cream mixed together.

(317)   Causative/Inchoative Alternation (most verbs):
     a. I mixed the soap into the water.
        The soap mixed into the water.
     b. I mixed the soap and the water.
        The soap and the water mixed.

(318)   Middle Alternation:
     a. I mixed the eggs with cream.
        Eggs mix well with cream.
     b. I mixed the eggs and cream (together).
        Eggs and cream mix well (together).

Comments: Unlike the *shake* verbs discussed below, the *mix* verbs describe the endstate of their direct object and not the way this endstate is reached. The most salient property of the *mix* verbs is that they undergo both the simple reciprocal alternation and the *together* reciprocal alternation. These verbs fall into different subclasses according to which preposition(s) they select when they take a prepositional phrase complement. When they do not take a prepositional phrase complement, they need a collective NP as object when transitive or a collective NP as subject when intransitive. It is possible that some of these verbs require *together* when they take a collective NP object in the absence of a prepositional phrase complement and should have been included among the *shake* verbs instead. Judgments about this do not always seem to be clear. The causative/inchoative alternation is possible with many of these verbs; the intransitive form of the two reciprocal alternations is possible only with those verbs that participate in the causative/inchoative alternation.

22.2 *Amalgamate* Verbs

Class Members:
with: affiliate, alternate, amalgamate, associate, coalesce, coincide, compare, confederate, confuse, conjoin, consolidate, contrast, correlate, criss-cross, entwine, entangle, harmonize, incorporate, integrate, interchange, interconnect, interlace, interlink, interlock, intermingle, interrelate, intersperse, intertwine, interweave, mate, muddle, ?pair, rhyme, ?team, total, unify, unite
to: engage, introduce, marry, oppose, wed

Properties:

(319)   Simple Reciprocal Alternation (transitive):
     a.   Harriet alternated folk songs with pop songs.
     b.   Harriet alternated folk songs and pop songs.

(320)   Simple Reciprocal Alternation (intransitive):
     a.   Plays alternate with ballets.
     b.   Plays and ballets alternate.

(321)   *Together* Reciprocal Alternation (transitive):
     a.   Harriet alternated folk songs with pop songs.
     b.   *Harriet alternated folk songs and pop songs together.

(322)   *Together* Reciprocal Alternation (intransitive):
     a.   Plays alternate with ballets.
     b.   *Plays and ballets alternate together.

(323)   Causative/Inchoative Alternation (most verbs):
     a.   Harriet interconnected the pieces.

The pieces interconnected.
   b.   Harriet alternated folk songs with pop songs.
       Folk songs alternated with pop songs.

(324)   Middle Alternation:
      a.   Harriet interconnected the pieces.
         The pieces interconnect easily.
      b.   Harriet alternated folk songs with pop songs.
         Folk songs alternate well with pop songs.

Comments: The most salient property of the *amalgamate* verbs is that they undergo the simple reciprocal alternation, but they are set apart from the other verbs of combining and attaching in not being found in the *together* reciprocal alternation. Unlike the *shake* verbs discussed below, the *amalgamate* verbs describe the endstate of the direct object and not the way this endstate is reached. These verbs fall into different subclasses according to which prepositions they select when they take a prepositional phrase as complement. When they do not take a prepositional phrase complement, they need a collective NP as object when transitive and a collective NP as subject when intransitive. The causative/inchoative alternation is possible with many of the verbs in this class that take the preposition *with* as head of their prepositional phrase complement; the intransitive form of the simple reciprocal alternation is only found with those verbs that participate in the causative/inchoative alternation.

22.3   *Shake* Verbs

References: Leitner (1974)

Class Members:
with: band, beat, bundle, cluster, collate, gather, glom, group, herd, jumble, lump, mass, package, pair, roll, scramble, shake, shuffle, stir, whip, whisk
into: beat, collect, scramble, shake, shuffle, splice, stir, swirl, whip, whisk
to: append, attach, baste, bind, bond, fasten, fuse, graft, moor, sew, splice, stick, weld

Properties:

(325)   Herman whipped the cream.

(326)   *Together* Reciprocal Alternation (transitive):
      a.   Herman whipped the sugar into the cream.
      b.   Herman whipped the sugar and the cream together.

(327)   * Simple Reciprocal Alternation (transitive):
      a.   Herman whipped the sugar into the cream.
      b. * Herman whipped the sugar and the cream.

(328)   * Causative Alternations (with a few exceptions):
     a.   Herman whipped the sugar into the cream.
       * The sugar whipped into the cream.
     b.   Herman whipped the sugar and the cream together.
       * The sugar and the cream whipped together.

(329)   Middle Alternation:
     a.   Herman whipped the sugar into the cream.
        Sugar whips into cream easily.
     b.   Herman whipped the sugar and the cream together.
        Sugar and cream whip together easily.

Comments: The *shake* verbs differ from the *mix* verbs discussed above in specifying the manner in which things are combined, rather than the result of the combining. These verbs only participate in the *together* reciprocal alternation, not in the simple reciprocal alternation. They fall into different subclasses according to which prepositions they select when they take a prepositional phrase as complement, although many of the verbs listed above take either *with* or *into*. The verbs taking *to* do not seem to allow other choices of preposition while retaining the same sense. When the *shake* verbs do not take a prepositional phrase complement, they need a collective NP as object. Most of these verbs are not found in the causative alternations and, therefore, do not show the intransitive form of any of the reciprocal alternations. Some of those verbs which do have an intransitive use are included under the *herd* verbs; the properties relating to this use are described there (sec. 47.5.2). Many of these verbs are also listed under other classes. The *tape* verbs discussed below behave exactly like those *shake* verbs that take the preposition *to*, except that they are all related to nominals that name types of fasteners.

22.4   *Tape* Verbs

References: Duszak (1980), Green (1972), Jespersen (1942), Kiparsky (1982), Lehrer (1990), Leitner (1974), Marchand (1969, 1974), J. McCawley (1971), Sehnert and Sharwood-Smith (1973), Watt (1973)

Class Members: anchor, band, belt, bolt, bracket, buckle, button, cement, chain, clamp, clasp, clip, epoxy, fetter, glue, gum, handcuff, harness, hinge, hitch, hook, knot, lace, lash, lasso, latch, leash, link, lock, loop, manacle, moor, muzzle, nail, padlock, paste, peg, pin, plaster, rivet, rope, screw, seal, shackle, skewer, solder, staple, stitch, strap, string, tack, tape, tether, thumbtack, tie, trammel, wire, yoke, zip

Properties:

(330)   Linda taped the picture to/on/onto the wall.

(331)   * Locative Alternation:
   a.   Linda taped the picture onto the wall.
   b. * Linda taped the wall with the picture.

(332)   * Simple Reciprocal Alternation (transitive):
   a.   Linda taped the label to the cover.
   b. * Linda taped the label and the cover.

(333)   *Together* Reciprocal Alternation (transitive):
   a.   Linda taped the label to the cover.
   b.   Linda taped the label and the cover together.

(334)   * Causative Alternations:
   a.   Linda taped the label to the cover.
       * The label taped to the cover.
   b.   Linda taped the label and the cover together.
       * The label and the cover taped together.

(335)   Middle Alternation:
   a.   Linda taped the label to the cover.
       Labels tape easily to that kind of cover.
   b.   Linda taped the label and the cover together.
       Labels and covers tape together easily.

(336)   Resultative Phrase:
   Linda taped the box shut.

(337)   Cognate *With* Phrase:
   Linda taped the box with two-sided tape.
   ? Linda taped the box with tape.

(338)   Zero-related Nominal:
   tape

Comments: These verbs are like those *shake* verbs which take *to* prepositional phrases, except that they are all zero-related to nouns that name fasteners—instruments used to attach one thing to another. The meanings of these verbs, like those of the *shake* verbs but unlike those of the *mix* verbs, relate to the manner/means in which things are combined, rather than the result of the combining. Although these verbs do not participate in the simple reciprocal alternation, they participate in the *together* reciprocal alternation. When they do not take a prepositional phrase complement, they need a collective NP as object. When they do take a prepositional phrase complement, they may allow some locative prepositions other than *to* to head this PP. Since these verbs are not found in the causative alternations, they do not show the intransitive form of the *together* reciprocal alternation. Like the *butter* verbs (sec. 9.9), they allow cognate *with* phrases; the object of *with* is an NP headed by the noun that the verb derives its name from. Such *with* phrases are typically best if they contribute additional information about the fastener through the use of a modifier of some kind.

22.5 *Cling* Verbs

Class Members: adhere, cleave, cling

Properties:

(339)   The child clung to her mother.

(340)   ∗ Simple Reciprocal Alternation (intransitive):
     a.   The child clung to her mother.
     b. ∗ The child and her mother clung.

(341)   *Together* Reciprocal Alternation (intransitive):
     a.   The child clung to her mother.
     b.   The child and her mother clung together.

(342)   ∗ Causative Alternations:
     a.   The child clung to her mother.
     b. ∗ The war clung the child to her mother.

Comments: These verbs are intransitive verbs describing the attachment of one entity to a second. Like the *shake* verbs, they show the *together* reciprocal alternation, but since they are intransitive, they show the intransitive version of this alternation. In the *together* reciprocal alternation, these verbs need a collective NP as subject when they do not take a prepositional phrase complement. They do not have a transitive use.

23   Verbs of Separating and Disassembling

References: Condoravdi (1990)

These verbs are all related to separating or disassembling. They fall into subclasses according to the participation of their members in the simple reciprocal alternations or the *apart* reciprocal alternations. Verbs in this class are never found in the *together* reciprocal alternations. The various subclasses differ according to whether their meanings involve results or means.

23.1 *Separate* Verbs

Class Members: decouple, differentiate, disconnect, disentangle, dissociate, distinguish, divide, divorce, part, segregate, separate, sever

Properties:

(343)   Simple Reciprocal Alternation (transitive):
       a.   I separated the yolk from the white.
       b.   I separated the yolk and the white.

(344)   Simple Reciprocal Alternation (intransitive):
       a.   The yolk separated from the white.
       b.   The yolk and the white separated.

(345)   * *Apart* Reciprocal Alternation (transitive):
       a.   I separated the yolk from the white.
       b.?? I separated the yolk and the white apart.

(346)   * *Apart* Reciprocal Alternation (intransitive):
       a.   The yolk separated from the white.
       b. * The yolk and the white separated apart.

(347)   Causative/Inchoative Alternation (some verbs):
       a.   I separated the cream from the milk.
          The cream separated from the milk.
       b.   I separated the egg yolk and the egg white.
          The egg yolk and the egg white separated.

(348)   Middle Alternation:
       a.   I separated the cream from the milk.
          Cream separates easily from milk.
       b.   I separated the egg yolks and the egg whites.
          Egg yolks and egg whites separate easily.

(349)   * Locative Alternation:
       a.   I separated the cream from the milk.
       b. * I separated the milk of the cream.

Comments: The characteristic property of the *separate* verbs is that they undergo the simple reciprocal alternation, but they are not found in the *apart* reciprocal alternation, the inverse of the *together* reciprocal alternation. Unlike the *split* verbs discussed below, the *separate* verbs have meanings that specify the endstate of their direct object and not the means or manner in which this endstate is reached. When these verbs do not take a prepositional phrase complement, they need a collective NP as object when used transitively and a collective NP subject when used intransitively. The causative/inchoative alternation is possible with the verbs in this class.

23.2 *Split* Verbs

Class Members: blow, break, cut, draw, hack, hew, kick, knock, pry, pull, push, rip, roll, saw, shove, slip, split, tear, tug, yank

Properties:

(350) * Simple Reciprocal Alternation (transitive):
      a.   I broke the twig off (of) the branch.
      b. * I broke the twig and the branch.
         (on roughly the interpretation of the (a) sentence)

(351) * Simple Reciprocal Alternation (intransitive):
      a.   The twig broke off (of) the branch.
      b. * The twig and the branch broke.
         (on roughly the interpretation of the (a) sentence)

(352) *Apart* Reciprocal Alternation (transitive):
      a.   I broke the twig off (of) the branch.
      b.   I broke the twig and the branch apart.
         (on roughly the interpretation of the (a) sentence)

(353) *Apart* Reciprocal Alternation (intransitive):
      a.   The twig broke off (of) the branch.
      b.   The twig and the branch broke apart.
         (on roughly the interpretation of the (a) sentence)

(354) Causative/Inchoative Alternation (most verbs):
      a.   I broke the twig off (of) the branch.
         The twig broke off (of) the branch.
      b.   I broke the twig and the branch apart.
         The twig and the branch broke apart.

(355) Middle Alternation:
      a.   I broke twigs off (of) those branches.
         Twigs break off of those branches easily.
      b.   I broke those twigs and branches apart.
         Those twigs and branches break apart easily.

Comments: These verbs are also listed under a variety of other classes, including the *break* verbs (sec. 45.1), the *cut* verbs (sec. 21.1), and the *push/pull* verbs (sec. 12). In the use illustrated here, each of these verbs manifests an extended sense which might be paraphrased "separate by V-ing," where "V" is the basic meaning of that verb. It is possible that additional verbs from these other classes might qualify as *split* verbs. The *split* verbs do not describe inherently reciprocal actions. This property is probably reflected in the fact that these verbs show the *apart* reciprocal alternation but not the simple reciprocal alternation. In the *apart* reciprocal alternation, they need a collective NP as object when they do not take a prepositional phrase complement. Many of these verbs participate in the causative/inchoative alternation, and they are also found in the intransitive version of the *apart* reciprocal alternation.

23.3   *Disassemble* Verbs

References: Bladin (1911), Cruse (1979), Marchand (1973, 1974)

Class Members: detach, disassemble, disconnect, partition, sift, sunder, unbolt, unbuckle, unbutton, unchain, unclamp, unclasp, unclip, unfasten, unglue, unhinge, unhitch, unhook, unlace, unlatch, unlock, unleash, unpeg, unpin, unscrew, unshackle, unstaple, unstitch, untie, unzip

Properties:

(356)   I unscrewed the handle.

(357)   * Simple Reciprocal Alternation (transitive):
      a.   I unscrewed the handle from the box.
      b. * I unscrewed the handle and the box.

(358)   * *Apart* Reciprocal Alternation (transitive):
      a.   I unscrewed the handle from the box.
      b. * I unscrewed the handle and the box apart.

(359)   * Causative Alternations (a few exceptions):
      a.   I unscrewed the handle from the box.
      b. * The handle unscrewed from the box.

(360)   Middle Alternation:
      a.   I unscrewed that new handle (from the box).
      b.   That new handle unscrews (*from the box) easily.

Comments: The meaning of these verbs includes a specification of the manner or means in which a separation can be brought about, without specifying the result of this process. Many of these verbs are formed by attaching the reversative prefix *un–* to verbs that belong to the *tape* class (sec. 22.4); it is possible that additional members of the *tape* class might allow for this. The *disassemble* verbs are not found in any reciprocal alternations.

23.4   *Differ* Verbs

Class Members: differ, diverge

Properties:

(361)   The winter schedule differed from the spring schedule.

(362)   Simple Reciprocal Alternation (intransitive):
     a.   This flyer differs from that flyer.
     b.   This flyer and that flyer differ.

(363)   * *Apart* Reciprocal Alternation (intransitive):
     a.   This flyer differs from that flyer.
     b. * This flyer and that flyer differ apart.

(364)   * Causative Alternations:
     a.   This flyer differs from that flyer.
     b. * I differed this flyer from that flyer.

Comments: These verbs are intransitive verbs describing a difference, but not necessarily an actual separation, between one entity and a second. Like the *separate* verbs, they show the simple reciprocal alternation, but since they are intransitive, they show the intransitive version of this alternation. In the simple reciprocal alternation, these verbs need a collective NP as subject when they do not take a prepositional phrase complement. They do not have a transitive counterpart.

24   Verbs of Coloring

Class Members: color, distemper, dye, enamel, glaze, japan, lacquer, paint, shellac, spraypaint, stain, tint, varnish

Properties:

(365)   Phyllis dyed the dress.

(366)   Resultative Phrase:
     Phyllis dyed the dress blue.
     Phyllis dyed the dress a very pale shade of blue.

(367)   Cognate *With* Phrase:
     Phyllis dyed the dress with a new colorfast blue dye.

Comments: These verbs describe changing the color of an entity, usually by the application of some coating that covers the surface of the entity and, therefore, changes its color. All of these verbs are zero-related to nouns that name such coatings. Some works have included these verbs among the *butter* verbs (cf. sec. 9.9) since their meaning could be paraphrased as "put X on (something)," where X is the coating that the verb takes its name from. And these verbs do show the properties of *butter* verbs. For instance, like them, they may take a cognate *with* phrase; the object of *with* is an NP headed by the noun that the verb derives its name from, or a noun that bears the hyponym relation to the noun that the verb derives its name from. Such *with* phrases are typically most acceptable if they include a modifier that contributes additional information about the thing that is being put somewhere. However, unlike the *butter* verbs, most verbs of coloring may be found with a resultative phrase, specifically a phrase expressing the color of the entity that becomes coated as a result of the action referred to by the verb.

25 Image Creation Verbs

References: Dowty (1991), Fellbaum and Kegl (1989), Fillmore (1977b), Fraser (1971), Rappaport and B. Levin (1985)

This set of verb classes contains verbs relating to the creation of images on surfaces.

25.1 Verbs of Image Impression

Class Members: appliqué, emboss, embroider, engrave, etch, imprint, incise, inscribe, mark, paint, set, sign, stamp, tattoo

Properties:

(368)   Smith inscribed his name on the ring.

(369)   Smith inscribed his name over the door/under the picture.

(370)   Image Impression Alternation:
      a.   Smith inscribed his name on the ring. (locative variant)
      b.   Smith inscribed the ring with his name. (*with* variant)

(371)   Unspecified Object Alternation:
      a.   Smith was inscribing the rings.
      b.   Smith was inscribing.

(372)   Process Nominal:
      the inscription of the motto
     * the inscription of the wall

(373)   Result Nominal:
         the inscription (on the wall)

Comments: The hallmark of this subset of the image creation verbs is the ability to show the image impression alternation (sec. 2.7). This alternation has sometimes been considered to be an instance of the locative alternation since it superficially resembles the form of the locative alternation shown by the *spray/load* verbs; however, the image impression verbs do not appear to show the "holistic/partitive" effect associated with the *spray/load* verbs. This difference may not warrant the recognition of the image impression verbs as a distinct class if the lack of the "holistic/partitive" effect can receive an independent explanation. Nevertheless, the image impression verbs have been included as a distinct class since they form a semantically coherent subset of verbs whose meaning differs from that of the *spray/load* verbs. The acceptability of the image impression verbs in the unspecified object construction varies.

25.2 *Scribble* Verbs

Class Members: carve, chalk, charcoal, copy, crayon, doodle, draw, forge, ink, paint, pencil, plot, print, scratch, scrawl, scribble, sketch, spraypaint, stencil, trace, type, write

Properties:

(374)   The jeweller printed the name.

(375)   a.   The jeweller printed the name on the ring.
         b.   The jeweller printed the name over the door/under the picture/onto the cup.

(376)   * Image Impression Alternation:
         a.   The jeweller scribbled his name on the contract.
         b. * The jeweller scribbled the contract with his name.

(377)   Unspecified Object Alternation (some verbs):
         a.   Smith was scribbling his notes.
         b.   Smith was scribbling.

(378)   Zero-related Nominal:
         a scribble, a sketch
         a crayon, chalk

Comments: Although these verbs belong to the larger class of image creation verbs, they show only one of the variants of the image impression alternation. The meaning of most of these verbs includes a specification of a manner or instrument; a number of them are zero-related to nouns that name instruments used for writing or drawing. Those verbs which are not zero-related to nouns naming instruments have related result nominals, often zero-related nominals. Some of these verbs also take "effected objects;" they are cross-listed under the *build* verbs (sec. 26.1). A few of these verbs—primarily the denominal ones—do not participate in the unspecified object alternation.

25.3   *Illustrate* Verbs

Class Members: address, adorn, autograph, brand, date, decorate, embellish, endorse, illuminate, illustrate, initial, label, letter, monogram, ornament, tag

Properties:

(379)   The jeweller decorated the ring.

(380)   The jeweller decorated the ring with the name.

(381)   * Image Impression Alternation:
      a.   * The jeweller decorated the name on the ring.
      b.   The jeweller decorated the ring with the name.

(382)   Process Nominal (some verbs):
      the decoration of the room

(383)   Result Nominal (some verbs):
      a decoration

(384)   Zero-related Nominal (some verbs):
      a monogram, an address

Comments: Although these verbs belong to the larger class of image creation verbs, they show only one of the variants of the image impression alternation. The meaning of most of these verbs includes a specification of the result of the image impression process. A number of these verbs, such as *autograph* and *monogram,* are zero-related to a noun that names the "image." Some works have included verbs like *autograph* among the *butter* verbs because their meaning can be paraphrased as "put X on (something)," where X is the noun the verb takes its name from; however, they have not been cross-listed under the *butter* verbs, since the zero-related noun appears to be a so-called "effected object."

25.4   *Transcribe* Verbs

References: Sehnert and Sharwood-Smith (1973)

Class Members: copy, film, forge (signature), microfilm, photocopy, photograph, record, tape, televise, transcribe, type

Properties:

(385)   The secretary transcribed the speech.

(386)   * Image Impression Alternation:
           a.   The secretary transcribed the speech into the record.
           b. * The secretary transcribed the record with the speech.

(387)   Zero-related Nominal:
           a record, a transcript
           a tape, a microfilm

Comments: As discussed by Dowty (1991), these verbs take as their direct object a "representation source"; that is, their object refers to the source that will be used to create a "representation." This set of verbs differs somewhat from the other verbs included in the larger class of image creation verbs, and it might actually belong elsewhere in the larger organizational scheme. *Transcribe* verbs do not show the image impression alternation. A few may cooccur with a locative prepositional phrase, but the exact function of this prepositional phrase requires further investigation. Some of these verbs are zero-related to nouns that name the medium on which the representation is made. Many have related result nominals; often these are zero-related nominals.

26   Verbs of Creation and Transformation

References: Atkins, Kegl, and B. Levin (1988), Bertram (1992), Croft (1985), Dixon (1991), Dowty (1991), Farsi (1974), Fellbaum (1990), Fellbaum and Kegl (1989), Gawron (1983), Grimshaw and Vikner (1990), Hopper (1985), Jackendoff (1990b), Jespersen (1949), Jolly (1987), Langacker (1991), G. Miller and Fellbaum (1991), Napoli (1989a), Nash-Webber (1971), Parsons (1989, 1990), Wierzbicka (1980)

The members of most of the verb classes identified in this section are transitive verbs, taking as one argument an agent that creates or transforms an entity; however, the *turn* verbs can be used as intransitive verbs that simply describe the transformation of an entity, without reference to an agent. A subset of the *build* verbs, listed separately as the *grow* verbs, can also be used intransitively.

A number of verbs listed in the various subclasses of verbs of creation and transformation are also found listed as members of other verb classes. Typically, these are verbs that have other uses describing activities that might result in the creation or assembly of an entity; usually, the other uses of these verbs are more basic. This is particularly true of certain verbs of change of state (especially, verbs of change of shape and verbs of cooking), verbs of writing, and verbs of attaching. In their use as verbs of creation and transformation, these verbs take what are called "effected objects"—objects brought into existence as a result of the action named by the verb—as well as objects that qualify as either raw material or Dowty's (1991) "representation source": *paint a picture* vs. *paint a view*, *carve a doll* vs. *carve wood*.

26.1 *Build* Verbs

Class Members: arrange, assemble, bake, blow (bubbles, glass), build, carve, cast, chisel, churn, compile, cook, crochet, cut, develop, embroider, fashion, fold, forge (metal), grind, grow, hack, hammer, hatch, knit, make, mold, pound, roll, sculpt, sew, shape, spin (wool), stitch, weave, whittle

Properties:

(388)   Material/Product Alternation (transitive):
    a.   Martha carved a toy out of the piece of wood.
    b.   Martha carved the piece of wood into a toy.

(389)   * Total Transformation Alternation (transitive):
    a.   Martha carved the piece of wood into a toy.
    b.   * Martha carved the piece of wood from a branch into a toy.

(390)   Unspecified Object Alternation:
    a.   Martha carves toys.
    b.   Martha carves.

(391)   Benefactive Alternation:
    a.   Martha carved a toy (out of a piece of wood) for the baby.
         Martha carved the baby a toy (out of a piece of wood).
    b.   Martha carved a piece of wood (into a toy) for the baby.
       * Martha carved the baby a piece of wood (into a toy).

(392)   * Causative Alternations:
    a.   Martha carved a toy out of the piece of wood.
      * A toy carved out of the piece of wood.
    b.   Martha carved the piece of wood into a toy.
      * The piece of wood carved into a toy.

(393)   Raw Material Subject Alternation (some verbs):
    a.   Martha carved beautiful toys out of this wood.
    b.   This wood carves beautiful toys.

(394)   Sum of Money Subject Alternation (few verbs):
         a.   The contractor will build (you) a house for $100,000.
         b. $100,000 will build (you) a house.

Comments: These verbs describe the creation of a product through the transformation of raw materials. If the creation is done on someone's behalf, then
these verbs are like verbs of obtaining and, like the *get* verbs, are found in the
benefactive alternation; however, these verbs have not been cross-listed among
the *get* verbs. Many of the verbs listed here belong to a variety of other classes
in their basic sense (verbs of cooking, verbs of cutting, etc.) and show extended
senses as *build* verbs. It is possible that additional verbs from these classes
might also show such extended uses. A small subset of *build* verbs can be used
intransitively; these verbs are listed below as the *grow* verbs, together with a
description of the properties related to their intransitive use.

26.2 *Grow* Verbs

Class Members: develop, evolve, grow, hatch, mature

Properties:

(395)   Material/Product Alternation (intransitive):
         a.   That acorn will grow into an oak tree.
         b.   An oak tree will grow from that acorn.

(396)   * Total Transformation Alternation (intransitive):
         a.   That acorn will grow into an oak tree.
         b. * That acorn will grow from a seed into an oak tree.

(397)   Causative/Inchoative Alternation:
         a.   The gardener grew that acorn into an oak tree.
              That acorn will grow into an oak tree.
         b.   The gardener grew an oak tree from that acorn.
              An oak tree will grow from that acorn.

Comments: These verbs simply describe the transformation of an entity from
one form to another; either the source or the goal may be the subject of the verb,
with the other being expressed in a prepositional phrase. Thus the members
of this class show an alternation that might be considered the intransitive
(unaccusative) counterpart of the material/product alternation shown by the
build verbs. With the possible exception of *mature*, these verbs participate
in the causative/inchoative alternation. When used transitively, they show the
behavior of *build* verbs and are cross-listed with these (cf. above); the properties
related to their transitive use are described under *Build* Verbs.

26.3   Verbs of Preparing

References: Jackendoff (1990a, 1990b), Wierzbicka (1988c)

Class Members: bake (cake), blend (drink), boil (egg, tea), brew (coffee), clean, clear (path), cook (meal), fix (meal), fry (egg), grill, hardboil (egg), iron, light (fire), mix (drink), poach (egg), pour (drink), prepare (meal), roast (chicken), roll, run (bath), scramble (egg), set (table), softboil (egg), toast, toss (salad), wash

Properties:

(398)   Donna fixed a sandwich.

(399)   * Material/Product Alternation (transitive):
      a. ? Donna fixed a sandwich from last night's leftovers.
      b. * Donna fixed last night's leftovers into a sandwich.

(400)   Benefactive Alternation:
      a.   Donna fixed a sandwich for me.
      b.   Donna fixed me a sandwich.

(401)   * Causative Alternations:
      a.   Donna fixed a sandwich.
      b. * A sandwich fixed.

Comments: The term "verbs of preparing" comes from Wierzbicka (1988c). Many of these verbs describe the preparation of food; most of the remainder deal with other types of household activities. These verbs describe the creation of a product, usually through the transformation of raw materials. However, they are not found in the material/product alternation, since they may only take the product ("effected object") as direct object. The raw material may be expressed in a prepositional phrase, though often these verbs seem best when the raw material is not expressed at all. Some of these verbs take as direct objects NPs that can refer to either the raw material or the product (e.g., *cake* can refer to either the batter or the baked cake), although with these verbs such NPs have the product interpretation.

    When the preparation is done on someone's behalf, then these verbs are like verbs of obtaining and, like the *get* verbs, are found in the benefactive alternation; however, they have not been cross-listed. A number of these verbs are verbs of cooking in their basic sense (cf. sec. 45.3) and are cross-listed here; possibly, more verbs of cooking could have been included here.

26.4   *Create* Verbs

Class Members: coin, compose, compute, concoct, construct, create, derive, design, dig, fabricate, form, invent, manufacture, mint, model, organize, produce, recreate, style, synthesize

Properties:

(402)   * Material/Product Alternation (transitive):
    a.   David constructed a house (out of/from bricks).
    b. * David constructed the bricks into a house.

(403)   * Benefactive Alternation (most verbs):
    a.   David constructed a house for me.
    b. * David constructed me a house.

(404)   * Causative Alternations:
    a.   David constructed the house.
    b. * The house constructed.

(405)   * Raw Material Subject Alternation:
    a.   David constructed a house from those new bricks.
    b. * Those new bricks constructed a house.

(406)   * David constructed the mansion [from bricks] [into a house].

Comments: This set of verbs of creation and transformation takes an "effected object"—an NP that refers to the created object. Many of them can take a *from* phrase specifying the raw material that the product was created from, but none of them can express the raw material as a direct object. Thus, these verbs are not found in the material/product alternation. Although they are found with benefactive *for* phrases, few, if any, of them are found in the double object construction; this might be due to the so-called Latinate restriction on this construction (see sec. 2.1, Dative Alternation).

26.5 *Knead* Verbs

Class Members: beat, bend, coil, collect, compress, fold, freeze, knead, melt, shake, squash, squish, squeeze, twirl, twist, wad, whip, wind, work

Properties:

(407)   * Material/Product Alternation (transitive):
    a.   I kneaded the dough (into a loaf).
    b. * I kneaded a loaf (from the dough).

(408)   Causative/Inchoative Alternation (some verbs):
    a.   I kneaded the dough (into a loaf).
      * The dough kneaded (into a loaf).
    b.   I twirled the dough into a pretzel.
      The dough twirled into a pretzel.

(409)   * Raw Material Subject Alternation:
      a. * I kneaded a good loaf from this dough.
      b. * This dough kneads a good loaf.

(410)   * Total Transformation Alternation (transitive):
      a.   I kneaded the dough into a loaf.
      b. * I kneaded [the dough] [from a lump] [into a loaf].

Comments: The members of this subset of the verbs of creation and transformation are also not found in the material/product alternation. These verbs describe the bringing about of a change of shape in an entity; this transformation can be viewed as a type of creation. They take the raw material/original shape as their direct object and express the product/resultant shape in a prepositional phrase. They do not allow the product to be expressed as their direct object. Many of these verbs are also listed as verbs of change of state (sec. 45) or as verbs of combining (sec. 22); it is possible that more verbs from those classes would also show the behavior of this set of verbs. Some of the verbs that are cross-listed require the *into* phrase in this sense (e.g., *twirl*).

26.6 *Turn* Verbs

Class Members: alter, change, convert, metamorphose, transform, transmute, turn

Properties:

(411)   The witch turned him from a prince into a frog.

(412)   Total Transformation Alternation (transitive):
      a.   The witch turned him into a frog.
      b.   The witch turned him from a prince into a frog.

(413)   Total Transformation Alternation (intransitive; most verbs):
      a.   He turned into a frog.
      b.   He turned from a prince into a frog.

(414)   Causative/Inchoative Alternation (most verbs):
      a.   The witch turned him into a frog.
         He turned into a frog.
      b.   The witch turned him from a prince into a frog.
         He turned from a prince into a frog.

(415)   * Material/Product Alternation (transitive):
      a. * The witch turned him from a prince.
      b.   The witch turned him into a frog.

(416) * Material/Product Alternation (intransitive):
      a. * He turned from a prince.
      b.   He turned into a frog.

(417) * The witch turned him.

Comments: These verbs describe a complete transformation; most of them participate in the causative/inchoative alternation and, therefore, are found in transitive and intransitive forms. These verbs take the following three arguments, whether transitive or intransitive: the entity undergoing the transformation, as well as the initial ("source") and final ("goal") forms of this entity. When transitive, these verbs also take an agent. The entity undergoing the transformation is always expressed as the direct object if the verb is transitive, and as the subject if the verb is intransitive; the other arguments are expressed in prepositional phrases. The final state always must be expressed, while the initial state can only be expressed if the final state is expressed. These verbs do not participate in the material/product alternation.

26.7   Performance Verbs

References: P. Austin (1982), Dowty (1991)

Class Members: chant (prayer), choreograph (dance), compose (symphony), dance (waltz), direct (movie, play), draw (picture), hum (tune), intone (prayer), perform (play), paint (picture), play (music, game), produce (movie), recite (poem), silkscreen, sing (song), spin (story), take (picture), whistle (tune), write (book)

Properties:

(418)   Sandy sang.

(419)   Sandy sang a song/a ballad.

(420)   Dative Alternation (some verbs):
      a.   Sandy sang a song to me.
      b.   Sandy sang me a song.

(421)   Benefactive Alternation (some verbs):
      a.   Sandy sang a song for me.
      b.   Sandy sang me a song.

(422)   Unspecified Object Alternation:
      a.   Sandy sang a song.
      b.   Sandy sang.

(423)   * Causative Alternations:
      a.   Sandy sang a song.
      b.   * The song sang.

Comments: Like many of the other verbs of creation and transformation, all of these verbs take effected objects and do not allow the expression of a raw material argument. These verbs describe performances, broadly speaking, and these performances are themselves the effected object. Some of these verbs appear to allow either the benefactive or the dative alternation. When these verbs are found in the double object form, it may not always be clear whether it is the benefactive or the dative interpretation that is intended; the alternating verbs have only been listed under the benefactive alternation in Part I. Further study is needed to determine whether it is simply difficult to distinguish these two interpretations with this set of verbs or whether there are in fact two interpretations. It is also possible that if the double object construction is associated with two interpretations, these interpretations are associated with different senses of these verbs. The *waltz* verbs, although listed under verbs of motion (sec. 51.5), could also be viewed as performance verbs.

27   *Engender* Verbs

Class Members: beget, cause, create, engender, generate, shape, spawn

Properties:

(424)   Racial inequality engenders conflict.

(425)   * Causative Alternations:
      a.   Racial inequality engenders conflict.
      b.   * Conflict engenders.

Comments: These verbs describe a causal relationship between the two arguments, which are typically both abstract NPs. One argument brings about the existence of the other.

28   *Calve* Verbs

References: Bladin (1911), E.V. Clark and H.H. Clark (1979), Duszak (1980), Hale and Keyser (1991, 1992), Jespersen (1942), Karius (1985), Marchand (1969, 1974)

Class Members: calve, cub, fawn, foal, kitten, lamb, litter, pup, spawn, whelp

Properties:

(426)   The cat kittened.

Comments: The verbs in this class are zero-related to nominals, which are the names of the young of certain animals. Each of these verbs relates to giving birth to the animal from which the verb takes its name.

29   Verbs with Predicative Complements

References: J.L. Austin (1962), Bolinger (1973), Borkin (1973, 1984), Curme (1931), Dixon (1991), Dowty (1991), Emonds (1985), J. McCawley (1977), Poutsma (1904), Quirk et al. (1985), Sinha (1973), Stowell (1989, 1991a, 1991b), Vendler (1972), Wierzbicka (1987)

The verbs in this section are used to characterize or describe properties of entities. The hallmark of these verbs is that they all take predicative complements. Most of the subclasses include verbs which have the predicative complement predicated of the immediately postverbal NP. The *masquerade* verbs are the exception; they have the predicative complement predicated of their subject.

The verbs in this class are found in a variety of frames. The most well-represented are the frames 'NP V NP NP', 'NP V NP *as* NP', 'NP V NP *to be* NP', as well as their counterparts with adjective phrases 'NP V NP AP', 'NP V NP *as* AP', 'NP V NP *to be* AP'; the adjectival frames are not treated here. In each of these frames, a predicative complement expressed by the second NP or the AP is predicated of the immediately postverbal NP. The frame associated with two postverbal NPs ('NP V NP NP') superficially resembles the double object variant associated with the dative alternation. Despite the superficial similarity, the two frames are given different syntactic analyses. The 'NP NP' sequence associated with the *as* alternation is often analyzed as a small clause. None of the verbs in this class show the dative alternation.

The verbs fall into subclasses according to the frames they are found in. Since it is sometimes difficult to determine which of the possible frames a given verb is associated with, the classification will need to be refined. Some of these verbs also take other types of sentential complements, but these are not treated systematically here. Further study is needed to identify the finer semantic criteria that distinguish between the verb classes identified in this section.

29.1 *Appoint* Verbs

Class Members: acknowledge, adopt, appoint, consider, crown, deem, designate, elect, esteem, imagine, mark, nominate, ordain, proclaim, rate, reckon, report, want

Properties:

(427)   *As* Alternation:
    a.   The president appointed Smith press secretary.
    b.   The president appointed Smith as press secretary.

(428)   * Dative Alternation:
    a.   The president appointed Smith press secretary.
    b.   * The president appointed press secretary to Smith.

(429)   Infinitival Copular Clause (some verbs):
    The president appointed Smith to be press secretary.

Comments: These verbs may take two postverbal NPs or a postverbal NP followed by an *as* phrase. It is not clear what determines whether a verb belongs to this class or to the *characterize* or *dub* classes below. Possibly, this class should not be recognized as a separate class; it may be preferable to list the verbs in it under both the *dub* verbs and the *characterize* verbs. Some of the listed verbs take other types of sentential complements, but those are not treated here.

29.2 *Characterize* Verbs

Class Members: accept, address, appreciate, bill, cast, certify, characterize, choose, cite, class, classify, confirm, count, define, describe, diagnose, disguise, employ, engage, enlist, enroll, enter, envisage, establish, esteem, hail, herald, hire, honor, identify, imagine, incorporate, induct, intend, lampoon, offer, oppose, paint, portray, praise, qualify, rank, recollect, recommend, regard, reinstate, reject, remember, represent, repudiate, reveal, salute, see, select, stigmatize, take, train, treat, use, value, view, visualize

Properties:

(430)   * *As* Alternation:
    a.   Angela characterized Shelly as a lifesaver.
    b.   * Angela characterized Shelly a lifesaver.

(431)   Infinitival Copular Clause (few verbs):
         * Angela characterized Shelly to be a lifesaver.
         Angela imagined Shelly to be the perfect candidate.

Comments: These verbs allow only the frame 'NP V NP *as* NP' and not the frame involving two postverbal NPs. Some of these verbs also figure among the *admire*-type psych-verbs and the judgment verbs. Interestingly, very few of these verbs are found in the 'NP V NP *to be* NP' frame. Some of them may take other kinds of sentential complements. The impossibility of the dative alternation is not illustrated here, since the verbs appear in neither of the frames associated with this alternation.

29.3 *Dub* Verbs

Class Members: anoint, baptize, brand, call, christen, consecrate, crown, decree, dub, label, make, name, nickname, pronounce, rule, stamp, style, term, vote

Properties:

(432)   * *As* Alternation:
         a.   The captain named the ship Seafarer.
         b. * The captain named the ship as Seafarer.

(433)   * Dative Alternation:
         a.   The captain named the ship Seafarer.
         b. * The captain named Seafarer to the ship.

(434)   * Infinitival Copular Clause:
         * The captain named the ship to be Seafarer.

Comments: Almost all of these verbs relate to the bestowing of names. These verbs allow only the frame involving two postverbal NPs, and not the frame 'NP V NP *as* NP'. None of these verbs are found in the infinitival copular clause frame, 'NP V NP *to be* NP'. There may be some differences of opinion concerning whether all of the *dub* verbs really do not allow infinitival complements; if some do allow them, those verbs should be included with the *declare* verbs below, which differ from the *dub* verbs in this respect.

29.4 *Declare* Verbs

Class Members: adjudge, adjudicate, assume, avow, believe, confess, declare, fancy, find, judge, presume, profess, prove, suppose, think, warrant

Properties:

(435)   * *As* Alternation:
         a.   The president declared Smith press secretary.
         b. * The president declared Smith as press secretary.

(436)   * Dative Alternation:
     a. The president declared Smith press secretary.
     b. * The president declared Smith to press secretary.

(437)   Infinitival Copular Clause:
     The president declared Smith to be press secretary.

(438)   The president declared that Smith would be press secretary.

Comments: Like the *dub* verbs above, these verbs allow only the frame involving two postverbal NPs and not the frame 'NP V NP *as* NP'. However, unlike the *dub* verbs, these verbs are found in the infinitival copular clause frame, 'NP V NP *to be* NP'. Some of them may take other kinds of sentential complements. There may be some differences of opinion concerning whether all of the *declare* verbs really do allow infinitival complements; if some do not allow them, they should be included with the *dub* verbs, which differ from the *declare* verbs in this respect.

29.5   *Conjecture* Verbs

Class Members: admit, allow, assert, conjecture, deny, discover, feel, figure, grant, guarantee, guess, hold, know, maintain, mean, observe, recognize, repute, show, suspect

Properties:

(439)   * *As* Alternation:
     a. * The press conjectured Smith the appointee.
     b. * The press conjectured Smith as the appointee.

(440)   Infinitival Copular Clause:
     The press conjectured Smith to be the appointee.

(441)   The press conjectured that Smith would be the appointee.

Comments: These verbs allow neither the frame involving two postverbal NPs nor the frame 'NP V NP *as* NP'; however, they are found in the infinitival copular clause frame, 'NP V NP *to be* NP'. Some of these verbs take types of sentential complements other than those listed here. The impossibility of the dative alternation is not illustrated here, since the verbs appear in neither of the frames associated with this alternation.

29.6   *Masquerade* Verbs

Class Members: act, behave, camouflage, count, masquerade, officiate, pose, qualify, rank, rate, serve

Properties:

(442)   Dina masqueraded as a lawyer.

(443)   * Dina masqueraded a lawyer.

Comments: The verbs in this class take a predicative complement predicated of their subject. They require *as* to introduce this complement.

29.7   *Orphan* Verbs

References: Bladin (1911), E.V. Clark and H.H. Clark (1979), Jespersen (1942), Karius (1985), Leitner (1974), Marchand (1969, 1974)

Class Members: apprentice, canonize, cripple, cuckold, knight, martyr, orphan, outlaw, pauper, recruit, widow

Properties:

(444)   The king knighted the brave soldier.
         (i.e., The king made the brave soldier a knight.)

(445)   Passive:
         The soldier was knighted (by the king).

Comments: With the exception of *canonize*, the verbs in this class are zero-related to nouns. The meaning of these verbs can be paraphrased so that the zero-related noun is a predicative complement of a verb like *make*. For example, the meaning of the verb *knight* is roughly "make (someone) a knight"; the noun *knight* is being predicated of the surface object of the verb. These verbs are often used in the passive, typically the adjectival passive.

29.8   *Captain* Verbs

References: Bladin (1911), E.V. Clark and H.H. Clark (1979), Jespersen (1942), Karius (1985), Lehrer (1990), Leitner (1974), Marchand (1969, 1974)

Class Members: boss, bully, butcher, butler, caddy, captain, champion, chaperone, chauffeur, clerk, coach, cox, crew, doctor, emcee, escort, guard, host, model, mother, nurse, partner, pilot, pioneer, police, referee, shepherd, skipper, sponsor, star, tailor, tutor, umpire, understudy, usher, valet, volunteer, witness

Properties:

(446)   Miriam tutored her brother.
         (i.e., Miriam acted as a tutor for her brother.)

(447)   Her cousin clerked for Judge Davis.
         (i.e., Her cousin acted as a clerk for Judge Davis.)

Comments: The verbs in this class are zero-related to nouns. The meaning of these verbs can be paraphrased so that the zero-related noun is a predicative complement of a verb like *act*. For instance, the verb *tutor* means roughly "act as a tutor for/toward." In the paraphrase, the noun zero-related to the verb is being predicated of the surface subject of the verb. The person toward whom the action is directed may be expressed as the object of the verb or the object of a prepositional phrase complement of the verb; the actual expression depends on the verb.

30 Verbs of Perception

References: Akmajian (1977), J.L. Austin (1962), Bach (1980), Barss (1985), Barwise (1981), Barwise and Perry (1983), Bennis and T. Hoekstra (1989), Borkin (1973), Brekke (1988), Caplan (1973), M.V. Clark (1971), Cooper (1974, 1975), Croft (1986, 1990), Declerck (1981, 1982, 1983), Dirven (1989), Dixon (1991), van der Does (1991), Emonds (1985), Faber (1985), Fellbaum (1990), Gee (1977), Goldsmith (1979), Gruber (1967), Gussenhoven (1992), Higginbotham (1983), Jørgensen (1990), Joshi (1974), Kearns (1991), Kirsner (1977), G. Lakoff (1987), Landau and Gleitman (1985), van der Leek and Jong (1982), Lehrer (1990), Ljung (1980), G. Miller and Johnson-Laird (1976), Mittwoch (1990), Na (1986), Parsons (1989, 1990), Quirk (1970), Rogers (1971, 1972, 1973, 1974), Ryle (1966), Sag (1973), Sibley (1955), Sundén (1916a, 1916b), Thalberg (1977), Thompson and Kirsner (1976), Tinker et al. (1989), Van Develde (1977), Van Voorst (1992), Viberg (1984), Wierzbicka (1980)

30.1 *See* Verbs

Class Members: detect, discern, feel, hear, notice, see, sense, smell, taste

Properties:

(448)   I saw the play.

(449)   ? I am seeing Sylvia.

(450)   * I saw at the play.

(451)   I can see that you are feeling great.

(452)   I see someone running down the street.
         Someone was seen running down the street.

(453)   I saw Jane run down the street.
         * Jane was seen run down the street.

(454)   * Middle Alternation:
         a. I saw the Mona Lisa.
         b. * The Mona Lisa sees easily.

(455)   * Possessor Object Possessor-Attribute Factoring Alternation:
         a. I sensed his eagerness.
         b. * I sensed him for his eagerness.

(456)   Attribute Object Possessor-Attribute Factoring Alternation:
         a. I sensed his eagerness.
         b. I sensed the eagerness in him.

Comments: The verbs in this subset of the verbs of perception describe the actual perception of some entity. They take the perceiver as subject and what is perceived as direct object. Some of these verbs are tied to a particular sense modality, but others are not. These verbs take a variety of sentential complements; however, there is no attempt to deal fully with the range of possible sentential complements here, although much of the discussion of these verbs in the literature focuses on this issue. (The verbs *taste* and *smell* are exceptional; they do not show as wide a range of options as the other class members, possibly because only a limited range of things can be apprehended through the sense of taste and smell.) The question of whether or not these verbs are stative has also received substantial attention; this issue arises because these verbs are often odd in the progressive, unless they receive a special interpretation.

30.2 *Sight* Verbs

Class Members: descry, discover, espy, examine, eye, glimpse, inspect, investigate, note, observe, overhear, perceive, recognize, regard, savor, scan, scent, scrutinize, sight, spot, spy, study, survey, view, watch, witness

Properties:

(457)   The crew spotted the island.

(458)   * The crew is spotting the island.

(459)   * The crew spotted at the island.

(460)   * We spotted that they were running. (except: *observe, note, perceive*)

(461)   We spotted them running.

(462)   * We spotted them run.

(463) * Middle Alternation:
    a.   I spotted the runaway cat.
    b. * Runaway cats spot easily.

Comments: This subset of the verbs of perception again take the perceiver as subject and what is perceived as direct object. Although some of these verbs are tied to a particular sense modality, others are not. These verbs are set apart from the *see* verbs above because they take a more limited range of complement types. Again, no attempt is made here to deal fully with the range of possible sentential complements, even though much of the discussion of these verbs in the literature focuses on this issue.

30.3 *Peer* Verbs

Class Members: check (on), gape, gawk, gaze, glance, glare, goggle, leer, listen (to), look, ogle, peek, peep, peer, sniff, snoop (on), squint, stare

Properties:

(464)   We peered at the baby/around the room/through the screen/into the closet.
        We listened to the baby.
        We checked/snooped on them.

(465) * We peered the baby.

(466) * We peered that all was well.

(467)   We peered at them running.

(468) * We peered at them run.

Comments: Unlike the *see* and *sight* verbs above, the verbs in this subset of the verbs of perception are not used transitively; rather they take a prepositional phrase complement. These verbs do not necessarily describe the apprehension of something via a sense: one can look at something without seeing it. The members of this subset show a limited range of sentential complements. All the verbs in this set involve sight, except for the verbs *sniff* and *listen*. Almost all of the verbs in this set take the preposition *at* or one of the locative prepositions as the head of their prepositional phrase complement. However, the verb *listen* differs in requiring the preposition *to* and in allowing infinitival complements (*We listened to them playing*), while the verbs *check* and *snoop* require the preposition *on*.

30.4   Stimulus Subject Perception Verbs

Class Members: feel, look, smell, sound, taste

Properties:

(469)   That pea soup tasted delicious.

(470)   That pea soup tasted delicious to me.

(471)   * Passive:
          * I was tasted delicious to (by the pea soup).

Comments: The members of this set of verbs of perception, like the *peer* verbs above, are intransitive. But unlike the other types of verbs of perception, they do not take the perceiver as their subject. Rather, these verbs take the stimulus as their subject and express the perceiver in a *to* prepositional phrase. In addition, these verbs take an adjective phrase complement predicated of the stimulus.

Due to the use of a *to* phrase to express the perceiver, these verbs are sometimes discussed in the context of psych-verbs; compare the use of the *to* phrase with psych-verbs to express an experiencer, as in *The outcome was perplexing to me.* In fact, with this set of verbs the perceiver is often referred to as the experiencer.

31   Psych-Verbs (Verbs of Psychological State)

References: Abney (1987), Aijmer (1972), Albury (1973), Amritavalli (1980a, 1980b), M. Baker (1988c), Belletti (1988), Belletti and Rizzi (1988), Berman (1970), Boguraev (1991), Bolinger (1967, 1972b), Bouchard (1990), Bowerman (1990), Brekke (1988), Brown and Fish (1983), Campbell and Martin (1989), Carlson (1977), Condoravdi and Sanfilippo (1990), Croft (1986, 1991), DiDesidero (1992), Dirven (1989), Dixon (1991), Emonds (1991), Fabb (1984), Geis (1973), Giorgi (1984), Grimshaw (1990), Haïk (1990), Hatcher (1951), Hermon (1986), E. Hoekstra (1991a), Jackendoff (1990a), Johnson (1986), Jørgensen (1987, 1991), Kearns (1991), Kegl and Fellbaum (1988), Kenny (1963), Keyser and Roeper (1992), Kuno (1987), G. Lakoff (1970a), Lee (1971), Lehrer (1990), Lightfoot (1991), Ljung (1980), Martin (1991), N. McCawley (1975, 1976), ter Meulen and Rooryck (1991), Mukhin (1985), Nissenbaum (1985), Norrick (1978), Pesetsky (1987, 1992), Pollard and Sag (1992), Postal (1971), Pullum (1987), Pustejovsky (1988, 1991a, 1991b), Rappaport (1983), Reinhart (1983), Rizzi and Belletti (1988), Roberts (1989), J.R. Ross (1969), Rozwadowska (1988), Rudanko (1991), Ruwet (1972), Ryle (1966), Snell-Hornby (1983), Talmy (1985), Tenny (1992), Thalberg (1977),

Tinker et al. (1989), Valesio (1971), Van Oosten (1980, 1986), Van Voorst (1992), Wall (1968), Wierzbicka (1972, 1973, 1980, 1988b), Zubizarreta (1987)

Verbs of psychological state typically take two arguments. Although there is some controversy over how best to characterize the "semantic roles" of these two arguments, most frequently these arguments are characterized as the experiencer and the stimulus (or sometimes theme, cause, object of emotion, or target of emotion). In terms of the expression of these arguments, it is possible to distinguish four classes of psychological verbs in English: the members of two classes are transitive verbs, and the members of the other two classes are intransitive verbs taking prepositional phrase complements. The transitive psych-verbs are the most numerous. They fall into two classes according to whether the experiencer is the subject (the *admire* verbs) or the object (the *amuse* verbs). The intransitive psych-verbs fall into two classes according to whether the experiencer is expressed as the subject (the *marvel* verbs) or as the object of the preposition heading a prepositional phrase complement (the *appeal* verbs). In addition to the references listed above, there are also many studies that deal with psychological verbs in other languages.

31.1 *Amuse* Verbs   *exp. ⌐) obj*

Class Members: abash, affect, afflict, affront, aggravate, agitate, agonize, alarm, alienate, amaze, amuse, anger, annoy, antagonize, appall, appease, arouse, assuage, astonish, astound, awe, baffle, beguile, bewilder, bewitch, boggle, bore, bother, bug, calm, captivate, chagrin, charm, cheer, chill, comfort, concern, confound, confuse, console, content, convince, cow, crush, cut, daunt, daze, dazzle, deject, delight, demolish, demoralize, depress, devastate, disappoint, disarm, discombobulate, discomfit, disconcert, discompose, discourage, disgrace, disgruntle, disgust, dishearten, disillusion, dismay, dispirit, displease, disquiet, dissatisfy, distract, distress, disturb, dumbfound, elate, electrify, embarrass, embolden, enchant, encourage, engage, engross, enlighten, enliven, enrage, enrapture, entertain, enthrall, enthuse, entice, entrance, exasperate, excite, exhaust, exhilarate, fascinate, faze, flabbergast, flatter, floor, fluster, frighten, frustrate, gall, galvanize, gladden, gratify, grieve, harass, haunt, hearten, horrify, humble, humiliate, hurt, hypnotize, impress, incense, infuriate, inspire, insult, interest, intimidate, intoxicate, intrigue, invigorate, irk, irritate, jar, jollify, jolt, lull, madden, mesmerize, miff, mollify, mortify, move, muddle, mystify, nauseate, nettle, numb, obsess, offend, outrage, overawe, overwhelm, pacify, pain, peeve, perplex, perturb, pique, placate, plague, please, preoccupy, provoke, puzzle, rankle, reassure, refresh, relax, relieve, repel, repulse, revitalize, revolt, rile, ruffle, sadden, satisfy, scandalize, scare, shake, shame, shock, sicken, sober, solace, soothe, spellbind, spook, stagger, startle, stimulate, sting, stir, strike, stump, stun, stupefy, surprise, tantalize, tease, tempt, terrify, terrorize, threaten, thrill, throw, tickle, tire, titillate, torment, touch, transport, trouble, try, unnerve, unsettle, uplift, upset, vex, weary, worry, wound, wow

Properties:

(472) The clown amused the children.

(473) *Causative Alternations (most verbs):
  a. The clown amused the children.
  b. *The children amused (at the clown).

(474) Middle Alternation (most verbs):
  a. The clown amused the little children.
  b. Little children amuse easily.

(475) PRO-Arb Object Alternation:
  a. That joke never fails to amuse little children.
  b. That joke never fails to amuse.

(476) Possessor Subject Possessor-Attribute Factoring Alternation (transitive):
  a. The clown amused the children with his antics.
  b. The clown's antics amused the children.

(477) Extraposition of sentential complements:
  a. That the clown had a red nose amused the children.
    It amused the children that the clown had a red nose.
  b. To win the prize would thrill me.
    It would thrill me to win the prize.

(478) Choice of prepositions in the "passive" depends on the verb:
  The children were amused at/by/with the clown.

(479) Resultative Phrase:
  That movie bored me silly/to tears.

(480) The clown was amusing to the children. (most verbs)

(481) an amusing joke

(482) Derived nominal has "passive" interpretation only:
  the children's amusement (at the clown)
  *the clown's amusement of the children

(483) *-er* Nominal (some verbs):
  baffler, disturber, enchanter, flatterer, startler, teaser
  *astonisher, *depresser, *disconcerter, *disguster, *fazer

(484)   *–able* Adjectives (some verbs):
         * amusable, *agitatable, *surprisable, *charmable, *delightable
         excitable, irritable, upsettable

Comments: The members of this subclass of the psych-verbs describe the
bringing about of a change in psychological or emotional state. They are transitive verbs whose object is the experiencer of the emotion and whose subject
is the cause of the change in psychological state. It is possible that the verbs included in this class should be further subdivided. For instance, Grimshaw (1990)
argues that some of these verbs, such as *amuse*, allow the subject/stimulus argument to receive an agentive interpretation, while others, such as *concern*, do
not; this distinction could be the basis for further subdivision of these verbs.
Some of the verbs in this class also are used in a physical action sense; among
them are *agitate, depress, hit, strike* (e.g., *The carpenter depressed the lever*).
In English, unlike in some languages, few *amuse*-type psych-verbs are found
in transitive/intransitive pairs of the type associated with the causative alternations; that is, the only intransitive use of these verbs with an experiencer
subject receives a middle interpretation. However, there are some exceptions,
including the verbs *cheer, delight, enthuse, gladden, grieve, madden, obsess,
puzzle, sadden, sicken, thrill, tire, weary, worry*; these verbs are also listed
among the *marvel* verbs below.

The binding properties of these verbs have received much attention recently;
see Belletti and Rizzi (1988), Giorgi (1984), Grimshaw (1990), Johnson (1986),
Pesetsky (1987, 1992), among others, for some discussion. The references cited
at the beginning of this section also discuss various properties of these verbs that
are not included here, since they do not directly involve their argument-taking
properties.

31.2 *Admire* Verbs $exp. \rightarrow subj$

Class Members:
POSITIVE VERBS: admire, adore, appreciate, cherish, enjoy, esteem, exalt, fancy,
favor, idolize, like, love, miss, prize, respect, relish, revere, savor, stand, support,
tolerate, treasure, trust, value, venerate, worship
NEGATIVE VERBS: abhor, deplore, despise, detest, disdain, dislike, distrust,
dread, envy, execrate, fear, hate, lament, loathe, mourn, pity, regret, resent,
?rue,

Properties:

(485)   The tourists admired the paintings.

(486)   * Middle Alternation:
         a.   Tourists admire paintings.
         b. * Paintings admire easily.

(487)   Possessor Object Possessor-Attribute Factoring Alternation:
         a.   I admired his honesty.
         b.   I admired him for his honesty.

(488)   Attribute Object Possessor-Attribute Factoring Alternation:
         a.   I admired his honesty.
         b.   I admired the honesty in him.

(489)   *As Alternation:
         a.   I admired him as a teacher.
         b.   *I admired him a teacher.

(490)   Sentential Complements (some verbs):
         The children liked that the clown had a red nose.

(491)   Extraposition of Sentential Complements (some verbs):
         The children liked it that the clown had a red nose.
         The children liked it when the clown tripped over his shoes.

(492)   Derived nominal has "active" interpretation only:
         the children's enjoyment of the movie
         *the movie's enjoyment by the children

(493)   –able Adjective:
         detestable, enjoyable, hatable, likable

(494)   –er Nominal:
         admirer of Roman ruins, dog-hater, music-lover, respecter of privacy

Comments: The members of this subclass of the psych-verbs are transitive verbs with an experiencer subject. There are a variety of opinions as to the best characterization of the "semantic role" of their direct object; the labels used include theme, target of emotion, stimulus, and subject matter. These verbs vary as to whether they allow sentential complements and, if so, which types. Some of the verbs that take sentential complements allow expletive *it* in object position with an extraposed sentential complement.

31.3   *Marvel* Verbs

Class Members:
about: bother, care, fret, mind, moon, rage, rejoice, rhapsodize, worry
at: cheer, cringe, enthuse, exult, fume, gladden, madden, marvel, rage, rejoice, sadden, sicken, swoon, thrill, wonder
for: bleed, care, cry, fear, feel, grieve, mourn, weep
from: ache, hurt, suffer
in: bask, delight, exult, glory, luxuriate, rejoice, revel, wallow

of: approve, beware, despair, disapprove, sicken, tire, weary
on: groove
over: anger, anguish, delight, enthuse, exult, fret, fume, gloat, grieve, gush, hunger, marvel, moon, mope, mourn, obsess, puzzle, rage, rave, rejoice, rhapsodize, salivate, seethe, sorrow, wonder, worry
to: react, thrill

Properties:

(495)   Megan marveled at the beauty of the Grand Canyon.

(496)   Passive (some verbs):
         The beauty of the Grand Canyon has been marveled over by countless tourists.

Comments: The members of this set of psych-verbs are intransitive verbs. Each takes an experiencer subject and expresses the stimulus/object of emotion in a prepositional phrase headed by one of a variety of prepositions. These verbs are not often singled out for discussion, and if they are mentioned, they are often lumped with the *admire* verbs. However, they do not show as wide a range of behavior as either of the types of transitive psych-verbs. Some of these verbs are used transitively as *amuse* verbs (cf. above); these are cross-listed.

31.4   *Appeal* Verbs

Class Members:
at: niggle
on: grate, jar
to: appeal, matter

Properties:

(497)   This painting appeals to Malinda.

(498)   * Passive:
         * Malinda is appealed to (by this painting).

Comments: This class is the smallest of the four psych-verb subclasses. Its members are intransitive verbs taking the stimulus as subject and expressing the experiencer in a prepositional phrase headed by one of a variety of prepositions. These verbs do not show the range of behavior that either of the transitive types of psych-verbs show. Their pattern of argument expression in some ways resembles a pattern that is more prevalent in other languages, where psych-verbs often express the stimulus as a nominative NP and the experiencer as a dative NP.

32   Verbs of Desire

References: Bolinger (1972b), Borkin (1972), Dirven (1989), Dixon (1991), Partee (1974), Quine (1960), Rudanko (1988), Snell-Hornby (1983), Talmy (1985), Wierzbicka (1988b). See Psych-Verbs above for further references.

These verbs are sometimes included among the psych-verbs that take an experiencer subject, that is, the *admire*-type and *marvel*-type psych-verbs. Like them, these verbs take two arguments and fall into two classes: a transitive class and an intransitive class. In addition, one of the two arguments, the person that desires something, is often considered to be a type of experiencer, and like the experiencer argument of the *admire* and *marvel* verbs, this argument is expressed as the subject of the verbs of desire. These verbs express their second argument, the thing desired, differently according to whether they are transitive (the *want* verbs) or intransitive (the *long* verbs); this argument is expressed as the direct object of the verb if the verb is transitive, or as the object of a preposition heading a prepositional phrase complement if the verb is intransitive.

32.1   *Want* Verbs

Class Members: covet, crave, desire, fancy, need, want

Properties:

(499)   Dorothy needs new shoes.

(500)   * Dorothy is needing new shoes.

(501)   Possessor Object Possessor-Attribute Factoring Alternation:
    a.   Dorothy needs her skills.
    b.   Dorothy needs her for her skills.

(502)   * Attribute Object Possessor-Attribute Factoring Alternation:
    a.   Dorothy needs her skills.
    b.   * Dorothy needs the skills in her.

(503)   * *As* Alternation:
    a.   Dorothy needs that dress as a costume.
    b.   * Dorothy needs that dress a costume.

(504)   ? Passive:
    ? New shoes were needed by Dorothy.

32.2   *Long* Verbs

Class Members:
after: dangle, hanker, lust, thirst, yearn

for: ache, crave, fall, hanker, hope, hunger, itch, long, lust, pine, pray, thirst, wish, yearn

Properties:

(505)   Dana longs for a sunny day.

(506)   Dana is longing for a sunny day.

(507)   ? Passive:
         ? An end to world hunger has always been longed for.

33   Judgment Verbs

References: J.L. Austin (1962), Fillmore (1971b, 1972), Gawron (1983), J. McCawley (1975, 1977), Vendler (1972), Wierzbicka (1987), Willems (1973)

Class Members:
POSITIVE VERBS: acclaim, applaud, bless, celebrate, commend, compensate, compliment, congratulate, eulogize, excuse, extol, felicitate, forgive, greet, hail, honor, laud, pardon, praise, recompense, remunerate, repay, reward, salute, thank, toast, welcome
NEGATIVE VERBS: abuse, backbite, calumniate, castigate, censure, chasten, chastise, chide, condemn, criticize, decry, defame, denigrate, denounce, deprecate, deride, disparage, fault, fine, impeach, insult, lambaste, malign, mock, penalize, persecute, prosecute, punish, rebuke, reprimand, reproach, reprove, revile, ridicule, scold, scorn, shame, snub, upbraid, victimize, vilify

Properties:

(508)   They praised the volunteers.

(509)   * Middle Alternation:
         a.   The director praised the volunteers.
         b.   * Volunteers praise easily.

(510)   Possessor Object Possessor-Attribute Factoring Alternation:
         a.   They praised the volunteers' dedication.
         b.   They praised the volunteers for their dedication.

(511)   * Attribute Object Possessor-Attribute Factoring Alternation:
         a.   They praised the volunteers' dedication.
         b.   * They praised the dedication in the volunteers.

(512)   *As* Alternation (some verbs):
         a.   They praised them as volunteers.
         b. * They praised them volunteers.

(513)   Process Derived Nominal (some verbs):
         the committee's condemnation of the policy
         the policy's condemnation by the committee
         the condemnation of the policy by the committee

Comments: These verbs share some properties with the *admire*-type psych-verbs (sec. 31.2). While the *admire* verbs relate to a particular feeling that someone may have in reaction to something, these verbs relate to a judgment or opinion that someone may have in reaction to something. Unlike the *admire*-type psych-verbs, they do not typically take sentential complements as objects, but they may take gerunds expressed in a *for* phrase. Although judgment verbs can have related *–able* adjectives and *–er* nominals, these forms do not always sound very natural. Many of these verbs do not have derived nominals with a process interpretation.

34   Verbs of Assessment

References: Deane and Wheeler (1984)

Class Members: analyze, assess, audit, evaluate, review, scrutinize, study

Properties:

(514)   The inspector analyzed the building.

(515)   Possessor Object Possessor-Attribute Factoring Alternation:
         a.   The inspector analyzed the building's soundness.
         b.   The inspector analyzed the building for its soundness.

(516)   * Attribute Object Possessor-Attribute Factoring Alternation:
         a.   The inspector analyzed the building's soundness.
         b. * The inspector analyzed the soundness in the building.

Comments: These verbs relate to making an assessment of something with respect to some attribute. They are found in one of the possessor-attribute factoring alternations: the possessor object alternation. These verbs differ from the *admire*-type psych-verbs (sec. 31.2) and the judgment verbs above, which also participate in this alternation, in simply indicating the assessment, without specifying a judgment or a feeling that reflects the outcome of the assessment.

35   Verbs of Searching

References: Bach (1968), Carlson (1977), Croft (1986, 1991), Dixon (1989, 1991), Dowty (1979), Ljung (1980), J. McCawley (1968a, 1973, 1974), Partee (1974), Quine (1960), Quirk (1970), Sibley (1955)

All the verbs in this section relate to searching. There seem to be three ways in which these verbs can express their arguments: 'NP1 V NP2 *in* NP3', 'NP1 V NP3 *for* NP2', 'NP1 V *for* NP2 *in* NP3'; this collection of frames is discussed in Part I under *Search* Alternations (sec. 2.11). Different verbs are found in different combinations of these patterns. With the exception of the *ferret* verbs, all of these verbs permit the use of a *for* phrase to express the object being searched for. In general, the argument that refers to the entity that is being searched for is something whose existence is not presupposed. When a PP is used to expressed the place where the search is being carried out, this PP can usually be headed by one of a variety of locative prepositions; the prepositions *in*, *through*, and *among* are particularly common.

One of the controversies that has surrounded these verbs is whether *look for* is the same as "try to find," as proposed in Quine (1960), Bach (1968), and J. McCawley (1968a), and criticized in Dougherty (1970), followed by a response in J. McCawley (1973).

35.1   *Hunt* Verbs

Class Members: dig, feel, fish, hunt, mine, poach, scrounge

Properties:

(517)   a.   I hunted the woods for game.
         b.   I hunted for game in the woods.
              I hunted in the woods for game.
         c.   I hunted game in the woods.

(518)   Unspecified Object Alternation:
         a.   I was hunting game (in the woods).
         b.   I was hunting (in the woods).

Comments: The members of this class show all three of the possible patterns of argument expression available to verbs of searching. With the possible exception of *scrounge*, these verbs allow the unspecified object alternation. They may take a range of locative prepositions heading the locative prepositional phrase.

35.2 *Search* Verbs

Class Members: advertise, check, comb, dive, drag, dredge, excavate, patrol, plumb, probe, prospect, prowl, quarry, rake, rifle, scavenge, scour, scout, search, shop, sift, trawl, troll, watch

Properties:

(519) a. I searched the cave for treasure.
       b. I searched for treasure in the cave.
          I searched in the cave for treasure.
       c. * I searched treasure in the cave.

Comments: The members of this class show two of the three possible patterns of expressing arguments. They do not show the pattern where the object being searched for is the direct object of the verb. Many of these verbs are most often found with *through* as the preposition heading the locative prepositional phrase.

35.3 *Stalk* Verbs

Class Members: smell, stalk, taste, track

Properties:

(520) a. I stalked the woods for game.
       b. * I stalked for game in the woods.
         * I stalked in the woods for game.
       c. I stalked game in the woods.

Comments: The members of this class show two of the three possible patterns of argument expression available to verbs of searching. They do not show the pattern where both arguments are expressed in prepositional phrases. These verbs may take a range of locative prepositions heading the locative prepositional phrase.

35.4 *Investigate* Verbs

Class Members: canvass, explore, examine, frisk, inspect, investigate, observe, quiz, raid, ransack, riffle, scan, scrutinize, survey, tap

Properties:

(521) a. We investigated the area for bombs.
       b. * We investigated for bombs in the area.
         * We investigated in the area for bombs.
       c. * We investigated bombs in the area.

Comments: The members of this class show only one of the three possible patterns of expressing arguments, the pattern where the place being searched is the direct object of the verb; that is, the place cannot be expressed via a prepositional phrase.

35.5 *Rummage* Verbs

Class Members: bore, burrow, delve, forage, fumble, grope, leaf, listen, look, page, paw, poke, rifle, root, rummage, scrabble, scratch, snoop, thumb, tunnel

Properties:

(522) a. * We rummaged the drawer for important documents.
　　　 b.   We rummaged in the drawer for important documents.
　　　 ? We rummaged for important documents in the drawer.
　　　 c. * We rummaged important documents in the drawer.

Comments: The members of this class show only one of the three possible patterns of argument expression available to verbs of searching, the pattern where both arguments are expressed using prepositional phrases. With some verbs, the order of prepositional phrases in which the prepositional phrase expressing the object being looked for precedes the prepositional phrase expressing the location being searched seems more awkward than the reverse order.

35.6 *Ferret* Verbs

Class Members: ferret, nose, seek, tease

Properties:

(523) a. * I ferreted the woods for game.
　　　 b. * I ferreted for game in the woods.
　　　 c.   I ferreted the secret out of him.

Comments: The members of this class show only one of the three possible patterns available to verbs of searching for argument expression, the pattern where the object being looked for is the direct object of the verb. This subclass is the only one whose members do not allow the entity being sought to be expressed in a *for* prepositional phrase. Unlike the situation with the other subclasses, one of the source prepositions is preferred as the preposition heading the locative prepositional phrase.

36   Verbs of Social Interaction

References: Condoravdi (1990), Dong (1970), Dowty (1991), Fellbaum (1990), Ginzburg (1990), Snell-Hornby (1983)

Most of these verbs relate to group activities—activities that inherently involve more than one participant—and even those verbs that do not inherently involve a group require more than one participant in the use described here. A significant number of these verbs relate to fighting; another large group relates to verbal interactions. When one of these verbs takes a subject that refers to a single person, then it must take either a direct object (the *marry* verbs) or a *with* phrase (the *correspond* verbs); it need not take a complement if its subject is a collective NP. In addition, those verbs that relate to verbal interactions can take a prepositional phrase describing the content of the communication (*They bargained over the price*), while those verbs that relate to fighting can take prepositional phrases describing the reason for the fight (*They fought over the land*). The prepositions most commonly heading such phrases are *over* and *about*; the choice of preposition depends on the verb and the content of the prepositional phrase itself.

36.1   *Correspond* Verbs

Class Members: agree, argue, banter, bargain, bicker, brawl, clash, coexist, collaborate, collide, combat, commiserate, communicate, compete, concur, confabulate, conflict, consort, cooperate, correspond, dicker, differ, disagree, dispute, dissent, duel, elope, feud, flirt, haggle, hobnob, jest, joke, joust, mate, mingle, mix, neck, negotiate, pair, plot, quarrel, quibble, rendezvous, scuffle, skirmish, spar, spat, spoon, squabble, struggle, tilt, tussle, vie, war, wrangle, wrestle

Properties:

(524)   Brenda bantered with Molly.

(525)   Collective NP Subject:
         * Brenda bantered.
         The committee bantered.

(526)   Simple Reciprocal Alternation (intransitive):
         a.   Brenda bantered with Molly.
         b.   Brenda and Molly bantered.

(527)   * Understood Reciprocal Object Alternation:
         a.   * Brenda bantered Molly.
         b.   Brenda and Molly bantered.

(528)   * *With* Preposition Drop Alternation:
   a. Brenda bantered with Molly.
   b. * Brenda bantered Molly.

(529)   Brenda and Molly bantered about the party. (most verbs)

Comments: The members of this subset of the verbs of social interaction take a *with* phrase complement when they do not take a collective NP as subject. They cannot be used transitively when they do not take a collective NP as subject. There are significant subclasses dealing with verbal interactions and fighting. The *chitchat* verbs (sec. 37.6) behave in most respects like these verbs, but they have been included among the verbs of communication below to illustrate that there are some verbs of communication that do not take sentential complements.

36.2 *Marry* Verbs

Class Members: court, cuddle, date, divorce, embrace, hug, kiss, marry, nuzzle, pass, pet

Properties:

(530)   * Simple Reciprocal Alternation (intransitive):
   a. * Bill married with Kathy.
   b. Bill and Kathy married.

(531)   Understood Reciprocal Object Alternation:
   a. Bill married Kathy.
   b. Bill and Kathy married.

(532)   * *With* Preposition Drop Alternation:
   a. Bill married Kathy.
   b. * Bill married with Kathy.

Comments: The members of this subset of the verbs of social interaction are used transitively when they do not take a collective NP as subject. Unlike the *correspond* verbs above, they cannot be used intransitively with a *with* phrase when they do not take a collective NP as subject.

36.3 *Meet* Verbs

Class Members: battle, box, consult, debate, fight, meet, play, visit

Properties:

(533)   Brenda met with Molly.

(534)   * Brenda met.
   The committee met.

(535)   Simple Reciprocal Alternation (intransitive):
         a.   Brenda met with Molly.
         b.   Brenda and Molly met.

(536)   Understood Reciprocal Object Alternation:
         a.   Anne met Cathy.
         b.   Anne and Cathy met.

(537)   *With* Preposition Drop Alternation:
         a.   Anne met with Cathy.
         b.   Anne met Cathy.

Comments: These verbs are also related to group activities. They show a combination of the properties of the *correspond* and *marry* verbs discussed above: they are found both in the intransitive simple reciprocal alternation and the understood reciprocal object alternation. That is, when the verbs in this subclass do not take a collective NP as subject, they can be used transitively as well as intransitively with a *with* phrase.

37   Verbs of Communication

References: J.L. Austin (1962), Dixon (1991), Fellbaum (1990), Kirsner (1972), Ljung (1980), J. McCawley (1977), G. Miller and Johnson-Laird (1976), Mufwene (1978), Munro (1982), Snell-Hornby (1983), Vendler (1972), Wierzbicka (1987, 1988b), Zwicky (1971a, 1971b)

This section provides an abbreviated treatment of some of the classes of verbs relating to communication and the transfer of ideas. The reason for this briefness is that sentential complements will figure prominently in any full description of the properties of these verbs, but a systematic treatment of such complements is outside the scope of this book. The verbs included here are those which show noteworthy properties that do not involve sentential complements; for example, some of these verbs are found in the dative alternation.

37.1   Verbs of Transfer of a Message

References: Workgroup on Functional Grammar (1981)

Class Members: ask, cite, demonstrate, dictate, explain, explicate, narrate, ?pose, preach, quote, read, recite, relay, show, teach, tell, write

Properties:

(538)   Wanda taught the students.

(539)   Dative Alternation (most verbs):
          a.   Wanda taught French to the students.
          b.   Wanda taught the students French.

(540)   Wanda taught the students that the earth was round.

Comments: These verbs are described by Gropen et al. (1989) as "verbs of type of communicated message (differentiated by something like 'illocutionary force')." As this description makes clear, they differ with respect to the nature of the message and the way it is communicated. This set of verbs is not treated fully here, but has been included to exemplify a set of verbs of communication that may take a *to* phrase indicating the addressee (goal) of a communication and that allow the dative alternation (assuming they meet the Latinate restriction on the dative alternation). Most of these verbs may take sentential complements, but this aspect of their behavior is not explored here.

37.2   *Tell*

References: Haïk (1990)

Class Members: tell (only)

Properties:

(541)   Ellen told a story.

(542)   Ellen told a story to Helen.

(543)   Dative Alternation:
          a.   Ellen told a story to Helen.
          b.   Ellen told Helen a story.

(544)   Ellen told Helen. (elliptical)
          * Ellen told to Helen.

(545)   Ellen told Helen about the situation.

(546)   * Ellen told a story at Helen.

(547)   Sentential Complement with Goal Object:
          Ellen told Helen that the party would be tonight.
          Ellen told Helen how to avoid the crowd.
          Ellen told Helen to come.

(548)   * Sentential Complement with Goal *To* Phrase:
          * Ellen told to Helen that the party would be tonight.

* Ellen told to Helen how to avoid the crowd.
* Ellen told to Helen to come.

(549)   * Sentential Complement without Goal Phrase:
        * Ellen told that the party would be tonight.
        * Ellen told how to avoid the crowd.
        * Ellen told to come.

(550)   * Ellen told for Helen to come.

(551)   Direct Speech:
        Ellen told me, "Leave the room."
        * Ellen told to me, "Leave the room."

(552)   Parenthetical Use of the Verb:
        The winner, Ellen told me, would be announced tonight.
        * The winner, Ellen told to me, would be announced tonight.

(553)   Passive:
        I was told that the winner would be announced tonight.

(554)   * Impersonal Passive:
        * It was told that the winner would be announced tonight.

(555)   * Zero-related Nominal:
        * a tell

Comments: Although the verb *tell* is included among the verbs of transfer of a message above, it is given a fuller treatment in this section. The focus here is on *tell* as a simple verb of communication. Its meaning does not include any further specification, such as a manner or instrument component, unlike that of the verbs of manner of speaking below, for example. Most of the properties listed above are further elaborated in Zwicky (1971a).

37.3   Verbs of Manner of Speaking

References: Atkins and B. Levin (1991), Barkaï (1972), Bolinger (1972b), Duszak (1980), Emonds (1985), G. Lakoff (1970a), B. Levin (1991), G. Miller and Johnson-Laird (1976), Moltmann (1989), Mufwene (1978), Penhallurick (1984), Poutsma (1904), Rudzka-Ostyn (1988), Safir (1985), Snell-Hornby (1983), Stowell (1981), Wierzbicka (1987), Zwicky (1971a, 1986)

Class Members: babble, bark, bawl, bellow, bleat, boom, bray, burble, cackle, call, carol, chant, chatter, chirp, cluck, coo, croak, croon, crow, cry, drawl, drone, gabble, gibber, groan, growl, grumble, grunt, hiss, holler, hoot, howl, jabber, lilt, lisp, moan, mumble, murmur, mutter, purr, rage, rasp, roar, rumble, scream, screech, shout, shriek, sing, snap, snarl, snuffle, splutter, squall, squawk, squeak, squeal, stammer, stutter, thunder, tisk, trill, trumpet, twitter, wail, warble, wheeze, whimper, whine, whisper, whistle, whoop, yammer, yap, yell, yelp, yodel

Properties:

(556)   Susan whispered.

(557)   Susan whispered to Rachel.

(558)   Susan whispered the news/a few words.

(559)   * Dative Alternation:
      a.   Susan whispered the news to Rachel.
      b. * Susan whispered Rachel the news.

(560)   Susan whispered at Rachel.

(561)   Susan whispered about the party.

(562)   Sentential Complement with Optional Goal *To* Phrase:
      Susan whispered (to Rachel) that the party would be tonight.
      Susan whispered (to Rachel) how to avoid the crowd.
      Susan whispered (to Rachel) to come.

(563)   Susan whispered for me to come.

(564)   Direct Speech:
      Susan whispered (to Rachel), "Leave the room."

(565)   Parenthetical Use of the Verb:
      The winner, Susan whispered, would be announced tonight.

(566)   * Passive:
      a.   Susan whispered "Shut up" (at them).
      ?? "Shut up" was whispered (at them) by Susan.
      b.   They whispered that the winner would be announced tonight.
      * It was whispered that the winner would be announced tonight.

(567)   Reaction Object:
      Susan whispered her consent.

(568)   ? Cognate Object:
      ? Susan whispered a piercing whisper.

(569)   Zero-related Nominal:
      a whisper/give a whisper

Comments: This set of verbs has been referred to as "verbs of manner of speaking," and as this label suggests, they are distinguished from each other by the manner in which the sound is expressed. In fact, many of these verbs are also used as verbs of animal sound (cf. sec. 38) and/or verbs of sound emission (cf. sec. 43.2) if sounds with similar characteristics are associated with animals and/or inanimate entities. In principle, all verbs listed here could potentially be found in all three classes, although only a subset of them commonly show one or both of these other uses. In addition, some of the verbs included here are also listed under verbs of nonverbal expression (sec. 40.2), as they are probably basically verbs of nonverbal expression. In fact, even though most of the verbs of nonverbal expression have not been cross-listed under the verbs of manner of speaking here, most of those that involve making a sound (and some of the others, too) can potentially be used as verbs of manner of speaking.

These verbs show an extremely complex set of properties. Most of the properties given above are drawn from Zwicky (1971a) and are elaborated there. Zwicky writes that these verbs take cognate objects, but there seem to be differences of opinion about whether such objects are indeed permitted; it is also possible that the different verbs in the class might behave differently. Zwicky points out that these verbs can be used either communicatively or noncommunicatively. Certain choices of complements disambiguate the verbs. For example, the presence of a *to* phrase forces the communicative interpretation, while passivization forces the noncommunicative interpretation. A careful consideration of the communicative/noncommunicative distinction will undoubtedly lead to a more refined analysis of these verbs. The *that* complements found with these verbs are understood nonfactively.

37.4   Verbs of Instrument of Communication

References: Leitner (1974), Marchand (1969), Sehnert and Sharwood-Smith (1973). For more discussion of these verbs see also studies of the dative alternation (cf. sec. 2.1).

Class Members: cable, e-mail, fax, modem, netmail, phone, radio, relay, satellite, semaphore, sign, signal, telephone, telecast, telegraph, telex, wire, wireless

Properties:

(570)   Heather cabled the news.

(571)   Heather cabled Sara.

(572)   Dative Alternation:
      a.   Heather cabled the news to Sara.
      b.   Heather cabled Sara the news.

(573)   * Heather cabled to Sara.

(574)   * Heather cabled the news at Sara.

(575)   Heather cabled Sara about the situation.

(576)   Sentential Complement with Optional Goal Object:
        Heather cabled (Sara) that the party would be tonight.
        Heather cabled (Sara) when to send the package.
        Heather cabled (Sara) to come.

(577)   Sentential Complement with Optional Goal *To* Phrase:
        Heather cabled (to Sara) that the party would be tonight.
        Heather cabled (to Sara) when to send the package.
        Heather cabled (to Sara) to come.

(578)   Heather cabled for Sara to come.

(579)   Direct Speech:
        Heather cabled (Sara), "Come immediately."
        Heather cabled (to Sara), "Come immediately."

(580)   Parenthetical Use of the Verb:
        The winner, Heather cabled (Sara), would be announced tonight.
        The winner, Heather cabled (to Sara), would be announced tonight.

(581)   Zero-related Nominal:
        a cable (result—some verbs only)
        a satellite (instrument)

Comments: Each of these verbs is zero-related to a noun that names an instrument of communication, although some of them also have zero-related nominals with a result interpretation (e.g., *cable*). They relate to communication via these instruments of communication. The means of communication need not involve the use of voice. The verbs in this class are set apart from other verbs of communication in manifesting the dative alternation (with some exceptions, which are likely to vary from speaker to speaker). This property suggests that these verbs might be considered verbs of change of possession like other dative verbs (cf. sec. 13); this is possible if communication is viewed as the acquisition of information. The verbs included here have not, however, been cross-listed under verbs of giving.

37.5 *Talk* Verbs

Class Members: speak, talk

Properties:

(582)   Ellen talked.

(583)   Ellen talked to Helen.

(584)   Ellen talked to Helen about the problem.

(585)   * Sentential Complement:
         * Ellen talked (to Helen) that the party was tomorrow.
         * Ellen talked (to Helen) how to avoid the crowd.
         * Ellen talked (to Helen) to come.

(586)   * Ellen talked for Helen to come.

(587)   Ellen talked with Helen (about the problem).

(588)   Simple Reciprocal Alternation (intransitive):
         a.   Ellen talked with Helen.
         b.   Ellen and Helen talked.

(589)   *Together* Reciprocal Alternation (intransitive):
         a.   Ellen talked with Helen.
         b.   Ellen and Helen talked together.

(590)   * Understood Reciprocal Object Alternation:
         a.   Ellen and Helen talked.
         b.   * Ellen talked Helen.

(591)   * *With* Preposition Drop Alternation:
         a.   Ellen talked with Helen.
         b.   * Ellen talked Helen.

(592)   Zero-related Nominal:
         a talk/have a talk
         * a speak

Comments: These verbs have been grouped together here, even though a more extensive examination of their properties reveals differences between them, because the meanings of both relate to speaking but do not involve a means or manner specification. These verbs do not take sentential complements. They can take a *to* phrase to express the goal that the communication is directed to. They can also take a *with* phrase, which indicates another participant in a conversation. In contrast, the *chitchat* verbs below cannot take a *to* phrase.

37.6   *Chitchat* Verbs

Class Members: argue, chat, chatter, chitchat, confer, converse, gab, gossip, rap, schmooze, yak

Properties:

(593)   Ellen was chitchatting.

(594)   Ellen chitchatted with Helen (about the problem).

(595)   * Ellen chitchatted to Helen (about the problem).

(596)   * Sentential Complement:
         * Ellen chitchatted that the party was tomorrow.
         * Ellen chitchatted how to avoid the crowd.
         * Ellen chitchatted to come.

(597)   * Ellen chitchatted for Helen to come.

(598)   Simple Reciprocal Alternation (intransitive):
         a.   Ellen chitchatted with Helen.
         b.   Ellen and Helen chitchatted.

(599)   * *Together* Reciprocal Alternation (intransitive):
         a.   Ellen chitchatted with Helen.
         b.   * Ellen and Helen chitchatted together.

(600)   * Understood Reciprocal Object Alternation:
         a.   Ellen and Helen chitchatted.
         b.   * Ellen chitchatted Helen.

(601)   * *With* Preposition Drop Alternation:
         a.   Ellen chitchatted with Helen.
         b.   * Ellen chitchatted Helen.

Comments: Most of these verbs can be used to describe spoken interactions between two or more participants. These verbs are found with *with* phrases but not usually with *to* phrases. They do not take sentential complements. The *chitchat* verbs behave in most respects like the *correspond* verbs (sec. 36.1), but they have been included among the verbs of communication to illustrate that there are some verbs in that class that do not take sentential complements.

37.7 *Say* Verbs

Class Members: announce, articulate, blab, blurt, claim, confess, confide, convey, declare, mention, note, observe, proclaim, propose, recount, reiterate, relate, remark, repeat, report, reveal, say, state, suggest

Properties:

(602)   Ellen said that melons were selling well.

(603)   Ellen said to Helen that melons were selling well.

(604)   Ellen said something/a few words to Helen.

(605)   *Dative Alternation:
       a. Ellen said something to Helen.
       b. *Ellen said Helen something.

(606)   *Ellen said to Helen.

(607)   *Ellen said about the present conditions.

Comments: Verbs such as these are described as "verbs of communication of propositions and propositional attitudes" by Gropen et al. (1989). This set of verbs has been included to exemplify a set of verbs of communication that may take a *to* phrase indicating the addressee (goal) of a communication but that do not allow the dative alternation. They allow a very limited range of noun phrases as objects. These verbs may also take finite sentential complements. Some of these verbs can take other types of sentential complements, but these possibilities are not explored here. A careful and more extensive study of these verbs is needed.

37.8 *Complain* Verbs

Class Members: boast, brag, complain, crab, gripe, grouch, grouse, grumble, kvetch, object

Properties:

(608)   Ellen complained.

(609)   Ellen complained to Helen.

(610)   Sentential Complement with Optional Goal *To* Phrase:
      Ellen complained (to Helen) that melons were selling.
    *Ellen complained (to Helen) how to avoid the crowd.
    *Ellen complained (to Helen) to come.

(611)   *Ellen complained for Helen to come.

(612)   Direct Speech:
      Ellen complained (to Helen), "The mail didn't come today."

(613)   Parenthetical Use of the Verb:
      The mail, Ellen complained (to Helen), didn't come today.

(614)   Ellen complained about the situation.

(615)   Ellen complained about the situation to Helen.

(616)   *Cognate Object:
    *Ellen complained a complaint (to Helen).

(617) * Ellen complained at Helen.
Ellen grouched at Helen.

(618) Zero-related Nominal (most verbs):
a gripe, a complaint

Comments: These verbs specify the speaker's attitude or feelings toward what is said. They only take finite sentential complements. Some of these verbs allow *at* phrases, as well as *to* phrases, to express the person the communication is directed to; others do not. Some of these verbs have zero-related nominals, while others have other types of derived nominals; the exception is *crab*, which does not have a related nominal.

37.9 *Advise* Verbs

References: J.L. Austin (1962), J. McCawley (1977), Vendler (1972), Wall (1968), Wierzbicka (1987)

Class Members: admonish, advise, alert, caution, counsel, instruct, warn

Properties:

(619) Ellen warned Helen.

(620) * Ellen warned to Helen.

(621) Ellen warned (Helen) against skating on thin ice.

(622) PRO-arb Object Alternation (except *alert*):
a. Ellen warned Helen that melons were selling.
b. Ellen warned that melons were selling.

(623) Sentential Complement with Optional Goal Object:
Ellen warned (Helen) that melons were selling.
Ellen warned (Helen) how to avoid the crowd.
Ellen warned (Helen) not to skate on thin ice.

(624) * Ellen warned for Helen to come.

(625) Direct Speech:
Ellen warned (Helen), "Avoid that hole in the sidewalk."

(626) Parenthetical Use of the Verb:
The assignment, Ellen warned (Helen), must be finished by tomorrow.

(627) Ellen warned (Helen) about the traffic jam.

(628) * Zero-related Nominal (most verbs):
* an admonish

Comments: These verbs relate to giving advice or warnings. The verbs in this class are among the verbs in English that allow a PRO-arb object interpretation when used intransitively. The exception is the verb *alert*, which requires an obligatory object.

38 Verbs of Sounds Made by Animals

References: Atkins and B. Levin (1991), Duszak (1980), B. Levin (1991), Salkoff (1983), Snell-Hornby (1983)

Class Members: baa, bark, bay, bellow, blat, bleat, bray, buzz, cackle, call, caw, chatter, cheep, chirp, chirrup, chitter, cluck, coo, croak, crow, cuckoo, drone, gobble, growl, grunt, hee-haw, hiss, honk, hoot, howl, low, meow, mew, moo, neigh, oink, peep, pipe, purr, quack, roar, scrawk, scream, screech, sing, snap, snarl, snort, snuffle, squawk, squeak, squeal, stridulate, trill, tweet, twitter, wail, warble, whimper, whinny, whistle, woof, yap, yell, yelp, yip, yowl

Properties:

(629)   The dog barked.

(630)   The dog barked at the cat. (*at:* directed toward)
         The dog barked at the commotion. (*at:* in reaction to)

(631)   * Directional Phrase:
         * The duck quacked down the path.

(632)   Reaction Object:
         The dog barked a warning.

(633)   Resultative Phrase:
         The rooster crowed everyone awake.

Comments: These verbs describe the expression of sounds by animals; each verb describes the sound characteristic of some type of animal. Some of these verbs are also used as verbs of sound emission (cf. sec. 43.2) and/or verbs of manner of speaking (cf. sec. 37.3), if a sound with the same characteristics is associated with an inanimate entity and/or a person. In principle, all verbs listed here could potentially be found in all three classes, although only a subset of them commonly show one or both of those other uses. When some of these verbs are used as verbs of sound emission they may take directional phrase complements, but this possibility is not open to them when they are used as verbs of animal sound.

39   Verbs of Ingesting

References: Brame (not dated), Dixon (1991), Fellbaum (1990), Fellbaum and Kegl (1989), G. Miller and Fellbaum (1991), Rice (1988), Snell-Hornby (1983), Wierzbicka (1982)

The following verb classes relate to the ingestion of food or drink. These classes of verbs vary as to whether or not they allow the unspecified object alternation and the conative alternation. In addition, the members of some of these classes show an intransitive use that resembles the conative construction but involves the preposition *on* rather than the typical conative preposition *at*; this use of *on* has been noted in Part I in the discussion of the conative alternation (sec. 1.3). Some studies of these verbs in other languages lump them together with verbs of acquisition of information such as *learn*, because the acquisition of information may be viewed as a type of ingesting and because the subject of verbs in both these classes does not behave like the subject of most intransitive agentive verbs with respect to causativization.

39.1   *Eat* Verbs

Class Members: drink, eat (only)

Properties:

(634)   Cynthia ate the peach.

(635)   Unspecified Object Alternation:
     a.   Cynthia ate the peach.
     b.   Cynthia ate.

(636)   Conative Alternation:
     a.   Cynthia ate the peach.
     b.   Cynthia ate at the peach.

(637)   * Cynthia ate on the peach.

(638)   * Instrument Subject Alternation:
     a.   Cynthia ate the peach with a fork.
     b.   * The fork ate the peach.

(639)   Resultative Phrase:
     Cynthia ate herself sick.

(640)   Zero-related Nominal:
     a drink/take a drink/have a drink
     * an eat/*take an eat/*have an eat

Comments: These two verbs are the simple verbs of ingesting: *eat* involves ingesting solids and *drink* liquids. Their meaning does not specify the manner of ingesting or the meal involved.

39.2   *Chew* Verbs

Class Members: chew, chomp, crunch, gnaw, lick, munch, nibble, pick, peck, sip, slurp, suck

Properties:

(641)   Cynthia nibbled the carrot.

(642)   Unspecified Object Alternation:
    a.   Cynthia nibbled the carrot.
    b.   Cynthia nibbled.

(643)   Conative Alternation:
    a.   Cynthia nibbled the carrot.
    b.   Cynthia nibbled at the carrot.

(644)   Cynthia nibbled on the carrot.

(645)   Zero-related Nominal:
    a nibble

Comments: The meaning of these verbs involves a specification of the manner of ingesting. These verbs participate in what appears to be the conative alternation, although some of them allow both the prepositions *at* and *on*, while others only take the preposition *on*.

39.3   *Gobble* Verbs

Class Members: bolt, gobble, gulp, guzzle, quaff, swallow, swig, wolf

Properties:

(646)   Cynthia gobbled the pizza.

(647)   Cynthia gobbled the pizza down.

(648)   * Unspecified Object Alternation:
    a.   Cynthia gobbled the pizza.
    b. * Cynthia gobbled.

(649)   * Conative Alternation:
    a.   Cynthia gobbled the pizza.
    b. * Cynthia gobbled at/on the pizza.

(650)   Zero-related Nominal (some verbs):
         a swallow

Comments: The meaning of these verbs involves the complete, and usually speedy, consumption of something. These verbs do not participate in either the conative alternation or the unspecified object alternation. There may be a preference for using some of these verbs with the particle *down*.

39.4   *Devour* Verbs

Class Members: consume, devour, imbibe, ingest, swill

Properties:

(651)   Cynthia devoured the pizza.

(652)   * Unspecified Object Alternation:
         a.   Cynthia devoured the pizza.
         b. * Cynthia devoured.

(653)   * Conative Alternation:
         a.   Cynthia devoured the pizza.
         b. * Cynthia devoured at the pizza.

(654)   * Cynthia devoured on the pizza.

(655)   * Zero-related Nominal:
         * a devour

Comments: These verbs show a more limited set of properties then some of the other subclasses of the verbs of ingesting. They must be used transitively and, unlike the *gobble* verbs above, they are not found with the particle *down*. Like the *gobble* verbs, they do not allow either the conative alternation or the unspecified object alternation. Interestingly, these verbs are almost all Latinate.

39.5   *Dine* Verbs

References: E.V. Clark and H.H. Clark (1979)

Class Members: banquet, breakfast, brunch, dine, feast, graze, lunch, luncheon, nosh, picnic, snack, sup

Properties:

(656)   Cynthia breakfasted.

(657)   Cynthia breakfasted on peaches.

(658)   * Unspecified Object Alternation:
      a.   Cynthia breakfasted.
      b. * Cynthia breakfasted peaches.

(659)   * Conative Alternation:
      a. * Cynthia breakfasted peaches.
      b. * Cynthia breakfasted at peaches.

Comments: These verbs all refer to eating particular meals, and most of them are zero-related to nouns that name meals. These verbs cannot be used transitively. They are not found in the conative alternation with the preposition *at*, although they may take *on*.

39.6   *Gorge* Verbs

Class Members: exist, feed, flourish, gorge, live, prosper, survive, thrive

Properties:

(660)   * Cynthia gorged.

(661)   Cynthia gorged on peaches.

(662)   * Unspecified Object Alternation:
      a. * Cynthia gorged.
      b. * Cynthia gorged peaches.

(663)   * Conative Alternation:
      a. * Cynthia gorged peaches.
      b. * Cynthia gorged at peaches.

Comments: These verbs are used to describe what a person's diet consists of. They pattern almost exactly like the *dine* verbs above, except that they are not zero-related to nouns and cannot be used without a prepositional phrase (at least not while maintaining the same sense). These verbs cannot be used transitively. They are not found in the conative alternation with the preposition *at*, although they may take *on*. All of these verbs, except *feed* and *gorge,* are basically not verbs of eating, but rather verbs of existence; they are cross-listed (cf. sec. 47).

39.7   Verbs of Feeding

References: Fellbaum (1990)

Class Members: bottlefeed, breastfeed, feed, forcefeed, handfeed, spoonfeed

Properties:

(664)   Teresa bottlefed the baby.

(665)   Dative Alternation:
      a.   Teresa bottlefed soy milk to the baby.
      b.   Teresa bottlefed the baby soy milk.

(666)   ? Teresa bottlefed the baby on/with soy milk.

(667)   * Teresa bottlefed soy milk.

Comments: The verbs in this set describe causing someone to eat. The verb *feed* does not specify a particular means or manner, although the other verbs, which are compounds with the verb *feed* as the right-hand member, do. The acceptability of the use of the prepositions *with* or *on* to head a prepositional phrase specifying the type of food varies with the different verbs; such prepositional phrases appear to be most acceptable with the verb *feed*.

40   Verbs Involving the Body

40.1   Verbs of Bodily Processes

References: Dixon (1991), Fellbaum (1990), McClure (1990), Rice (1988), Snell-Hornby (1983), Thalberg (1972)

40.1.1   *Hiccup* Verbs

Class Members: belch, blush, burp, flush, hiccup, pant, sneeze, sniffle, snore, snuffle, swallow, wheeze, yawn

Properties:

(668)   Paul hiccuped.

(669)   ? Cognate Object:
      ? Paul hiccuped a loud hiccup.

(670)   * Paul hiccuped at/on Mary.

(671)   ?? Resultative Phrase:
      ?? Paul hiccuped himself sick.

(672)   Zero-related Nominal:
      a hiccup
      * give a hiccup (most verbs)

Comments: These verbs relate to involuntary bodily processes; that is, processes that are typically not under the control of the person that experiences them.

40.1.2   *Breathe* Verbs

Class Members: bleed, breathe, cough, cry, dribble, drool, puke, spit, sweat, vomit, ?weep

Properties:

(673)   Paul breathed.

(674)   Cognate Object (few verbs):
        Paul breathed a deep breath.
        * Paul sweated a cold sweat.

(675)   Substance Object (most verbs):
        The dragon breathed fire.

(676)   Paul breathed on Mary.

(677)   * Paul breathed at Mary. (most verbs)

(678)   * Resultative Phrase:
        * Paul breathed Mary awake.

(679)   Zero-related Nominal (most verbs):
        a breath/*give a breath

Comments: These verbs also relate to bodily processes. With the exception of *breathe*, which can also describe taking air *into* the body, they relate to emitting a substance *from* the body. Most of them take *on* complements. The emitted substance may be optionally expressed as the object of the verb; however, few of these verbs can take cognate objects even though some of them have zero-related nominals. Among those that have zero-related nominals, only *cough* is found in the light verb construction headed by *give*, but this might be because *cough* is also a verb of nonverbal expression (cf. below).

40.1.3   *Exhale* Verbs

Class Members: exhale, inhale, perspire

Properties:

(680)   Paul exhaled.

(681)   * Cognate Object:
        * Paul exhaled a deep breath.

(682)   * Paul exhaled at Mary.

(683)   * Paul exhaled on Mary.

(684)   * Zero-related Nominal:
        * an exhale

Comments: These verbs relate to emitting some substance from the body or taking some substance into the body. They show a limited set of properties. All of these verbs are of Latinate origin.

40.2   Verbs of Nonverbal Expression

References: B. Levin and Rapoport (1988), Snell-Hornby (1983)

Class Members: beam, cackle, chortle, chuckle, cough, cry, frown, gape, gasp, gawk, giggle, glare, glower, goggle, grimace, grin, groan, growl, guffaw, howl, jeer, laugh, moan, pout, scowl, sigh, simper, smile, smirk, sneeze, snicker, sniff, snigger, snivel, snore, snort, sob, titter, weep, whistle, yawn

Properties:

(685)   Paul laughed.

(686)   Cognate Object (some verbs):
        Paul laughed a cheerful laugh.

(687)   Reaction Object:
        She laughed her excitement.

(688)   Paul laughed at Mary. (*at:* directed toward)
        Paul laughed at the story. (*at:* in reaction to)

(689)   She laughed in/from embarrassment.

(690)   Resultative Phrase (most verbs):
        Paul laughed himself sick.
        The audience laughed the actor off the stage.

(691)   Zero-related Nominal (most verbs):
        a laugh/give a laugh

Comments: These verbs can be described as verbs of "nonverbal expression." Most of them involve facial expressions that are associated with a particular emotion. Although almost all of these verbs have zero-related nominals, some of them take these nominals as cognate objects more freely than others. Some of these verbs are used as manner of speaking verbs and have been included in the list of manner of speaking verbs (sec. 37.3); in principle, all of these verbs could show properties of manner of speaking verbs. The verbs in this class often take *at* phrases; some *at* phrases seem to indicate the person the action is directed at, while others seem to indicate what the action is a reaction to. The verbs vary as to whether or not they allow both types of *at* phrases.

40.3   Verbs of Gestures/Signs Involving Body Parts

References: Bresnan (1982b), Rice (1988), Ross (1970), Snell-Hornby (1983), Thalberg (1977). See Hatcher (1944a, 1944b) and Junker and Martineau (1987) for discussion of similar phenomena in French and J.S. Levine (1980) for discussion of similar phenomena in Russian.

40.3.1   *Wink* Verbs

Class Members: blink (eye), clap (hands), nod (head), point (finger), shrug (shoulders), squint (eyes), wag (tail), wave (hand), wink (eye)

Properties:

(692)   Linda winked her eye/*lip/*nose.

(693)   Linda winked her/*his eye.

(694)   Understood Body-Part Object Alternation:
         a.   Linda winked her eye.
         b.   Linda winked.

(695)   * Passive:
         * Her$_i$ eye was winked (by Linda$_i$).
         * Many eyes were winked when the curtain rose.

(696)   Linda winked at the audience. (*at:* directed toward)
         ? Linda winked at his behavior. (*at:* in reaction to)

(697)   Linda winked in agreement.

(698)   * Cognate Object:
         * Linda winked a bold wink.

(699)   Reaction Object:
         Linda winked her agreement.

(700)   Zero-related Nominal:
         a wink (of complicity)
         give a wink

Comments: These verbs relate to gestures or signs made with specific body parts. The direct object of these verbs is typically a body part possessed by the subject of the verb; this object is optionally expressed, and when it is not expressed, it is understood. These verbs are also found with reaction objects. However, they do not typically take cognate objects, although almost all have zero-related nominals. These verbs often take *at* phrases; some *at* phrases seem to describe the person the action is directed at, while others seem to indicate what the action is a reaction to. The verbs vary as to whether or not they allow both types of *at* phrases. A few of these verbs, including *point* and *wave*, also take *to* phrases.

40.3.2 *Crane* Verbs

Class Members: arch (back, neck), bare (teeth), bat (eyelashes), beat (feet), blow (nose), clench (fists), click (heels, tongue), close (eyes), cock (head), crane (neck), crook (finger), cross (arms, eyes, legs), drum (finger), flap (wings), flash (teeth), flex (muscles), flick (finger), flutter (eyelashes), fold (arms), gnash (teeth), grind (teeth), hang (head), hunch (shoulders), kick, knit (eyebrows), open (eyes), pucker (lips), purse (lips), raise (eyebrows, hand), roll (eyes), rub (hands), shake (head, fist, hands), show (teeth), shuffle (feet), smack (lips), snap (fingers), stamp (foot), stretch (legs), toss (mane), turn (head), twiddle (thumbs), twitch (ears, nose), wag (finger, tail), waggle (ears), wiggle (ears, hips, nose), wring (hands), wrinkle (forehead, nose)

Properties:

(701)   Jennifer craned her/*his neck.

(702)   Jennifer craned her neck/*arm.

(703)   Understood Body-Part Object Alternation:
          a.   Jennifer craned her neck.
          b. * Jennifer craned.

(704)   * Cognate Object:
          * Jennifer shook a determined shake of the head.

(705)   * Passive:
          * Her$_i$ neck was craned (by Jennifer$_i$).
          * Necks were craned throughout the restaurant when the star walked in.

(706)   Jennifer wagged her finger at the naughty child. (*at:* directed at; some verbs)
          Jennifer rolled her eyes at his behavior. (*at:* in reaction to; some verbs)

(707)   Zero-related Nominals (some verbs):
          * a crane (of the neck)/*give a crane (of the neck)
          a shake of the head/give a shake of the head

Comments: These verbs describe gestures or signs made with specific body parts. The direct object of these verbs is a body part possessed by the subject of the verb. Unlike the object of the *wink* verbs above, this object must be obligatorily expressed. Given the obligatoriness of the object, it is not unexpected that *crane* verbs do not take cognate objects. Many of these verbs are found with *at* phrases designating the person the action is directed to or the person/thing the action is in reaction to. Few of these verbs have zero-related nominals, at least on the relevant interpretation.

40.3.3 *Curtsey* Verbs

Class Members: bob, bow, curtsey, genuflect, kneel, salaam, salute

Properties:

(708)   The princess curtseyed.

(709)   The princess curtseyed to the queen.

(710)   *Cognate Object:
        *The princess curtseyed a beautiful curtsey.

(711)   Reaction Object:
        The princess curtseyed her assent.

(712)   Zero-related Nominal:
        a curtsey (most verbs)

Comments: The verbs in this class describe signs made with the entire body. They differ from each other with respect to the movement involved and the position attained. Unlike the *wink* and *crane* verbs above, they do not take a body part as object. They do not take cognate objects either. Many of these verbs are found with *to* phrases designating the person the action is directed toward. Most of them have zero-related nominals.

40.4 *Snooze* Verbs

Class Members: catnap, doze, drowse, nap, sleep, slumber, snooze

Properties:

(713)   Gloria snoozed.

(714)   *Causative Alternations:
        a. *The heavy meal snoozed Gloria.
        b. Gloria snoozed.

(715)   *Cognate Object (except *sleep*):
        *Gloria snoozed a light snooze.

(716)   Zero-related Nominal (some verbs):
        a snooze

Comments: These verbs describe different types of sleeping. With the exception of the verb *sleep* itself, they do not appear to take cognate objects. Some of the *snooze* verbs do not have zero-related nominals. The verbs *doze* and *drowse* are found with the particle *off*, indicating a transition from a state of being awake to a state of being asleep.

40.5   *Flinch* Verbs

Class Members: ?balk, cower, cringe, flinch, recoil, shrink, wince

Properties:

(717)   Sharon flinched.

(718)   Sharon flinched at the sight of the accident.

(719)   * Causative Alternations:
      a. * The shock flinched Sharon.
      b.   Sharon flinched.

(720)   * Cognate Object:
      * Sharon flinched a flinch.

(721)   * Reaction Object:
      * Sharon flinched her pain.

Comments: These verbs describe body movements that reflect an emotional or physical reaction. For instance, these movements might be triggered by fear, dislike, shame, cold, or pain. *Flinch* verbs do not take objects, whether cognate objects or reaction objects. The verbs in this class often take *at* phrases indicating what triggered the body movement.

40.6   Verbs of Body-Internal States of Existence

References: Snell-Hornby (1983)

Class Members: convulse, cower, quake, quiver, shake, shiver, shudder, tremble, writhe

Properties:

(722)   Sharon shivered.

(723)   Sharon shivered from fear.

(724)   Sharon shivered at the thought of the cold sea.

(725)   * Causative Alternations:
      a.   Sharon shivered.
      b. * The fear shivered Sharon.

Comments: These verbs typically take animate subjects. They describe a physical state of the subject that typically is a reflex of a particular psychological or physiological state. (Some of these verbs may have another sense involving an inanimate subject.) The verbs in this class often take *at* and *from* phrases indicating what the state is in reaction to.

40.7   *Suffocate* Verbs

Class Members: asphyxiate, choke, drown, ?stifle, suffocate

Properties:

(726)   Causative Alternation:
    a.   The pirates drowned the sailor.
    b.   The sailor drowned.

(727)   ? Middle Alternation:
    a.   The seamonster drowned the sailors.
    b.   ? Sailors drown easily.

(728)   Resultative Phrase (some verbs):
    He choked/suffocated to death.
    * The sailor asphyxiated/drowned to death.

Comments: These verbs relate to the disruption of breathing; they differ from each other with respect to means. These verbs are found in the causative alternation. The verbs *asphyxiate*, *drown*, and *suffocate* are often considered to either lexicalize or entail death and, consequently, have sometimes been included among the verbs of killing; they are cross-listed with the *poison* verbs (sec. 42.2). These three verbs, unlike the other verbs in the class, do not occur with resultative phrases.

40.8   Verbs of Bodily State and Damage to the Body

40.8.1   *Pain* Verbs

References: Campbell and Martin (1989), Deane (1984), Dixon (1991), Hatcher (1951), Martin (1991), Snell-Hornby (1983), Wierzbicka (1980)

Class Members: ache, bother, hurt, itch, pain

Properties:

(729)   My eyes are itching (me).

(730)   * My eyes are itching my brother.

(731)   * Cognate Object:
    * My eyes are itching an intense itch.

(732)   My eyes are itching from the smoke.

(733)   * Passive:
         * I am being itched by my eyes.

Comments: These verbs of bodily state can be used either transitively or intransitively. The subject of these verbs is a body part whose possessor experiences the state. When they are used transitively, the object is the experiencer of the state and, therefore, understood as the possessor of the body part expressed in subject position.

40.8.2   *Tingle* Verbs

References: Campbell and Martin (1989), Deane (1984), Hatcher (1951), Wierzbicka (1980)

Class Members: (mouth) burn, hum, (head, heart) pound, prickle, (lips) pucker, (head) reel, (eyes) smart, (head) spin, (head) split, sting, (head) swim, throb, (throat) tickle, tingle

Properties:

(734)   My heart is pounding.

(735)   * My heart is pounding me.

(736)   * My heart is pounding my brother.

(737)   * Cognate Object:
         * My heart is pounding an intense pound.

(738)   My heart is pounding from fear.

Comments: These verbs of bodily state are only used intransitively. Their subject is a body part whose possessor experiences the state. The subject does not receive an agent or cause interpretation. Some of these verbs have other, more basic senses and are cross-listed; some are also intransitive verbs of manner of motion (*swim*, *spin*), while others are drawn from various classes of transitive verbs that take agentive subjects.

40.8.3   *Hurt* Verbs

References: Abney (1987), Junker and Martineau (1987)

Class Members: bark (shin), bite (lip), bump, burn, break, bruise, chip (tooth), cut, fracture, hurt, injure, nick (chin, leg), prick (finger), pull (muscle), rupture, scald, scratch (chin), skin (knee), split (lip), sprain (ankle, back, knee, wrist), strain, stub (toe), turn (ankle), twist (ankle)

(739)   Tessa sprained her ankle.

(740)   * Tessa sprained Mary's ankle. (on a non-agentive interpretation)

(741)   * Cognate Object:
          * Tessa sprained a sprain.

(742)   * Passive:
          * Her$_i$ ankle was sprained (by Tessa$_i$).
          * Tessa's ankle was sprained when she tripped over the rug.

(743)   Unintentional interpretation available:
          a.   Reflexive Object (some verbs):
               Tessa hurt herself.
                 * Tessa sprained herself.
          b.   Body-Part Object:
               Tessa hurt her ankle.
               Tessa sprained her ankle.

(744)   * Understood Reflexive Object Alternation:
          a.   Tessa cut herself.
          b. * Tessa cut.

(745)   * Understood Body-Part Object Alternation:
          a.   Tessa sprained her ankle.
          b. * Tessa sprained.

(746)   Adjectival Passive Participle:
          a sprained ankle

(747)   Zero-related Nominal (some verbs):
          a sprain

Comments: These verbs relate to the occurrence of damage to the body through a process that is not under control of the person that suffers the damage. Although some of these verbs may take agentive subjects, the subject does not receive an agentive interpretation on the use considered here. The subject involuntarily injures himself or herself and does not intentionally inflict an injury on himself or herself. These verbs resemble the *crane* verbs above in taking body-part objects that are possessed by the subject and in often being restricted to a few specific body parts as objects. Although these verbs are not found in the verbal passive, some of them may be used in the adjectival passive.

40.8.4   Verbs of Change of Bodily State

Class Members: blanch, faint, sicken, swoon

Properties:

(748)   Sharon fainted.

(749)   Sharon fainted from hunger.

(750)   Sharon fainted at the sight of the accident.

(751)   * Causative Alternations:
        a. * Hunger fainted Sharon.
        b.   Sharon fainted.

(752)   * Cognate Object:
        * Sharon fainted a faint.

Comments: These verbs describe changes in the states of humans, and hence take an animate subject.

41   Verbs of Grooming and Bodily Care

References: Atkins, Kegl, and B. Levin (1986), Fellbaum (1990), Geniušienė (1987), Poutsma (1904), Sigler (1985)

41.1   Verbs of Caring for the Whole Body

41.1.1   *Dress* Verbs

Class Members: bathe, change, disrobe, dress, exercise, preen, primp, shave, shower, strip, undress, wash

Properties:

(753)   Marlene dressed.

(754)   Causative Alternation:
        a.   The baby dressed.
        b.   Marlene dressed the baby. (except *preen* and *primp*)
           (does not mean: Marlene caused the baby to dress.)

(755)   Understood Reflexive Object Alternation:
        a.   Marlene dressed herself.
        b.   Marlene dressed.

(756)   * Marlene dressed her body.

Comments: These verbs relate to taking care of or grooming the whole body. They can be found with either X*self* or with the appropriate body part as direct object. This set of verbs shows the understood reflexive object alternation; when they are used intransitively, the action is understood to be directed at the subject.

41.1.2 *Groom* Verbs

Class Members: curry, groom

Properties:

(757)   Sheila groomed the horse.

(758)   * Understood Reflexive Object Alternation:
      a. * The horse groomed itself.
      b. * The horse groomed.

Comments: These verbs also relate to taking care of or grooming the whole body, but they always refer to actions performed on another individual. They are not used intransitively, nor are they found with X*self* as object.

41.2 Verbs of Caring for a Specific Body Part

41.2.1 *Floss* Verbs

Class Members: brush (teeth), floss (teeth), shave (beard, legs), wash (hands, face)

Properties:

(759)   The hygienist flossed my teeth.

(760)   I flossed my teeth.

(761)   * Understood Reflexive Object Alternation:
      a.   I flossed.
      b. * I flossed myself.

(762)   Understood Body-Part Object Alternation:
      a.   I flossed my teeth.
      b.   I flossed.

Comments: These verbs relate to taking care of or grooming a part of the body. They cannot be found with X*self* as object, but they may be found with the appropriate body part as object. When these verbs are used intransitively, the body part that would typically be the object of the verb is understood as the object. These verbs are not found in the understood reflexive object alternation.

41.2.2 *Braid* Verbs

Class Members: bob (hair), braid (hair), brush (hair), clip (nails), coldcream (face), comb (hair), condition (hair), crimp (hair), crop (hair), curl (hair), cut (hair), dye (hair), file (nails), henna (hair), lather (hair, body), manicure (nails), part (hair), perm (hair), plait (hair), pluck (eyebrows), powder (face, nose), rinse (hair, mouth), rouge (cheeks, face), set (hair), shampoo (hair), soap (hands, body), talc (body), tease (hair), towel (face, hands), trim (hair, beard), wave (hair)

Properties:

(763)   Celia brushed the baby's hair.

(764)   Celia brushed her hair.

(765)   * Understood Body-Part Object Alternation:
     a.   Celia brushed her hair.
     b. * Celia brushed.

(766)   * Understood Reflexive Object Alternation:
     a. * Celia brushed herself.
     b. * Celia brushed.

Comments: These verbs relate to taking care of or grooming a part of the body. With a few exceptions (e.g., *to soap oneself*), these verbs do not allow X*self* as object, but they may be found with the appropriate body part as object. Unlike the *floss* verbs above, these verbs cannot be used intransitively.

41.3   Verbs of Dressing

41.3.1   Simple Verbs of Dressing

Class Members: don, doff, wear

Properties:

(767)   She always wore purple dresses.

(768)   * Understood Reflexive Object Alternation:
     a. * She always wore herself (in purple).
     b. * She always wore.

Comments: These verbs relate to wearing, putting on, or taking off clothes.

41.3.2   Verbs of Dressing Well

Class Members: doll, dress, spruce, tog

Properties:

(769)   She spruced herself up before the job interview.

(770)   She spruced up before the job interview.

(771)   * She spruced (herself) before the job interview.

(772)   Adjectival Passive:
         She was all spruced up for the job interview.

Comments: These verbs relate to dressing well. They must occur with the particle *up*. It is likely that when these verbs are found in the passive participle form, they are being used as adjectival, rather than verbal, passives.

41.3.3   Verbs of Being Dressed

Class Members: attire, clad, garb, robe

Properties:

(773)   She was always clad in black.

(774)   * Her stepmother always clad her in black.

(775)   * Understood Reflexive Object Alternation:
         a. * She always clad herself in black.
         b. * She always clad in black.

Comments: These verbs of dressing usually occur in the passive participle form to describe the state of being dressed. This form shows the hallmarks of being an adjectival, rather than a verbal, passive participle.

42   Verbs of Killing

42.1   *Murder* Verbs

References: Brousseau and Ritter (1991), Carter (1976, 1988), Dixon (1991), Dowty (1979), Fodor (1970), Kac (1972a, 1972b), G. Lakoff (1970a), J.D. Mc-Cawley (1970b, 1972a, 1972b, 1976), Morgan (1969), Morreall (1976), Parsons (1990), Ravin (1990), Shibatani (1972, 1976b), Wierzbicka (1980)

Class Members: assassinate, butcher, dispatch, eliminate, execute, immolate, kill, liquidate, massacre, murder, slaughter, slay

Properties:

(776)   Brutus murdered Julius Caesar.

(777)   * Causative Alternations:
          a.   Brutus murdered Julius Caesar.
          b. * Julius Caesar murdered.

(778)   * Middle Alternation:
          a.   The bandits murdered innocent victims.
          b. * Innocent victims murder easily.

(779)   * Instrument Subject Alternation (except *kill*):
          a.   Brutus murdered Julius Caesar with a dagger.
               * The dagger murdered Julius Caesar.
          b.   The exterminators killed the insects with DDT.
               The DDT killed the insects.

(780)   * Resultative Phrase (except *kill*):
          * Brutus murdered Julius Caesar dead.
          Brutus killed Julius Caesar dead.

(781)   Zero-related Nominal (some verbs):
          a murder
          * an assassinate

Comments: The verbs in this class all describe killing. The verb *kill* is the class member with the least specific meaning: it lexicalizes nothing about the specific means, manner, or purpose involved in bringing about death; it also differs from the other class members in its behavior. Unlike *kill*, the other verbs in this class lexicalize something about the purpose or manner of killing. None of the verbs in this class lexicalizes a means component; that is, none provides any information about how the killing came about. This property sets these verbs apart from the *poison* verbs below, which lexicalize a means, but not a result.

Few members of this class of verbs appear to be able to take instrumental phrases headed by the preposition *with*. Fewer still allow instrumental subjects; their absence might reflect the fact that many of the allowable instruments are merely so-called "enabling" or "facilitating" instruments. The verb *kill* itself allows the widest range of instruments. In fact, it generally allows a wider range of behavior than some of the other class members; for example, it is also found in the resultative construction.

The verb *kill* has received substantially more attention than most of the other members of this class; however, this attention has been directed at it not in relation to its membership in the class of verbs of killing, but rather in relation to issues concerning the nature of semantic and syntactic representations.

Specifically, this verb has figured prominently in discussions of the pros and cons of predicate decomposition. The question that has been frequently asked is whether *kill* can be given a predicate decomposition along the lines of "cause to die." There is a large literature on this question; some representative and central works are included in the references listed above, which, with few exceptions, focus on the verb *kill*. Additional discussion of the predicate decomposition issue will be found in many of the references listed under Causative Alternations (sec. 1.1.2), since the causative/inchoative verbs also play an important part in this debate.

42.2 *Poison* Verbs

References: Carter (1976, 1988), Dixon (1991)

Class Members: asphyxiate, crucify, drown, electrocute, garrotte, hang, knife, poison, shoot, smother, stab, strangle, suffocate

Properties:

(782)   The witch poisoned Snow White.

(783)   * Causative Alternations (except *asphyxiate, drown, suffocate*):
            a.   The witch poisoned Snow White.
            b. * Snow White poisoned.

(784)   * Middle Alternation:
            a.   The witch poisoned the children.
            b. * Children poison easily.

(785)   Resultative Phrase (some verbs):
            The Boston Strangler strangled his victims to death.
         ?? The weak swimmer was drowned to death.

(786)   * Zero-related Nominal:
            * a drown (result; cf. *a drowning*)

Comments: The verbs in this class relate to actions which can be ways of killing. Thus they each lexicalize a means component, and it is this means which differentiates among them. In principle, as means verbs, these verbs need not entail that the action they denote results in death; however, some of them do appear to have this entailment. Their differing behavior in this respect probably reflects our conception of how effective the means involved is in causing death. Therefore, although the entailment of death suggests that some of the verbs in this class could have been included among the *murder* verbs above, they have been kept distinct since, strictly speaking, they lexicalize a means. This same variation in behavior is probably responsible for the fact that some of these verbs are more likely than others to be found with resultative phrases such as *to death*.

Few members of this class are found with instrumental phrases, probably because they already lexicalize a means. Those that are in fact found with an instrumental phrase typically take what might be described as a "cognate" instrumental phrase (e.g., *poison with rat poison*) or an instrumental phrase involving a hyponym of *poison*. Fewer still allow instrumental subjects; their absence might reflect the fact that most of the allowable instruments are merely so-called "enabling" or "facilitating" instruments.

Some of these verbs are not exclusively verbs of killing, since they describe actions that have death as only one of their possible results. These include the verb *shoot*, which is cross-listed under the *swat* verbs (sec. 18.2), as well as the verbs *asphyxiate*, *drown*, and *suffocate*, which are cross-listed under the *suffocate* verbs (sec. 40.7) and are the only verbs in the *poison* class to show one of the causative alternations.

43   Verbs of Emission

References: Brekke (1988), B. Levin (1991), B. Levin and Rappaport (1988), B. Levin and Rappaport Hovav (1992b), Merlan (1985), Perlmutter (1978), Pinker (1989), Salkoff (1983), Zoeppritz (1971)

The verbs in this class involve the emission of a stimulus or substance that is particular to some entity, and consequently, these verbs take a very limited range of subjects. For instance, typically brooks babble and the wind whistles, but not vice versa. There is a sense in which verbs in this class describe intrinsic properties of their subjects. In this respect, these verbs resemble the verbs of entity-specific modes of being (cf. sec. 47.2). Verbs of emission typically take inanimate subjects.

43.1   Verbs of Light Emission

Class Members: beam, blink, burn, blaze, flame, flare, flash, flicker, glare, gleam, glimmer, glint, glisten, glitter, glow, incandesce, scintillate, shimmer, shine, sparkle, twinkle

Properties:

(787)   The jewel sparkled.

(788)   Locative Alternation:
    a.   Jewels sparkled on the crown.
    b.   The crown sparkled with jewels.

(789)   Locative Inversion:
    a.   A magnificent diamond sparkled on his finger.
    b.   On his finger sparkled a magnificent diamond.

(790)   *There*-Insertion:
    a.   A magnificent diamond sparkled on his finger.
    b.   On his finger there sparkled a magnificent diamond.

(791)   Causative Alternation (some verbs):
    a.   The stagehand flashed the lights.
        The lights flashed.
    b. * The stagehand sparkled the lights.
        The lights sparkled.

(792)   a sparkling jewel

(793)   * Adjectival Perfect Participle:
    * a sparkled jewel

(794)   *-er* Nominal:
    sparkler

(795)   Zero-related Nominal:
    a sparkle (of excitement)

Comments: The members of this subset relate to the emission of light. They show the intransitive *swarm* form of the locative alternation (cf. sec. 2.3.4). Like other verbs found in the locative alternation, they show a "holistic" interpretation in the *with* variant. These verbs are also found in the locative inversion and *there*-insertion constructions. Some verbs of light emission clearly allow a transitive use with a causative interpretation. A variety of factors determine whether the causative use is available, so that it is possible that in the right circumstances additional members of this class could show such a use. For this reason, this set of verbs has not been separated into two subsets on the basis of the availability of a causative transitive use. The verbs *scintillate* and *incandesce* are more restricted in their behavior than the other verbs in this class; interestingly, these are the only two clearly Latinate members of the set.

43.2   Verbs of Sound Emission

References: Atkins and B. Levin (1991), Duszak (1980), B. Levin (1991), Salkoff (1983), Snell-Hornby (1983)

Class Members: babble, bang, beat, beep, bellow, blare, blast, blat, boom, bubble, burble, burr, buzz, chatter, chime, chink, chir, chitter, chug, clack, clang, clank, clap, clash, clatter, click, cling, clink, clomp, clump, clunk, crack, crackle, crash, creak, crepitate, crunch, cry, ding, dong, explode, fizz, fizzle, groan, growl, gurgle, hiss, hoot, howl, hum, jangle, jingle, knell, knock, lilt, moan, murmur, patter, peal, ping, pink, pipe, plink, plonk, plop, plunk, pop, purr, putter, rap, rasp, rattle, ring, roar, roll, rumble, rustle, scream, screech, shriek, shrill, sing, sizzle, snap, splash, splutter, sputter, squawk, squeak, squeal, squelch, strike, swish, swoosh, thrum, thud, thump, thunder, thunk, tick, ting, tinkle, toll, toot, tootle, trill, trumpet, twang, ululate, vroom, wail, wheeze, whine, whir, whish, whistle, whoosh, whump, zing

Properties:

(796)   The door hinges squeaked.

(797)   Locative Alternation (most verbs):
      a.   Birds sang in the trees.
      b.   The trees sang with birds.

(798)   Locative Inversion (some verbs):
      a.   A grandfather clock ticked in the hallway.
      b.   In the hallway ticked a grandfather clock.

(799)   *There*-Insertion (some verbs):
      a.   A grandfather clock ticked in the hallway.
      b.   In the hallway there ticked a grandfather clock.

(800)   Causative Alternation:
      a.   I buzzed the bell.
          The bell buzzed.
      b. * I squeaked the door.
          The door squeaked.

(801)   The bell chimed the hour. (some)
    * The hour was chimed by the bell.

(802)   Directional Phrase:
    The cart rumbled down the street.

(803)   a squeaking door

(804)   * Adjectival Perfect Participle:
    * a squeaked door

(805)   *-er* Nominal:
    a squeaker

(806)   Zero-related Nominal:
         the squeak (of unoiled hinges)

Comments: The members of this subset of the verbs of emission relate to the emission of sounds. Many of these verbs also figure among the verbs of manner of speaking (sec. 37.3) and/or the verbs of sounds made by animals (sec. 38). Some of these verbs allow an object; with some verbs, such as *toll* or *chime*, this object may express a time. Some members of this class are found with directional phrases; generally, this option is only allowed if the sound is a necessary concomitant of the motion of some entity (*Shelly whistled down the street/The train whistled into the station*). Verbs of sound emission show the intransitive *swarm* form of the locative alternation (cf. sec. 2.3.4). Like other verbs found in the locative alternation, they show a "holistic" interpretation in the *with* variant. Some of these verbs are also found in the locative inversion and *there*-insertion constructions. Some verbs of sound emission allow a transitive use with a causative interpretation. A variety of factors determine whether the causative use is available, so that it is possible that in the right circumstances more members of the set could show such a use. For this reason, this set of verbs has not been separated into two subsets on the basis of the availability of a causative transitive use.

43.3   Verbs of Smell Emission

References: Ljung (1980), Quirk (1970)

Class Members: reek, smell, stink

Properties:

(807)   The onions reeked.

(808)   Locative Alternation:
         a.   The onions reeked (??in the room).
         b.   The room reeked (of onions).

(809)   * Causative Alternations:
         a.   * Kelly reeked the onions.
         b.   The onions reeked.

(810)   Zero-related Nominal:
         a reek (of onions)

Comments: These verbs relate to the emission of smells. The set of verbs of smell emission is much smaller than the other subsets of the verbs of emission. These verbs also show a much more limited range of properties. Although they allow both the emitter of the smell and the location of the smell to turn up as their subject, as in the intransitive form of the locative alternation, with these verbs the alternation does not show all the hallmarks of the locative alternation, and may in fact be a different alternation. More specifically, when these verbs express the location of the smell as the subject, the emitter of the smell is expressed in an *of* phrase, in contrast to the *with* phrase found with the analogous variant of the other types of verbs of emission. However, when the subject of the verb is the emitter of the smell, a co-occurring locative phrase seems awkward; this is not the case with other subclasses of verbs of emission.

43.4   Verbs of Substance Emission

References: Duszak (1980), B. Levin (1991), Pinker (1989), Snell-Hornby (1983)

Class Members: belch, bleed, bubble, dribble, drip, drool, emanate, exude, foam, gush, leak, ooze, pour, puff, radiate, seep, shed, slop, spew, spill, spout, sprout, spurt, squirt, steam, stream, sweat

Properties:

(811)   The fountain gushed.

(812)   The well gushed oil.

(813)   Causative Alternation (some verbs):
     a. *I gushed the fountain.
       The fountain gushed.
     b. I bled him.
       He bled.

(814)   Substance/Source Alternation:
     a.   The well gushed oil.
     b.   Oil gushed from the well.

(815)   Locative Alternation (some verbs):
     a.   Water gushed through the streets.
     b.   The streets gushed with water.

(816)   Locative Inversion (some verbs):
     a.   A fragrant stew bubbled over the fire.
     b.   Over the fire bubbled a fragrant stew.

(817)   *There*-Insertion (some verbs):
     a.   A fragrant stew bubbled over the fire.
     b.   Over the fire there bubbled a fragrant stew.

(818)   a gushing fountain

(819)   * Adjectival Perfect Participle:
     * a gushed fountain

(820)   *-er* Nominal:
     a gusher

(821)   Zero-related Nominal (some verbs):
     a gush (of water)

Comments: The members of this subset of the verbs of emission relate to the emission of substances from something (the emitter); there is a sense in which the emitter can be viewed as a source, as reflected in one of the possible expressions of the arguments of these verbs. The verbs of substance emission differ from the other verbs of emission in showing more options for expressing their arguments. Like other verbs of emission, these verbs take the emitter/source as subject; but unlike other verbs of emission, they may optionally express the substance emitted as direct object. These verbs also are used intransitively with the substance emitted as subject and the emitter/source expressed via a *from* phrase, giving rise to their participation in the substance/source alternation. Some of them can be viewed as describing entity-specific modes of being and are cross-listed under the verbs of existence (sec. 47.2).

Some members of this class show the intransitive *swarm* form of the locative alternation (cf. sec. 2.3.4). These verbs, like other verbs found in the locative alternation, show a "holistic" interpretation in the *with* variant. Verbs of substance emission seem to participate in the *there*-insertion and locative inversion constructions less readily than some of the other types of verbs of emission.

Some members of this subset of the verbs of emission allow a transitive use with a causative interpretation, in which an agent causes some entity (the direct object) to emit a substance. A variety of factors determine whether the causative use is available, so that it is possible that under the right circumstances more members of the set could show such a use. For this reason, this set of verbs has not been separated into two subsets on the basis of the availability of a causative transitive use. Some of these verbs also have a transitive use which involves an agent causing a substance to be emitted from the entity (e.g., *spew* and *squirt*); that is, in this use the substance, rather than the emitter, is the object. Verbs with this use are cross-listed under the *pour* verbs (sec. 9.5) and the *spray/load* verbs (sec. 9.7).

44   *Destroy* Verbs

References: Dixon (1991), Jackendoff (1990b)

Class Members: annihilate, blitz, decimate, demolish, destroy, devastate, exterminate, extirpate, obliterate, ravage, raze, ruin, waste, wreck

Properties:

(822)   The Romans destroyed the city.

(823)   * Causative Alternations:
   a.   The Romans destroyed the city.
   b.   * The city destroyed.

(824)   * Middle Alternation:
   a.   The Romans destroyed the city.
   b.   * Cities destroy easily.

(825)   * Material/Product Alternation (transitive):
   a.   * The Romans destroyed the city into ruins.
   b.   * The Romans destroyed ruins from the city.

(826)   * Total Transformation Alternation:
   a.   * The Romans destroyed the city into a ruin.
   b.   * The Romans destroyed the city from a capital into a ruin.

(827)   Instrument Subject Alternation:
   a.   The builders destroyed the warehouse with explosives.
   b.   The explosives destroyed the warehouse.

(828)   * Conative Alternation:
   a.   The builders destroyed the warehouse.
   b.   * The builders destroyed at the warehouse.

(829)   * Resultative Phrase:
   * The builders destroyed the warehouse flat.
   * The builders destroyed the warehouse to smithereens.

(830)   * Zero-related Nominal:
   * a destroy

Comments: These verbs relate to the total destruction of entities. In some respects, they might seem similar to the *break* verbs (cf. sec. 45.1), which also appear to describe the destruction of entities; but the *break* verbs describe specifics of the resulting physical state of an entity (e.g., whether something is broken, splintered, cracked, and so on) rather than simply describing the fact that it is totally destroyed. The *destroy* verbs also differ from the *break* verbs in not being found in the causative/inchoative alternation, nor, for that matter, in any of the other causative alternations.

Jackendoff (1990b) points out that the *destroy* verbs could be viewed as verbs of creation, since the destruction of an entity can result in the creation of another; however, these verbs cannot express a created "product." Jackendoff proposes that this property arises because *destroy* verbs "totally incorporate the goal" (p. 117); that is, they describe some facet of the resulting state of destruction. These verbs are further distinguished from verbs of creation in not being found in either the material/product or the total transformation alternations. Jackendoff's observation may also figure in an explanation of why these verbs are not found in the resultative construction, another property that distinguishes them from the *break* verbs.

45 Verbs of Change of State

References: Abusch (1985, 1986), Anderson (1977), Binnick (1974), Boguraev (1991), Borer (1991), Bowerman (1976, 1982), Brousseau and Ritter (1991), Burzio (1986), Chafe (1970), Chitoran (1986), Croft (1986, 1990, 1991), Cruse (1972, 1973), Curme (1931), Davidse (1992), Dezsö (1980), Dixon (1982b, 1991), Dowty (1979), Farsi (1974), Fellbaum (1990), Fillmore (1966, 1967, 1968a, 1968b, 1977a, 1977b), Fodor (1970), Fodor et al. (1980), Fontenelle and Vanandroye (1989), Gawron (1983), Geis (1973), Gergely and Bever (1986), Guerssel et al. (1985), Hale and Keyser (1986, 1987, 1988, 1992), Halliday (1967, 1968), T. Hoekstra (1992), Ikegami (1988), Jackendoff (1990b), Jespersen (1927, 1942), Jolly (1987), Kastovsky (1973), Keyser and Roeper (1984), Kilby (1984), Kirchner (1955, 1959), G. Lakoff (1968, 1970a), G. Lakoff and J.R. Ross (1972), Langacker (1991), Lee (1971), B. Levin and Rappaport Hovav (1992b), Lipka (1976), Lord (1979), Manzini (1992), Marantz (1984, 1988), Marchand (1969, 1974), J. McCawley (1968a), G. Miller and Fellbaum (1991), Morgan (1969), Mukhin (1985), Parsons (1990), Pinker (1989), Pustejovsky (1988, 1991b), Ravin (1990), Richardson (1983), C.S. Smith (1970, 1972), Sundén (1916a, 1916b), Vendler (1972), Wall (1968), Wasow (1977), Zubizarreta (1987). See Rothemberg (1974) and Ruwet (1972) for an in-depth discussion of a similar phenomenon in French.

The verb classes in this section all relate to changes of state. Several subsets of this class that have been singled out in other studies, or that show distinguishing properties, are treated separately. However, subsection 45.4, "Other Alternating

Verbs of Change of State," provides a general treatment of the properties of this class of verbs as a whole.

45.1 *Break* Verbs

References: Brousseau and Ritter (1991), Dixon (1991), Fillmore (1967, 1968a, 1968b, 1977a, 1977b), Guerssel et al. (1985), Hale and Keyser (1986, 1987), Ney (1990), Pinker (1989), Ravin (1990), Richardson (1983), Ruhl (1972, 1979)

Class Members: break, chip, crack, crash, crush, fracture, rip, shatter, smash, snap, splinter, split, tear

Properties:

(831)   Tony broke the window with a hammer.

(832)   Causative/Inchoative Alternation:
    a.   Tony broke the window.
    b.   The window broke.

(833)   Middle Alternation:
    a.   Tony broke the crystal vase.
    b.   Crystal vases break easily.

(834)   Instrument Subject Alternation:
    a.   Tony broke the window with a hammer.
    b.   The hammer broke the window.

(835)   * *With/Against* Alternation:
    a.   Tony broke the cup against the wall.
    b.   * Tony broke the wall with the cup.

(836)   * Conative Alternation:
    a.   Tony broke the window.
    b.   * Tony broke at the window.

(837)   * Body-Part Possessor Ascension Alternation:
    a.   * Tony broke herself on the arm.
    b.   Tony broke her arm.

(838)   Unintentional interpretation available (some verbs):
    a.   Reflexive Object:
        * Tony broke himself.
    b.   Body-Part Object:
        Tony broke his finger.

(839)   Resultative Phrase:
         Tony broke the piggy bank open.
         Tony broke the glass to pieces.

(840)   Zero-related Nominal:
         a break
         a break in the window
         * the break of a window

Comments: These verbs refer to actions that bring about a change in the
"material integrity" of some entity (Hale and Keyser (1987)). They are often
contrasted with the *cut* verbs (cf. sec. 21.1), which also involve a change in
"material integrity;" but the *break* verbs, unlike the *cut* verbs, are pure verbs
of change of state, and their meaning, unlike that of the *cut* verbs, provides
no information about how the change of state came about. The most widely
cited property of the *break* verbs, and one that distinguishes them from the *cut*
verbs, is their ability to turn up in the causative/inchoative alternation. Both
types of verbs, however, are found in the middle alternation. Some of the *break*
verbs, like the *cut* verbs, allow unintentional, as well as intentional, action
interpretations with body-part objects; some of these verbs are also listed as
hurt verbs (sec. 40.8.3). However, unlike the *cut* verbs, they do not allow this
interpretation with reflexive objects; this property may be related to the fact
that the *break* verbs also differ from the *cut* verbs in not allowing body-part
possessor ascension.

Not all the *break* verbs have zero-related nominals. When they do, the
nominals describe the result of the action named by the verb. This interpretation
is also associated with nominals zero-related to the *cut* verbs.

45.2   *Bend* Verbs

Class Members: bend, crease, crinkle, crumple, fold, rumple, wrinkle

Properties:

(841)   Tony bent the rod with pliers.

(842)   Causative/Inchoative Alternation:
         a.   Tony bent the rod.
         b.   The rod bent.

(843)   Middle Alternation:
         a.   Tony bent the copper rod.
         b.   Copper rods bend easily.

(844)   Instrument Subject Alternation:
         a.   Tony bent the rod with pliers.
         b.   The pliers bent the rod.

(845)   * *With/Against* Alternation:
      a.   Tony bent the rod against the table.
      b. * Tony bent the table with the rod.

(846)   * Conative Alternation:
      a.   Tony bent the rod.
      b. * Tony bent at the rod.

(847)   * Body-Part Possessor Ascension Alternation:
      a. * Tony bent Mary in the arm.
      b.   Tony bent Mary's arm.

(848)   Resultative Phrase (some verbs):
      Tony bent the rod into a U.
      Tony folded the flaps open.

(849)   Zero-related Nominal (most verbs):
      a bend
      a bend in the rod
    * a bend of a rod

Comments: Unlike the *break* verbs above, the *bend* verbs relate to a change in the shape of an entity that does not disrupt its material integrity. These verbs show the same properties as the *break* verbs, except that they name reversible actions; thus one could "unbend" something but not "unbreak" it. Not all these verbs have zero-related nominals; when they do, the nominals describe the result of the action named by the verb.

45.3   Cooking Verbs

References: Atkins, Kegl, and B. Levin (1988), Ingria and Pustejovsky (1990), Lehrer (1969, 1974), Ilson and Mel'čuk (1990), Newman (1975), Pustejovsky (1991a), Schentke (1977), Sundén (1916b)

Class Members: bake, barbecue, blanch, boil, braise, broil, brown, charbroil, charcoal-broil, coddle, cook, crisp, deep-fry, French fry, fry, grill, hardboil, heat, microwave, oven-fry, oven-poach, overcook, pan-broil, pan-fry, parboil, parch, percolate, perk, plank, poach, pot-roast, rissole, roast, sauté, scald, scallop, shirr, simmer, softboil, steam, steam-bake, stew, stir-fry, toast

Properties:

(850)   Causative/Inchoative Alternation:
      a.   Jennifer baked the potatoes.
      b.   The potatoes baked.

(851)   Middle Alternation:
     a.   Jennifer baked Idaho potatoes.
     b.   Idaho potatoes bake beautifully.

(852)   Instrument Subject Alternation:
     a.   Jennifer baked the potatoes in the oven.
     b.   This oven bakes potatoes well.

(853)   * Conative Alternation:
     a.   Jennifer baked the potatoes.
     b.   * Jennifer baked at the potatoes.

(854)   * Cognate Object:
     * The cake baked a bake.

(855)   Resultative Phrase:
     Jennifer boiled the pot dry.
     Jennifer baked the potatoes to a crisp.

(856)   Adjectival Passive Participle:
     a baked potato

Comments: These verbs describe different ways of cooking food. Many of these verbs show properties of both change of state verbs and the *prepare*-type (or sometimes the *build*-type) verbs of creation and transformation; they have been cross-listed (sec. 26.1, 26.3). That is, in addition to the properties illustrated in this section, they participate in the benefactive, the unspecified object, and the material/product alternations. These properties are not listed here, since they are associated with this other class membership. Other verbs of cooking simply describe the cooking process and are not also used as verbs of creation and transformation; these verbs do not easily allow the benefactive, unspecified object, or material/product alternations.

Some of the verbs listed above have been included even though they do not seem to be found in the causative/inchoative alternation (e.g., *plank* and *shirr*); however, some verbs that might appear to resist the inchoative use can show this use in the progressive. The verbs *cook*, *bake*, *boil*, and *fry*—those verbs which describe the basic methods of cooking—are the ones that show the widest range of properties.

45.4   Other Alternating Verbs of Change of State

Class Members:
abate, advance, age, air, alter, atrophy, awake, balance, blast, blur, burn, burst, capsize, change, char, chill, clog, close, collapse, collect, compress, condense, contract, corrode, crumble, decompose, decrease, deflate, defrost, degrade, diminish, dissolve, distend, divide, double, drain, ease, enlarge, expand, explode,

fade, fill, flood, fray, freeze, frost, fuse, grow, halt, heal, heat, hush, ignite, improve, increase, inflate, kindle, light, loop, mature, melt, multiply, overturn, pop, quadruple, rekindle, reopen, reproduce, rupture, scorch, sear, short, short-circuit, shrink, shrivel, singe, sink, soak, splay, sprout, steep, stretch, submerge, subside, taper, thaw, tilt, tire, topple, triple, unfold, vary, warp

ZERO-RELATED TO ADJECTIVE: blunt, clear, clean, cool, crisp, dim, dirty, double, dry, dull, empty, even, firm, level, loose, mellow, muddy, narrow, open, pale, quiet, round, shut, slack, slim, slow, smooth, sober, sour, steady, tame, tense, thin, triple, warm

CHANGE OF COLOR: blacken, brown, crimson, gray, green, purple, redden, silver, tan, whiten, yellow

−en VERBS: awaken, brighten, broaden, cheapen, coarsen, dampen, darken, deepen, fatten, flatten, freshen, gladden, harden, hasten, heighten, lengthen, lessen, lighten, loosen, moisten, neaten, quicken, quieten, ripen, roughen, sharpen, shorten, sicken, slacken, smarten, soften, steepen, stiffen, straighten, strengthen, sweeten, tauten, thicken, tighten, toughen, waken, weaken, widen, worsen

−ify VERBS: acetify, acidify, alkalify, calcify, carbonify, dehumidify, emulsify, fructify, gasify, humidify, intensify, lignify, liquefy, magnify, nitrify, ossify, petrify, purify, putrefy, silicify, solidify, stratify, vitrify

−ize VERBS: americanize, caramelize, carbonize, crystallize, decentralize, demagnetize, democratize, depressurize, destabilize, energize, equalize, fossilize, gelatinize, glutenize, harmonize, hybridize, iodize, ionize, magnetize, neutralize, oxidize, polarize, pulverize, regularize, stabilize, unionize, vaporize, volatilize, westernize

−ate VERBS: accelerate, agglomerate, ameliorate, attenuate, coagulate, decelerate, de-escalate, degenerate, desiccate, deteriorate, detonate, disintegrate, dissipate, evaporate, federate, granulate, incubate, levitate, macerate, operate, proliferate, propagate, ulcerate, vibrate

Properties:

(857)   Causative/Inchoative Alternation:
       a. Bill dried the clothes.
       b. The clothes dried.

(858)   Middle Alternation:
       a. Bill dried the cotton clothes.
       b. Cotton clothes dry easily.

(859)   Instrument Subject Alternation:
       a. Bill dried the clothes with a hairdryer.
       b. The hairdryer dried the clothes.

(860)   * Conative Alternation:
      a.   Bill dried the clothes.
      b. * Bill dried at the clothes.

(861)   * Locative Alternation (intransitive):
      a.   A lot of clothes are drying on the line.
      b. * The line is drying with a lot of clothes.

(862)   * Locative Alternation (transitive):
      a.   Bill is drying a lot of clothes on the line.
      b. * Bill is drying the line with a lot of clothes.

(863)   * Locative Inversion:
      a.   A lot of clothes are drying on the line.
      b. * On the line are drying a lot of clothes.

(864)   * *There*-Insertion:
      a.   A lot of clothes are drying on the line.
      b. * On the line there are drying a lot of clothes.

(865)   * Cognate Object:
      * The clothes dried a dry.

(866)   Resultative Phrase:
      The clothes dried wrinkled.

(867)   Adjectival Passive Participle:
      dried clothes (related to transitive *dry*)

Comments: This subsection includes a variety of verbs that relate to externally caused changes of state. Many of these changes of state involve changes
of physical state. Many of these verbs are de-adjectival; as noted in Dixon
(1982b), dimensional and physical property adjectives often give rise to such
verbs, while human propensity adjectives (e.g., *bold, proud, modest*) do not.
The most cited property of these verbs is their ability to participate in the
causative/inchoative alternation. They also permit instrument subjects. These
verbs differ from verbs of existence and appearance in not showing certain
alternations that are typically restricted to intransitive verbs: the *swarm*-type
locative alternation, locative inversion, and *there*-insertion (unless they also
permit a verb of appearance or existence sense). This behavior appears to be
characteristic of verbs of change of state in general, although it has not been
illustrated with the other subclasses of those verbs here.

45.5   Verbs of Entity-Specific Change of State

Class Members: blister, bloom, blossom, burn, corrode, decay, deteriorate,
erode, ferment, flower, germinate, molder, molt, rot, rust, sprout, stagnate,
swell, tarnish, wilt, wither

Properties:

(868)   The roses bloomed.

(869)   * Causative Alternations:
         a. * The sun bloomed the roses.
         b.   The roses bloomed.

(870)   * Cognate Object:
         * The roses bloomed a blossom.

(871)   Adjectival Perfect Participle (some verbs):
         sprouted wheat

Comments: These verbs describe changes of state that are specific to particular entities. That is, these verbs impose very narrow selectional restrictions on
their arguments. For example, silver and some other metals tarnish, flowers and
plants wilt, and so on. The changes of state these verbs describe often cannot
be directly caused, but rather are inherent to the entities that undergo them. In
contrast, the alternating verbs of change of state of secs. 45.1–45.4 describe
changes that can be brought about externally by an agent. A few of the verbs
listed here describe changes of state that can be brought about either through
inherent properties of the entity undergoing the change of state or by an external
cause; these verbs are cross-listed under other alternating verbs of change of
state (sec. 45.4). Usually such verbs show a causative form only with a very
narrow range of causers. Some of the verbs in this class, such as *blossom* and
burn, allow both an entity-specific change of state use and an entity-specific
mode of being use; these verbs are also cross-listed (cf. sec. 47.2).

45.6   Verbs of Calibratable Changes of State

Class Members: appreciate, balloon, climb, decline, decrease, depreciate,
differ, diminish, drop, fall, fluctuate, gain, grow, increase, jump, ?mushroom,
plummet, plunge, rocket, rise, skyrocket, soar, surge, tumble, vary

Properties:

(872)   The temperature soared.

(873)   Possessor Subject Possessor-Attribute Factoring Alternation (intran-
         sitive):
         a.   The price of oil soared.
         b.   Oil soared in price.

(874)   * Causative Alternations:
         a.   The temperature soared.
         b. * The heat soared the temperature.

(875)   * *There*-Insertion:
    a. Oil soared in price.
    b. * There soared oil in price.

(876)   * Locative Inversion:
    a. Oil soared in price.
    b. * In price soared oil.

(877)   * Cognate Object:
    * Oil soared a soar.

(878)   soaring temperatures

(879)   * Adjectival Perfect Participle:
    * soared prices

Comments: These verbs describe positive or negative changes along a scale. They involve entities that themselves have a measurable attribute. The change can be predicated directly of the attribute (i.e., the attribute is the subject) or the change can be predicated of the entity possessing the attribute (i.e., the entity itself is the subject). When the attribute is the subject, the possessor of the attribute is expressed as a genitive modifier, but when the possessor is the subject, the attribute is expressed in a prepositional phrase.

46   *Lodge* Verbs

Class Members: bivouac, board, camp, dwell, live, lodge, reside, settle, shelter, stop, stay

Properties:

(880)   Cornelia lodged with the Stevensons.

(881)   Cornelia lodged at Mrs. Parker's.

(882)   Cornelia lodged in the new boarding house.

(883)   * *There*-Insertion:
    a. An old woman lodged at Mrs. Parker's.
    b. * There lodged an old woman at Mrs. Parker's.

(884)   * Locative Inversion:
    a. An old woman lodged at Mrs. Parker's.
    b. * At Mrs. Parker's lodged an old woman.

(885)   * Locative Alternation:
      a.   Squatters lodged in these abandoned buildings.
      b. * These abandoned buildings lodged with squatters.

(886)   Causative Alternation (some verbs):
      a.   The soldiers lodged in the schoolhouse.
          The army lodged the soldiers in the schoolhouse.
      b.   An old woman lived in the forest.
        * The king lived an old woman in the forest.

(887)   * Adjectival Passive/Perfect Participle:
      * a lodged person

(888)   *-er* Nominal (some verbs):
      a lodger

Comments: These verbs are used to describe one's living situation. In the sense intended here, they involve protagonist control. However, some of these verbs can be used as verbs of existence—asserting little more than existence at a location—and are cross-listed (sec. 47). Although some *lodge* verbs are found in *there*-insertion or locative inversion contexts, this possibility arises only with those verbs that are also verbs of existence and can probably be attributed to the availability of this additional sense. Some of the verbs in this class also allow a transitive causative use.

47   Verbs of Existence

47.1   *Exist* Verbs

References: Firbas (1966), Kimball (1973b), B. Levin and Rappaport Hovav (1992b). For discussion of the verb *lurk*, see Harnish (1975) and Sobin (1976). See also references under *There*-Insertion and Locative Inversion (sec. 6).

Class Members: coexist, ?correspond, ?depend, dwell, endure, exist, extend, flourish, languish, linger, live, loom, lurk, overspread, persist, predominate, prevail, prosper, remain, reside, shelter, stay, survive, thrive, tower, wait

Properties:

(889)   Unicorns don't exist (on the Earth).

(890)   *There*-Insertion:
    a.   A solution to this problem exists.
    b.   There exists a solution to this problem.

(891)   Locative Inversion:
    a.   An old woman languished in the forest.
    b.   In the forest languished an old woman.

(892)   * Locative Alternation:
    a.   A crowd of people remained in the square.
    b.   * The square remained with a crowd of people.

(893)   * Causative Alternations:
    a.   A solution to this problem exists.
    b.   * The famous mathematician existed a solution to the problem.

(894)   the existing solution

(895)   * Adjectival Perfect Participle:
    * an existed solution

Comments: These verbs relate to the existence of an entity at some location. Some of them require a locative prepositional phrase complement. These verbs do not impose restrictions on the argument whose existence they assert that are as specific as those imposed by verbs of entity-specific modes of being. Unlike the verbs of entity-specific modes of being, *exist* verbs are not found in the locative alternation. However, these verbs do figure among the prototypical locative inversion and *there*-insertion verbs. Some of them are basically *lodge* verbs (cf. above). Other verbs in this class have an extended use as *gorge* verbs and are cross-listed (sec. 39.6).

47.2   Verbs of Entity-Specific Modes of Being

Class Members: billow, bloom, blossom, blow, breathe, bristle, bulge, burn, cascade, corrode, decay, decompose, effervesce, erode, ferment, fester, fizz, flow, flower, foam, froth, germinate, grow, molt, propagate, rage, ripple, roil, rot, rust, seethe, smoke, smolder, spread, sprout, stagnate, stream, sweep, tarnish, trickle, wilt, wither

Properties:

(896)   The beer foamed.

(897)   *There*-Insertion (some verbs):
    a.   A fire raged in the mountains.
    b.   In the mountains there raged a fire.

(898)   Locative Inversion (some verbs):
     a.   A fire raged all through the mountains.
     b.   All through the mountains raged a fire.

(899)   Locative Alternation (some verbs):
     a.   Roses flowered in the garden.
     b.   The garden flowered with roses.

(900)   * Causative Alternations (with a few exceptions):
     a.   A fire raged over the fields.
     b. * The farmers raged a fire over the fields.

(901)   a raging fire

(902)   * Adjectival Perfect Participle:
     * a raged fire

(903)   * –er Nominal:
     * a rager, *a foamer

Comments: Each of these verbs describes a state of existence that is typical of certain entities, and concomitantly, each of them occurs with a very limited set of subjects. In this respect, these verbs are like the verbs of emission. Some of these verbs can also be used as verbs of entity-specific change of state (sec. 45.5); they can describe an entity coming to be in a particular state of existence.

47.3   Verbs of Modes of Being Involving Motion

References: Jackendoff (1990b)

Class Members: bob, bow, creep, dance, drift, eddy, flap, float, flutter, hover, jiggle, joggle, oscillate, pulsate, quake, quiver, revolve, rock, rotate, shake, stir, sway, swirl, teeter, throb, totter, tremble, undulate, vibrate, waft, wave, waver, wiggle, wobble, writhe

Properties:

(904)   A large flag fluttered.

(905)   A large flag fluttered over the fort.

(906)   * Locative Alternation:
     a.   Many flags fluttered over the fort.
     b. * The fort fluttered with many flags.

(907)   *There*-Insertion (some verbs):
     a.   A large flag fluttered over the fort.
     b.   Over the fort there fluttered a large flag.

(908)   Locative Inversion (some verbs):
     a. A large flag fluttered over the fort.
     b. Over the fort fluttered a large flag.

(909)   Causative Alternation (some verbs):
     a. The tree trembled.
         * The foresters trembled the tree.
     b. The flag waved.
         The patriots waved the flag.

(910)   a trembling tree, a fluttering flag

(911)   * Adjectival Perfect Participle:
      * a trembled tree

Comments: These verbs describe states of existence of inanimate entities that involve types of motion typical of these entities. That is, a type of motion characterizes the existence of these entities. Reflecting this property, these verbs take a very limited range of subjects. Some of them can also be used with animate subjects as verbs of body-internal movement; these verbs are cross-listed (sec. 49). A few of the verbs included in this section can be used transitively to describe causing an entity to be in the state of existence named by the verb.

47.4   Verbs of Sound Existence

Class Members: ?din, echo, resonate, resound, reverberate, sound

Properties:

(912)   The voices echoed (through the hall).

(913)   Locative Alternation:
     a. The voices echoed in the hall.
     b. The hall is echoing with voices.

(914)   *There*-Insertion:
     a. A loud cry echoed through the hall.
     b. Through the hall there echoed a loud cry.

(915)   Locative Inversion:
     a. A loud cry echoed through the hall.
     b. Through the hall echoed a loud cry.

(916)   * Causative Alternations:
     a. The music echoed.
     b. * The magician echoed the music.

(917)   * an echoing voice

(918)   * Adjectival Perfect Participle:
        * an echoed voice

(919)   * -*er* Nominal:
        *an echoer

Comments: These verbs are often included among the verbs of sound emission (cf. sec. 43.2), but they do not actually seem to belong to this class. Rather than describing the emission of a particular sound, they describe the existence of a sound, although they are vague as to the exact nature of the sound. These verbs show the intransitive *swarm* form of the locative alternation (cf. sec. 2.3.4). The verb *sound* appears to behave slightly differently from the others, but its behavior may be attributable to the existence of several senses of this verb. For instance, *sound* does allow transitive causative uses, but it is possible that in its transitive use the verb does not simply describe the bringing into existence of a sound, but rather describes the bringing into existence of a particular type of sound. Evidence for this proposal is that the transitive use of *sound* appears to allow a more limited range of noun phrases as direct object than its intransitive use allows as subject.

47.5   Verbs of Group Existence

The verbs in the next three subclasses relate to the existence of a group or aggregate.

47.5.1   *Swarm* Verbs

References: Bach (1980), J. Lumsden (1991), Salkoff (1983). See also references under *Spray/Load* Verbs (sec. 9.7).

Class Members: abound, bustle, crawl, creep, hop, run, swarm, swim, teem, throng

Properties:

(920)   Locative Alternation:
        a.   Bees are swarming in the garden. (locative variant)
        b.   The garden is swarming with bees. (*with* variant)

(921)   Locative Inversion:
        a.   A striped fish swam in the aquarium.
        b.   In the aquarium swam a striped fish.

(922)   *There*-Insertion:
        a.   A striped fish swam in the aquarium.
        b.   In the aquarium there swam a striped fish.

(923) * Causative Alternations:
    a.   Bees are swarming in the garden.
       * The beekeeper swarmed bees in the garden.
    b.   The garden is swarming with bees.
       * The beekeeper swarmed the garden with bees.

Comments: These verbs participate in the form of the locative alternation displayed by intransitive verbs; specifically, the alternation they display is most similar to that shown by the *spray/load* verbs. These verbs show the "holistic/partitive" effect; the "holistic" interpretation is associated with the subject of the *with* variant. Some of these verbs are *run* verbs (sec. 51.3.2) in their basic sense, and are cross-listed here.

47.5.2 *Herd* Verbs

Class Members: accumulate, aggregate, amass, assemble, cluster, collect, congregate, convene, flock, gather, group, herd, huddle, mass

Properties:

(924) The cattle are herding in the pasture.

(925) * Locative Alternation:
    a.   The cattle are herding in the pasture.
    b. * The pasture is herding with cattle.

(926) Causative Alternation (some verbs):
    a.   The cattle herded.
    b.   I herded the cattle.

(927) Zero-related Nominal (some verbs):
    a herd

Comments: These verbs are found in a syntactic frame that resembles the locative variant associated with the intransitive form of the locative alternation shown by the *swarm* verbs (sec. 2.3.4). The verbs in this class take collective NPs as subjects, and some of them are zero-related to collective nouns. Some of these verbs have a transitive use which is included under the *shake* verbs (sec. 22.3); the properties relating to this use are described there.

47.5.3 *Bulge* Verbs

Class Members: bristle, bulge, seethe

Properties:

(928) The bag is bulging with groceries.

(929)   * Locative Alternation:
      a.   * Groceries are bulging in the bag.
      b.   The bag is bulging with groceries.

(930)   * Causative Alternations:
      a.   The bag is bulging (with groceries).
      b.   * I bulged the bag (with groceries).

Comments: These verbs are found in a syntactic frame that resembles the *with* variant associated with the intransitive *swarm* form of the locative alternation (cf. sec. 2.3.4). There is a "holistic" interpretation associated with the subject of these verbs.

47.6   Verbs of Spatial Configuration

References: Dixon (1991), Dowty (1975, 1979), Kearns (1991), G. Lakoff (1966), Lehrer (1990), B. Levin and Rappaport Hovav (1992b), Ljung (1980), Mulder and Wehrmann (1989), Snell-Hornby (1983)

Class Members: balance, bend, bow, crouch, dangle, flop, fly, hang, hover, jut, kneel, lean, lie, loll, loom, lounge, nestle, open, perch, plop, project, protrude, recline, rest, rise, roost, sag, sit, slope, slouch, slump, sprawl, squat, stand, stoop, straddle, swing, tilt, tower

Properties:

(931)   A statue stood on the corner/next to the building.

(932)   *There*-Insertion:
      a.   A statue of Jefferson stood on the corner.
      b.   There stood on the corner a statue of Jefferson.

(933)   Locative Inversion:
      a.   A statue of Jefferson stood on the corner of the two boulevards.
      b.   On the corner of the two boulevards stood a statue of Jefferson.

(934)   Causative Alternation (some verbs):
      a.   They stood the statue on the pedestal.
      b.   The statue stood on the pedestal.

(935)   the hanging gardens
      the leaning tower

(936)   * Adjectival Perfect Participle:
      * hung gardens

Comments: As part of their meaning, the members of this subset of the verbs of existence specify the spatial configuration of an entity with respect to some location. Some of these verbs have transitive uses as verbs of putting in a spatial configuration; the properties associated with this use are listed under Verbs of Putting in a Spatial Configuration (sec. 9.2). This transitive use has been included here under the label "causative alternation." This alternation is not the causative/inchoative alternation, since the intransitive use does not have the change of state or change of location interpretation that is associated with the intransitive variant of the prototypical verbs showing that alternation. In English, many verbs of spatial configuration, such as *hang* or *sit*, also have another intransitive use as verbs of assuming a position; these verbs are cross-listed (cf. sec. 50). However, there are some languages where verbs of spatial configuration and verbs of assuming a position are not lexicalized by a single verb form; see Talmy (1985) for a brief discussion of the lexicalization patterns associated with these verbs.

When those verbs that permit both intransitive uses are found in the *there*-insertion or locative inversion constructions, they only have the spatial configuration interpretation, although the same verbs might be open to both intepretations when used in other contexts.

47.7 *Meander* Verbs

References: D.C. Bennett (1975), Brugman and G. Lakoff (1988), Dowty (1979), Jackendoff (1990b), G. Lakoff (1987), B. Levin and Rappaport Hovav (1992b)

Class Members: cascade, climb, crawl, cut, drop, go, meander, plunge, run, straggle, stretch, sweep, tumble, turn, twist, wander, weave, wind

Properties:

(937)   The river runs from the lake to the sea.

(938)   The stream winds/twists/crawls through the valley.

(939)   Locative Inversion:
         a.   A rushing stream ran through the valley.
         b.   Through the valley ran a rushing stream.

(940)   *There*-Insertion:
         a.   A rushing stream ran through the valley.
         b.   There ran through the valley a rushing stream.

Comments: The verbs in this class have been described by Dowty (1979) as "pseudo-motional locative" verbs. This label reflects the fact that many of these verbs are verbs of motion that are being used to describe the location of a long continuous object such as a road or a river. A few of the verbs that are used to describe the location of such an object are not verbs of motion in their basic sense (e.g., *sweep*, *cut*), although even they do show an extended sense as a verb of motion. It is possible that verbs of motion other than the ones listed here could also show this use.

47.8   Verbs of Contiguous Location

References: Dixon (1991), Green (1971), Grimshaw (1990), Gruber (1965, 1976), Nunberg (1978), Pinker (1989), Rice (1987)

Class Members: abut, adjoin, blanket, border, bound, bracket, bridge, cap, contain, cover, cross, dominate, edge, encircle, enclose, fence, fill, flank, follow, frame, head, hit, hug, intersect, line, meet, miss, overhang, precede, rim, ring, skirt, span, straddle, support, surmount, surround, top, touch, underlie

Properties:

(941)   Italy borders France.

(942)   Adjectival Passive Participle:
         France is bordered by Italy.
         * France is bordered.

(943)   Understood Reciprocal Object Alternation (some verbs):
         a.   Italy touches France.
               Italy and France touch.
         b.   Snow caps the mountain.
               * Snow and the mountain cap.

Comments: These verbs are used to describe a spatial relation between two entities that are contiguous in space. They are basically transitive; the two entities are expressed as the subject and object of the verb, respectively. Some members of this class (e.g., *intersect, meet, touch*) describe a symmetric relationship between two entities; these verbs may show the understood reciprocal object alternation. A number of the verbs in this class have other senses; several are found among the *fill* verbs (sec. 9.8), while others are listed among the members of other verb classes. In their other uses, these verbs are agentive and mean roughly "cause something to be in a particular spatial relation that involves contiguity." As noted by Grimshaw (1990), these verbs require a *by* phrase in the passive.

48 Verbs of Appearance, Disappearance, and Occurrence

48.1 Verbs of Appearance

48.1.1 *Appear* Verbs

References: Faber (1987), Firbas (1966), Kimball (1973b), B. Levin and Rappaport Hovav (1992b). See also references under *There*-Insertion and Locative Inversion (sec. 6).

Class Members: appear, arise, awake, awaken, break, burst, come, dawn, derive, develop, emanate, emerge, erupt, evolve, exude, flow, form, grow, gush, issue, materialize, open, plop, result, rise, spill, spread, steal, stem, stream, supervene, surge, wax;

Class Members: pop up, show up, turn up

Properties:

(944)   A ship appeared.

(945)   A ship appeared on the horizon.

(946)   *There*-Insertion (most verbs):
    a.   A ship appeared on the horizon.
    b.   There appeared a ship on the horizon.

(947)   Locative Inversion (most verbs):
    a.   A large ship appeared on the horizon.
    b.   On the horizon appeared a large ship.

(948)   * Causative Alternations (many verbs):
    a.   A dove appeared from the magician's sleeve.
    b. * The magician appeared a dove from his sleeve.

(949)   Adjectival Perfect Participle:
    a recently appeared book

Comments: These verbs describe the appearance of an entity on the scene. Although all of these verbs can take prepositional phrase complements, some of them do not require them. These verbs also differ as to the types of prepositional phrases they allow. Some take various types of locative phrases; others are limited to *from* phrases.

In determining what verbs to include in this class, a rather broad definition of the notion "verb of appearance" was used. Further study might suggest that some of the verbs listed should not have been included. However, it is worth pointing out that some of the verbs listed, such as *break* and *open*, are basically verbs of change of state and are used as verbs of appearance in an extended, possibly figurative, sense. This dual class membership makes it difficult to determine whether the verbs in this class behave uniformly with respect to the causative alternations. As noted above, many of these verbs do not have transitive uses with a causative interpretation, and it seems that those verbs that do show transitive causative uses show them on a sense other than their appearance sense, but this needs to be more carefully studied.

For further discussion of these verbs, see the references listed under Locative Inversion and *There*-Insertion (sec. 6), since *appear* verbs are considered to belong to one of the canonical classes of verbs found in these constructions.

48.1.2   Reflexive Verbs of Appearance

References: Geniušienė (1987), Poutsma (1904), Sigler (1985)

Class Members: assert, declare, define, express, form, intrude, manifest, offer, pose, present, proffer, recommend, shape, show, suggest

Properties:

(950)   A solution immediately presented itself.

(951)   * A solution immediately presented.

(952)   A solution immediately presented itself to him.

(953)   * *There*-Insertion:
     a.   A wonderful opportunity presented itself yesterday.
     b.   * There presented itself a wonderful opportunity yesterday.

(954)   * Locative Inversion:
     a.   A wonderful opportunity presented itself to him yesterday.
     b.   * To him presented itself a wonderful opportunity.

(955)   Reflexive of Appearance Alternation (except *intrude*):
     a.   I presented a solution yesterday.
     b.   A solution presented itself yesterday.

Comments: The verbs in this class are being used as verbs of appearance. All of them (with the possible exception of *intrude*) can be used transitively as two-argument verbs; however, such a use of these verbs is obligatorily associated with the presence of a reflexive pronoun as object. When they are used as verbs of appearance, the subject of these verbs bears the same semantic relation to the verb as the object does in the ordinary transitive use. The argument that is the subject of the typical transitive use of the verb is not expressed. These verbs are set apart from the *appear* verbs above both by the existence of a transitive use and by the obligatory occurrence of a reflexive pronoun as object. These verbs appear not to be found in the *there*-insertion and locative inversion constructions.

48.2 Verbs of Disappearance

Class Members: die, disappear, expire, lapse, perish, vanish

Properties:

(956)   The crowd vanished.

(957) ?? *There*-Insertion:
   a.   A valuable 13th-century manuscript recently vanished from the library.
   b.?? There recently vanished from the library a valuable 13th-century manuscript.

(958) ?? Locative Inversion:
   a.   A valuable 13th-century manuscript recently vanished from the library.
   b.?? From the library vanished recently a valuable 13th-century manuscript.

(959) ∗ Causative Alternations:
   a.   The rabbit vanished into thin air.
   b. ∗ The magician vanished a rabbit into thin air.

(960)   Adjectival Perfect Participle:
        vanished civilizations

Comments: These verbs describe the disappearance or going out of existence of some entity. It has been noted in the literature on *there*-insertion and locative inversion that these verbs are not typically acceptable in either of these constructions; however, Kimball (1973b) observes that their acceptability can be improved in carefully constructed contexts, particularly those contrived so that these verbs take on an appearance sense.

48.3 Verbs of Occurrence

Class Members: ensue, eventuate, happen, occur, recur, transpire

Properties:

(961)   The accident happened at three o'clock.

(962)   *There*-Insertion:
   a.   A serious accident happened yesterday.
   b.   There happened a serious accident yesterday.

(963)   Locative Inversion:
   a. A serious accident happened in front of them.
   b. In front of them happened a serious accident.

(964)   * Causative Alternations:
   a. The accident happened.
   b. * The motorist happened the accident.

Comments: These verbs describe the occurrence of an event. They are some-times included among the *appear* verbs, and like the *appear* verbs, they are found in the locative inversion and *there*-insertion constructions. These verbs are not found in transitive uses with a causative interpretation.

49 Verbs of Body-Internal Motion

References: Cowper (1990a), Jackendoff (1990b), B. Levin and Rappaport Hovav (1992b)

Class Members: buck, fidget, flap, gyrate, kick, rock, squirm, sway, teeter, totter, twitch, waggle, wiggle, wobble, wriggle

Properties:

(965)   Sylvia fidgeted.

(966)   * Causative Alternations:
   a. Sylvia fidgeted.
   b. * The lecture fidgeted Sylvia.

(967)   * Body-Part Object:
   * Sylvia fidgeted her fingers.

(968)   Resultative Phrase (some verbs):
   Sylvia fidgeted herself into a tizzy.
   * Sylvia twitched the teacher angry.

(969)   Directional Phrase:
   Sylvia wriggled out of her seat.
   The sick man wobbled down the stairs.

Comments: These verbs, which describe movements of the body, take an-imate subjects. In isolation, they do not entail any displacement; however, in the presence of a goal or directional phrase, they may. Some of these verbs are also used as verbs describing modes of being involving motion; these verbs are cross-listed (sec. 47.3). Some of the verbs of body-internal motion, particularly those that involve the movement of a particular body part, can be used transitively, with the part of the body that is involved as the direct object. The verbs in this class are typically not found in any of the causative alternations.

50   Verbs of Assuming a Position

References: B. Levin and Rappaport Hovav (1992b)

Class Members: bend, bow, crouch, flop, hang, kneel, lean, lie, perch, plop, rise, sit, slouch, slump, sprawl, squat, stand, stoop, straddle

Properties:

(970)   The dog flopped in the corner/onto the bed.

(971)   * *There*-Insertion:
      a.   A dog lay in the corner.
      b. * There lay a dog in the corner. (on the relevant interpretation)
         * There lay in the corner a dog. (on the relevant interpretation)

(972)   * Locative Inversion:
      a.   A dog lay in the corner.
      b. * In the corner lay a dog. (on the relevant interpretation)

Comments: All of the verbs in this class have several senses. This section describes the properties these verbs show in the sense of "assume the spatial configuration specific to the verb." However, they all have another intransitive sense as verbs of being in a particular spatial configuration (cf. sec. 47.6), and many of them also have a transitive sense as verbs of putting in a spatial configuration (cf. sec. 9.2); all of the verbs in this class are cross-listed as appropriate. (Some languages morphologically distinguish these different senses; see Talmy (1985).) In the assume position sense these verbs are incompatible with locative inversion and *there*-insertion, even though in the being in a spatial configuration sense they are found in these constructions. These verbs cannot be used transitively in the sense of "cause to assume the spatial configuration specific to the verb." See also the discussion under Verbs of Spatial Configuration and Verbs of Putting in a Spatial Configuration.

51 Verbs of Motion

References: Amsler (1980), Aske (1989), D.C. Bennett (1975), Binnick (1971), Choi and Bowerman (1991), Collier and Fellbaum (1988), Cowper (1990a, 1990b), Croft (1991), Dixon (1991), Dowty (1979, 1991), Emonds (1991), Faber (1987), Fellbaum (1990), Fillmore (1972, 1977b, 1978, 1986), Gruber (1965, 1976), Heringer (1976), Ikegami (1970, 1973), Jackendoff (1972, 1976, 1983, 1990b), Kupferman (1985), Lehrer (1990), B. Levin and Rappaport (1989), B. Levin and Rappaport Hovav (1992a, 1992b), G. Miller (1972), G. Miller and Fellbaum (1991), G. Miller and Johnson-Laird (1976), Mukhin (1985), Ostler (1980a, 1980b), Radden (1988), Ravin (1990), Schlyter (1979), Snell-Hornby (1983), Stratton (1971), Talmy (1975, 1985)

51.1 Verbs of Inherently Directed Motion

Class Members: advance, arrive, ascend, ?climb, come, ?cross, depart, descend, enter, escape, exit, fall, flee, go, leave, plunge, recede, return, rise, tumble

Properties:

(973)   The convict escaped.

(974)   Locative Preposition Drop Alternation (some verbs):
        a.   The convict escaped from the police.
        b.   The convict escaped the police.

(975)   * Causative Alternations:
        a.   The convict escaped.
        b. * The collaborators escaped the convict.
           (on the interpretation "cause to escape")

(976)   * Measure Phrase:
       * The convict escaped three miles.

(977)   Adjectival Perfect Participle:
       an escaped convict (a convict that has escaped)
       * an escaped jail

(978)   Depictive Phrase:
       The convict escaped exhausted.
       (on the interpretation where the convict escapes feeling exhausted)

(979)   * Resultative Phrase:
       * The convict escaped exhausted.
       (on the interpretation where the escape exhausts the convict)

Comments: The meaning of these verbs includes a specification of the direction of motion, even in the absence of an overt directional complement. For some verbs this specification is in deictic terms; for others it is in nondeictic terms. None of these verbs specify the manner of motion. However, the members of this class do not behave uniformly in all respects. They differ as to how they can express the goal, source, or path of motion; depending on the verb, these may be expressed via a prepositional phrase, as a direct object, or both. The verb *cross* has been included here because of its meaning, but it does not behave in all respects like the other verbs in this class; for instance, it is always transitive. The verbs in this class have received a certain amount of attention in the literature on the Unaccusative Hypothesis.

51.2 *Leave* Verbs

Class Members: abandon, desert, leave

Properties:

(980)   We abandoned the area.

(981)   * We abandoned from the area.

(982)   Adjectival Passive Participle (some verbs):
         an abandoned house

Comments: These verbs do not specify a manner of motion; they simply indicate that motion away from a location has taken place. The direct object of these verbs is understood to be the location that has been left. The location cannot be expressed in a prepositional phrase.

51.3 Manner of Motion Verbs

These verbs describe motion that typically, though not necessarily, involves displacement, but none of them specifies an inherent direction as part of its meaning. All of these verbs have meanings that include a notion of manner or means of motion. They differ from each other in terms of the specific manner or means.

51.3.1 *Roll* Verbs

Class Members:
bounce, drift, drop, float, glide, move, roll, slide, swing
MOTION AROUND AN AXIS: coil, revolve, rotate, spin, turn, twirl, twist, whirl, wind

Properties:

(983)   The ball rolled.

(984)   The ball rolled down the hill/over the hill/into the gutter.

(985)   Causative/Inchoative Alternation (most verbs):
         a.   Bill rolled the ball down the hill.
         b.   The ball rolled down the hill.

(986)   * Locative Preposition Drop Alternation:
         a.   The ball rolled down the hill.
         b. * The ball rolled the hill.

(987)   Resultative Phrase:
         The drawer rolled open.
         * The cart rolled the rubber off its wheels.
         * The cart rolled its way down the hill.

(988)   Adjectival Passive Participle:
         a constantly rolled ball (related to transitive *roll*)

Comments: These verbs relate to manners of motion that are characteristic of inanimate entities (i.e., where there is not necessarily protagonist control on the part of the moving entity). In the absence of a prepositional phrase specifying direction, none of these verbs indicates the direction of motion. Many of the *roll* verbs that describe motion around an axis take a rather restricted range of prepositions heading the prepositional phrase that describes the path of motion.

Most of the verbs in this class show the causative/inchoative alternation. However, this alternation is possible only if the motion is externally controllable. This restriction may explain why some of the verbs are not eligible for this alternation. For instance, the verbs *glide* and *drift* do not participate in this alternation, and gliding and drifting are not typically externally controllable. Those verbs that do have a transitive causative use typically show the properties of the *coil* verb subclass of the verbs of putting if they describe motion around an axis (cf. sec. 9.6), or the *slide* verb subclass of the verbs of sending and carrying, otherwise (cf. sec. 11.2). (The verb *roll* is the exception, showing properties of both classes.) Those verbs with transitive uses are also listed under the appropriate transitive class. This section focuses on the properties related to their intransitive use; the properties related to their transitive use are discussed under *Slide* Verbs or *Coil* Verbs, as appropriate.

51.3.2   *Run* Verbs

Class Members: amble, backpack, bolt, bounce, bound, bowl, canter, carom, cavort, charge, clamber, climb, clump, coast, crawl, creep, dart, dash, dodder, drift, file, flit, float, fly, frolic, gallop, gambol, glide, goosestep, hasten, hike, hobble, hop, hurry, hurtle, inch, jog, journey, jump, leap, limp, lollop, lope, lumber, lurch, march, meander, mince, mosey, nip, pad, parade, perambulate,

plod, prance, promenade, prowl, race, ramble, roam, roll, romp, rove, run, rush,
sashay, saunter, scamper, scoot, scram, scramble, scud, scurry, scutter, scuttle,
shamble, shuffle, sidle, skedaddle, skip, skitter, skulk, sleepwalk, slide, slink,
slither, slog, slouch, sneak, somersault, speed, stagger, stomp, stray, streak,
stride, stroll, strut, stumble, stump, swagger, sweep, swim, tack, tear, tiptoe,
toddle, totter, traipse, tramp, travel, trek, troop, trot, trudge, trundle, vault,
waddle, wade, walk, wander, whiz, zigzag, zoom

Properties:

(989)   The horse jumped over/across/into/out of the stream.

(990)   Induced Action Alternation (some verbs):
         a.   The horse jumped over the fence.
               Tom jumped the horse over the fence.
         b.   The lions jumped through the hoop.
               The lion tamer jumped the lions through the hoop.

(991)   Locative Preposition Drop Alternation (some verbs):
         a.   The horse jumped over the stream.
         b.   The horse jumped the stream.

(992)   *There*-Insertion:
         a.   A little white rabbit jumped out of the box.
         b.   There jumped out of the box a little white rabbit.

(993)   Locative Inversion:
         a.   A little white rabbit jumped out of the box.
         b.   Out of the box jumped a little white rabbit.

(994)   Measure Phrase (some verbs):
         We walked five miles.

(995)   Resultative Phrase:
         a.   We walked ourselves into a state of exhaustion.
               * We walked into a state of exhaustion.
         b.   Tom ran the soles off his shoes.

(996)   Adjectival Passive Participle (some verbs):
         the jumped/run/galloped horse
         (a horse that has been jumped/run/galloped by someone)

(997)   * Adjectival Perfect Participle:
         * the jumped horse (on the interpretation: a horse that has jumped)

(998)   * Cognate Object:
         * The horse jumped a high jump.

(999)   Zero-related Nominal (some verbs):
         a jump, a run, a walk

Comments: Most of these verbs describe the manners in which animate
entities can move, although some of them may be used to describe the movement
of inanimate entities. Although these verbs describe the displacement of an
object in a particular manner or by a particular means, no specific direction of
motion is implied unless they occur with an explicit directional phrase. The *run*
verbs probably need to be further subdivided. For instance, not all of them can be
found in the induced action alternation, nor do they all allow locative preposition
drop. When these verbs are found in the induced action construction, they may
or may not show an accompanied motion interpretation, as the two examples
illustrate. The verbs in this class may be found in the locative inversion and
there-insertion constructions, particularly when they occur with a directional
phrase. (When they are found in these constructions with locative phrases, they
may be being used as verbs of existence; however, these verbs are not cross-
listed as verbs of existence, since further study of this phenomenon is necessary.)
The *run* verbs are found to a limited extent in resultative constructions in which
the resultative phrase is predicated of a nonsubcategorized object. However,
despite the fact that many have zero-related result nominals, they do not take
cognate objects.

51.4   Verbs of Motion Using a Vehicle

51.4.1   Verbs That Are Vehicle Names

References: Bladin (1911), E.V. Clark and H.H. Clark (1979), Jespersen
(1942), Leitner (1974), Marchand (1969, 1974), Ostler and Atkins (1991),
Sehnert and Sharwood-Smith (1973)

Class Members: balloon, bicycle, bike, boat, bobsled, bus, cab, canoe, cara-
van, chariot, coach, cycle, dogsled, ferry, gondola, helicopter, jeep, jet, kayak,
moped, motor, motorbike, motorcycle, parachute, punt, raft, rickshaw, rocket,
skate, skateboard, ski, sled, sledge, sleigh, taxi, toboggan, tram, trolley, yacht

Properties:

(1000)   They skated.

(1001)   They skated along the canal/across the lake.

(1002)   Induced Action Alternation (some verbs):
          a.   He skated Penny around the rink.
          b.   Penny skated around the rink.

(1003)   Locative Preposition Drop Alternation (some verbs):
          a.   They skated along the canals.
          b.   They skated the canals.

(1004)   Resultative Phrase:
          Penny skated her skate blades blunt.

Comments: These verbs are all zero-related to nouns that are vehicle names;
they mean roughly "go using the vehicle named by the noun." In principle, it
should be possible for any vehicle name to be used as a verb of this type. The
members of this set of verbs describe the motion of an entity, but no specific
direction of motion is implied unless there is an explicit directional phrase
present. These verbs have not been attested in the locative inversion or *there*-
insertion constructions, although it is possible that they might be found in these
constructions.

51.4.2   Verbs That Are Not Vehicle Names

Class Members: cruise, drive, fly, oar, paddle, pedal, ride, row, sail, tack

Properties:

(1005)   They rowed.

(1006)   They rowed along the canal/across the lake.

(1007)   Induced Action Alternation (some verbs):
          a.   He rowed Penny across the lake.
          b.   Penny rowed across the lake.

(1008)   Locative Preposition Drop Alternation (some verbs):
          a.   They rowed along the canals of Venice.
          b.   They rowed the canals of Venice.

(1009)   Resultative Phrase:
          Penny rowed her palms raw.

Comments: Although these verbs are not zero-related to vehicle names, they
all describe motion using a particular type of vehicle. Some of these verbs are
zero-related to nouns that name parts used in propelling these vehicles. The
members of this set of verbs describe the motion of an entity, but no specific
direction of motion is implied unless there is an explicit directional phrase
present. These verbs have not been attested in the locative inversion or *there*-
insertion constructions, although it is possible that they might be found in these
constructions.

51.5   *Waltz* Verbs

References: Fellbaum and Kegl (1989), Ostler and Atkins (1991)

Class Members: boogie, bop, cancan, clog, conga, dance, foxtrot, jig, jitterbug, jive, pirouette, polka, quickstep, rumba, samba, shuffle, squaredance, tango, tapdance, waltz

Properties:

(1010)   They waltzed.

(1011)   They waltzed across/into/through the room.

(1012)   Induced Action Alternation:
    a.   She waltzed across the floor.
    b.   He waltzed her across the floor. (if dance involves a partner)

(1013)   Resultative Phrase:
She waltzed the soles off her shoes.

(1014)   Cognate Object:
They waltzed every other waltz.

Comments: These verbs are zero-related to names of dances and mean roughly "perform the dance." In principle, any dance name should give rise to a zero-related verb of this type. Although the members of this set of verbs describe motion, no specific direction of motion is implied unless there is an explicit directional phrase present. In this respect, these verbs pattern like the *run* verbs above. Verbs taking their names from dances involving partners appear to show slightly different behavior from those that do not; these are the verbs most likely to be found in the induced action alternation. *Waltz* verbs have not been attested in the locative inversion or *there*-insertion constructions, although it is possible that they might be found in these constructions. These verbs, although only listed under verbs of motion here, could also be viewed as performance verbs (cf. sec. 26.7).

51.6   *Chase* Verbs

References: Dixon (1991), Gawron (1983), Gruber (1965)

Class Members: chase, follow, pursue, shadow, tail, track, trail

Properties:

(1015)   Jackie chased the thief (down the street).

(1016)   Jackie chased after the thief. (few verbs)

(1017)   * Causative Alternations:
    a.   Jackie chased the thief (down the street).
    b.   * The thief chased (down the street).

Comments: The *chase* verbs are typically transitive, with the chaser as subject and the person being chased as object. Some of these verbs allow an intransitive use, with the chaser as subject and a prepositional phrase headed by *after* expressing what is being chased.

51.7 *Accompany* Verbs

Class Members: accompany, conduct, escort, guide, lead, shepherd

Properties:

(1018)   Jackie accompanied Rose.

(1019)   Jackie accompanied Rose to the store.

(1020)   * Causative Alternations:
      a.   Jackie accompanied Rose.
      b.   * Rose accompanied. (on the interpretation "be accompanied")

Comments: These verbs relate to one person taking a second from one place to another. The verbs are differentiated by the nature of the relation between the two participants.

52 *Avoid* Verbs

Class Members: avoid, ?boycott, dodge, duck, elude, evade, shun, sidestep

Properties:

(1021)   We avoided the area.

(1022)   * We avoided from the area.

Comments: The verbs in this class are related to avoidance. Many of these verbs are also found with gerundive sentential complements.

53 Verbs of Lingering and Rushing

References: Dixon (1991), Snell-Hornby (1983)

The verbs in this class describe the shortening or the prolongation of the time course of an event.

53.1 Verbs of Lingering

Class Members: dally, dawdle, delay, dither, hesitate, linger, loiter, tarry

Properties:

(1023)   Sasha dawdled in the museum.

(1024)   Sasha dawdled over lunch.

(1025)   * Causative Alternations:
       a.   Sasha dawdled over lunch.
       b. * Phyllis dawdled Sasha over lunch.

Comments: These verbs describe types of "lingering," as the name of their class suggests. Some of them can appear with a prepositional phrase headed by *over* that describes the event whose duration is protracted as a consequence of an action carried out by the subject of the verb. Only *delay* can be used transitively, to describe causing a delay.

53.2 Verbs of Rushing

Class Members: hasten, hurry, rush

Properties:

(1026)   Maggie hurried through the museum.

(1027)   Maggie hurried with her lunch.

(1028)   Causative Alternation:
       a.   Her sister hurried.
       b.   Maggie hurried her sister.

Comments: These verbs describe doing something quickly. All of these verbs can be used transitively with a causative interpretation.

54   Measure Verbs

References: Anderson (1988), Bach (1980), Bowers (1989), Croft (1991), Fillmore (1977b), Kegl and Fellbaum (1988, 1989), Klooster (1972, 1973, 1978), Na (1986), Nunberg (1978), Rizzi (1990)

54.1   *Register* Verbs

Class Members: measure, read, register, total, weigh

Properties:

(1029)   The package weighed ten pounds.

(1030)   * Passive:
      a.   The package weighed ten pounds.
      b. * Ten pounds was weighed by the package.

(1031)   * Causative Alternation:
      a.   The package weighed ten pounds.
      b. * I weighed the package ten pounds.

(1032)   I weighed the package.

Comments: These verbs describe the value of some attribute of an entity (e.g., height, weight, temperature) along a scale relevant to the characterization of this property. The particular attribute is determined by the verb. Register verbs can be used intransitively with a postverbal noun phrase expressing the measurement; this noun phrase does not show the properties of a direct object. When these verbs are used transitively, the noun phrase specifying the measurement cannot be expressed. Due to their inability to passivize, these verbs are sometimes discussed briefly in studies of the passive.

54.2   *Cost* Verbs

Class Members: carry, cost, last, take

Properties:

(1033)   The book costs $10.

(1034)   * Passive:
      * $10 was cost (by the book).

(1035)   * Causative Alternations:
      a.   The book costs $10.
      b. * I costed the book $10.

(1036)   * I costed the book.

Comments: These verbs describe the value of some attribute of an entity (e.g., height, weight, temperature) along a scale relevant to the characterization of this property. The particular attribute is determined by the verb. *Cost* verbs can be used intransitively, with a postverbal noun phrase expressing the measurement; this noun phrase does not show the properties of a direct object. Unlike the *register* verbs above, these verbs cannot be used transitively. Due to their inability to passivize, these verbs are sometimes discussed briefly in studies of the passive.

54.3 *Fit* Verbs

References: Perlmutter and Postal (1984)

Class Members: carry, contain, fit, feed, hold, house, seat, serve, sleep, store, take, use

(1037) Each room sleeps five people.

(1038) Location Subject Alternation:
  a.   We sleep five people in each room.
  b.   Each room sleeps five people.

(1039) * Passive:
  * Five people are slept in each room.

Comments: All the verbs in this class belong to other classes in their basic use; many of them are verbs of putting (cf. sec. 9). However, this section considers their use with oblique subjects that are locations. They are used with such location subjects to describe the capacity of the location with respect to the action named by the verb. Due to their inability to passivize, these verbs are sometimes discussed briefly in studies of the passive.

54.4 *Price* Verbs

Class Members: appraise, assess, estimate, fix, peg, price, rate, value

Properties:

(1040) The dealer valued the book.

(1041) The dealer valued the book at $200.

(1042) * Causative Alternations:
  a.   The dealer valued the book at $200.
  b. * The book valued (at) $200.

Comments: These verbs describe an agent measuring the value of an attribute of an entity along a scale relevant to the characterization of that attribute. They allow for the specification of the value of the measurement. These verbs are always used transitively.

54.5 *Bill* Verbs

Class Members: bet, bill, charge, fine, mulct, overcharge, save, spare, tax, tip, undercharge, wager

Properties:

(1043)   The phone company billed me $10 for that phone call.

(1044)   * Dative Alternation:
      a. * The phone company billed $10 to me.
      b.   The phone company billed me $10.

(1045)   * *As* Alternation:
      a.   The phone company billed me $10.
      b. * The phone company billed $10 as me.

Comments: These verbs describe one person (or institution) bringing about a particular relationship between a second person (or institution) and a sum of money; the relationship depends on the verb. These verbs are found in the double object construction and do not permit the dative alternation.

55   Aspectual Verbs

References: Brinton (1988), Dixon (1991), Fischer and Marshall (1969), Freed (1979), Givón (1972), ter Meulen (1990), ter Meulen and Rooryck (1991), Newmeyer (1975), Perlmutter (1970), Pustejovsky (1991a), J.R. Ross (1972), Talmy (1991)

These verbs describe the initiation, termination, or continuation of an activity. They have been extensively discussed in the works above, particularly with respect to their sentential complement-taking properties; however, these properties are not discussed here.

55.1 *Begin* Verbs

Class Members: begin, cease, commence, continue, end, finish, halt, keep, proceed, repeat, resume, start, stop, terminate

Properties:

(1046)   The meeting began at 4 P.M.

(1047)   Causative Alternation (some verbs):
    a. The meeting began at 4 P.M.
    b. I began the meeting at 4 P.M.

Comments: The members of this subset of the aspectual verbs all have intransitive uses, and some of them also allow transitive causative uses. These verbs differ with respect to the types of sentential complements they take: some take only gerundive complements, while others take both gerundive and infinitival complements. Since this work is not concerned with sentential complement-taking properties, the *begin* verbs have not been further subdivided with respect to this facet of their behavior. When these verbs take nominal arguments, there is some variation among them as to the types of noun phrases that are allowable.

55.2   *Complete* Verbs

Class Members: complete, discontinue, initiate, quit

Properties:

(1048)   Wilma completed the assignment.

(1049)   * Causative Alternations:
    a. Wilma completed the assignment.
    b. * The assignment completed.

Comments: The members of this set of aspectual verbs again describe the initiation, continuation, or termination of an activity, but unlike the members of the other subset of aspectual verbs above, *complete* verbs are not used intransitively. These verbs may also take sentential complements, but this facet of their behavior is not explored further here.

56   *Weekend* Verbs

References: Bladin (1911), E.V. Clark and H.H. Clark (1979), Duszak (1980), Jespersen (1942), Karius (1985), Marchand (1969, 1974)

Class Members: December, holiday, honeymoon, overnight, sojourn, summer, vacation, weekend, winter

Properties:

(1050)   My family always summered at the seashore.

Comments: With the exception of *overnight*, the verbs in this class are zero-related to nominals. Each of these verbs relates to spending a period of time (either named by or associated with the noun from which the verb takes its name) at some location, which is expressed as a prepositional phrase complement of the verb. It is likely that more verbs of this type might be coined; for instance, the names of other months might be used as verbs of this type.

57   Weather Verbs

References: Bolinger (1972a, 1977a), Carter (1988), Darden (1973), Dixon (1991), Langacker (1991), Marchand (1969, 1974), Napoli (1989a), Pesetsky (1992), J.R. Ross (1973), Ruwet (1986, 1991)

Class Members: blow, clear, drizzle, fog, freeze, gust, hail, howl, lightning, mist, mizzle, pelt, pour, precipitate, rain, roar, shower, sleet, snow, spit, spot, sprinkle, storm, swelter, teem, thaw, thunder

Properties:

(1051)   It's raining.

(1052)   It's raining cats and dogs.

(1053)   It was pelting with rain.

Comments: These verbs describe different types of weather. They take the pronoun *it* as subject. This subject has been described as an expletive by some; it is described by Bolinger as "ambient" *it*. Some of these verbs are best if they occur with an aspectual particle, particularly *up* (*It's fogging up*). Some of these verbs, especially those that are not zero-related to nouns and that describe precipitation, can sometimes take a *with* phrase that expresses the type of precipitation.

References

Abbreviations:

BLS: Proceedings of the Annual Meeting of the Berkeley Linguistics Society
CLS: Papers from the Regional Meeting of the Chicago Linguistic Society
ESCOL: Proceedings of the Eastern States Conference on Linguistics
NELS: Proceedings of the North Eastern Linguistic Society
WCCFL: Proceedings of the West Coast Conference on Formal Linguistics

Abney, S.P. (1987) *The English Noun Phrase in its Sentential Aspect*, Doctoral dissertation, MIT, Cambridge, MA.

Abraham, W. (1983) "Heuristic Problems Concerning the Identification of Grammatical Relations: The Case of the Westgermania (Dutch-English-German)," in L. Tasmowski and D. Willems, eds. (1983), 29–53.

Abusch, D. (1985) *On Verbs and Time*, Doctoral dissertation, University of Massachusetts, Amherst.

Abusch, D. (1986) "Verbs of Change, Causation, and Time," Report CSLI-86-50, Center for the Study of Language and Information, Stanford University, Stanford, CA.

Aijmer, K. (1972) *Some Aspects of Psychological Predicates in English*, Almqvist and Wiksell, Stockholm.

Aissen, J. (1975) "Presentational-*There* Insertion: A Cyclic Root Transformation," *CLS* 11, 1–14.

Aissen, J. and J. Hankamer (1972) "Shifty Subjects: A Conspiracy in Syntax?" *Linguistic Inquiry* 3, 501–504.

Akmajian, A. (1977) "The Complement Structure of Perception Verbs in an Autonomous Framework," in P. Culicover et al., eds. (1977), 427–460.

Albury, D.H. (1973) "The Clause-Internal Sentence Squish," in C.-J.N. Bailey and R.W. Shuy, eds. (1973), 69–82.

Alexander, D. and W.J. Kunz (1964) "Some Classes of Verbs in English," Indiana University Linguistics Club, Bloomington.

Allen, K. (1971) "A Note on the Source of *There* in Existential Sentences," *Foundations of Language* 7, 1–18.

Allerton, D.J. (1975) "Deletion and Proform Reduction," *Journal of Linguistics* 11, 213–237.

Allerton, D.J. (1978) "Generating Indirect Objects in English," *Journal of Linguistics* 14, 21–33.

Amritavalli, R. (1980a) *Aspects of the Organization of Redundancy Rules in the Lexicon*, Doctoral dissertation, Simon Fraser University, Vancouver, British Columbia.

Amritavalli, R. (1980b) "Expressing Cross-Categorial Selectional Correspondences: An Alternative to the X-Bar Syntax Approach," *Linguistic Analysis* 6, 305–343.

Amsler, R.A. (1980) *The Structure of the Merriam-Webster Pocket Dictionary*, Doctoral dissertation, University of Texas, Austin.

Anderson, S.R. (1971) "On the Role of Deep Structure in Semantic Interpretation," *Foundations of Language* 7, 387–396.

Anderson, S.R. (1977) "Comments on the Paper by Wasow," in P. Culicover et al., eds. (1977), 361–377.

Anderson, S.R. (1988) "Objects (Direct and Not-So-Direct) in English and Elsewhere," in C. Duncan-Rose and T. Vennemann, eds. (1988), 287–314.

Andrews, E. (1986) "Analysis of *De–* and *Un–* in American English," *American Speech* 61, 221–232.

Anward, J. (1989) "Constraints on Passives in Swedish and in English," *Working Papers in Scandinavian Syntax* 44, 15–29.

Aoun, J. and Y.A. Li (1989) "Scope and Constituency," *Linguistic Inquiry* 20, 141–72.

Apresjan, J.D. (1973) "Regular Polysemy," *Linguistics* 142, 5–32.

Arnold, D., M. Atkinson, J. Durand, C. Grover, and L. Sadler, eds. (1989) *Essays on Grammatical Theory and Universal Grammar*, Oxford University Press, Oxford.

Aske, J. (1989) "Path Predicates in English and Spanish: A Closer Look," *BLS* 15, 1–14.

Atkins, B.T. and B. Levin (1991) "Admitting Impediments," in U. Zernik, ed., *Lexical Acquisition: Exploiting On-line Resources to Build a Lexicon*, Lawrence Erlbaum Associates, Hillsdale, NJ, 233–262.

Atkins, B.T., J. Kegl, and B. Levin (1986) "Explicit and Implicit Information in Dictionaries," *Advances in Lexicology*, Proceedings of the Second Conference of the Centre for the New OED, University of Waterloo, Waterloo, Ontario. A revised version appears as Lexicon Project Working Papers 12, Center for Cognitive Science, MIT, Cambridge, MA, and CSL Report 5, Cognitive Science Laboratory, Princeton University, Princeton, NJ.

Atkins, B.T., J. Kegl, and B. Levin (1988) "Anatomy of a Verb Entry: From Linguistic Theory to Lexicographic Practice," *International Journal of Lexicography* 1, 84–126.

Austin, J.L. (1962) *Sense and Sensibilia*, Oxford University Press, Oxford.

Austin, P. (1982) "Transitivity and Cognate Objects in Australian Languages," in P. Hopper and S. Thompson, eds. (1982), 37–47.

Babby, L.H. (1975) "A Transformational Analysis of Transitive *–Sja* Verbs in Russian," *Lingua* 35, 297–332.

Bach, E. (1968) "Nouns and Noun Phrases," in E. Bach and R.T. Harms, eds. (1968), 91–122.

Bach, E. (1980) "In Defense of Passive," *Linguistics and Philosophy* 3, 297–342.

Bach, E. (1981) "On Time, Tense, and Aspect: An Essay in English Metaphysics," in P. Cole, ed., *Radical Pragmatics*, Academic Press, New York, 63–81.

Bach, E. (1986) "The Algebra of Events," *Linguistics and Philosophy* 9, 5–16.

Bach, E. and R.T. Harms, eds. (1968) *Universals in Linguistic Theory*, Holt, Rinehart, and Winston, New York.

Bailey, C.-J.N. and R.W. Shuy, eds. (1973) *New Ways of Analyzing Variation in English*, Georgetown University Press, Washington, D.C.

Baker, C.L. (1992) "Review of S. Pinker: *Learning and Cognition: The Acquisition of Argument Structure*," *Language* 68, 402–413.

Baker, M. (1988a) *Incorporation: A Theory of Grammatical Function Changing*, University of Chicago Press, Chicago, IL.

Baker, M. (1988b) "Theta-Theory and the Syntax of Applicatives in Chichewa," *Natural Language and Linguistic Theory* 6, 353–390.

Baker, M. (1988c) "On the Theta-Roles of Psych-Verbs," unpublished ms., McGill University, Montreal, Quebec.

Baker, M., K. Johnson, and I. Roberts (1989) "Passive Arguments Raised," *Linguistic Inquiry* 20, 219–252.

Baldi, P. (1971) "Conjunction or Reflexives: Syntax or Semantics," *Linguistic Inquiry* 2, 603–604.

Baldi, P. (1974) "Reciprocal Verbs and Symmetric Predicates," *CLS* 10, 17–26.

Barkaï, M. (1972) "On the Shiftability of Past Participles in English," *Linguistic Inquiry* 3, 377–378.

Baron, N.S. (1971) "On Defining 'Cognate Object'," *Glossa* 5, 71–98.

Barss, A. (1985) "Remarks on Akmajian's 'The Complement Structure of Perception Verbs' and Gee's 'Comments on the Paper by Akmajian'," in B. Levin, ed. (1985a), 149–166.

Barss, A. and H. Lasnik (1986) "A Note on Anaphora and Double Objects," *Linguistic Inquiry* 17, 347–354.

Barwise, J. (1981) "Scenes and Other Situations," *The Journal of Philosophy* 78, 369–397.

Barwise, J. and J. Perry (1983) *Situations and Attitudes*, MIT Press, Cambridge, MA.

Bates, M. and R. Weischedel, eds. (1992) *Challenges in Natural Language Processing*, Cambridge University Press, Cambridge.

Becker, D.A. (1971) "Case Grammar and German *be*," *Glossa* 5, 125–145.

Beedham, C. (1979) "The Perfect Passive Participle in English," *Zeitschrift für Anglistik und Amerikanistik* 27, 75–81.

Beedham, C. (1982) *The Passive Aspect in English, German and Russian*, Gunter Narr, Tübingen.

Belletti, A. (1988) "The Case of Unaccusatives," *Linguistic Inquiry* 19, 1–34.

Belletti, A. and L. Rizzi (1988) "Psych-Verbs and Θ-Theory," *Natural Language and Linguistic Theory* 6, 291–352.

Bennett, D.C. (1975) *Spatial and Temporal Uses of English Prepositions: An Essay in Stratificational Semantics*, Longman, London.

Bennett, P.A. (1980) "English Passives: A Study in Syntactic Change and Relational Grammar," *Lingua* 51, 101–114.

Bennis, H. and T. Hoekstra (1989) "Why Kaatje Was Not Heard Sing a Song," in D. Jaspers et al., eds. (1989), 21–40.

Berman, A. (1970) "Agent, Experiencer, and Controllability," *Mathematical Linguistics and Machine Translation*, Report NSF-24, Aiken Computation Laboratory, Harvard University, Cambridge, MA.

Bertram, A. (1992) "Arranging the Data into the Paper: Material/Product Verbs and Dowty's Diagnostic for Incremental Theme," *Northwestern University Working Papers in Linguistics* 4, Northwestern University, Evanston, IL, 1–11.

Bhat, D.N.S. (1977) "Multiple Case Roles," *Lingua* 42, 365–377.

Bickerton, D. (1985) "Argument Domains as Binding Categories," *WCCFL* 4, 35–45.

Binnick, R. (1971) "*Bring* and *Come*," *Linguistic Inquiry* 2, 260–265.

Binnick, R. (1974) "Quantification in Transitivity," *CLS* 10, 62–72.

Birner, B.J. (1992) *The Discourse Function of Inversion in English*, Doctoral dissertation, Northwestern University, Evanston, IL.

Bladin, V. (1911) *Studies on Denominative Verbs in English*, Almqvist and Wiksell, Uppsala.

Blansitt, E.L., Jr. (1984) "Dechticaetiative and Dative," in F. Plank, ed. (1984), 127–150.

Bloomfield, L. (1933) *Language*, Holt, New York.

Boguraev, B.K. (1991) "Building a Lexicon: The Contribution of Computers," *International Journal of Lexicography* 4, 227–260. Also in M. Bates and R. Weischedel, eds. (1992).

Boguraev, B.K. and E. Briscoe, eds. (1989) *Computational Lexicography for Natural Language Processing*, Longman, London.

Bolinger, D. (1967) "Adjectives in English: Attribution and Predication," *Lingua* 18, 1–34.

Bolinger, D. (1971) *The Phrasal Verb in English*, Harvard University Press, Cambridge, MA.

Bolinger, D. (1972a) "Ambient *It* Is Meaningful Too," *Journal of Linguistics* 9, 261–270.

Bolinger, D. (1972b) *That's That*, Mouton, The Hague.

Bolinger, D. (1973) "Essence and Accident: English Analogs of Hispanic *Ser–Estar*," in B. Kachru et al., eds. (1973), 58–69.

Bolinger, D. (1975) "On the Passive in English," *The First LACUS Forum*, 57–80.

Bolinger, D. (1977a) *Form and Meaning*, Longman, London.

Bolinger, D. (1977b) "Transitivity and Spatiality: The Passive of Prepositional Verbs," in A. Makkai, V.B. Makkai, and L. Heilmann, eds., *Linguistics at the Crossroads*, Liviana Editrice, Padova.

Bolinger, D. (1978) "Passive and Transitivity Again," *Forum Linguisticum* 3, 25–8.

Boons, J.-P. (1974) "Acceptability, Interpretation and Knowledge of the World: Remarks on the Verb *Planter* (To Plant)," *Cognition* 2, 183–211.

Boons, J.-P. (1985) "Préliminaires à la Classification des Verbes Locatifs: Les Compléments de Lieu, leurs Critères, leurs Valeurs Aspectuelles," *Lingvisticae Investigationes* 9, 195–267.

Boons, J.-P. (1986) "Des Verbes au Compléments Locatifs 'Hamlet' à l'Effet du Même Nom," *Revue Québecoise de Linguistique* 15, 57–90.

Borer, H. (1983) *Parametric Syntax*, Foris, Dordrecht.

Borer, H. (1984) "The Projection Principle and Rules of Morphology," *NELS* 14, 16–33.

Borer, H. (1991) "The Causative-Inchoative Alternation: A Case Study in Parallel Morphology," *The Linguistic Review* 8, 119–158.

Borillo, A. (1971) "Remarques sur les Verbes Symétriques Français," *Langue Française* 11, 17–31.

Borkin, A. (1972) "Two Notes on *Want* and *Desire*," *Linguistic Inquiry* 3, 378–385.

Borkin, A. (1973) "*To Be* and *Not to Be*," *CLS* 9, 44–56.

Borkin, A. (1984) *Problems in Form and Function*, Ablex, Norwood, NJ.

Bouchard, D. (1990) "Psych Constructions and Linking to Conceptual Structures," unpublished ms., Université du Québec à Montréal, Montreal, Quebec.

Bouldin, J.M. (1990) "Attributive Postnominal Adjectives in a Categorial Grammar," *WCCFL* 9, 43–57.

Bouton, L.F. (1973) "Some Reasons for Doubting the Existence of a Passive Transformation," in B. Kachru et al., eds. (1973), 70–84.

Bowerman, M. (1976) "Learning the Structure of Causative Verbs: A Study in the Relationship of Cognitive, Semantic and Syntactic Development," *Papers and Reports on Child Language Development* 8, 142–178.

Bowerman, M. (1982) "Reorganizational Processes in Lexical and Syntactic Development," in E. Wanner and L.R. Gleitman, eds., *Language Acquisition: The State of the Art*, Cambridge University Press, Cambridge, 319–346.

Bowerman, M. (1990) "Mapping Thematic Roles onto Syntactic Functions: Are Children Helped by Innate Linking Rules?" *Linguistics* 28, 1253–1289.

Bowers, J.S. (1976) "On Surface Structure Grammatical Relations and the Structure-Preserving Hypothesis," *Linguistic Analysis* 2, 225–242.

Bowers, J.S. (1981) *The Theory of Grammatical Relations*, Cornell University Press, Ithaca, NY.

Bowers, J.S. (1989) "The Syntax and Semantics of Predication," unpublished ms., Cornell University, Ithaca, NY.

Brame, M. (not dated) "*eat*, Part I," unpublished ms., University of Washington, Seattle.

Branchadell, A. (1991) "Against Argument Augmentation," *Catalan Working Papers in Linguistics 1991*, 1–32.

Breivik, L.E. (1978) "Existential Sentences Revisited," in K. Gregersen, ed., *Papers from the Fourth Scandinavian Conference of Linguistics*, Odense University Press, Odense, 235–240.

Breivik, L.E. (1979) "Review of L. Jenkins: *The English Existential* and P. Erdmann: *THERE Sentences in English: A Relational Study Based on a Corpus of Written Texts*," *English Studies* 60, 216–230.

Breivik, L.E. (1981) "On the Interpretation of Existential *There*," *Language* 57, 1–25.

Breivik, L.E. (1983) "On the Use and Non-Use of Existential *There*," *Lingua* 61, 353–368.

Brekke, M. (1988) "The Experiencer Constraint," *Linguistic Inquiry* 19, 169–180.

Brekle, H.E. and D. Kastovsky, eds. (1977) *Perspektiven der Wortbildungsforschung*, Bouvier Verlag Herbert Grundmann, Bonn.

Bresnan, J. (1976) "Nonarguments for Raising," *Linguistic Inquiry* 7, 485–502.

Bresnan, J. (1980) "Polyadicity: Part I of a Theory of Lexical Rules and

Representations," in T. Hoekstra et al., eds. (1980). Also in J. Bresnan, ed. (1982a), 149–172.

Bresnan, J., ed. (1982a) *The Mental Representation of Grammatical Relations*, MIT Press, Cambridge, MA.

Bresnan, J. (1982b) "The Passive in Lexical Theory," in J. Bresnan, ed. (1982a), 3–86.

Bresnan, J. (1990) "Levels of Representation in Locative Inversion: A Comparison of English and Chicheŵa," unpublished ms., Stanford University and Xerox PARC, Stanford and Palo Alto, CA.

Bresnan, J. and J. Kanerva (1989) "Locative Inversion in Chicheŵa: A Case Study of Factorization in Grammar," *Linguistic Inquiry* 20, 1–50. Reprinted in T. Stowell and E. Wehrli, eds. (1992), 53–101.

Bresnan, J. and J. Kanerva (1992) "The Thematic Hierarchy and Locative Inversion in UG: A Reply to Schachter's Comments," in T. Stowell and E. Wehrli, eds. (1992), 111–125.

Bresnan, J. and A. Zaenen (1990) "Deep Unaccusativity in LFG," in K. Dziwirek et al., eds. (1990), 45–57.

Bridgeman, L.I., D. Dillinger, C. Higgins, P.D. Seaman, and F.A. Shank (1965) "More Classes of Verbs in English," Indiana University Linguistics Club, Bloomington.

Brinton, L.J. (1988) *The Development of English Aspectual Systems: Aspectualizers and Post-Verbal Particles*, Cambridge University Press, Cambridge.

Brittain, R.C. (1971) "Indirect Observations About Indirect Objects," *Working Papers in Linguistics* 10, The Ohio State University, Columbus, 72–84.

Brousseau, A.-M. and E. Ritter (1991) "A Non-Unified Analysis of Agentive Verbs," *WCCFL* 10, 53–64.

Brown, R. and D. Fish (1983) "The Psychological Causality Implicit in Language," *Cognition* 14, 237–273.

Browne, W. (1971) "Verbs and Unspecified NP Deletion," *Linguistic Inquiry* 2, 259–260.

Brugman, C. and G. Lakoff (1988) "Cognitive Topology and Lexical Networks," in S. Small, G. Cottrell, and M. Tanenhaus, eds., *Lexical Ambiguity Resolution*, Morgan Kaufmann, San Mateo, CA, 477–508.

Buck, R.A. (1993) "Affectedness and Other Semantic Properties of English Denominal Locative Verbs," *American Speech* 68. Also in *Northwestern University Working Papers in Linguistics* 3, 1991, Northwestern University, Evanston, IL, 31–49.

Burzio, L. (1981) *Intransitive Verbs and Italian Auxiliaries*, Doctoral dissertation, MIT, Cambridge, MA.

Burzio, L. (1986) *Italian Syntax: A Government-Binding Approach*, Reidel, Dordrecht.

Campbell, R. and J. Martin (1989) "Sensation Predicates and the Syntax of Stativity," *WCCFL* 8, 44–55.

Cantrall, W.R. (1974) *Viewpoint, Reflexives, and the Nature of Noun Phrases*, Mouton, The Hague.

Caplan, D. (1973) "A Note on the Abstract Readings of Verbs of Perception," *Cognition* 2, 269–277.

Carlson, G. N. (1977) *Reference to Kinds in English*, Doctoral dissertation, University of Massachusetts, Amherst.

Carrier, J. and J.H. Randall (1992) "The Argument Structure and Syntactic Structure of Resultatives," *Linguistic Inquiry* 23, 173–234.

Carrier, J. and J.H. Randall (in press) *From Conceptual Structure to Syntax*, Mouton de Gruyter, Berlin.

Carrier-Duncan, J. (1985) "Linking of Thematic Roles in Derivational Word Formation," *Linguistic Inquiry* 16, 1–34.

Carter, R.J. (1976) "Some Constraints on Possible Words," *Semantikos* 1, 27–66.

Carter, R.J. (1988) *On Linking: Papers by Richard Carter* (edited by B. Levin and C. Tenny), Lexicon Project Working Papers 25, Center for Cognitive Science, MIT, Cambridge, MA.

Catlin, J. and J.-C. Catlin (1972) "Intentionality: A Source of Ambiguity in English," *Linguistic Inquiry* 3, 504–508.

Cattell, R. (1985) "On Wierzbicka's 'The Semantics of 'Internal Dative' in English'," *Quaderni di Semantica* 7, 136–139.

Chafe, W. (1970) *Meaning and the Structure of Language*, University of Chicago Press, Chicago, IL.

Channon, R. (1982) "3 → 2 Advancement, Beneficiary Advancement, and *With*," *BLS* 8, 271–282.

Chitoran, D. (1986) "Metaphor in the English Lexicon: The Verb," in D. Kastovsky and A. Szwedek, eds., *Linguistics Across Historical and Geographical Boundaries: Descriptive, Contrastive and Applied Linguistics*, vol. 2, Mouton de Gruyter, Berlin, 837–49.

Choi, S. and M. Bowerman (1991) "Learning to Express Motion Events in English and Korean: The Influence of Language-Specific Lexicalization Patterns," *Cognition* 41, 83–121.

Chomsky, N.A. (1965) *Aspects of the Theory of Syntax*, MIT Press, Cambridge, MA.

Chomsky, N.A. (1981) *Lectures on Government and Binding*, Foris, Dordrecht.

Chomsky, N.A. (1986) *Knowledge of Language*, Praeger, New York.

Chomsky, N.A. (1991) "Some Notes on Economy of Derivation and Representation," in R. Freidin, ed., *Principles and Parameters in Comparative Grammar*, MIT Press, Cambridge, MA, 417–454. [Originally published (1989) in *MIT Working Papers in Linguistics* 10, Department of Linguistics and Philosophy, MIT, Cambridge, MA.]

Clark, E.V. (1978) "Locationals: Existential, Locative, and Possessive," in J.H. Greenberg, ed., *Universals of Human Language: Syntax*, vol. 4, Stanford University Press, Stanford, CA, 85–126.

Clark, E.V. and H.H. Clark (1979) "When Nouns Surface as Verbs," *Language* 55, 767–811.

Clark, M.V. (1971) "The Case Against Stative," *Working Papers in Linguistics* 10, The Ohio State University, Columbus, 149–56.

Collier, G.H. and C. Fellbaum (1988) "Exploring the Verb Lexicon with the Sensus Electronic Thesaurus," *Information in Text*, Proceedings of the Fourth Annual Conference of the UW Centre for the New Oxford English Dictionary, Waterloo, Ontario, 11–27.

Comorovski, I. (1991) "Partitives and the Definiteness Effect," *WCCFL* 10, 91–102.

Condoravdi, C. (1989) "The Middle: Where Semantics and Morphology Meet," *Student*

Conference in Linguistics 1989, MIT Working Papers in Linguistics 11, MIT, Cambridge, MA, 16–30.

Condoravdi, C. (1990) "Symmetric Predicates, Verbal Classes and Diathesis Alterations," unpublished ms., University of Cambridge, Cambridge.

Condoravdi, C. and Sanfilippo, A. (1990) "Notes on Psychological Predicates," unpublished ms., University of Cambridge, Cambridge.

Cooper, W.E. (1974) "Syntactic Flexibility Among English Sensation Referents," *Linguistics* 133, 33–38.

Cooper, W.E. (1975) "Primacy Relations Among English Sensation Referents," *Linguistics* 137, 5–12.

Coopmans, P. (1989) "Where Stylistic and Syntactic Processes Meet: Locative Inversion in English," *Language* 65, 728–751.

Coopmans, P. (1992) "Review of M.S. Rochemont and P.W. Culicover: *English Focus Constructions and the Theory of Grammar*," *Language* 68, 206–210.

Couper-Kuhlen, E. (1979) *The Prepositional Passive in English*, Niemeyer, Tübingen.

Cowper, E.A. (1990a) "Thematic Underspecification and Manner-of-Motion Verbs," *Toronto Working Papers* 12, University of Toronto, Toronto, Ontario.

Cowper, E.A. (1990b) "Apparent Polysemy and Thematic Underspecification," *Toronto Working Papers* 12, University of Toronto, Toronto, Ontario.

Croft, W.A. (1985) "Indirect Object 'Lowering'," *BLS* 11, 39–51.

Croft, W.A. (1986) *Categories and Relations in Syntax: The Clause-Level Organization of Information*, Doctoral dissertation, Stanford University, Stanford, CA.

Croft, W.A. (1990) "Possible Verbs and the Structure of Events," in S.L. Tsohatzidis, ed., *Meanings and Prototypes: Studies on Linguistic Categorization*, Routledge, London.

Croft, W.A. (1991) *Syntactic Categories and Grammatical Relations*, University of Chicago Press, Chicago, IL.

Cruse, D.A. (1972) "A Note on English Causatives," *Linguistic Inquiry* 3, 522–528.

Cruse, D.A. (1973) "Some Thoughts on Agentivity," *Journal of Linguistics* 9, 11–23.

Cruse, D.A. (1979) "Reversives," *Linguistics* 17, 957–966.

Culicover, P. and W. Wilkins (1984) *Locality in Linguistic Theory*, Academic Press, New York.

Culicover, P. and W. Wilkins (1986) "Control, PRO, and the Projection Principle," *Language* 62, 120–153.

Culicover, P., A. Akmajian, and T. Wasow, eds. (1977) *Formal Syntax*, Academic Press, New York.

Curme, G.O. (1931) *A Grammar of the English Language*, D.C. Heath, Boston. Reprinted 1977 by Verbatim, Essex, CT.

Czepluch, H. (1982) "Case Theory and the Dative Construction," *The Linguistic Review* 2, 1–38.

Darden, B. (1973) "What Rains," *Linguistic Inquiry* 4, 523–526.

Davidse, K. (1992) "Transitivity/Ergativity: The Janus-Headed Grammar of Actions and Events," in M. Davies and L. Ravelli, eds., *Advances in Systemic Linguistics*, Pinter, London, 105–135.

Davidson, D. and G.H. Harmon, eds. (1972) *The Semantics of Natural Language*, Reidel, Dordrecht.

Davison, A. (1980) "Peculiar Passives," *Language* 56, 42–66.

Deane, P. (1984) "Aspects of the Semantics of Part Terms," *Papers from the Parasession on Lexical Semantics*, Chicago Linguistic Society, Chicago, IL, 81–94.

Deane, P. and R.S. Wheeler (1984) "On the Use of Syntactic Evidence in the Analysis of Word Meaning," *Papers from the Parasession on Lexical Semantics*, Chicago Linguistic Society, Chicago, IL, 95–116.

Declerck, R. (1977) "Some Arguments in Favor of a Generative Semantics Analysis of Sentences with an Adverbial Particle or a Prepositional Phrase of Goal," *Orbis* 26, 297–340.

Declerck, R. (1979) "Aspect and the Bounded/Unbounded (Telic/Atelic) Distinction," *Linguistics* 17, 761–794.

Declerck, R. (1981) "On the Role of Progressive Aspect in Nonfinite Perception Verb Complements," *Glossa* 15, 83–114.

Declerck, R. (1982) "The Triple Origin of Participial Perception Verb Complements," *Linguistic Analysis* 10, 1–26.

Declerck, R. (1983) "The Structure of Infinitival Perception Verb Complements in a Transformational Grammar," in L. Tasmowski and D. Willems, eds. (1983), 105–128.

DeLancey, S. (1985) "Prototype Semantics and the 'Internal Dative': Comments on Wierzbicka," *Quaderni di Semantica* 7, 140–142.

Dezsö, L. (1980) "Middle and Causative Constructions in English and Hungarian," in W. Nemser, *Studies in English and Hungarian Contrastive Linguistics*, Akadémiai Kiadó, Budapest, 207–231.

DiDesidero, L. (1992) "On the Stativity of the FEAR Verbs of Psychological State," *Northwestern Working Papers in Linguistics* 4, Northwestern University, Evanston, IL, 31–40.

Dik, S.C. (1978) *Functional Grammar*, North-Holland, Amsterdam.

Dik, S.C. (1980) *Studies in Functional Grammar*, Academic Press, London.

Dirven, R. (1989) "A Cognitive Perspective on Complementation," in D. Jaspers et al., eds. (1989), 113–139.

Dixon, R.M.W. (1973) "The Semantics of Giving," in M. Gross, M. Halle, and M.P. Schutzenberger, eds., *The Formal Analysis of Natural Languages*, Mouton, The Hague, 205–223. Also in R.M.W. Dixon (1982b), 1–62.

Dixon, R.M.W. (1982a) "The Grammar of English Phrasal Verbs," *Australian Journal of Linguistics* 2, 1–42.

Dixon, R.M.W. (1982b) *Where Have All the Adjectives Gone? and Other Essays in Semantics and Syntax*, Mouton, Berlin.

Dixon, R.M.W. (1989) "Subject and Object in Universal Grammar," in D. Arnold et al., eds. (1989), 91–118.

Dixon, R.M.W. (1991) *A New Approach to English Grammar, On Semantic Principles*, Oxford University Press, Oxford.

Does, J. van der (1991) "A Generalized Quantifier Logic for Naked Infinitives," *Linguistics and Philosophy* 14, 241–294.

Dong, Q.P. (1970) "A Note on Conjoined Noun Phrases," *Journal of Philosophical Linguistics* 1, 31–40.

Doron, E. and M. Rappaport Hovav (1991) "Affectedness and Externalization," *NELS* 21, 81–94.

Dougherty, R.C. (1970) "Recent Studies on Language Universals," *Foundations of Language* 6, 505–561.

Dougherty, R.C. (1971) "A Grammar of Coördinate Conjoined Structures, II," *Language* 47, 298–339.

Dougherty, R.C. (1974) "The Syntax and Semantics of *Each Other* Constructions," *Foundations of Language* 12, 1–47.

Dowty, D.R. (1975) "The Stative in the Progressive and Other Essence/Accident Contrasts," *Linguistic Inquiry* 6, 579–589.

Dowty, D.R. (1978a) "Applying Montague's Views on Linguistic Metatheory to the Structure of the Lexicon," *Papers from the Parasession on the Lexicon*, Chicago Linguistic Society, Chicago, IL, 97–137.

Dowty, D.R. (1978b) "Lexically Governed Transformations as Lexical Rules in a Montague Grammar," *Linguistic Inquiry* 9, 393–426.

Dowty, D.R. (1979) *Word Meaning and Montague Grammar*, Reidel, Dordrecht.

Dowty, D.R. (1981) "Quantification and the Lexicon: A Reply to Fodor and Fodor," in M. Moortgat et al., eds., *The Scope of Lexical Rules*, Foris, Dordrecht, 79–106.

Dowty, D.R. (1982) "Grammatical Relations in Montague Grammar," in P. Jacobson and G.K. Pullum, eds., (1982), 79–130.

Dowty, D.R. (1991) "Thematic Proto-Roles and Argument Selection," *Language* 67, 547–619.

Dryer, M.S. (1985) "The Role of Thematic Relations in Adjectival Passives," *Linguistic Inquiry* 16, 320–326.

Dryer, M.S. (1987) "On Primary Objects, Secondary Objects and Antidative," *Language* 62, 808–845.

Dubinsky, S. and C. Rosen (1987) "A Bibliography on Relational Grammar through May 1987 with Selected Titles on Lexical-Functional Grammar," Indiana University Linguistics Club, Bloomington.

Duncan-Rose, C. and T. Vennemann, eds. (1988) *On Language: Rhetorica, Phonologica, Syntactica*, Routledge, London.

Duszak, A. (1980) "A Semantic Description of English Verbs with Semantically and Formally Related Nominal Counterparts in Present-Day English," *Kwartalnik Neofilologiczny* 27, 49–71.

Dziwirek, K., P. Farrell, and E. Mejías-Bikandi, eds. (1990) *Grammatical Relations: A Cross-Theoretical Perspective*, Center for the Study of Language and Information, Stanford University, Stanford, CA.

Emonds, J.E. (1972) "Evidence that Indirect-Object Movement Is a Structure-Preserving Rule," *Foundations of Language* 8, 546–561.

Emonds, J.E. (1976) *A Transformational Approach to English Syntax*, Academic Press, New York.

Emonds, J.E. (1985) *A Unified Theory of Syntactic Categories*, Foris, Dordrecht.

Emonds, J.E. (1991) "Subcategorization and Syntax-Based Theta-Role Assignment," *Natural Language and Linguistic Theory* 9, 369–429.

Erades, P.A. (1950) "Points of Modern English Syntax," *English Studies* 31, 153–157.

Erdmann, P. (1976) *There Sentences in English*, Tuduv, Munich.

Erteschik-Shir, N. (1979) "Discourse Constraints on Dative Movement," in T. Givón, ed., *Syntax and Semantics 12: Discourse and Syntax*, Academic Press, New York, 441–467.

Erteschik-Shir, N. (1991) "Review of M.S. Rochemont and P.W. Culicover: *English Focus Constructions and the Theory of Grammar*," *Journal of Linguistics* 27, 525–32.

Everaert, M., A. Evers, R. Huybregts, and M. Trommelen, eds. (1988) *Morphology and Modularity*, Foris, Dordrecht.

Fabb, N. (1984) *Syntactic Affixation*, Doctoral dissertation, MIT, Cambridge, MA.

Fabb, N. (1988) "Doing Affixation in the GB Syntax," in M. Everaert et al., eds. (1988), 129–145.

Faber, D. (1987) "The Accentuation of Intransitive Sentences in English," *Journal of Linguistics* 23, 341–358.

Fagan, S. (1988) "The English Middle," *Linguistic Inquiry* 19, 181–203.

Fagan, S.M.B. (1992) *The Syntax and Semantics of Middle Constructions*, Cambridge University Press, Cambridge.

Faltz, L.M. (1978) "On Indirect Objects in Universal Syntax," *CLS* 14, 76–88.

Faltz, L.M. (1985) *Reflexivization: A Study in Universal Syntax*, Garland, New York.

Farsi, A.A. (1974) "Change Verbs," *Language Sciences* 31, 21–23.

Fellbaum, C. (1985) "Adverbs in Agentless Actives and Passives," *Papers from the Parasession on Causatives and Agentivity*, CLS 21, Part 2, 21–31.

Fellbaum, C. (1989) "On the 'Reflexive Middle' in English," *CLS* 25, Part 1, 123–132.

Fellbaum, C. (1990) "English Verbs as a Semantic Net," *International Journal of Lexicography* 3, 278–301.

Fellbaum, C. (1992) "Review of R.M.W. Dixon: *A New Approach to English Grammar, On Semantic Principles*," *Language* 68, 642–645.

Fellbaum, C. and J. Kegl (1989) "Taxonomic Structures and Cross-Category Linking in the Lexicon," *ESCOL* '89, 93–104.

Fellbaum, C. and A. Zribi-Hertz (1989) "La Construction Moyenne en Français et en Anglais: Etude de Syntaxe et de Semantique Comparée," *Récherches Linguistiques de Vincennes* 18, 19–57.

Fiengo, R.W. (1977) "On Trace Theory," *Linguistic Inquiry* 8, 35–63.

Fiengo, R.W. (1980) *Surface Structure: The Interface of Autonomous Components*, Harvard University Press, Cambridge, MA.

Fiengo, R.W. and H. Lasnik (1973) "The Logical Structure of Reciprocal Sentences in English," *Foundations of Language* 9, 447–468.

Fillmore, C.J. (1965) *Indirect Object Constructions in English and the Ordering of Transformations*, Mouton, The Hague.

Fillmore, C.J. (1966) "A Proposal Concerning English Prepositions," in F.P. Dinneen, S.J., ed., *Report of the Seventeenth Annual Round Table Meeting on Linguistics and Language Studies*, Georgetown University Press, Washington, D.C., 19–34.

Fillmore, C.J. (1967) "The Grammar of *Hitting* and *Breaking*," in R. Jacobs and P. Rosenbaum, eds. (1967), 120–133.

Fillmore, C.J. (1968a) "The Case for Case," in E. Bach and R.T. Harms, eds. (1968), 1–88.

Fillmore, C.J. (1968b) "Lexical Entries for Verbs," *Foundations of Language* 4, 373–393.

Fillmore, C.J. (1971a) *Santa Cruz Lectures on Deixis*, Indiana University Linguistics Club, Bloomington.

Fillmore, C.J. (1971b) "Verbs of Judging: An Exercise in Semantic Description," in C.J. Fillmore and D.T. Langendoen, eds., *Studies in Linguistic Semantics*, Holt, Rinehart and Winston, New York, 273–289.

Fillmore, C.J. (1972) "Subjects, Speakers and Roles," in D. Davidson and G. Harman, eds. (1972), 1–24.

Fillmore, C.J. (1977a) "The Case for Case Reopened," in P. Cole and J.M. Sadock, eds., *Syntax and Semantics 8: Grammatical Relations*, Academic Press, New York, 59–81.

Fillmore, C.J. (1977b) "Topics in Lexical Semantics," in R.W. Cole, ed., *Current Issues in Linguistic Theory*, Indiana University Press, Bloomington, 76–138.

Fillmore, C.J. (1978) "On the Organization of Semantic Information in the Lexicon," *Papers from the Parasession on the Lexicon*, Chicago Linguistic Society, Chicago, IL, 148–173.

Fillmore, C.J. (1986) "Pragmatically Controlled Zero Anaphora," *BLS* 12, 95–107.

Firbas, J. (1966) "Non-Thematic Subjects in Contemporary English," *Travaux Linguistiques de Prague* 2, 239–256.

Fischer, S.D. and B.A. Marshall (1969) "The Examination and Abandonment of the Theory of *Begin* of D.M. Perlmutter as Carried Out by Two of the Inmates of Room Twenty E-Two-Fifteen, under the Direction of Divine Providence," unpublished ms., MIT, Cambridge, MA.

Fisiak, J., ed., (1985) *Historical Semantics: Historical Word-Formation*, Mouton, Berlin, 397–405.

Fodor, J.A. (1970) "Three Reasons for Not Deriving *Kill* from *Cause to Die*," *Linguistic Inquiry* 1, 429–438.

Fodor, J.A. and J.D. Fodor (1980) "Functional Structures, Quantifiers, and Meaning Postulates," *Linguistic Inquiry* 11, 759–770.

Fodor, J.A., M. Garrett, E. Walker, and C. Parkes (1980) "Against Definitions," *Cognition* 8, 263–367.

Foley, W.A. and R.D. Van Valin, Jr. (1984) *Functional Syntax and Universal Grammar*, Cambridge University Press, Cambridge.

Fontenelle, T. and J. Vanandroye (1989) "Retrieving Ergative Verbs from a Lexical Data Base," *Dictionaries* 11, 11–39.

Fraser, B. (1971) "A Note on the *Spray Paint* Cases," *Linguistic Inquiry* 2, 603–607.

Fraser, B. (1976) *The Verb Particle Construction in English*, Academic Press, New York.

Freed, A.F. (1979) *The Semantics of English Aspectual Complementation*, Reidel, Dordrecht.

Freeze, R. (1992) "Existentials and Other Locatives," *Language* 68, 553–595.

Freidin, R. (1975) "The Analysis of Passives," *Language* 51, 384-405.

Fukui, N., S. Miyagawa, and C. Tenny (1985) "Verb Classes in English and Japanese: A Case Study in the Interaction of Syntax, Morphology and Semantics," Lexicon Project Working Papers 3, Center for Cognitive Science, MIT, Cambridge, MA.

Gawron, M.J. (1983) *Lexical Representations and the Semantics of Complementation*, Doctoral dissertation, University of California, Berkeley, CA.

Gawron, M.J. (1986) "Valence Structure Preservation and Demotion," *CLS* 22, Part 1, 51–64.

Gee, J.P. (1977) "Comments on the Paper by Akmajian," in P. Culicover et al., eds. (1977), 461–481.

Geis, J.E. (1973) "Subject Complementation with Causative Verbs," in B. Kachru et al., eds., *Issues in Linguistics*, University of Illinois Press, Urbana, 210–230.

Geniušienė, E. (1987) *The Typology of Reflexives*, Mouton de Gruyter, Berlin.

Gentner, D. (1978) "On Relational Meaning: The Acquisition of Verb Meaning," *Child Development* 49, 988–998.

Gergely, G. and T.G. Bever (1986) "Related Intuitions and the Mental Representation of Causative Verbs in Adults and Children," *Cognition* 23, 211–277.

Gestel, F. van (1989) "Resultative Predication," distributed by LIPADIT.

Ginzburg, J. (1990) "Monadic Comitatives and Dyadic Equivalence Relations," *NELS* 20, 135–149.

Giorgi, A. (1984) "Toward a Theory of Long Distance Anaphors: A GB Approach," *The Linguistic Review* 3, 307–361.

Givón, T. (1972) "Forward Implications, Backward Presuppositions, and the Time Axis of Verbs," in J. Kimball, ed. (1972), 29–50.

Givón, T. (1984) "Direct Object and Dative Shifting: Semantic and Pragmatic Case," in F. Plank, ed. (1984), 151–182.

Gleitman, L.H. (1965) "Coordinating Conjunctions in English," *Language* 41, 260–293.

Goldberg, A.E. (1989) "A Unified Account of the Semantics of the English Ditransitive," *BLS* 15, 79–90.

Goldberg, A.E. (1991) "It Can't Go Down the Chimney Up: Paths and the English Resultative," *BLS* 17.

Goldberg, A.E. (1992) "In Support of a Semantic Account of Resultatives," unpublished ms., University of California, Berkeley, CA.

Goldberg, A.E. (in press) "The Inherent Semantics of Argument Structure: The Case of the English Ditransitive Construction," *Cognitive Linguistics*.

Goldsmith, J. (1979) "On the Thematic Nature of *See*," *Linguistic Inquiry* 10, 347–352.

Goldsmith, J. (1980) "Meaning and Mechanism in Grammar," in S. Kuno, ed., *Harvard Studies in Syntax and Semantics*, 423–449.

Grady, M. (1965) "The Medio-Passive Voice in Modern English," *Word* 21, 270–272.

Green, G. (1971) "On the Representation of *Contain*," *Papers in Linguistics* 4, 198–199.

Green, G. (1972) "Some Observations on the Syntax and Semantics of Instrumental Verbs," *CLS* 8, 83–97.

Green, G. (1973) "A Syntactic Syncretism in English and French," in B. Kachru et al., eds. (1973), 257–278.

Green, G. (1974) *Semantics and Syntactic Regularity*, Indiana University Press, Bloomington.

Green, G.M. (1976) "Main Clause Phenomena in Subordinate Clauses," *Language* 52, 382–397.

Green, G. (1980) "Some Wherefores of English Inversions," *Language* 56, 582–601.

Green, G. (1982) "Colloquial and Literary Uses of Inversions," in D. Tannen, ed., *Spoken and Written Language: Exploring Orality and Literacy*, Ablex, Norwood, NJ, 119–153.

Green, G. (1984) "Subcategorization and the Account of Inversions," *ESCOL '84*, 214–221.

Green, G. (1985) "The Description of Inversions in Generalized Phrase Structure Grammar," *BLS* 11, 117–145.

Green, G. (1986) "Comments on Anna Wierzbicka's 'The Semantics of 'Internal Dative' in English'," *Quaderni di Semantica* 7, 143–146.

Grimshaw, J. (1987) "Unaccusatives: An Overview," *NELS* 17, 244–259.

Grimshaw, J. (1989) "Getting the Dative Alternation," *MIT Working Papers in Linguistics* 10, MIT, Cambridge, MA.

Grimshaw, J. (1990) *Argument Structure*, MIT Press, Cambridge, MA.

Grimshaw, J. and A. Prince (1986) "A Prosodic Account of the *to*-Dative Alternation," unpublished ms., Brandeis University, Waltham, MA.

Grimshaw, J. and S. Vikner (1990) "Obligatory Adjuncts and the Structure of Events," unpublished ms., Brandeis University and University of Geneva, Waltham, MA and Geneva.

Grodzinsky, Y., A. Pierce, and S. Marakovitz (1991) "Neuropsychological Reasons for a Transformational Analysis of Verbal Passive," *Natural Language and Linguistic Theory* 9, 431–453.

Groot, C. de (1984) "Totally Affected. Aspect and Three-Place Predicates," in C. de Groot and H. Tommola, eds., *Aspect Bound*, Foris, Dordrecht, 133–151.

Gropen, J. (1989) *Learning Locative Verbs: How Universal Linking Rules Constrain Productivity*, Doctoral dissertation, MIT, Cambridge, MA.

Gropen, J., S. Pinker, M. Hollander, R. Goldberg, and R. Wilson (1989) "The Learnability and Acquisition of the Dative Alternation in English," *Language* 65, 203–257.

Gropen, J., S. Pinker, M. Hollander, and R. Goldberg (1991a) "Affectedness and Direct Objects: The Role of Lexical Semantics in the Acquisition of Verb Argument Structure," *Cognition* 41, 153–195.

Gropen, J., S. Pinker, M. Hollander, and R. Goldberg (1991b) "Syntax and Semantics in the Acquisition of Locative Verbs," *Journal of Child Language* 18, 115–151.

Gruber, J.S. (1965) *Studies in Lexical Relations*, Doctoral dissertation, MIT, Cambridge, MA. Also in Gruber (1976), 1–210.

Gruber, J.S. (1967) "*Look* and *See*," *Language* 43, 937–947.

Gruber, J.S. (1976) *Lexical Structures in Syntax and Semantics*, North-Holland, Amsterdam.

Guéron, J. (1980) "On the Syntax and Semantics of PP Extraposition," *Linguistic Inquiry* 11, 637–678.

Guéron, J. (1985) "Inalienable Possession, PRO-Inclusion and Lexical Chains," in J. Guéron et al., eds. (1985), 43–86.

Guéron, J., H.-G. Obenauer, and J.-Y. Pollock, eds. (1985) *Grammatical Representations*, Foris, Dordrecht.

Guerssel, M. (1986) "On Berber Verbs of Change: A Study of Transitivity Alternations,"

Lexicon Project Working Papers 9, Center for Cognitive Science, MIT, Cambridge, MA.

Guerssel, M., K. Hale, M. Laughren, B. Levin, and J. White Eagle (1985) "A Cross-linguistic Study of Transitivity Alternations," *Papers from the Parasession on Causatives and Agentivity*, CLS 21, Part 2, Chicago, IL, 48–63.

Gussenhoven, C. (1992) "Sentence Accents and Argument Structure," in I.M. Roca, ed. (1992), 79–106.

Haegeman, L. (1987) "Register Variation in English: Some Theoretical Observations," *Journal of English Linguistics* 20, 230–248.

Haider, H. (1992) "Branching and Discharge," unpublished ms., University of Stuttgart.

Haïk, I. (1990) "Telling *Tell*," unpublished ms., Université du Québec à Montréal, Montreal, Quebec.

Hale, K.L. (1982) "The Essential Features of Warlpiri Main Clauses," in S. Swartz, ed., *Papers in Warlpiri Grammar: In Memory of Lothar Jagst, Work-Papers of SIL-AAB*, Series A, Volume 6, Summer Institute of Linguistics, Berrimah, N.T.

Hale, K.L. and S.J. Keyser (1986) "Some Transitivity Alternations in English," Lexicon Project Working Papers 7, Center for Cognitive Science, MIT, Cambridge, MA.

Hale, K.L. and S.J. Keyser (1987) "A View from the Middle," Lexicon Project Working Papers 10, Center for Cognitive Science, MIT, Cambridge, MA.

Hale, K.L. and S.J. Keyser (1988) "Explaining and Constraining the English Middle," in C. Tenny, ed. (1988), 41–58.

Hale, K.L. and S.J. Keyser (1991) "On the Syntax of Argument Structure," unpublished ms., MIT, Cambridge, MA.

Hale, K.L. and S.J. Keyser (1992) "The Syntactic Character of Thematic Structure," in I.M. Roca, ed. (1992), 107–143.

Hall, B. (1965) *Subject and Object in English*, Doctoral dissertation, MIT, Cambridge, MA.

Halliday, M.A.K. (1967) "Notes on Transitivity and Theme in English Part I," *Journal of Linguistics* 3, 37–81.

Halliday, M.A.K. (1968) "Notes on Transitivity and Theme in English Part III," *Journal of Linguistics* 4, 179–215.

Hanks, P., ed. (1986) *Collins English Dictionary*, Collins Publishers, London and Glasgow.

Hannay, M. (1985) *English Existentials in Functional Grammar*, Foris, Dordrecht.

Harnish, R.M. (1975) "The Argument from *Lurk*," *Linguistic Inquiry* 6, 145–154.

Hartvigson, H.H. and L.K. Jakobsen (1974) *Inversion in Present-Day English*, Odense University Studies in English 2, Odense University Press, Odense.

Hasegawa, K. (1968) "The Passive Construction in English," *Language* 44, 230–243.

Hasegawa, N. (1981) "On the Passive as a Lexical Process," *NELS* 11, 96–112.

Hasegawa, N. (1988) "Passives, Verb Raising, and the Affectedness Condition," *WCCFL* 7, 99–114.

Hatcher, A.G. (1943) "'Mr. Howard Amuses Easy'," *Modern Language Notes* 58, 8–17.

Hatcher, A.G. (1944a) "*Il Me Prend Le Bras* vs. *Il Prend Mon Bras*," *The Romanic Review* 35, 156–164.

Hatcher, A.G. (1944b) "*Il Tend les Mains* vs. *Il Tend ses Mains*," *Studies in Philology* 41, 457–481.

Hatcher, A.G. (1951) "The Use of the Progressive Form in English: A New Approach," *Language* 27, 254-280. Also appears in A. Schupf, ed. (1974) *Der Englische Aspekt*, Wissenschaftliche Buchgesellschaft, Darmstadt, 177–216.

Hawkins, R. (1981) "On 'Generating Indirect Objects in English': A Reply to Allerton," *Journal of Linguistics* 17, 1–9.

Herbert, R.K. (1975) "Observations on a Class of Instrumental Causatives," *CLS* 11, 260–271.

Heringer, J.T. (1976) "Idioms and Lexicalization in English," in M. Shibatani, ed. (1976a), 205–216.

Hermon, G. (1986) *Syntactic Modularity*, Foris, Dordrecht.

Hestvik, A. (1986) "Case Theory and Norwegian Impersonal Constructions: Subject-Object Alternations in Active and Passive Verbs," *Nordic Journal of Linguistics* 9, 181–197.

Hestvik, A. (1991) "Subjectless Binding Domains," *Natural Language and Linguistic Theory* 9, 455–496.

Hetzron, R. (1971) "Presentative Function and Presentative Movement," *Papers from the Second Conference on African Linguistics*, Studies in African Linguistics Suppl. 2, 79–105.

Higginbotham, J.T. (1983) "The Logic of Perceptual Reports: An Extensional Alternative to Situation Semantics," *Journal of Philosophy* 80, 100–127.

Hinrichs, E. (1985) *A Compositional Semantics for Aktionsarten and NP Reference in English*, Doctoral dissertation, The Ohio State University, Columbus.

Hoard, J.E. (1979) "On the Semantic Representation of Oblique Complements," *Language* 55, 319–332.

Hoekstra, E. (1989) "Binding, Objects and the Structure of English VP," in H. Bennis and A. van Kemenade, eds., *Linguistics in the Netherlands 1989*, Foris, Dordrecht, 71–80.

Hoekstra, E. (1991a) *Licensing Conditions on Phrase Structure*, Doctoral dissertation, Rijksuniversiteit Groningen, Groningen.

Hoekstra, E. (1991b) "On Double Objects in English and Dutch," in K. Leffel and D. Bouchard, eds. (1991), 83–95.

Hoekstra, T. (1984) *Transitivity*, Foris, Dordrecht.

Hoekstra, T. (1986) "Passives and Participles," *Linguistics in the Netherlands 1986*, Foris, Dordrecht, 95–104.

Hoekstra, T. (1988) "Small Clause Results," *Lingua* 74, 101–139.

Hoekstra, T. (1992) "Aspect and Theta Theory," in I.M. Roca, ed. (1992), 145–174.

Hoekstra, T., H. van der Hulst, and M. Moortgat, eds. (1980) *Lexical Grammar*, Foris, Dordrecht.

Hoekstra, T. and R. Mulder (1990) "Unergatives as Copular Verbs: Locational and Existential Predication," *The Linguistic Review* 7, 1–79.

Hoffman, M.C. (1991) *The Syntax of Argument-Structure-Changing Morphology*, Doctoral dissertation, MIT, Cambridge, MA.

Holmback, H. (1984) "An Interpretive Solution to the Definiteness Effect Problem," *Linguistic Analysis* 13, 195–215.

Hook, P.E. (1983) "The English Abstrument and Rocking Case Relations," *CLS* 19, 183–194.

Hooper, J. and S. Thompson (1973) "On the Applicability of Root Transformations," *Linguistic Inquiry* 4, 465–498.

Hopper, P.J. (1985) "Cause and Affects," *Papers from the Parasession on Causatives and Agentivity*, CLS 21, Part 2, 67–88.

Hopper, P.J. and S.A. Thompson, eds. (1982) *Syntax and Semantics 15: Studies in Transitivity*, Academic Press, New York.

Horn, L.R. (1988) "Morphology, Pragmatics, and the *Un*-verb," *ESCOL '88*, 216–233.

Hornstein, N. and A. Weinberg (1981) "Case Theory and Preposition Stranding," *Linguistic Inquiry* 12, 55–92.

Huddleston, R. (1970) "Some Remarks on Case Grammar," *Linguistic Inquiry* 1, 501–511.

Hudson, R. (1991) "Double Objects, Grammatical Relations and Proto-Roles," *UCL Working Papers in Linguistics* 3, University College, London, 331–368.

Hudson, R. (1992) "So-Called 'Double Objects' and Grammatical Relations," *Language* 68, 251–276.

Ikegami, Y. (1970) *The Semological Structure of the English Verbs of Motion*, Sanseido, Tokyo.

Ikegami, Y. (1973) "A Set of Basic Patterns for the Semantic Structure of the Verb," *Linguistics* 117, 15–58.

Ikegami, Y. (1985) "'Activity'-'Accomplishment'-'Achievement'—A Language that Can't Say 'I Burned It, but It Didn't Burn' and One that Can," in A. Makkai and A.K. Melby, eds., *Linguistics and Philosophy*, Benjamins, Amsterdam, 266–304.

Ikegami, Y. (1988) "Transitivity: Intransitivization vs. Causativization: Some Typological Considerations Concerning Verbs of Action," in C. Duncan-Rose and T. Vennemann, eds. (1988), 389–401.

Ike-uchi, M. (1990) "On Extraction of Secondary Predicates in English," *MIT Working Papers in Linguistics* 13, MIT, Cambridge, MA, 125–162.

Ilson, R. and I. Mel'čuk (1989) "English *Bake* Revisited," *International Journal of Lexicography* 2, 325–346.

Ingria, R. (1987) "Survey of Verb Complement Types in English," unpublished ms., Bolt Beranek and Newman, Inc., Cambridge, MA.

Ingria, R. and J. Pustejovsky (1990) "Active Objects in Syntax, Semantics, and Parsing," in C. Tenny, ed., *The MIT Parsing Volume, 1988-1989*, Parsing Project Working Papers 2, Center for Cognitive Science, MIT, Cambridge, MA, 147–169.

Iordanskaja, L.N. and I.A. Mel'čuk (1981) "On a Class of Russian Verbs Which Can Introduce Direct Speech," in P. Jacobsen and H.L. King, eds., *The Slavic Verb*, Rosenkilde and Bagger, Copenhagen, 51–66.

Iwakura, K. (1978) "On the Role of the Empty Node in the Structure-Preserving Hypothesis," *Linguistic Analysis* 5, 247–292.

Jackendoff, R.S. (1972) *Semantic Interpretation in Generative Grammar*, MIT Press, Cambridge, MA.

Jackendoff, R.S. (1973) "The Base Rules for Prepositional Phrases," in S.R. Anderson and P. Kiparsky, eds., *A Festschrift for Morris Halle*, Holt, Rinehart and Winston, New York, 345–356.

Jackendoff, R.S. (1974) "A Deep Structure Projection Rule," *Linguistic Inquiry* 5, 481–506.

Jackendoff, R.S. (1976) "Toward an Explanatory Semantic Representation," *Linguistic Inquiry* 7, 89–150.

Jackendoff, R.S. (1983) *Semantics and Cognition*, MIT Press, Cambridge, MA.

Jackendoff, R.S. (1985a) "The Argument Structure of *Put*," unpublished ms., Brandeis University, Waltham, MA.

Jackendoff, R.S. (1985b) "Multiple Subcategorization and the Theta-Criterion: The Case of *Climb*," *Natural Language and Linguistic Theory* 3, 271–295.

Jackendoff, R.S. (1987) "The Status of Thematic Relations in Linguistic Theory," *Linguistic Inquiry* 18, 369–411.

Jackendoff, R.S. (1990a) "On Larson's Treatment of the Double Object Construction," *Linguistic Inquiry* 21, 427–456.

Jackendoff, R.S. (1990b) *Semantic Structures*, MIT Press, Cambridge, MA.

Jackendoff, R.S. (1992a) "Babe Ruth Homered His Way into the Hearts of America," in T. Stowell and E. Wehrli, eds. (1992), 155–178.

Jackendoff, R.S. (1992b) *Languages of the Mind: Essays on Mental Representation*, MIT Press, Cambridge, MA.

Jackendoff, R.S. (1992c) "On the Role of Conceptual Structure in Argument Selection: A Reply to Emonds," unpublished ms., Brandeis University, Waltham, MA.

Jackendoff, R.S. and P. Culicover (1971) "A Reconsideration of Dative Movements," *Foundations of Language* 7, 397–412.

Jacobs, R. and P. Rosenbaum, eds. (1967) *Readings in English Transformational Grammar*, Ginn, Waltham, MA.

Jacobson, P. and G.K. Pullum, eds. (1982) *The Nature of Syntactic Representation*, Reidel, Dordrecht.

Jaeggli, O.A. (1986) "Passive," *Linguistic Inquiry* 17, 587–622.

Jaspers, D., W. Klooster, Y. Putseys, and P. Seuren, eds. (1989) *Sentential Complementation and the Lexicon*, Foris, Dordrecht.

Jeffries, L. and P. Willis (1984) "A Return to the Spray Paint Issue," *Journal of Pragmatics* 8, 715–729.

Jenkins, L. (1975) *The English Existential*, Niemeyer, Tübingen.

Jespersen, O. (1927) *A Modern English Grammar on Historical Principles*, Part 3 Syntax, Vol. 2, Carl Winter, Heidelberg.

Jespersen, O. (1942) *A Modern English Grammar on Historical Principles*, Part 6 Morphology, Munksgaard, Copenhagen.

Jespersen, O. (1949) *A Modern English Grammar on Historical Principles*, Part 7 Syntax, Munksgaard, Copenhagen.

Johnson, K. (1986) "Subjects and Theta-Theory," unpublished ms., MIT, Cambridge, MA.

Johnson, K. (1991) "Object Positions," *Natural Language and Linguistic Theory* 9, 577–636.

Jolly, J.A. (1987) "An Analysis of Selected English Prepositions Within the Framework of Role and Reference Grammar," *Davis Working Papers in Linguistics 2*, University of California, Davis, CA, 60–114.

Jones, M. (1988) "Cognate Objects and the Case-Filter," *Journal of Linguistics* 24, 89–110.

Jørgensen, E. (1987) "To Amuse Oneself—To Enjoy Oneself," *English Studies* 68, 274–279.

Jørgensen, E. (1990) "Verbs of Physical Perception Used in the Progressive Tenses," *English Studies* 71, 439–445.

Jørgensen, E. (1991) "The Progressive Tenses and the So-Called 'Non-Conclusive' Verbs," *English Studies* 72, 173–182.

Joshi, A. (1974) "Factorization of Verbs," in C.H. Heidrich, ed., *Semantics and Communication*, North-Holland, Amsterdam, 251–283.

Junker, M.-O. and F. Martineau (1987) "Les Possessions Inaliénables dans les Constructions Objet," *Revue Romane* 22, 194–209.

Kac, M.B. (1972a) "Action and Result: Two Aspects of Predication in English," in J.P. Kimball, ed. (1972), 117–124.

Kac, M.B. (1972b) "Reply to McCawley," in J.P. Kimball, ed. (1972), 151–156.

Kachru, B., R.B. Lees, Y. Malkiel, A. Pietrangeli, and S. Saporta, eds. (1973) *Issues in Linguistics*, University of Illinois Press, Urbana.

Kageyama, T. (1980) "The Role of Thematic Relations in the Spray Paint Hypallage," *Papers in Japanese Linguistics* 7, 35–64.

Kaisse, E.M. (1985) *Connected Speech*, Academic Press, Orlando, FL.

Karius, I. (1985) *Die Ableitung der denominalen Verben mit Nullsuffigierung im Englischen*, Niemeyer, Tübingen.

Kastovsky, D. (1973) "Causatives," *Foundations of Language* 10, 255–315.

Kayne, R.S. (1975) *French Syntax*, MIT Press, Cambridge, MA.

Kayne, R.S. (1981) "Unambiguous Paths," in J. Koster and R. May, eds., *Levels of Syntactic Representation*, Foris, Dordrecht, 143–183. Also in R. Kayne (1984), 129–163.

Kayne, R.S. (1984) *Connectedness and Binary Branching*, Foris, Dordrecht.

Kayne, R.S. (1987) "Principles of Particle Constructions," in J. Guéron et al., eds. (1987), 101–140.

Kearns, K.S. (1991) "The Semantics of the English Progressive," Doctoral dissertation, MIT, Cambridge, MA.

Keenan, E.L. (1975) "Some Universals of Passive in Relational Grammar," *CLS* 11, 340–352.

Keenan, E.L. (1985) "Passive in the World's Languages," in T. Shopen, ed., *Language Typology and Syntactic Description* 1, Cambridge University Press, Cambridge, 243–280.

Kegl, J. and C. Fellbaum (1988) "Non-Canonical Argument Identification," *WCCFL* 7, 187–202. Also appears as CSL Report 25, Cognitive Science Laboratory, Princeton University, Princeton, NJ.

Kegl, J. and C. Fellbaum (1989) "An Analysis of Obligatory Adjuncts: Evidence from the Class of Measure Verbs," *ESCOL '88*, 275–288.

Kenny, A. (1963) *Action, Emotion, and Will*, Routledge and Kegan Paul, London.

Keyser, S.J. and T. Roeper (1984) "On the Middle and Ergative Constructions in English," *Linguistic Inquiry* 15, 381–416.

Keyser, S.J. and T. Roeper (1992) "Re: The Abstract Clitic Hypothesis," *Linguistic Inquiry* 23, 89–125.

Kilby, D. (1984) *Descriptive Syntax and the English Verb*, Croom Helm, London.

Kimball, J.P., ed. (1972) *Syntax and Semantics 1*, Seminar Press, New York.

Kimball, J.P. (1973a) "Get," in J.P. Kimball, ed. (1973c), 205–215.

Kimball, J.P. (1973b) "The Grammar of Existence," *CLS* 9, 262–270.

Kimball, J.P., ed. (1973c) *Syntax and Semantics 2*, Seminar Press, New York.

Kimball, J.P., ed. (1975) *Syntax and Semantics 4*, Academic Press, New York.

Kiparsky, P. (1982) "Word-Formation and the Lexicon," *Proceedings of the 1982 Mid-American Linguistics Conference*, University of Kansas, Lawrence, 3–29.

Kipka, P.F. (1990) *Slavic Aspect and its Implications*, Doctoral dissertation, MIT, Cambridge, MA.

Kirchner, G. (1955) "Direct Transitivation," *English Studies* 36, 15–23.

Kirchner, G. (1959) "Zur Transitiven und intransitiven Verwendung des englischen Verbums," *Zeitschrift für Anglistik und Amerikanistik* 7, 342–399.

Kirsner, R.S. (1972) "About 'About' and the Unity of 'Remind'," *Linguistic Inquiry* 3, 489–499.

Kirsner, R.S. (1973) "Natural Focus and Agentive Interpretation: On the Semantics of Dutch Expletive *er*," *Stanford Occasional Papers in Linguistics* 3, Stanford University, Stanford, CA, 101–114.

Kirsner, R.S. (1977) "On the Passive of Sensory Verb Complement Sentences," *Linguistic Inquiry* 8, 173–179.

Kirsner, R.S. (1986) "Comments on Professor Wierzbicka's Paper," *Quaderni di Semantica* 7, 146–151.

Klooster, W.G. (1972) *The Structure Underlying Measure Phrase Sentences*, Reidel, Dordrecht.

Klooster, W.G. (1973) "Reduction in Dutch Measure Phrase Sentences," in F. Kiefer and N. Ruwet, eds., *Generative Grammar in Europe*, Reidel, Dordrecht, 243–283.

Klooster, W.G. (1978) "Much in Dutch," *CLS* 14, 217–229.

Kuno, S. (1971) "The Position of Locatives in Existential Sentences," *Linguistic Inquiry* 2, 333–378.

Kuno, S. (1972) "Functional Sentence Perspective," *Linguistic Inquiry* 3, 269–320.

Kuno, S. (1983) "Reflexivization in English," in L. Tasmowski and D. Willems, eds. (1983), 257–272.

Kuno, S. (1987) *Functional Syntax: Anaphora, Discourse and Empathy*, University of Chicago Press, Chicago, IL.

Kupferman, L. (1985) "En Observant des Allées et Venues," *Folia Linguistica* 19, 463–497.

Kuroda, S.-Y. (1968) "Review of C.J. Fillmore: *Indirect Object Constructions in English and the Ordering of Transformations*," *Language* 44, 374–378.

Lakoff, G. (1966) "Stative Adjectives and Verbs in English," in A.G. Oettinger, ed., *Mathematical Linguistics and Automatic Translation*, Report NSF-17, The Computation Laboratory, Harvard University, Cambridge, MA.

Lakoff, G. (1968) "Some Verbs of Change and Causation," in S. Kuno, ed., *Mathematical Linguistics and Automatic Translation*, Report NSF-20, Aiken Computation Laboratory, Harvard University, Cambridge, MA.

Lakoff, G. (1970a) *Irregularity in Syntax*, Holt, Rinehart and Winston, New York.

Lakoff, G. (1970b) "A Note on Vagueness and Ambiguity," *Linguistic Inquiry* 1, 357–359.

Lakoff, G. (1977) "Linguistic Gestalts," *CLS* 13, 225–235.

Lakoff, G. (1987) *Women, Fire, and Dangerous Things*, University of Chicago Press, Chicago, IL.

Lakoff, G. and S. Peters (1969) "Phrasal Conjunction and Symmetric Predicates," in D.A. Reibel and S.A. Schane, eds. (1969), 113–142.

Lakoff, G. and J.R. Ross (1972) "A Note on Anaphoric Islands and Causatives," *Linguistic Inquiry* 3, 121–125.

Lakoff, R. (1971) "Passive Resistance," *CLS* 7, 149–162.

Landau, B. and L.R. Gleitman (1985) *Language and Experience*, Harvard University Press, Cambridge, MA.

Langacker, R.W. (1991) *Foundations of Cognitive Grammar*, Vol. 2: Descriptive Application, Stanford University Press, Stanford, CA.

Langendoen, D.T. (1973) "The Problem of Grammatical Relations in Surface Structure," in K.R. Jankowsky, ed., *Georgetown University Round Table 1973: Language and International Studies*, Georgetown University Press, Washington, D.C., 27–37.

Langendoen, D.T. (1978) "The Logic of Reciprocity," *Linguistic Inquiry* 9, 177–197.

Langendoen, D.T. (1979) "More on Locative-Inversion Sentences and the Structure-Preserving Hypothesis," *Linguistic Analysis* 5, 421–437.

Larson, R.K. (1988a) "Light Predicate Raising," Lexicon Project Working Papers 27, Center for Cognitive Science, MIT, Cambridge, MA.

Larson, R.K. (1988b) "On the Double Object Construction," *Linguistic Inquiry* 19, 335–391.

Larson, R.K. (1990) "Double Objects Revisited: Reply to Jackendoff," *Linguistic Inquiry* 21, 589–632.

Lasnik, H. (1988) "Subjects and the Theta-Criterion," *Natural Language and Linguistic Theory* 6, 1–17.

Lasnik, H. (1990) "Case and Expletives," unpublished ms., University of Connecticut, Storrs.

Laughren, M. (1988) "Towards a Lexical Representation of Warlpiri Verbs," in W. Wilkins, ed. (1988a), 215–242.

Lee, G. (1971) "Subjects and Agents II," *Working Papers in Linguistics* 7, The Ohio State University, Columbus, OH, L1–L118.

Leek, F. van der and J.A. Jong (1982) "The Complement Structure of Perception Verbs in English," in S. Daalder and M. Gerritsen, eds., *Linguistics in the Netherlands 1982*, North Holland, Amsterdam, 103–114.

Lees, R.B. and E. Klima (1963) "Rules for English Pronominalization," *Language* 39, 17–28.

Leffel, K. and D. Bouchard, eds. (1991) *Views on Phrase Structure*, Kluwer, Dordrecht.

Lehrer, A. (1969) "Semantic Cuisine," *Journal of Linguistics* 5, 39–55.

Lehrer, A. (1970) "Verbs and Deletable Objects," *Lingua* 25, 227–253.

Lehrer, A. (1974) *Semantic Fields and Lexical Structure*, North-Holland, Amsterdam.

Lehrer, A. (1990) "Polysemy, Conventionality, and the Structure of the Lexicon," *Cognitive Linguistics* 1, 207–246.

Leitner, G. (1974) *Denominale Verbalisierung im Englischen*, Niemeyer, Tübingen.

Leitner, G. (1977) "Zur Vorhersagbarkeit von Derivation: Teil-von Nomina als Basen," in H.E. Brekle and D. Kastovsky, eds. (1977), 140–154.

Levin, B., ed. (1985a) *Lexical Semantics in Review*, Lexicon Project Working Papers 1, Center for Cognitive Science, MIT, Cambridge, MA.

Levin, B. (1985b) "Introduction," in B. Levin, ed. (1985a), 1–62.

Levin, B. (1991) "Building a Lexicon: The Contribution of Linguistic Theory," *International Journal of Lexicography* 4, 205–226. Also in M. Bates and R. Weischedel, eds. (1992).

Levin, B. (in prep.) "Approaches to Lexical Semantic Representation," in D. Walker, A. Zampolli, and N. Calzolari, eds., *Automating the Lexicon*, Oxford University Press, Oxford.

Levin, B. and S. Pinker (1991) "Introduction to Special Issue of *Cognition* on Lexical and Conceptual Semantics," *Cognition* 41, 1–7.

Levin, B. and T. Rapoport (1988) "Lexical Subordination," *CLS* 24, Part 1, 275–289.

Levin, B. and M. Rappaport (1986) "The Formation of Adjectival Passives," *Linguistic Inquiry* 17, 623–661.

Levin, B. and M. Rappaport (1988) "Non-event *–er* Nominals: A Probe into Argument Structure," *Linguistics* 26, 1067–1083.

Levin, B. and M. Rappaport (1989) "Approaches to Unaccusative Mismatches," *NELS* 19, 314–328.

Levin, B. and M. Rappaport Hovav (1991) "Wiping the Slate Clean: A Lexical Semantic Exploration," *Cognition* 41, 123–151.

Levin, B. and M. Rappaport Hovav (1992a) "The Lexical Semantics of Verbs of Motion: The Perspective from Unaccusativity," in I. Roca, ed. (1992), 247–269.

Levin, B. and M. Rappaport Hovav (1992b) *Unaccusativity: At the Syntax-Semantics Interface*, unpublished ms., Northwestern University and Bar Ilan University, Evanston, IL and Ramat Gan.

Levin, L. (1986) *Operations on Lexical Forms: Unaccusative Rules in Germanic Languages*, Doctoral dissertation, MIT, Cambridge, MA.

Levin, L. (1987) "Towards a Linking Theory of Relation Changing Rules in LFG," Report CSLI-87-115, Center for the Study of Language and Information, Stanford University, Stanford, CA.

Levin, L. and J. Simpson (1981) "Quirky Case and the Structure of Icelandic Lexical Entries," *CLS* 17, 185–196.

Levin, L., M. Rappaport, and A. Zaenen, eds. (1983) *Papers in Lexical-Functional Grammar*, Indiana University Linguistics Club, Bloomington.

Levine, J.S. (1980) "Observations on 'Inalienable Possession' in Russian," *Folia Slavica* 4, 7–24.

Levine, R.D. (1989) "On Focus Inversion: Syntactic Valence and the Role of a SUBCAT List," *Linguistics* 27, 1013-1055.

Lichtenberk, F. (1985) "Multiple Uses of Reciprocal Constructions," *Australian Journal of Linguistics* 5, 19–41.

Lieber, R. (1983) "Argument Linking and Compounds in English," *Linguistic Inquiry* 14, 251–285.

Lightfoot, D. (1991) *How to Set Parameters: Arguments from Language Change*, MIT Press, Cambridge, MA.

Lipka, L. (1976) "Topicalization, Case Grammar, and Lexical Decomposition in English," *Archivum Linguisticum* 7, 118–141.

Ljung, M. (1970) *English Denominal Adjectives: A Generative Study of the Semantics of a Group of High-Frequency Denominal Adjectives in English*, Almqvist and Wiksell, Stockholm.

Ljung, M. (1977) "Problems in the Derivation of Instrumental Verbs," in H.E. Brekle and D. Kastovsky, eds. (1977), 165–179.

Ljung, M. (1980) *Reflections on the English Progressive*, Gothenburg Studies in English 46, University of Gothenburg, Gothenburg.

Long, R.B. (1968) "Expletive *There* and the *There* Transformation," *Journal of English Linguistics* 2, 12–22.

Lord, C. (1979) "'Don't You Fall Me Down': Children's Generalizations Regarding Cause and Transitivity," *Papers and Reports on Child Language Development* 17, 81–89.

Lumsden, J.S. (1991) "The Locative Alternations," unpublished ms., Université du Québec à Montréal, Montreal, Quebec.

Lumsden, M. (1988) *Existential Sentences: Their Structure and Meaning*, Croom Helm, London.

Lyons, C. (1989) "Review of M. Lumsden: *Existential Sentences: Their Structure and Meaning*," *Journal of Linguistics* 25, 267–269.

Lys, F. (1988) *An Analysis of Aspectual Compositionality in English and German*, Doctoral dissertation, Northwestern University, Evanston, IL.

Machonis, P.A. (1985) "Transformations of Verb Phrase Idioms: Passivization, Particle Movement, Dative Shift," *American Speech* 60, 291–308.

Manzini, M.R. (1992) "The Projection Principle(s): A Reexamination," in I.M. Roca, ed. (1992), 271–291.

Marantz, A.P. (1982) "Whither Move NP," *MIT Working Papers in Linguistics 4: Papers in Syntax*, MIT, Cambridge, MA, 123–162.

Marantz, A.P. (1984) *On the Nature of Grammatical Relations*, MIT Press, Cambridge, MA.

Marantz, A.P. (1988) "Apparent Exceptions to the Projection Principle," in M. Everaert et al., eds. (1988), 217–232.

Marantz, A.P. (1992) "The *Way* Construction and the Semantics of Direct Arguments in English," in T. Stowell and E. Wehrli, eds. (1992), 179–188.

Marchand, H. (1969) *The Categories and Types of Present-Day English Word-Formation*, 2nd ed., C.H. Beck, Munich.

Marchand, H. (1973) "Reversative, Ablative, and Privative Verbs in English, French and

German," in B. Kachru et al., eds. (1973), 636–643. Also in H. Marchand (1974), 405–415.

Marchand, H. (1974) *Studies in Syntax and Word-Formation* (edited by D. Kastovsky), Wilhelm Fink, Munich.

Martin, W. (1991) "On the Dynamic Organization of (Computer) Lexicons," *Cahiers de l'Institut de Linguistique de Louvain* 17, 43–50.

Maruta, T. (1985) "Is Stylistic Inversion Stylistic?" *Cahiers Linguistiques d'Ottawa* 14, 111–120.

Massam, D. (1985) *Case Theory and the Projection Principle*, Doctoral dissertation, MIT, Cambridge, MA.

Massam, D. (1989) "Part/Whole Constructions in English," *WCCFL* 8, 236–246.

Massam, D. (1990) "Cognate Objects as Thematic Objects," *Canadian Journal of Linguistics* 35, 161–190.

Massam, D. and Y. Roberge (1989) "Recipe Context Null Objects in English," *Linguistic Inquiry* 20, 134–139.

McCawley, J.D. (1968a) "Lexical Insertion in a Transformational Grammar Without Deep Structure," *CLS* 4, 71–80. Reprinted with notes in J.D. McCawley (1973), 154–166.

McCawley, J.D. (1968b) "The Role of Semantics in a Grammar," in E. Bach and R.T. Harms, eds. (1968), 124–169. Reprinted with notes in J.D. McCawley (1973), 59–98.

McCawley, J.D. (1970a) "English as a VSO Language," *Language* 46, 286–299. Reprinted with notes in J.D. McCawley (1973), 211–228.

McCawley, J.D. (1970b) "Semantic Representation," in P.M. Garvin, ed., *Cognition: A Multiple View*, Spartan Books, New York, 227–247. Reprinted with notes in J.D. McCawley (1973), 240–256.

McCawley, J.D. (1971) "Prelexical Syntax," *Report of the 22nd Annual Roundtable Meeting on Linguistics and Language Studies*, Georgetown University Press, Washington DC, 19–33. Reprinted with notes in J.D. McCawley (1973), 343–356.

McCawley, J.D. (1972a) "A Program for Logic," in D. Davidson and G.H. Harmon, eds. (1972), 498–544. Reprinted with notes in J.D. McCawley (1973), 285–319.

McCawley, J.D. (1972b) "Kac and Shibatani on the Grammar of Killing," in J.P. Kimball, ed. (1972), 151–157.

McCawley, J.D. (1973) *Grammar and Meaning*, Taishukan, Tokyo.

McCawley, J.D. (1974) "On Identifying the Remains of Deceased Clauses," *Language Research* 9, 73–85. Also in J.D. McCawley (1979), 84–95.

McCawley, J.D. (1975) "Verbs of Bitching," in D. Hockey, W. Harper, and B. Freed, eds., *Contemporary Research in Philosophical Logic and Linguistic Semantics*, Reidel, Dordrecht, 313–332. Also in J.D. McCawley (1979), 135–150.

McCawley, J.D. (1976) "Remarks on What Can Cause What," in M. Shibatani, ed. (1976a), 117–129. Also in J.D. McCawley (1979), 101–112.

McCawley, J.D. (1977) "Remarks on the Lexicography of Performative Verbs," in A. Rogers, R. Wall, and J. Murphy, eds., *Proceedings of the Texas Conference on Performatives, Implicature, and Presupposition*, Center for Applied Linguistics, Washington, D.C., 13–25. Also in J.D. McCawley (1979), 151-164.

McCawley, J.D. (1979) *Adverbs, Vowels, and Other Objects of Wonder*, University of Chicago Press, Chicago, IL.

McCawley, J.D. (1981) "A Selection of *There*-Insertion Verbs," unpublished ms., University of Chicago, Chicago, IL.

McCawley, J.D. (1988) *The Syntactic Phenomena of English*, University of Chicago Press, Chicago, IL.

McCawley, N. (1975) "What Strikes Me about Psych-Movement," *The Second LACUS Forum*, 320–328.

McCawley, N. (1976) "On Experiencer Causatives," in M. Shibatani, ed. (1976a), 181–203.

McCawley, N. (1977) "What is the 'Emphatic Root Transformation' Phenomenon?" *CLS* 13, 384–400.

McCloskey, J. (1991) *"There, It*, and Agreement," *Linguistic Inquiry* 22, 563–567.

McConnell-Ginet, S. (1982) "Adverbs and Logical Form," *Language* 58, 144–184.

McClure, W. (1990) "A Lexical Semantic Explanation for Unaccusative Mismatches," in K. Dziwirek et al., eds. (1990), 305–318.

McNally, L. (1992) *An Interpretation for the English Existential Construction*, Doctoral dissertation, University of California, Santa Cruz, CA.

Merlan, F. (1985) "Split Intransitivity: Functional Oppositions in Intransitive Inflection," in J. Nichols and A.C. Woodbury, eds., *Grammar Inside and Outside the Clause*, Cambridge University Press, Cambridge, 324–362.

Merlo, P. (1988) "Secondary Predicates in Italian and English," *ESCOL* '88.

Merlo, P. (1989) "Risultative in Italiano ed Inglese," *Rivista di Grammatica Generativa* 14, 29–53.

Meulen, A.G.B. ter (1990) "English Aspectual Verbs as Generalized Quantifiers," *NELS* 20, 378–390.

Meulen, A.G.B. ter and J. Rooryck (1991) "The Quantificational Force of Static and Dynamic Predication," *WCCFL* 10, 459–469.

Miller, G.A. (1972) "English Verbs of Motion: A Case Study in Semantics and Lexical Memory," in A.W. Melton and E. Martin, eds., *Coding Processes in Human Memory*, Winston, Washington, D.C., 335–372.

Miller, G.A. and C. Fellbaum (1991) "Semantic Networks of English," *Cognition* 41, 197–229.

Miller, G.A. and P.N. Johnson-Laird (1976) *Language and Perception*, Harvard University Press, Cambridge, MA.

Miller, J.E. (1989) "Participant Roles, Synonymy, and Truth Conditions," in D. Arnold et al., eds. (1989), 187–202.

Milsark, G. (1974) *Existential Sentences in English*, Doctoral dissertation, MIT, Cambridge, MA.

Milsark, G. (1977) "Towards an Explanation of Certain Peculiarities of the Existential Construction in English," *Linguistic Analysis* 3, 1–29.

Milsark, G. (1990) "Review of M. Lumsden: *Existential Sentences: Their Structure and Meaning*," *Language* 66, 850–854.

Mish, F.C., ed. (1986) *Webster's Ninth New Collegiate Dictionary*, Merriam-Webster, Springfield, MA.

Mittwoch, A. (1982) "On the Difference Between Eating and Eating Something: Activities versus Accomplishments," *Linguistic Inquiry* 13, 113–122.

Mittwoch, A. (1990) "On the Distribution of Bare Infinitive Complements in English," *Journal of Linguistics* 26, 103–31.

Moltmann, F. (1989) "Nominal and Clausal Event Predicates," *CLS* 25, Part 1, 300–314.

Moravcsik, E.A. (1978) "Agreement," in J.H. Greenberg, ed., *Universals of Human Language: Syntax*, Vol. 4, Stanford University Press, Stanford, CA, 331–374.

Morgan, J.L. (1969) "On Arguing About Semantics," *Papers in Linguistics* 1, 49–70.

Moro, A. (1989) "*There* as Raised Predicate," unpublished ms., Università di Venezia, Venezia.

Morreall, J. (1976) "The Nonsynonymy of *Kill* and *Cause to Die*," *Linguistic Inquiry* 7, 516–518.

Mourelatos, A.P.D. (1978) "Events, Processes and States," *Linguistics and Philosophy* 2, 415–434. Also in P. Tedeschi and A. Zaenen, eds. (1981) *Syntax and Semantics 14: Tense and Aspect*, Academic Press, New York, 191–212.

Mufwene, S.S. (1978) "English Manner-of-Speaking Verbs Revisited," *Papers from the Parasession on the Lexicon*, CLS, Chicago, IL, 278–289.

Mufwene, S.S. (1979) "A Revisitation to Causation," *The Elements: A Parasession on Linguistic Units and Levels*, CLS, Chicago, IL, 132–143.

Mukhin, A.M. (1985) "Lexical and Syntactic Semantics in Historical Aspect," in J. Fisiak, ed. (1985), 397–405.

Mulder, R. and P. Wehrmann (1989) "Locational Verbs as Unaccusatives," in H. Bennis and A. van Kemenade, eds., *Linguistics in the Netherlands 1989*, Foris, Dordrecht, 111–22.

Munro, P. (1982) "On the Transitivity of 'Say' Verbs," in P.J. Hopper and S.A. Thompson, eds. (1982), 301–318.

Na, Y. (1986) "The Conventionalization of Semantic Distinctions," *CLS* 22, Part 1, 166–178.

Napoli, D.J. (1988a) "The Double Object Construction in English: A Reply," unpublished ms., Swarthmore University, Swarthmore, PA.

Napoli, D.J. (1988b) "Subjects and External Arguments: Clauses and Non-Clauses," *Linguistics and Philosophy* 11, 323–354.

Napoli, D.J. (1989a) *Predication Theory: A Case Study for Indexing Theory*, Cambridge University Press, Cambridge.

Napoli, D.J. (1989b) "Secondary Resultative Predicates in Italian," unpublished ms., Swarthmore College, Swarthmore, PA.

Napoli, D.J. and E. Rando (1978) "Definites in *There*-Sentences," *Language* 54, 300–313.

Nash-Webber, B. (1971) "Verbs of Composition," unpublished ms., Harvard University, Cambridge, MA.

Newman, A. (1975) "A Semantic Analysis of English and Hebrew Cooking Terms," *Lingua* 37, 53–79.

Newmeyer, F.J. (1975) *English Aspectual Verbs*, Mouton, The Hague.

Newmeyer, F.J. (1987) "Presentational *There*-Insertion and the Notions 'Root Transformation' and 'Stylistic Rule'," *CLS* 23, Part 1, 295–308.

Ney, J.W. (1990) "Polysemy and Syntactic Variability in the Surface Verb 'Break'," *The Seventeenth LACUS Forum*, 264–278.

Nilsen, D.L.F. (1973) *The Instrumental Case in English: Syntactic and Semantic Considerations*, Mouton, The Hague.

Nissenbaum, H.F. (1985) *Emotion and Focus*, Center for the Study of Language and Information, Stanford University, Stanford, CA.

Norrick, N.R. (1978) *Factive Adjectives and the Theory of Factivity*, Niemeyer, Tübingen.

Norvig, P. and G. Lakoff (1987) "Taking: A Study in Lexical Network Theory," *BLS* 13, 195–206.

Nunberg, G.D. (1978) *The Pragmatics of Reference*, Indiana University Linguistics Club, Bloomington.

Nwachukwu, P.A. (1987) "The Argument Structure of Igbo Verbs," Lexicon Project Working Papers 18, Center for Cognitive Science, MIT, Cambridge, MA.

Oehrle, R.T. (1976) *The Grammatical Status of the English Dative Alternation*, Doctoral dissertation, MIT, Cambridge, MA.

Oehrle, R.T. (1977) "Review of G.M. Green: *Semantics and Syntactic Regularity*," *Language* 53, 198–208.

Oehrle, R.T. (1983) "Czepluch on the English Dative Constructions: A Case for Reanalysis," *The Linguistic Review* 3, 165–180.

Ostler, N.D.M. (1980a) "Origins, Orientations and Endpoints: Evidence for a Finer Analysis of Thematic Relations," *Studies in English Linguistics* 8, Asahi Press, Tokyo.

Ostler, N.D.M. (1980b) *A Theory of Case Linking and Agreement*, Indiana University Linguistics Club, Bloomington.

Ostler, N.D.M. and B.T.S. Atkins (1991) "Predictable Meaning Shift: Some Linguistic Properties of Lexical Implication Rules," in J. Pustejovsky and S. Bergler, eds., *Lexical Semantics and Knowledge Representation*, ACL SIG Workshop Proceedings, 76–87.

Parsons, T. (1989) "The Progressive in English: Events, States, and Processes," *Linguistics and Philosophy* 12, 213–241.

Parsons, T. (1990) *Events in the Semantics of English*, MIT Press, Cambridge, MA.

Partee, B.H. (1974) "Opacity and Scope," in M.K. Munitz and P.K. Unger, eds., *Semantics and Philosophy*, New York University Press, New York, 81–101.

Penhallurick, J. (1984) "Full-Verb Inversion in English," *Australian Journal of Linguistics* 4, 33–56.

Perlmutter, D.M. (1970) "On the Two Verbs *Begin*," in R. Jacobs and P. Rosenbaum, eds. (1970), 107–119.

Perlmutter, D.M. (1978) "Impersonal Passives and the Unaccusative Hypothesis," *BLS* 4, 157–189.

Perlmutter, D.M. and P.M. Postal (1983) "The Relational Succession Law," in D.M. Perlmutter, ed., *Studies in Relational Grammar 1*, University of Chicago Press, Chicago, IL, 30–80.

Perlmutter, D.M. and P.M. Postal (1984) "The 1-Advancement Exclusiveness Law," in D.M. Perlmutter and C. Rosen, eds. (1984), 81–125.

Perlmutter, D.M. and C. Rosen, eds. (1984) *Studies in Relational Grammar 2*, University of Chicago Press, Chicago, IL.

Pesetsky, D. (1987) "Binding Problems with Experiencer Verbs," *Linguistic Inquiry* 18, 126–140.

Pesetsky, D. (1992) *Zero Syntax*, Vol. 1: Experiencers and Cascades, unpublished ms., MIT, Cambridge, MA.

Pinker, S. (1989) *Learnability and Cognition: The Acquisition of Argument Structure*, MIT Press, Cambridge, MA.

Plank, F., ed. (1984) *Objects*, Academic Press, London.

Platzack, C. (1983) "Existential Sentences in English, German, Icelandic and Swedish," *Papers from the 7th Scandinavian Conference in Linguistics*, 80–100.

Pollard, C. and I.A. Sag (1992) "Anaphors in English and the Scope of Binding Theory," *Linguistic Inquiry* 23, 261–303.

Poser, W.J. (1982) "Lexical Rules May Exchange Internal Arguments," *The Linguistic Review* 2, 97–100.

Postal, P.M. (1971) *Cross-Over Phenomena*, Holt, Rinehart and Winston, New York.

Postal, P.M. (1977a) "About a 'Nonargument' for Raising," *Linguistic Inquiry* 8, 141–155.

Postal, P.M. (1977b) "Antipassive in French," *Lingvisticae Investigationes* 1, 333–374.

Postal, P.M. (1982) "Some Arc Pair Grammar Descriptions," in P. Jacobson and G.K. Pullum, eds. (1982), 341–425.

Postal, P.M. (1990) "Some Unexpected English Restrictions," in K. Dziwirek et al., eds. (1990), 365–385.

Postal, P.M. and G.K. Pullum (1988) "Expletive Noun Phrases in Subcategorized Positions," *Linguistic Inquiry* 19, 635–670.

Pouradier, F. Duteil, and J. François (1981) "Les Equivalents Prépositionnels des Biprédications Résultatives Réfléchies: *Sich Krank Arbeiten* vs. *Tomber Malade à Force de Travailler*," in C. Schwarze, ed., *Analyse des Prépositions*, Niemeyer, Tübingen, 111–138.

Poutsma, H. (1904) *A Grammar of Late Modern English*, P. Noordhoff, Groningen.

Pullum, G.K. (1987) "Implications of English Extraposed Irrealis Clauses," *ESCOL '87*, 260–270.

Pusch, L.F. (1972) "Bemerkungen über Partitive and Holistische Konstruktionen im Deutschen und Englischen," in G. Nickel, *Reader zur Kontrastiven Linguistik*, Athenäum Fischer Taschenbuch, Frankfurt, 122–35.

Pustejovsky, J. (1988) "The Geometry of Events," in C. Tenny, ed. (1988), 19–40.

Pustejovsky, J. (1991a) "The Generative Lexicon," *Computational Linguistics* 17, 409–441.

Pustejovsky, J. (1991b) "The Syntax of Event Structure," *Cognition* 41, 47–81.

Quine, W.V.O. (1960) *Word and Object*, MIT Press, Cambridge, MA.

Quirk, R. (1970) "Taking a Deep Smell," *Journal of Linguistics* 6, 119–124.

Quirk, R., S. Greenbaum, G. Leech, and J. Svartvik (1985) *A Comprehensive Grammar of the English Language*, Longman, London.

Radden, G. (1988) "The Concept of Motion," in W. Hüllen and R. Schulze, eds.,

Understanding the Lexicon: Meaning, Sense and World Knowledge in Lexical Semantics, Niemeyer, Tübingen, 380–394.

Randall, J.H. (1982) "A Lexical Approach to Causatives," *Journal of Linguistic Research* 2, 77–105.

Randall, J.H. (1990) "Catapults and Pendulums: The Mechanics of Language Acquisition," *Linguistics* 28, 1381–1406.

Rapoport, T.R. (1986) "Nonverbal Predication in Hebrew," *WCCFL* 5, 207–218.

Rapoport, T.R. (1990) "Secondary Predication and the Lexical Representation of Verbs," *Machine Translation* 4, 31–55.

Rappaport, M. (1983) "On the Nature of Derived Nominals," in L. Levin et al., eds. (1983), 113–142.

Rappaport, M. and B. Levin (1985) "A Case Study in Lexical Analysis: The Locative Alternation," unpublished ms., Lexicon Project, Center for Cognitive Science, MIT, Cambridge, MA.

Rappaport, M. and B. Levin (1988) "What to Do with Theta-Roles," in W. Wilkins, ed. (1988a), 7–36.

Rappaport, M., B. Levin, and M. Laughren (1988) "Niveaux de Representation Lexicale," *Lexique* 7, 13–32. An English translation appears as "Levels of Lexical Representation," Lexicon Project Working Papers 20, Center for Cognitive Science, MIT, Cambridge, MA.

Rappaport Hovav, M. and B. Levin (1992) "–er Nominals: Implications for a Theory of Argument Structure," in T. Stowell and E. Wehrli, eds. (1992), 127–153.

Ravin, Y. (1990) *Lexical Semantics Without Thematic Roles*, Oxford University Press, Oxford.

Reibel, D.A. and S.A. Schane, eds. (1969) *Modern Studies in English*, Prentice-Hall, Englewood Cliffs, NJ.

Reinhart, T. (1983) *Anaphora and Semantic Interpretation*, University of Chicago Press, Chicago, IL.

Reinhart, T. and E. Reuland (1991) "Anaphors and Logophors: An Argument Structure Perspective," in J. Koster and E. Reuland, eds., *Long-Distance Anaphora*, Cambridge University Press, Cambridge.

Reuland, E. and A.G.B. ter Meulen, eds. (1987) *The Representation of (In)definiteness*, MIT Press, Cambridge, MA.

Rice, S. (1987) "Towards a Transitive Prototype: Evidence from Some Atypical English Passives," *BLS* 13, 422–434.

Rice, S. (1988) "Unlikely Lexical Entries," *BLS* 14, 202–212.

Richardson, J.F. (1983) "Smash Bang," *BLS* 9, 221–217.

Riddle, E. and G. Sheintuch (1983) "A Functional Analysis of Pseudo-passives," *Linguistics and Philosophy* 6, 527–563.

Riddle, E., G. Sheintuch, and Y. Ziv (1977) "Pseudo-Passivization: On the Role of Pragmatics in Determining Rule Unity," *Studies in the Linguistic Sciences* 7, 147–156.

Ritchie, W.C. (1985) "Word-Formation, Learned Vocabulary and Linguistic Maturation," in J. Fisiak, ed. (1985), Mouton, Berlin, 463–482.

Rivière, C. (1981) "Résultatifs Anglais et Transitivité," *Modèles Linguistiques* 1981, 162–179.

Rivière, C. (1982) "Objectionable Objects," *Linguistic Inquiry* 13, 685–689.

Rizzi, L. (1986) "Null Objects in Italian and the Theory of *pro*," *Linguistic Inquiry* 17, 501–557.

Rizzi, L. (1990) *Relativized Minimality*, MIT Press, Cambridge, MA.

Rizzi, L. and A. Belletti (1988) "Remarques sur les Verbes Psychologiques, la Θ-Théorie et le Principe de Liage," *Lexique* 7, 13–32.

Roberts, I.G. (1987) *The Representation of Implicit and Dethematized Subjects*, Foris, Dordrecht.

Roberts, I.G. (1988) "Predicative APs," *Linguistic Inquiry* 19, 703–710.

Roberts, I.G. (1989) "Psych-Adjectives and the Ergative Hypothesis," *NELS* 19, 358–374.

Roca, I., ed. (1992) *Thematic Structure: Its Role in Grammar*, Mouton de Gruyter, Berlin.

Rochemont, M.S. (1978) *A Theory of Stylistic Rules in English*, Doctoral dissertation, University of Massachusetts, Amherst.

Rochemont, M.S. (1979) "Stylistic Rules in English," *NELS* 9, Part 2, 168–176.

Rochemont, M.S. (1986) *Focus in Generative Grammar*, Benjamins, Amsterdam.

Rogers, A. (1971) "Three Kinds of Physical Perception Verbs," *CLS* 7, 206–223.

Rogers, A. (1972) "Another Look at Flip Perception Verbs," *CLS* 8, 302–315.

Rogers, A. (1973) *Physical Perception Verbs in English: A Study in Lexical Relatedness*, Doctoral dissertation, UCLA, Los Angeles, CA.

Rogers, A. (1974) "A Transderivational Constraint on Richard?" *CLS* 10, 551–558.

Rose, J. (1973) "Principled Limitations on Productivity in Denominal Verbs," *Foundations of Language* 10, 509–526.

Rosen, C. (1984) "The Interface between Semantic Roles and Initial Grammatical Relations," in D.M. Perlmutter and C. Rosen, eds. (1984), 38–77.

Ross, A.S.C. (1976) "Meaningless *De–* in English," *American Speech* 23, 310–311.

Ross, J.R. (1966) "On the Cyclic Nature of English Pronominalization," in D.A. Reibel and S.A. Schane, eds. (1966), 187–200.

Ross, J.R. (1970) "Two Types of Idioms," *Linguistic Inquiry* 1, 144.

Ross, J.R. (1972) "More on *Begin*," *Foundations of Language* 8, 574–577.

Ross, J.R. (1973) "A Fake NP Squish," in C.-J.N. Bailey and R.W. Shuy, eds. (1973), 96–140.

Ross, J.R. (1974) "There, There, (There, (There, (There, …)))," *CLS* 10, 569–587.

Rothemberg, M. (1974) *Les Verbes à la Fois Transitifs et Intransitifs en Français Contemporain*, Mouton, The Hague.

Rothstein, S. (1983) *The Syntactic Forms of Predication*, Doctoral dissertation, MIT, Cambridge, MA.

Rozwadowska, B. (1988) "Thematic Restrictions on Derived Nominals," in W. Wilkins, ed. (1988a), 147–165.

Rudanko, J. (1988) "On the Grammar of *For* Clauses in English," *English Studies* 69, 433–452.

Rudanko, J. (1989) *Complementation and Case Grammar: A Syntactic and Semantic*

Study of Selected Patterns of Complementation in Present-Day English, State University of New York Press, Albany.

Rudanko, J. (1991) "On Verbs Governing *in –ing* in Present-Day English," *English Studies* 72, 55–72.

Rudzka-Ostyn, B. (1988) "Semantic Extensions into the Domain of Verbal Communication," in B. Rudzka-Ostyn, ed., *Topics in Cognitive Grammar*, Benjamins, Amsterdam, 507–553.

Ruhl, C. (1972) "'The Grammar of Hitting and Breaking' Revisited," *Glossa* 6, 147–154.

Ruhl, C. (1979) "The Semantic Field of *Break*, *Cut*, and *Tear*," *The Sixth LACUS Forum*, 200-214.

Ruhl, C. (1989) *On Monosemy: A Study in Linguistic Semantics*, State University of New York Press, Albany.

Ruwet, N. (1972) *Théorie Syntaxique et Syntaxe du Français*, Editions du Seuil, Paris.

Ruwet, N. (1986) "On Weather Verbs," *CLS* 22, Part 1, 195–215.

Ruwet, N. (1991) *Syntax and Human Experience*, University of Chicago Press, Chicago, IL.

Ryle, G. (1949) *The Concept of Mind*, Hutchinson, London.

Sadock, J.M. (1974) "Read at Your Own Risk: Syntactic and Semantic Horrors You Can Find in Your Medicine Chest," *CLS* 10, 599–607. Also in E. Schiller, B. Need, D. Varley, and W.H. Eilfort, eds. (1988) *The Best of CLS*, Chicago Linguistic Society, Chicago, IL, 202–208.

Safir, K. (1985) *Syntactic Chains*, Cambridge University Press, Cambridge.

Safir, K. (1987) "So *There*! A Reply to Williams' Analysis of *There*-Sentences," *MIT Working Papers in Linguistics* 9, Cambridge, MA.

Sag, I.A. (1973) "On the State of Progress on Progressives and Statives," in C.-J.N. Bailey and R.W. Shuy, eds. (1983), 83–95.

Sager, N. (1981) *Natural Language Information Processing: A Computer Grammar of English and Its Applications*, Addison-Wesley, Reading, MA.

Salkoff, M. (1983) "Bees Are Swarming in the Garden," *Language* 59, 288–346.

Sato, H. (1987) "Resultative Attributes and GB Principles," *English Linguistics* 4, 91–106.

Sawyer, J. (1973) "Existential Sentences: A Linguistic Universal?" *American Speech* 48, 239–245.

Schachter, P. (1977) "Constraints on Coördination," *Language* 53, 86–103.

Schachter, P. (1992) "Comments on Bresnan and Kanerva's 'Locative Inversion in Chicheŵa: A Case Study of Factorization in Grammar'," in T. Stowell and E. Wehrli, eds. (1992), 103–110.

Schentke, M. (1977) "Zur Wortsemantik: Verbklassen—Verben Boil/Cook," *Linguistische Studien* 42, 157–179.

Schlesinger, I.M. (1989) "Instruments as Agents: On the Nature of Semantic Relations," *Journal of Linguistics* 25, 189–210.

Schlyter, S. (1979) "Point of Observation and Time Indications with Movement Verbs," in T. Pettersson, ed., *Aspectology*, Almqvist and Wiksell, Stockholm.

Schreiber, P. (1978) "*There*-Insertion and Number Agreement," *Linguistic Inquiry* 9, 318–325.

Schwartz, L. (1990) "Review of R.R. van Oirsouw: *The Syntax of Coordination*," *Language* 66, 844–850.

Schwartz-Norman, L. (1976) "The Grammar of 'Content' and 'Container'," *Journal of Linguistics* 12, 279–287.

Sehnert, J. and M. Sharwood-Smith (1973) "The Verbalization of Instrumentals in English," *Studia Anglica Posnaniensia* 5, 37–46.

Sheintuch, G. (1980) "The *There*-Insertion Construction in English — A Pragmatic Strategy for Promoting Certain Syntactic Structures," *Glossa* 14, 168–188.

Shibatani, M. (1972) "Three Reasons for Not Deriving 'Kill' from 'Cause to Die' in Japanese," in J.P. Kimball, ed. (1972), 125–137.

Shibatani, M., ed. (1976a) *Syntax and Semantics 6: The Grammar of Causative Constructions*, Academic Press, New York.

Shibatani, M. (1976b) "The Grammar of Causative Constructions: A Conspectus," in M. Shibatani, ed. (1976a), 1–40.

Shopen, T. (1986) "Comments on 'The Semantics of 'Internal Dative' in English' by Anna Wierzbicka," *Quaderni di Semantica* 7, 151–154.

Sibley, F. N. (1955) "Seeking, Scrutinizing and Seeing," *Mind* 64, 455–478.

Siegel, D. (1973) "Nonsources for Unpassives," in J. Kimball, ed. (1973c), 301–317.

Siewierska, A. (1984) *The Passive: A Comparative Linguistic Analysis*, Croom Helm, London.

Sigler, M. (1985) "Optionally Reflexive Verbs," unpublished ms., MIT, Cambridge, MA.

Silva, C.M. (1973) "Adverbial *-ing*," *Working Papers in Linguistics* 16, The Ohio State University, Columbus, 90–94.

Simpson, J. (1983) "Resultatives," in L. Levin et al., eds. (1983), 143–157.

Sinha, A.K. (1973) "On Stative Passives and Treatment of Some Idioms," *CLS* 9, 615–626.

Sinha, A.K. (1974) "How Passive Are Passives?" *CLS* 10, 631–642.

Sinha, A.K. (1978) "Another Look at the Universal Characterization of the Passive Voice," *CLS* 14, 445–458.

Smith, C.S. (1970) "Jespersen's 'Move and Change' Class and Causative Verbs in English," in M.A. Jazayery, E.C. Palome, and W. Winter, eds., *Linguistic and Literary Studies in Honor of Archibald A. Hill*, Vol.2: Descriptive Linguistics, Mouton, The Hague, 101–109.

Smith, C.S. (1972) "On Causative Verbs and Derived Nominals in English," *Linguistic Inquiry* 3, 136–138.

Smith, D.L. (1981) "On the Order of Objects in Two Argument Predicates," *Descriptive and Applied Linguistics* 14, 185–198.

Snell-Hornby, M. (1983) *Verb Descriptivity in German and English*, Carl Winter, Heidelberg.

Sobin, N. (1976) "The Pragmatics of Lurking," *Linguistic Inquiry* 7, 726–728.

Spangler, W.E. (1970) "Locative Restraints on the English Reflexive," *Word* 26, 114–118.

Speas, M. (1990) *Phrase Structure in Natural Language*, Kluwer, Dordrecht.

Sproat, R.W. (1985) *On Deriving the Lexicon*, Doctoral dissertation, MIT, Cambridge, MA.

Stanley, J.P. (1975) "Passive Motivation," *Foundations of Language* 13, 25–39.

Stein, G. (1979) *Studies in the Functions of the Passive*, Gunter Narr, Tübingen.

Stowell, T. (1978) "What Was There Before There Was There," *CLS* 14, 457–471.

Stowell, T. (1979) "Restricting Modifiers," *NELS* 9, Part 2, 193–213.

Stowell, T. (1981) *Origins of Phrase Structure*, Doctoral dissertation, MIT, Cambridge, MA.

Stowell, T. (1989) "Subjects, Specifiers, and X-Bar Theory," in M. Baltin and A. Kroch, eds., *Alternative Conceptions of Phrase Structure*, University of Chicago Press, Chicago, IL, 232–262.

Stowell, T. (1991a) "Determiners in NP and DP," in K. Leffel and D. Bouchard, eds. (1991), 37–56.

Stowell, T. (1991b) "Small Clause Restructuring," in R. Freidin, ed., *Principles and Parameters in Comparative Grammar*, MIT Press, Cambridge, MA, 182–218.

Stowell, T. and Wehrli, E., eds. (1992) *Syntax and Semantics 26: Syntax and the Lexicon*, Academic Press, New York.

Stratton, C.R. (1971) "The Pathological Case," *Working Papers in Linguistics* 10, The Ohio State University, Columbus, 221–230.

Stroik, T. (1990) "Expletive NPs in Object-Position," *Canadian Journal of Linguistics* 35, 13–27.

Stroik, T. (1992) "Middles and Movement," *Linguistic Inquiry* 23, 127–137.

Styan, E.M. (1984) "Theta-Roles in the Lexicon: Linguistic Evidence," *McGill Working Papers in Linguistics* 1, Montreal, Quebec, 118–147.

Sundén, K.F. (1916a) *The Predicational Categories in English* (Essay I), The University Press, Uppsala.

Sundén, K.F. (1916b) *A Category of Predicational Change in English* (Essay II), The University Press, Uppsala. (Published together with Sundén (1916a).)

Svartvik, J. (1966) *On Voice and the English Verb*, Mouton, The Hague.

Szabolcsi, A. (1986) "From the Definiteness Effect to Lexical Integrity," in W. Abraham and J. de Mey, eds., *Topic, Focus, and Configurationality*, Benjamins, Amsterdam.

Talmy, L. (1975) "Semantics and Syntax of Motion," in J.P. Kimball, ed. (1975), 181–238.

Talmy, L. (1985) "Lexicalization Patterns: Semantic Structure in Lexical Forms," in T. Shopen, ed., *Language Typology and Syntactic Description* 3: *Grammatical Categories and the Lexicon*, Cambridge University Press, Cambridge, 57–149.

Talmy, L. (1991) "Path to Realization: A Typology of Event Conflation," unpublished ms., State University of New York, Buffalo.

Tasmowski, L. and D. Willems, eds. (1983) *Problems in Syntax*, Plenum, New York.

Tenny, C. (1987) *Grammaticalizing Aspect and Affectedness*, Doctoral dissertation, MIT, Cambridge, MA.

Tenny, C., ed. (1988) *Studies in Generative Approaches to Aspect*, Lexicon Project Working Papers 24, Center for Cognitive Science, MIT, Cambridge, MA.

Tenny, C. (1992) "The Aspectual Interface Hypothesis," in I.A. Sag and A. Szabolcsi, eds., *Lexical Matters*, CSLI Lecture Notes 24, Center for the Study of Language and

Information, Stanford University, Stanford, CA, 1–27. An earlier version appeared in *NELS* 18, 490-508.

Thalberg, I. (1972) *Enigmas of Agency*, George Allen and Unwin, London.

Thalberg, I. (1977) *Perception, Motion and Action*, Blackwell, Oxford.

Thompson, S. and R. Kirsner (1976) "The Role of Pragmatic Inference in Semantics: A Study of Sensory Verb Complements in English," *Glossa* 10, 200–40.

Thorne, J.P. (1973) "On the Grammar of Existential Sentences," in P. Suppes, L. Henkin, A. Joja, and G.R.C. Moisil, eds., *Logic, Methodology and Philosophy of Science IV*, North-Holland, Amsterdam, 863–81.

Tinker, E., R. Beckwith, and R. Dougherty (1989) "Markedness and the Acquisition of Psych Verbs," *ESCOL '89*, 252–263.

Travis, L. (to appear) "Notes on Case and Expletives: A Discussion of Lasnik's Paper," in R. Freidin, ed., *Comparative Syntax: Princeton Workshop II*, MIT Press, Cambridge, MA.

Tremblay, M. (1990) "An Argument Sharing Approach to Ditransitive Constructions," *WCCFL* 9, 549–563.

Tremblay, M. (1991) "Alternances D'Arguments Internes en Français et en Anglais," *Revue Québécoise de Linguistique* 20, 39–53.

Valesio, P. (1971) "The Distinction of Active and Passive," *Linguistic Inquiry* 2, 407–414.

Van Develde, R. (1977) "Mistaken Views of *See*," *Linguistic Inquiry* 8, 767–771.

Van Oosten, J. (1977) "Subjects and Agenthood in English," *CLS* 13, 459–471.

Van Oosten, J. (1980) "Subjects, Topics and Agents: Evidence from Property-Factoring," *BLS* 6, 479–494.

Van Oosten, J. (1986) *The Nature of Subjects, Topics and Agents: A Cognitive Explanation*, Indiana University Linguistics Club, Bloomington.

Van Valin, R.D., Jr. (1990) "Semantic Parameters of Split Intransitivity," *Language* 66, 221–260.

Van Voorst, J. (1986) *Event Structure*, Doctoral dissertation, University of Ottawa, Ottawa, Ontario.

Van Voorst, J. (1992) "The Aspectual Semantics of Psychological Verbs," *Linguistics and Philosophy* 15, 65–92.

Vendler, Z. (1957) "Verbs and Times," *Philosophical Review* 56, 143–160. Also in Z. Vendler (1967) *Linguistics in Philosophy*, Cornell University Press, Ithaca, NY, 97–121.

Vendler, Z. (1972) *Res Cogitans: An Essay in Rational Psychology*, Cornell University Press, Ithaca, NY.

Verhaar, J.W.M. (1990) "How Transitive Is Intransitive?" *Studies in Language* 14, 93–168.

Verkuyl, H.J. (1972) *On the Compositional Nature of the Aspects*, Reidel, Dordrecht.

Verkuyl, H.J. (1989) "Aspectual Classes and Aspectual Composition," *Linguistics and Philosophy* 12, 39–94.

Vestergaard, T. (1973) "A Note on Objective, Instrumental, and Affected in English," *Studia Linguistica* 27, 85–89.

Veyrenc, J. (1976) "Sur la Double Diathèse d'Objet des Enoncés Translocatifs," *Bulletin de la Société de Linguistique de Paris* 72, 241–273.

Viberg, A. (1984) "The Verbs of Perception: A Typological Study," in B. Butterworth, B. Comrie, and O. Dahl, eds., *Explanations for Language Universals*, Mouton, Berlin, 123–162.

Vikner, S. (1991) "*Be* is Selected Over *Have* If and Only If It is Part of an A-Chain," in W. Abraham, W. Kosmeijer, and E. Reuland, eds., *Issues in Germanic Syntax*, Mouton de Gruyter, Berlin, 365–381.

Wall, R. (1968) "Selectional Restrictions on Subjects and Objects of Transitive Verbs," Indiana University Linguistics Club, Bloomington.

Wasow, T. (1977) "Transformations and the Lexicon," in P. Culicover et al., eds. (1977), 327–360.

Wasow, T. (1978) "Remarks on Processing Constraints and the Lexicon," *Theoretical Issues in Natural Language Processing* 2, 247–251.

Wasow, T. (1980) "Major and Minor Rules in Lexical Grammar," in T. Hoekstra et al., eds. (1980), 285–312.

Watt, W.C. (1973) "Late Lexicalizations," in K.J.J. Hintikka, J.M.E. Moravcsik, and P. Suppes, eds., *Approaches to Natural Language*, Reidel, Dordrecht, 457–489.

Wechsler, S. (1991) "A Non-Derivational Account of the English Benefactive Alternation," paper presented at the 65th LSA Annual Meeting, Chicago, IL.

Weydt, H. (1973) "On G. Lakoff, 'Instrumental Adverbs and the Concept of Deep Structure'," *Foundations of Language* 10, 569–578.

Wierzbicka, A. (1972) *Semantic Primitives*, Athenäum, Frankfurt.

Wierzbicka, A. (1973) "The Semantic Structure of Words for Emotions," in R. Jakobson, C.H. Van Schooneveld, and D.S. Worth, eds., *Slavic Poetics: Essays in Honor of Kiril Taranovsky*, Mouton, The Hague, 500–505.

Wierzbicka, A. (1979) "Ethno-Syntax and the Philosophy of Grammar," *Studies in Language* 3, 313–383. Also in A. Wierzbicka (1988a), 169–236.

Wierzbicka, A. (1980) *Lingua Mentalis: The Semantics of Natural Language*, Academic Press, New York.

Wierzbicka, A. (1982) "Why Can You *Have a Drink* When You Can't *Have an Eat*?" *Language* 58, 753–799. Also in A. Wierzbicka (1988a), 293–358.

Wierzbicka, A. (1986) "The Semantics of the 'Internal Dative'—a Rejoinder," *Quaderni di Semantica* 7, 155–165.

Wierzbicka, A. (1987) *English Speech Act Verbs*, Academic Press, New York.

Wierzbicka, A. (1988a) *The Semantics of Grammar*, Benjamins, Amsterdam.

Wierzbicka, A. (1988b) "The Semantics of English Complementation in a Cross-Linguistic Perspective," in A. Wierzbicka (1988a), 23–168.

Wierzbicka, A. (1988c) "The Semantics of 'Internal Dative' in English," in A. Wierzbicka (1988a), 359–387. An earlier version appears in *Quaderni di Semantica* 7, 121–135.

Wilkins, W. (1987) "On the Linguistic Function of Event Roles," *BLS* 13, 460–472.

Wilkins, W., ed. (1988a) *Syntax and Semantics 21: Thematic Relations*, Academic Press, New York.

Wilkins, W. (1988b) "Thematic Structure and Reflexivization," in W. Wilkins, ed. (1988a), 191–213.

Willems, D. (1973) "Syntaxe et Semantique du Français. Les Verbes de Jugement. A Propos de Ch.J. Fillmore, *Verbs of Judging: An Exercise in Semantic Description,*" *Travaux de Linguistique* 3, 187–197.

Williams, E. (1981) "Argument Structure and Morphology," *The Linguistic Review* 1, 81–114.

Williams, E. (1982) "Another Argument That Passive is Transformational," *Linguistic Inquiry* 13, 160–163.

Williams, E. (1984) "*There* Insertion," *Linguistic Inquiry* 15, 131–153.

Wojcik, R. (1976) "Where Do Instrumental NPs Come From?" in M. Shibatani, ed. (1976a), 165–180.

Woolford, E. (1984) "Datives with Unspecified Objects," *The Linguistic Review* 3, 389–409.

Workgroup on Functional Grammar (1981) "On the Functional Grammar of Teaching Verbs," in T. Hoekstra, H. van der Hulst, and M. Moortgat, eds., *Perspectives on Functional Grammar*, Foris, Dordrecht, 203–231.

Zaenen, A. (in press) "Unaccusativity in Dutch: An Integrated Approach," in J. Pustejovsky, ed., *Semantics and the Lexicon*, Kluwer, Dordrecht.

Ziv, Y. (1982a) "Another Look at Definites in Existentials," *Journal of Linguistics* 18, 73–88.

Ziv, Y. (1982b) "Getting More Mileage out of Existentials in English," *Linguistics* 20, 747–762.

Ziv, Y. and G. Sheintuch (1979) "Indirect Objects—Reconsidered," *CLS* 15, 390–403.

Ziv, Y. and G. Sheintuch (1981) "Passives of Obliques over Direct Objects," *Lingua* 54, 1–17.

Zoeppritz, V.M. (1971) "On the Requirement That Agentives Be Animate," *Beiträge zur Linguistik und Informationsbearbeitung* 21, 65–78.

Zribi-Hertz, A. (1989) "Anaphor Binding and Narrative Point of View: English Reflexive Pronouns in Sentence and Discourse," *Language* 65, 695–727.

Zubizarreta, M.L. (1987) *Levels of Representation in the Lexicon and in the Syntax*, Foris, Dordrecht.

Zwicky, A.M. (1971a) "In a Manner of Speaking," *Linguistic Inquiry* 2, 223–232.

Zwicky, A.M. (1971b) "On Reported Speech," in C. J. Fillmore and D.T. Langendoen, eds., *Studies in Linguistic Semantics*, Holt, Rinehart and Winston, New York, 73–77.

Zwicky, A.M. (1986) "The Unaccented Pronoun Constraint in English," *Working Papers in Linguistics* 32, The Ohio State University, Columbus, 100–113.

Zwicky, A.M. and G.K. Pullum (1986) "Two Spurious Counterexamples to the Principle of Phonology-Free Syntax," *Working Papers in Linguistics* 32, The Ohio State University, Columbus, 92–99.

Zwicky, A.M. and J.M. Sadock (1975) "Ambiguity Tests and How to Fail Them," in J.P. Kimball, ed. (1975), 1–36.

Verb Index

The index includes an alphabetical listing of the verbs referred to in Part I and Part II of the book. Each verb is followed by a list of the sections that it is mentioned in. There has been no attempt to distinguish and give separate entries to the different senses of a verb. Similarly, there is only one entry in the index for verbs that are homographs. For instance, the entry in the index for *jar* includes a list of all sections discussing *jar*, whether in the sense of "put in a jar" or in the sense of "have a disagreeable effect on."